International Political Theory

Series Editor
Gary Browning
Oxford Brookes University
Oxford, UK

The Palgrave International Political Theory Series provides students and scholars with cutting-edge scholarship that explores the ways in which we theorise the international. Political theory has by tradition implicitly accepted the bounds of the state, and this series of intellectually rigorous and innovative monographs and edited volumes takes the discipline forward, reflecting both the burgeoning of IR as a discipline and the concurrent internationalisation of traditional political theory issues and concepts. Offering a wide-ranging examination of how International Politics is to be interpreted, the titles in the series thus bridge the IR-political theory divide. The aim of the series is to explore international issues in analytic, historical and radical ways that complement and extend common forms of conceiving international relations such as realism, liberalism and constructivism.

More information about this series at
http://www.palgrave.com/gp/series/14842

Petr Urban • Lizzie Ward
Editors

Care Ethics, Democratic Citizenship and the State

palgrave
macmillan

Editors
Petr Urban
Institute of Philosophy
Czech Academy of Sciences
Prague, Czech Republic

Lizzie Ward
School of Applied Social Science
University of Brighton
Brighton, UK

Chapter 1 was supported by the project "Towards a New Ontology of Social Cohesion", grant number GA19-20031S of the Czech Science Agency (GA ČR), realised at the Institute of Philosophy of the Czech Academy of Sciences in Prague. Chapter 11 was supported by the Wellcome Trust [203363/Z/16/Z]. Chapter 13 was supported by the Slovak Research and Development Agency under the Contract No. APVV-15-0234. Chapter 14 was supported by the project "Measures for Developing an Ethical Culture in the Czech State Administration", grant number TL01000430 of the Technology Agency of the Czech Republic (TA ČR) realised at the Institute of Philosophy of the Czech Academy of Sciences in Prague.

ISSN 2662-6039 ISSN 2662-6047 (electronic)
International Political Theory
ISBN 978-3-030-41436-8 ISBN 978-3-030-41437-5 (eBook)
https://doi.org/10.1007/978-3-030-41437-5

Cover illustration: Oleksiy Maksymenko / Alamy Stock Photo

This Palgrave Macmillan imprint is published by the registered company Springer Nature Switzerland AG.
The registered company address is: Gewerbestrasse 11, 6330 Cham, Switzerland

Acknowledgements

We want to thank many fellow care ethicists, colleagues, and friends who encouraged and supported us in various ways during the work on this project. This volume is a collective result of an enjoyable cooperation between us, the editors, and the authors of the following chapters. We want to thank them all for their effort and contribution.

Praise for *Care Ethics, Democratic Citizenship and the State*

"*Care Ethics, Democratic Citizenship and the State* wonderfully demonstrates the evolving maturation of care theory, and its application as an international collection of leading care scholars extends the boundaries of thinking on relationality in world democracies at a moment when traditional liberal theories have proven inadequate to ameliorate social and political life."

—Maurice Hamington, *Professor in Philosophy, Portland State University, USA*

"An important book: these interesting explorations show why the new moral approaches of the ethics of care should transform our politics and our institutions."

—Virginia Held, *Emeritus Professor, City University of New York, USA*

Contents

Notes on Contributors

Sophie Bourgault is Associate Professor of Political Science in the School of Political Studies, University of Ottawa, Canada. Bourgault's work has appeared in the *International Journal of Care and Caring*; *Etica & Politica*; the *European Journal of Women's Studies*; and *Frontiers*, among other journals. She is also the co-editor of several edited volumes on care ethics, such as *Le care: Éthique féministe actuelle* (2015), *Emotions and Care* (2018), *Éthiques de l'hospitalité, du don et du care: Actualité, regards croisés* (2020); and *In yet a Different Voice: Francophone Contributions* (2020).

Fabienne Brugère is Professor of Philosophy at Paris 8 University, France. Brugère has written many books in French: *L'éthique du* care, Presses Universitaires de France, 2011; *La politique de l'individu*, Seuil/ La République des idées, 2013; *La fin de l'hospitalité*, Flammarion, 2017, with Guillaume le Blanc; and *On ne naît pas femme, on le devient*, Stock, 2019. Her book has been published in English: *Care Ethics: The Introduction of Care as a Political Category* (2019).

Brunella Casalini is Associate Professor of Political Philosophy in the Department of Political and Social Science, University of Florence, Italy. Casalini was a visiting scholar at UVA—Research Centre for Gender and Sexuality, Amsterdam University in 2016 and a visiting professor at School of Political Studies, University of Ottawa in 2017. Her recent publications include "The Market, Social Justice and Elderly Care: A Reflection Starting from the Italian Case" (2016) and "The Weight of the Body on the Scales of Justice" (2016).

Jorma Heier is Junior Lecturer in Political Theory, PhD candidate in the Institute of Social Sciences, University of Osnabrück, Germany, and Equal Opportunities and Diversity person at the University of Applied Sciences Flensburg, Germany. Heier's recent papers on the political theory of care include "Towards a political theory of care" (2014, with Elisabeth Conradi), "Disabling Constraints on Democratic Participation: Challenges for a Political Theory of Care" (2015), and "Relationale Verantwortung" (2016).

Adriana Jesenková is Junior Lecturer in Philosophy and Applied Ethics in the Faculty of Arts, Pavol Jozef Šafárik University in Košice, Slovakia. Jesenková is the author of *The Ethics of Care* (2016 Unibook, in Slovak) and several articles on feminist philosophy, ethics of care, and issues of power, care, and justice in the teaching profession and in medical practice. Her research project focuses on sex education in the context of ethics of care.

Kanchana Mahadevan is Professor in the Department of Philosophy, University of Mumbai, India. Her areas of research and teaching include feminist philosophy, decolonisation, critical theory, political thought, aesthetics, and film. She has explored reinterpretations of care ethics with reference to migration, caste, Indian feminism, and intersectionality. Her book *Between Femininity and Feminism: Colonial and Postcolonial Perspectives on Care* (2014) examines the relevance of Western feminist philosophy in the Indian context.

Satomi Maruyama is Associate Professor of Sociology at Kyoto University, Japan. Maruyama is the author of *Josei Homeless toshite Ikiru* (2013); English version of this book is *Living on the Streets in Japan: Homeless Women Break Their Silence* (2018).

Yayo Okano is Professor of Political Philosophy at the Doshisha University, Kyoto, Japan. Okano is the author of *Senso ni Kousuru* (Against War, 2015), *Feminizumu no Seijigaku* (The Politics of Feminism: Introducing the Ethics of Care to the Global Society, 2012), and other works. Her English publications include "Prime Minister Abe's Constitutional Campaign and the Assault on Individual Rights" (2018), "Why has the Ethics of Care Become an Issue of Global Concern?" (2016).

Mo Ray is Professor of Health and Social Care in the School of Health and Social Care, University of Lincoln, UK. After qualifying as a social worker, Ray worked for many years as a social worker, care manager, and team manager. On completion of her PhD, Ray was awarded an ESRC Fellowship and subsequently secured her first post as a social work lecturer. Ray's research interests focus on social work and social care with older people, social relationships in older age, and participatory approaches to research.

Marion Smiley is J. P. Morgan Chase Professor of Ethics in the Philosophy Department, Brandeis University, USA. Smiley is the author of *Moral Responsibility and the Boundaries of Community* (1992) and numerous articles on free will and determinism, moral agency, collective responsibility, and feminist social and political thought. She is the recipient of several research fellowships from Princeton University and Harvard University.

Helena Olofsdotter Stensöta is Associate Professor of Political Science in the Quality of Government Institute, University of Gothenburg, Sweden. Stensöta's work has been published in *Administration & Society* (2017), *Governance* (2015), *Ethics and Social Welfare* (2015), *Child Indicators Research* (2014), *Journal of Public Administration Research and Theory* (2012), *Social Politics* (2011), and *Public Administration Review* (2010), among other journals. In 2018, she published *Gender and Corruption. Historical Roots and New Avenues of Research* (edited with Lena Wängnerud, Palgrave Macmillan).

Denise Tanner is Senior Lecturer in Social Work in the School of Social Policy, University of Birmingham, UK. Tanner is a registered social worker and worked for 14 years in social work practice before joining academia. Her research interests encompass the following areas: promoting the well-being of older people, social work policy and practice with adults, and participatory methodologies.

Joan C. Tronto is Professor of Political Science Emerita at the University of Minnesota, USA, and the City University of New York, USA. She is the author of many articles and two pathbreaking books in the political theory of care—*Moral Boundaries: A Political Argument for an Ethic of Care* (1993) and *Caring Democracy: Markets, Equality, and Justice* (2013). In 2014 she was awarded an honorary doctorate by the University for Humanistic Studies in Utrecht and in 2015 she won the Brown Prize for

Democracy, which resulted in the publication of a short book—*Who Cares? How to Reshape a Democratic Politics* (2015).

Petr Urban is Senior Researcher in the Institute of Philosophy of the Czech Academy of Sciences, Czech Republic. Urban is the author of three books on phenomenology, philosophy of intersubjectivity and political theory: *Raný Husserl a filosofie jazyka* (The Early Husserl and His Philosophy of Language, 2014), *Jak rozumíme druhým?* (How Do We Understand Others?, 2016) and *Winnicot a politická teorie* (Winnicott and Political Theory, 2020). His work has appeared in *Frontiers in Psychology*; *Ethics and Social Welfare*; *Environmental Philosophy*; *Horizon: Studies in Phenomenology*; and *Filozofia*, among other journals. His English publications on care ethics include “Toward an Expansion of an Enactive Ethics with the Help of Care Ethics” (2014), “Enacting Care” (2015), and “Ethical Dimensions of Play and Care” (2020).

Lizzie Ward is Principal Research Fellow in the School of Applied Social Science at the University of Brighton, UK. Ward is a qualitative researcher and her interests include age and ageing, care ethics, participatory research and experiential knowledge, and gender and feminist methodologies. She works in the field of community participatory research and has a particular interest in co-production and working with older people as co-researchers. Her work has been published in the areas of applying care ethics to research practice and social care practice with older people.

Julie Anne White is Professor of Political Science and Women’s, Gender, and Sexuality Studies at Ohio University, USA. Her work has appeared in the *Journal of Politics, Law and Social Inquiry and Affilia: Journal of Women and Social Work*. She is the author of *Democracy, Justice, and the Welfare State: Reconstructing Public Care* (2000).

CHAPTER 1

Introducing the Contexts of a Moral and Political Theory of Care

Petr Urban and Lizzie Ward

Our aim in this chapter is to introduce the reader to the contexts of a moral and political theory of care by telling a less common version of the story about care ethics. There are numerous stories about care ethics that differ from each other depending on what the person who tells the story foregrounds, which plots and connections she decides to include or leave aside. The localisation of the beginning of the story plays an important role as it often determines the plot line and the style of the narration. One of the main stories about care ethics is that it began in moral psychology with Carol Gilligan (1982), then it slowly made its way into the realm of theorising about the social and political, and became engaged in the debates in political theory only in the 1990s (cf. Pettersen 2008; Molinier

P. Urban (✉)
Institute of Philosophy, Czech Academy of Sciences, Prague, Czech Republic
e-mail: urban@flu.cas.cz

L. Ward
School of Applied Social Science, University of Brighton, Brighton, UK
e-mail: E.Ward@brighton.ac.uk

P. Urban, L. Ward (eds.), *Care Ethics, Democratic Citizenship and the State*, International Political Theory,
https://doi.org/10.1007/978-3-030-41437-5_1

et al. 2009; Hamington and Miller 2006a; Koggel and Orme 2010; Dingler 2016; Timmerman et al. 2019). This is why numerous authors (cf. Hankivsky 2004, 2014; Engster and Hamington 2015b; Vosman 2016) draw a distinction between two (or three) generations of care ethics arguing that the first generation focused mainly on one-to-one personal relationships, whereas the second generation shifted attention to the social and political dimensions of care. As our story demonstrates, the birth of care ethics against the background of second-wave feminism precedes the famous work of Gilligan (1982) and is not confined to the narrow view of care as a private dyadic relation and women's activity. The social and political dimension of care was a focus of care ethics from the outset (Ruddick 1980) and received the explicit attention of care ethicists as early as about the mid-1980s (Ruddick, Tronto, Held). Moreover, most of the recent developments and applications of a political theory of care—especially in the field of public policy and public ethics—that occurred over the past two decades were clearly prefigured in the seminal works of the 1990s (e.g. Tronto 1993; Sevenhuijsen 1998; Kittay 1999). This is why we want to suggest moving beyond the schematism of the widely spread categorisation of care ethics' generations and rethinking the complex development of care ethics with a special focus on the prominent role of a political concept of care.

Maternal Thought Transformed by Feminist Consciousness

Our story begins in 1980, two years before the term "an ethic of care" would appear in Carol Gilligan's widely celebrated book *In a Different Voice*. In 1980, an American philosopher Sara Ruddick published her essay 'Maternal Thinking'.[1] Let us be clear about two things from the outset. First, our reading of this essay which we provide on the following pages does not primarily aim at historical and textual adequacy. Our aim is to reveal several motifs of the essay that we consider as most relevant to our story. Some of them are to be found only in the footnotes of the essay, some are even in tension with other motifs and arguments of the same essay. Second, as we locate the beginning of the story of care ethics in

[1] We are indebted to Virginia Held for drawing our attention to the pioneering character and relevance of Ruddick's 1980 essay (Held 2006, 26; personal conversations with Virginia Held between 2013 and 2014).

Ruddick's early reflections on maternal practice and thought, we do not by any means want to foreground motherhood as the moral and political ideal of care ethics, let alone equate care ethics with the concept of 'women's morality'.[2]

Ruddick (1980) conceives of 'maternal thinking' as a distinctive style of reflecting, judging and feeling which is guided by distinctive goals and interests of 'maternal practice'. Though Ruddick links the concept of maternal practice primarily to the activity of taking care of and raising a child, she concedes that maternal thinking expresses itself "in various kinds of working and caring with others" (Ruddick 1980, 346). Maternal practice that gives rise to maternal thinking, Ruddick argues, is a response to three basic interests or demands of a child, namely for preservation, growth and acceptability. What style of reflecting, judging and feeling corresponds to a practice governed by these interests? First, it is important to note that Ruddick makes a distinction between degenerative and non-degenerative forms of maternal practice which correspond to degenerative and non-degenerative forms of maternal thought. Ruddick characterises these through typical attitudes, values and capacities of the actor of the respective form of maternal practice. In Ruddick's view, the actor of the non-generative form of maternal practice would typically feature attentive love, humility, understanding, respect for the other, sense of complexity and reality, the capacity to change along with the changing reality, to explore, create and insist upon one's own values and to see and name the existing forms of oppression and domination. In contrast, the actor of the degenerative form of maternal practice is characterised by rigid and excessive control over the other, self-refusal, uncritical acceptance of the values of the dominant culture or obedience—a sense of wanting to 'be good' in the 'eyes' of the dominant culture and society (Ruddick 1980, 354f.).

What motivates Ruddick's focus on maternal practice and thinking? Ruddick insists that the practice of 'working and caring with others' and the corresponding thought plays a crucial role in human life. Her point is

[2] Robinson's (2014) interpretation of Ruddick's thought is in many respects similar to the arguments that we propose in what follows. Robinson contends that "the importance of Ruddick's contribution, not just to feminist thought but to the transformation of the entire terrain of moral philosophy, cannot be underestimated" and that "the moral and political import of the intellectual legacy left by Sara Ruddick has yet to be fully recognized" (Robinson 2014, 102 and 106). However, while Robinson's focus is on Ruddick's 1989 book *Maternal Thinking*, we make our case exclusively on the reading of Ruddick's 1980 essay.

that although this practice and activity forms the core of human existence it has historically been marginalised and devalued and its description suffered from sentimentalisation and romanticisation. Thus, Ruddick's aim is to *provide an adequate description* of this practice and thought, *point out its distinctiveness* and *explain its value* and potential as an important source of an alternative moral, social and political theory.

An attentive reading of 'Maternal Thinking' reveals that its author is well aware of the fact that the description of maternal practice and thinking, as well as the description of any other form of human practice and corresponding rationality, is inevitably *bound to the position and situation* of the one who is describing. This position is determined by a given historical, cultural, social and political context, which in Ruddick's case is the context of the "heterosexual nuclear family" within the "middle-class, white, Protestant, capitalist, patriarchal America" of the second half of the twentieth century (Ruddick 1980, 347). Ruddick's awareness of the necessary particularity and limitation of her description of maternal practice and thought is clearly demonstrated by the following statement: "I am dependent on others, morally as well as intellectually, for the statement of differences, the assessment of their effects on every aspect of maternal lives, and finally for radical correction as well as for expansion of any general theory I would offer" (Ruddick 1980, 365, note 15). Ruddick is also explicit about the theoretical and intellectual situatedness of her account, as she traces its roots back to the notions of thought and practice in the philosophy of Wittgenstein and Habermas, the feminist critiques of the oppressive structures of the dominant society (Rich 1976; Bartky 1975), feminist psychology and psychoanalysis (Miller 1976; Chodorow 1978), feminist epistemology (Rose 1971), Weil's account of attention (Weil 1952) or Murdoch's notion of love (Murdoch 1970).

An important question is whether Ruddick constructs her account of maternal practice and thinking as necessarily related to 'womanhood' in either the biological or any other naturalist or essentialist sense. For Ruddick "'maternal' is a social category" (Ruddick 1980, 346), which entails that her account focuses on the practice itself and, by "concentrating on what mothers *do*" rather than on what they *are*, suspends any question about the 'essence' of this practice. Ruddick rejects "the ideology of womanhood" and argues that it was invented by men and caused the oppression of women (Ruddick 1980, 345). Moreover, any identification of maternal practice with biological or adoptive motherhood is false, Ruddick argues, since it "obscures the many kinds of mothering performed by those who do not parent particular children in families" (Ruddick 1980, 363, note 11). Together with 'the ideology of womanhood' Ruddick rejects "all accounts of gender difference or maternal nature which would claim an essential and ineradicable difference between female and male parents" (Ruddick 1980, 346).[3] Hence, we contend that what Ruddick describes as maternal practice is in her view *a fundamental human practice* that has been *historically* associated with women (and other marginalised groups) but in fact has *no essential relation* to any sex or gender identity.[4]

Ruddick finally borrows the notion of 'feminist consciousness' from Sandra Bartky (1975) and concludes her essay by envisioning 'maternal thought transformed by feminist consciousness'. It is a task of the 'feminist consciousness' to critique the current economic, social and political structures that perpetuate the marginalisation and devaluation of the practice of 'working and caring with others' and which foster the dominant association of this practice with women and other oppressed groups. When shaped by 'feminist consciousness' maternal thinking reveals "the damaging effects of the prevailing sexual arrangements and social hierarchies on maternal lives" (Ruddick 1980, 356) and raises a voice "affirming its own criteria of acceptability, insisting that the dominant values are unacceptable and need not to be accepted" (Ruddick 1980, 357). In order to create a society based on the values and rationality of this practice, Ruddick argues, we must "work to bring *transformed* maternal thought into the public realm" and to make it "a work of public conscience and legislation" (Ruddick 1980, 361). This would require, on the practical level, a transformation of politics and "moral reforms of economic life" (Ruddick 1980, 360) and, on the theoretical level, "articulating a theory of justice shaped by and incorporating maternal thinking" (Ruddick 1980, 361).

[3] Ruddick quotes in an affirmative tone Chodorow's claim that "we cannot know what children would make of their bodies in a nongender or nonsexually organized social world. … It is not obvious that there would be major significance to biological sex differences, to gender difference or to different sexualities" (Chodorow 1979, 66, cited in Ruddick 1980, 364, note 13).

[4] Robinson (2014) similarly concludes that "contrary to the arguments of some critics, Ruddick's work neither upholds gender roles nor idealizes the values and activities of mothering. On the contrary, Ruddick's philosophy politicizes motherhood and draws our attention to the ambivalent relationship that mothers have with the societies in which they live" (Robinson 2014, 106).

As we already said, our decision to tell the story of care ethics starting with Ruddick's 1980 essay is an important move in our attempt to understand both the core and the development of care ethics. It is our contention that Ruddick's essay not only is an exemplifying instance of a particular intellectual, historical, cultural, social and political constellation from which care ethics arose but also clearly expresses several key elements that became central for the subsequent forty years of care ethics' development.

Let us highlight the following six elements which are evident in Ruddick's account:

1. the aim to describe a human practice which, though fundamental to the human condition, was historically marginalised, devalued and kept outside the scope of the dominant Western moral, social and political thought;
2. the aim to provide an adequate description of 'the rationality' of this practice, which would replace the widespread sentimentalising and romanticising distortions that go often hand in hand with the socio-cultural and political devaluating of the practice;
3. the focus on the practice itself, which entails a rejection of the naturalistic and essentialist accounts[5];
4. the awareness of the socio-cultural and political positionality of the description;
5. the transformative potential of the description, which inspires critique of the social, economic and political structures that hinder realisation of the non-degenerative forms of this practice and rationality; and
6. the insight that the ideals of this practice and rationality are connected with the ideals of justice and that promoting both requires a transformation of our social and political institutions.

[5] We certainly do not want to claim that care ethicists have always rejected the view of care as an essentially feminine practice, perspective and attitude. Some care theorists have proposed accounts of caring that build on an essentialist view of the difference between the sexes and conceived of care ethics as a distinctive 'feminine approach to ethics' (Noddings 1984). Other care theorists have strongly opposed this view and argued against the link between care ethics and feminist essentialism (cf. Tronto 1987; Ruddick 1989; Fisher and Tronto 1990). It is our claim here that it was the latter approach which was decisive for the success and further development of a moral and political theory of care.

The Different Voice of an Ethic of Care

It goes without saying that the idea of focusing on care as a core human practice, whose values and goals inspire a profound critique of the prevailing moral, social and political devaluation of this practice, cannot be considered as a discovery of a single author, let alone a single theoretical work. It obviously arose from a particular historical, intellectual and socio-political situation of North America and Europe in the 1970s and 1980s, especially from second-wave feminism with its critique of the dominant 'hegemonic masculinity', which manifested itself in the image of an autonomous independent individual as the cultural, social and political paradigm. In the early 1980s, the shift to the description and revaluation of care and caring labour was reinforced by numerous works across many academic disciplines, such as epistemology (Rose 1983), sociology (Ungerson 1983; Graham 1983; Waerness 1984), social policy (Finch and Groves 1983; Finch 1984; Parker 1985), political economy (Hartsock 1984), philosophy of education (Noddings 1984), social philosophy (Held 1983, 1987) and developmental psychology (Gilligan 1982). It was the field of developmental psychology where Carol Gilligan coined the term 'an ethic of care', which strongly affected the following development of theories and accounts of an ethic of care.

In her widely read book *In a Different Voice* (1982), Gilligan, as is well known, characterises an ethic of care as a distinctive style of moral judging and constructing moral problems. In this view, an ethic of care centres around the responsibility for human relationships, builds moral judgement on concrete knowledge of a particular situation and context, emphasises the priority of connection and starts from the insight that there is no contradiction in acting responsibly towards oneself and others. An ethic of care, which "ties the activity of thought to the activity of care" (Gilligan 1982/2003, 149), foregrounds the ideal of non-violent and non-hierarchical relationships based on responsibility, respect, understanding, cooperation, sensitivity to the needs of the others, compassion and tolerance. Or, as Gilligan puts it, "the ideal of care is thus an activity of relationship, of seeing and responding to need, taking care of the world by sustaining the web of connection that no one is left alone" (Gilligan 1982/2003, 62).

Gilligan formulates her idea of an ethic of care within a conceptual and theoretical framework, which is fundamentally characterised by a duality. An ethic of care is the 'different voice', which differs from the voice of an ethic of justice (or rights). In contrast to an ethic of care, in Gilligan's view, an ethic of justice emphasises the priority of the individual, derives moral judgement from formal and abstract rules, foregrounds the ideal of equality and impartiality and considers the struggle for individual rights as the fundamental dynamics of social relations. Despite the numerous harsh contrasts in her exposition of an ethic of care and an ethic of justice, Gilligan ultimately contends that the "two views of morality ... are complementary rather than sequential or opposed" (Gilligan 1982/2003, 33) and that "to understand how the tension between responsibilities and rights sustains the dialectic of human development is to see the integrity of two disparate modes of experiences that are in the end connected" (Gilligan 1982/2003, 174). Yet, perhaps due to the fact that she expresses this view with restraint, or due to her failure to provide an account of how the two views of morality should be connected in the real life of individuals and communities, most of the critics as well as admirers of Gilligan's work have focused on the contrast and opposition of the "two different constructions of the moral domain" (Gilligan 1982/2003, 69).[6]

As we know, Gilligan's conceptual and theoretical framework is fundamentally marked by yet another duality, namely the duality of the female and male 'voices', the female and male ways of telling the story of what it means to be oneself, to be an adult human being. On Gilligan's account, the male voice typically speaks "of the role of separation as it defines and empowers the self", whereas the female voice typically speaks "of the ongoing process of attachment that creates and sustains the human community" (Gilligan 1982/2003, 156). This dual way of defining the self and its relationships to other selves and the world, Gilligan argues, is rooted in the difference between the psychology of men and "the psychology of women that has constantly been described as distinctive" (Gilligan 1982/2003, 22). Gilligan considers this view as supported by a body of previous work in psychology of feminine and masculine identity formations (McClelland 1975; Miller 1976; Lever 1976; Chodorow 1978; Erikson 1968) and as confirmed by the evidence gained through her own empirical research. However, this highly debated and contested aspect of Gilligan's theory is not our concern here. We rather want to draw

[6] However, it is fair to note that in her later work Gilligan did elaborate on how care and justice may be connected in the real life of individuals and communities. See in particular her studies on patriarchy and democracy (Gilligan and Richards 2009) and African-American young women (Taylor et al. 1995).

attention to the question of whether and how Gilligan connects the two distinctions or dualities that are firmly rooted at the heart of her project.

On the opening pages of her book, Gilligan assures the reader that the different voice of an ethic of care, which this book describes, "is characterized not by gender but theme" and that "the contrasts between male and female voices are presented here to highlight a distinction between two modes of thought and to focus a problem of interpretation rather than to represent a generalization about either sex" (Gilligan 1982/2003, 2). Yet, the rest of the book abounds with passages that reveal a strong identification between women's voices, distinctive female personal identity and an ethic of care as a "different construction of the moral problem by women" (Gilligan 1982/2003, 19). It is obvious that the more or less clear traces of this identification inspired the widely spread interpretation of Gilligan's work as proving and advocating a distinctive 'women's morality'. Although we sympathise with Tronto's view that "the equation of Gilligan's work with women's morality is a cultural phenomenon, and not of Gilligan's making" (Tronto 1987, 646),[7] we think that the conceptual and theoretical ambiguity of Gilligan's early work laid the ground for the formation of this cultural phenomenon.

Gilligan's (1982) view of an ethic of care bears certain similarities with Ruddick (1980) as regards our six points listed earlier. However, as a consequence of the dualistic framework of Gilligan's theory and the more or less overt identification of the 'voice' of an ethic of care with distinctive feminine personality, the interpretation of her early work as an argument for 'women's morality' (cf. Voet 1998, 118; Wendel 2003, 40) obscured its potential for building a full-fledged moral and political theory of care.[8]

Towards a Full-Fledged Theory of Care

In her important though rarely cited paper "Beyond Gender Difference to a Theory of Care", which appeared as early as in 1987, Joan Tronto proposes to look critically at the philosophical promises of an ethic of care and construct "a full-fledged moral and political theory of care" (Tronto 1987, 657). In particular, Tronto argues that "only when care is assessed in its

[7] Soon after her 1982 book, Gilligan herself made it clear that this was a very limited interpretation of her research (cf. Gilligan 1986).

[8] For a thoughtful early criticism of the dualistic framework of Gilligan's account, see Broughton (1983).

relative importance to other values can it begin to serve as a critical standpoint from which to evaluate public life" (Tronto 1987, 656). Tronto especially warns against the risk of confusing an ethic of care with private-life-oriented women's morality and presenting it as a supplemental moral theory, both of which she identifies in Noddings (1984) and the dominant interpretation of Gilligan (1982). Such a confusion not only leads to an easy dismissal of the 'different voice' in the context of dominant moral and political theories, but it can also have potentially harmful consequences such as sidestepping the structural problems of domination, exploitation, oppression and marginalisation, and reinforcing the reductive view of care as a private activity of women. Tronto (1987) suggests dissociating an ethic of care from the maternal ideal of caring, since it entails a fundamentally hierarchical view of human relationships and obscures power relations that often affect the content, distribution and boundaries of caring activities (cf. Dietz 1985).

Fisher and Tronto (1990) took up the task of constructing a full moral and political theory of care by offering a broad definition and analysis of caring that enables the inclusion of the whole range of human activities that serve to sustain human life and allows for taking into account the political dimensions of power and conflict entailed in all caring activities. Finally, it problematises the traditional division of the world into public and private spheres where care is usually associated with private life.[9] Fisher and Tronto (1990) famously define caring as "a species activity that includes everything we do to maintain, continue, and repair our 'world' so that we can live in it as well as possible. That world includes our bodies, our selves, and our environment, all of which we seek to interweave in a complex, life-sustaining web" (Fisher and Tronto 1990, 40). This definition, which emphasises the processual dimension of care and implies that the caring process may be directed not only towards people but also other living being and things, has been widely influential in further development

[9]Virginia Held's valuable work (cf. Held 1990, 1993) represents a parallel attempt to construct a full-blown feminist moral theory as an alternative to dominant moral and social theories. Held's approach, in contrast to Fisher and Tronto (1990), foregrounds mothering as the paradigm caring practice and puts greater emphasis on the feminist origin and core of this new ethic. Held views the feminist debates as a 'transformation' of moral theory, as she contends that "feminist reconceptualizations and recommendations concerning the relation between reason and emotion, the distinction between public and private, and the concept of the self, are providing insights deeply challenging to standard moral theory" (Held 1990, 342).

of a moral and political theory of care and served as a starting point for numerous applications of a care ethical perspective which we will discuss later on. The same holds true for Fisher and Tronto's related distinction and analysis of four intertwining phases or components of the caring process: (1) *caring about* (paying attention to something with a focus on continuity, maintenance and repair); (2) *taking care of* (taking responsibility for activities responding to the facts noticed in caring about); (3) *care-giving* (the concrete tasks and the hands-on care work); and (4) *care-receiving* (the responses of those towards whom caring is directed) (Fisher and Tronto 1990, 40).

In a way similar to Ruddick's reflection on degenerative forms of 'maternal practice', Fisher and Tronto describe ineffective and destructive patterns in caring activities. They think of them as characterised by fragmentation and alienation in the caring process, as opposed to the integrity of caring where the four phases of the care process fit together into a whole. Such ineffective patterns in caring occur, for example, when caregivers suffer a shortage of time and/or other resources necessary for caring, or when care-receivers have little control over how their needs are defined in the caring process. Against the background of the insight that how we think about care is deeply affected by existing social and political structures of power and inequality, Fisher and Tronto conclude that the patterns of fragmentation and imbalance of the caring process are mainly created by deficient social and political arrangements. Hence, a full-fledged moral theory of care needs to be developed hand in hand with a social and political theory of care that scrutinises the workings of our social and political institutions (e.g. the household, the market, the state) from a critical perspective inspired by the ideal of good caring. Such a social and political theory must address the following questions: "Where does caring come from. ... Who determines who can be a member of the caring society? What should be the role of the market in a caring society? Who should bear responsibility for education? How much inequality is acceptable before individuals become indifferent to those who are too different in status?" or "How to make sure that the web of relationships is spun widely enough so that some are not beyond its reach?" (Tronto 1987, 661).

While an ethic of care envisions "a different world, one where the daily caring of people for each other is a valued premise of human existence, ... an alternative vision of life, one centred on human care and interdependence" (Tronto 1993, x), a *political* theory of care reveals that "what this vision requires is that individuals and groups be frankly assessed in terms of the extent to which they are permitted to be care demanders and required to be care providers" (Tronto 1993, 168). In her path-breaking book *Moral Boundaries* (1993), Tronto lays ground for a full-fledged political theory of care that aims to explicate what "a just distribution of caring tasks and benefits" (Tronto 1993, 169) entails and which social and political arrangements facilitate caring and contribute to creating "a more just world that embodies good caring" (Tronto 1993, xii). A political theory of care sheds light on the close relationship between care and justice, which we mentioned earlier in the last point of our summary of Ruddick's ideas. On the one hand, to address the problems of care and to conceptualise the prerequisites of good caring requires concepts of justice, equality and democracy, since caring is always deeply affected by unequal power and access to material conditions and recourses necessary for caring. Thus, Tronto argues, "only in a just, pluralistic, democratic society can care flourish" (Tronto 1993, 162). On the other hand, "care as a practice can inform the practices of democratic citizenship" (Tronto 1993, 177), since it describes "the qualities necessary for democratic citizens to live together well in a pluralistic society" (Tronto 1993, 161f.). Reflection on the mutually enabling relationship, foregrounded by Tronto (1993), between good caring and democratic citizenship in a just society is a thread that connects most subsequent developments in a political theory of care.

Revised Concepts of Citizenship, Equality, Justice and Solidarity

In her book *Citizenship and the Ethics of Care* (1998) the Dutch political philosopher Selma Sevenhuijsen offered an influential revision of the concepts of citizenship, equality and solidarity from the perspective of a political theory of care, by drawing from the feminist work of Ruddick, Gilligan, Tronto, Fraser, Okin, Young and Nedelsky, the postmodern criticism of identity ethics and politics (Foucault, Lyotard, Bauman), and the neo-republican notion of active citizenship. In accord with Tronto (1993), Sevenhuijsen emphasises that "power and conflict are involved in every phase of the caring process, as well as in our collective discussions about the way social institutions should care about and for human beings" (Sevenhuijsen 1998, 141) and that a politically formulated ethics of care should not aim to eliminate power in caring relations, but to provide an understanding that helps to differentiate between power and domination by making power recognisable and manageable. It is Sevenhuijsen's contention that such a goal can be achieved "only by situating the ethics of care in ideas and practices of democratic citizenship" (Sevenhuijsen 1998, 67). In the context of Western political theory, at least in its modern version, citizenship has been a central normative ideal for human personhood, whereas care was considered as a matter of private life that lies outside the scope of the questions concerning citizenship. A political theory of care, in contrast, places the considerations regarding care firmly in the public domain and incorporates care, vulnerability and interdependency into the concept of a 'normal' subject of politics, as Eva Feder Kittay (1999) puts it in accord with Sevenhuijsen. The content of the care-oriented notion of citizenship differs from both the liberal and the neoliberal notion by including caregiving and care-receiving on the list of 'primary social goods'. It is 'a good of citizens' "to be cared for in a responsive dependency relation if and when one is unable to care for oneself, and to meet the dependency needs of others without incurring undue sacrifices oneself" (Kittay 1999, 103).[10]

As a key notion in political theory, the notion of citizenship is closely linked to the notion of equality, for at least in the modern liberal view all citizens are conceived as fundamentally equal in terms of their individual rights and duties. Sevenhuijsen (1998) and Kittay (1999), drawing on the feminist criticism of the liberal idea of equality as sameness (Okin 1979; Fineman 1991) and Tronto's analysis of a political concept of care (Tronto 1993, 1996), propose a revised care-oriented notion of equality. A political theory of care reveals that the failure to secure the conditions of good caregiving and care-receiving in a society impairs the capability of many—especially the most vulnerable and dependent ones—to participate as equals in an otherwise well-ordered society. Thus, as Kittay puts it, "a commitment to the equality of *all* requires an equality that is connection-based, and equality that acknowledges a common fate and shared humanity which lies as much in our need to care for others and be attended to in caring relationships as in properties we possess as individuals" (Kittay 1999, 183). Such a connection-based equality implies 'full social

[10] By juxtaposing Sevenhuijsen (1998) and Kittay (1999) in these paragraphs we do not aim to claim that their positions are perfectly comparable. However, we contend that their views on the topics of citizenship, care and equality merge to a great extent. We also want to highlight that both Sevenhuijsen and Kittay should be credited with this particular contribution to the development of a political theory of care shortly before the turn of the millennium.

citizenship' as participation in collective deliberations and decisions about the availability of, and access to, good care. The equality of voice in the public domain would again be impossible without equal access to social services that provide a safeguard against processes of marginalisation and exclusion and without paying sufficient attention to the diversity of needs (Sevenhuijsen 1998, 147f.). This is why the questions of social and political inclusion, "the politics of needs interpretation" (Fraser 1987) and deliberation gain a central place in a political theory of care.[11]

Finally, a 'democratic politics of care' (White 2000) implies a renewed notion of justice. A politically formulated ethics of care, as we have outlined earlier, does not aim to replace the ideal of justice by the ideal of care. It rather aims to broaden and transform the modern liberal view of justice as impartiality and fairness by stressing that "justice which does not incorporate the need to respond to vulnerability with care is incomplete, and a social order which ignores care will itself fail to be just" (Kittay 1999, 102). Full democratic citizenship requires connection-based equality which, as argued earlier, can be only achieved in a "society in which care is publicly acknowledged as a good which the society as a whole bears a responsibility to provide in a manner that is just to all" (Kittay 1999, 109). Such a view entails a notion of 'social justice' that is "based on values such as reconciliation, reciprocity, diversity and responsibility, and on the willingness and ability of citizens to accept responsibility for each other's well-being" (Sevenhuijsen 1998, 149). By envisioning social justice as a matter of collective responsibility with respect to ensuring an equal voice about and access to caregiving and care-receiving in a society, a political theory of care arrives at a revised notion of solidarity. In contrast to both the view of solidarity as mutual exchange and the view of solidarity as charity, Sevenhuijsen proposes the notion of 'caring solidarity' as a collective responsibility for care. Only through adopting and institutionalising collective responsibility for care can a society avoid the risks of privatising and marginalising care and devaluing care as a mere preparation for full citizenship. At the same time, by speaking in terms of 'caring solidarity' "we can do justice to the idea that people are differently situated and that this is exactly what makes public dialogue and collective support so necessary" (Sevenhuijsen 1998, 151).

[11] For a wider context of feminist debates on citizenship, see Voet (1998) or a more recent collection edited by Friedman (2005).

The exploration of a close relationship between caring, democracy, citizenship and equality inspired Tronto's more recent reflection on the practice of 'caring with' as constitutive for a 'caring democracy' (Tronto 2013). To be a citizen in a democracy means, Tronto argues, "to care for citizens and to care for democracy itself" (Tronto 2013, x). This requires that citizens take seriously the collective responsibility for 'caring with' each other and that democratic politics recognises the centrality of "assigning responsibilities for care, and for ensuring that democratic citizens are as capable as possible of participating in this assignment of responsibilities" (Tronto 2013, 30). Tronto expands the original distinction of the four phases of caring (Fisher and Tronto 1990) by adding 'caring with' as the final fifth phase of the care process and identifying plurality, communication, trust, respect and solidarity as the key moral qualities that 'caring with' requires (Tronto 2013, 35f.).

Recent Developments and a Look Back

This section concludes our story by sketching a bird's eye view on the recent developments in a moral and political theory of care after the turn of the millennium. Over the past two decades, care ethics has grown into "a burgeoning field of study" (Engster and Hamington 2015b, 4) and moved beyond its place of origin in several ways—geographical, intellectual, scientific, socio-political and so on. After its early European reception, which developed into several care ethics 'schools' across Europe,[12] care ethics made its way into other parts of the world including Asia, Africa, Latin America and Australia. A care approach has been adopted by scholars from a number of different disciplines and applied to various fields, such as international relations and global studies (Robinson 1999; Held 2006; Pulcini 2009), educational psychology (Noddings 2003; Bozalek et al. 2014), medical ethics (Mol 2008; Kohlen 2009; Leget 2013; Groenhout 2019; Timmerman et al. 2019), animal ethics (Donovan and Adams 2007; Laugier 2012), legal studies (Nedelsky 2011), organisational studies and business ethics (Hamington and Sander-Staudt 2011),

[12] The European reception of care ethics started as early as in the late 1980s (cf. Sevenhuijsen 1988, 1991). However, we shall not overlook the previous independent European tradition of research on care, especially the British and Norwegian studies in the field of sociology and public policy (cf. Finch and Groves 1983; Waerness 1984). For a detailed account of the European reception and development of care ethics, see Vosman (2016). For a reflection on a 'Francophone voice' in care ethics literature, see Bourgault and Vosman (2020).

public administration (Davidson 1994; De Burnier 2003; Stensöta 2010; Bourgault 2017), social policy and social work (Kittay 1999; Noddings 2002; Hankivsky 2004; Barnes 2006, 2012), youth and childhood research (Rauner 2000; Langford 2019) and many others. Care ethics has been compared and brought into dialogue with several related approaches and theories, including moral sentimentalism (Baier 1995), virtue ethics (Slote 2007), Levinasian ethics (Groenhout 2004), communitarianism (Kittay 2001a), ethics of hospitality (Hamington 2010; Bourgault et al. 2020), Confucianism (Sander-Staudt 2015) or African ethics (Gouws and van Zyl 2015). The richness, diversity and international dimension of the latest developments and applications of care ethics are well documented in three recent collections (Mahon and Robinson 2011; Barnes et al. 2015; Conradi and Vosman 2016).

Political care theorists have been increasingly interested in the role of the state and the questions of public policy with regard to the arrangements of the care provision. The idea of 'a public ethic of care' (Clement 1996; Kittay 2001b; Noddings 2002) served as a starting point for both the criticism of the paternalistic modes of the welfare state care provision and the neoliberal models of market-oriented care arrangements (e.g. Kittay 1999; White 2000; Tronto 2001; Hankivsky 2004; Hamington and Miller 2006a; Held 2006; Engster 2015; Barnes 2006, 2012; Tronto 2013, 2017). A number of care theorists focused on contemporary policy documents and offered care-oriented analyses and criticisms of normative assumptions of these documents (Sevenhuijsen 1998; Barnes 2006). The book *Care Ethics and Political Theory* (Engster and Hamington 2015a) provides a valuable selection of the recent research on both basic and applied questions in a political theory of care.

Looking back at the forty years of the development of care ethics, one can hardly avoid being confronted with the issue of the unity and identity of care ethics. Is there one referent of the term 'care ethics'? If so, what makes it distinctive? As should be clear from the above, it is our contention that there in not a single referent of the term 'care ethics' and any story of care ethics has to build a narrative by foregrounding certain ideas and authors and sidelining other ideas and authors from a diverse 'family' of related approaches. Thus, the narrative of care ethics which we provided in this chapter cannot obscure the diversity of perspectives and contexts out of which care ethics grew as well as the plurality of versions and approaches into which it has developed. Frans Vosman's (2016) account of socio-culturally and linguistically conditioned plurality of moral and political theories of care, in our view, serves as a useful analytical tool for understanding the complex developments of care ethics and assessing its diversity as a strength rather than a weakness. This said, we are happy to present Tronto's reflection on the question of whether and how the concepts of care ethics should travel outside the place and time of their birth and the ethical and epistemological challenges this implies (Tronto this volume).

We believe that our version of the story of care ethics has the potential to inspire new reflections among those who are familiar with care ethics or even contributed themselves to its development. We equally hope that our version of the story will provide a reliable guide and source of information to all our readers who encounter care ethics for the first time through this book. In the last section of this chapter we map the content and the structure of this collection.

The Contribution and Organisation of This Book

This book aims to contribute to the development of care ethics, continuing the thread we traced back to Ruddick on the centrality of the social and political dimension of care. The authors of the following chapters take up the debates in care ethics by providing original and fresh perspectives on the seminal notions and topics of a politically formulated ethics of care. Some chapters elaborate in a more theoretical way on the concepts of democratic citizenship, social and political participation, moral and political deliberation, solidarity and situated attentive knowledge, while other more practice-oriented chapters explore the risks of marketising and privatising care or deal with the issues of state care provision and democratic caring institutions. In addition, this volume has an ambition to speak to current political and societal challenges. This includes in particular the contemporary crisis of Western democracy which is related to the rise of populism and identity politics worldwide. Some of the chapters speak to the issue of an ageing population and the 'care crisis' in the Global North, while other contributions aim to contribute to revealing the destructive effects of globalised neoliberalism. The breadth of the contributions is also reflected in that it brings together perspectives of (both junior and senior) care theorists from three different continents and ten different countries and gives voice to their unique local insights from very different sociopolitical and cultural contexts. Many of these theorists gathered in Prague to discuss the above-mentioned concepts of a political theory of care at the conference 'Caring Democracy: Current Topics in the Political Theory of Care', which was hosted by the Institute of Philosophy of the Czech Academy of Sciences in November 2017. This meeting gave an initial impulse for the creation of this collection.

The outline of this volume is as follows. The book is divided into two parts—the first elaborates on core concepts in a political theory of care and the second offers case studies which apply and expand on a political ethic of care in different contexts.

The first part opens with Chap. 2 by Sophie Bourgault (University of Ottawa, Canada) which offers a deep exploration of the concept of attentiveness within democratic practice. Highlighting the challenges that post-truth politics presents for political theory, Bourgault urges us to consider the significance of 'attentive listening' for socio-political life as a matter of urgency. Drawing on hermeneutics and Gadamerian care-based listening she proposes the notion of 'caring to deliberate' as a form of caring for democracy itself.

The theme of deliberation is taken up by Jorma Heier (University of Flensburg, Germany) in Chap. 3. For Heier, care theory needs to address the ways in which those who are most impacted by exclusionary processes of responsibility-setting are the least able to participate in the very political deliberations that impact them. To remedy this Heier proposes 'democratic caring with' to address structural inequality and recognise the political and epistemological dimensions of democratic inclusion.

Next in Chap. 4 Helena Olofsdotter Stensöta (University of Gothenburg, Sweden) considers the question of equal access to care within democratic societies and the possibilities of meeting care 'for all'. Stensöta examines three different spheres of care provision: civil society, the market and the state and the extent to which they meet the ethical demands of care. She concludes that an 'encompassing welfare state' and publicly funded care offer the best alternative to provide democratic care 'for all'.

In Chap. 5 Marion Smiley (Brandeis University, USA) takes us further into considering the barriers of democratic modes of care at the level of the state. Turning her focus to paternalism, the chapter aims to make explicit how paternalism, conceptualised in political and philosophical thought, conceals its structural dimensions, and so threatens the development of caring democracy. By understanding paternalism as a 'distinctly paternal kind of hierarchical governance' she reconceptualises paternalism to suggest how a non-paternalistic system of democratic state care can be developed.

Reminding us of the intrinsic connections between feminist thought and care ethics in Chap. 6, Brunella Casalini (University of Florence, Italy) explores these connections in relation to other currents in feminist thought. She examines the commonalities between feminist approaches of 'affective equality', 'social flesh', 'social reproduction' and care ethics. She contrasts these different approaches and argues that by considering care ethics alongside these other feminist approaches core aspects of care ethics are strengthened.

Neoliberalism and to a lesser extent neo-populism are themes which provide the backdrop to all of the contributions, but in Chap. 7 by Fabienne Brugère (University Paris 8, France) the focus is more explicit. Here Brugère deals with two main questions: how do neoliberalism and neo-populism appear as solutions to the current care crisis and how can care ethics offer a different solution.

The temporal aspects of neoliberalism are explored in Chap. 8 by Julie White (Ohio University, USA). White argues that the neoliberal organisation of time is "out of synch" with caring practices and at odds with the slow deliberation required for democratic practices. 'Making time for democracy requires making time for care' argues White, and the processes of 'reclaiming care time' will lead to a more equal distribution of care work. Moreover, caring democracy will require a different temporal frame that rejects the commodification of care and care workers.

Part II illustrates our earlier point that care ethics is moving beyond its origins geographically and intellectually. In each chapter we see authors using care ethics to think through a range of issues related to care and democratic practice in specific contexts. These include a diverse range of areas such as education, welfare, care services, public institutions, migration, healthcare and constitutional reform. In these contributions, the authors consider the role of the state and the relationship between care and citizenship in national contexts or as wider global issues.

Joan Tronto (University of Minnesota, USA) in Chap. 9 opens this part by considering the conceptual and ethical challenges of applying care ethics beyond the time and place where it first emerged. The dangers of Western discourses as conduits for colonial and imperial power are well recognised, so Tronto asks how can care ethics 'leave domination behind' in its travels? To address this question Tronto discusses the notions of dislocation, solidarity, cosmopolitanism and virtue in relation to global responsibilities for democratic practices. Underlying these issues is the 'epistemic dimension' and the question of who gets to define what knowledge *is* and the power that this bestows. As Tronto observes this needs to be acknowledged and addressed if care ethicists are to embark on the journey 'from imperious observer or caregiver to accepting traveler'.

In Chap. 10 Kanchana Mahadevan (University of Mumbai, India) brings us directly to some of these key tensions in her consideration of global responsibilities for care drawing on the context of Indian healthcare workers. India is not only one of the largest exporters of healthcare workers, it is also a major destination for 'medical tourists'. The implications for care-receivers in India (and other 'home' countries of migrating care workers) of these dimensions of the global commodification of care are largely absent in current debates on cosmopolitanism. Mahadevan demonstrates the limitations of a cosmopolitan model which overlooks complex interdependencies and emphasise individual citizenship. In contrast to this Mahadevan reimagines cosmopolitanism and care from the perspective of mutual dependencies highlighted by the migration crisis of Indian healthcare workers.

In contrast, Chap. 11 reflects on the impact of the commodification of care and neoliberal restructuring in a developed welfare state. Lizzie Ward (University of Brighton, UK), Mo Ray (University of Lincoln, UK) and Denise Tanner (University of Birmingham, UK) look at the social care system in England and the dual impacts of austerity and commodification. They draw on empirical research about the lived experiences of older people who need care to discuss the epistemic dimension of care and question the ways that 'knowledge' is produced and/or even recognised within neoliberal welfare systems of audit and measurement. Using examples drawn from their empirical research they argue that lived experiences of care challenge assumptions of individual consumer choice and responsibility, the ideological backbone of neoliberal care policy.

Japan is the focus of Chap. 12, in which Yayo Okano (Doshisha University, Japan) and Satomi Maruyama (Ritsumeikan University, Japan) apply care ethics concepts related to caring democracy to the Japanese political and socio-economic context. In considering the allocation of caring responsibilities within Japan, they argue that the social protection system provided by employment and strongly gendered family norms leave the extent and existence of women's poverty largely invisible. In this context they explore how the concept of 'protection' has been mobilised in recent political debates on the reform of the Japanese constitution and consider this in relation to Tronto's 'protection pass' out of care responsibilities.

We turn next to education reform in Slovakia where Adriana Jesenková (Pavol Jozef Šafárik University, Slovakia) in Chap. 13 applies care ethics to the democratisation process and the role of education in democratic citizenship. She argues that the deficit of care in the Slovak education system results in a deficit of inclusive citizenship. Using a care ethics lens, she discusses inclusion and protection and how these have been interpreted within reforms to the education system. Jesenková argues that the example of Slovakia illustrates the need to link democratic care in education to citizenship and caring democracy, and that the application of care ethics demonstrates the need to critically rethink the notion of protection as a dimension of democratic care.

In the final chapter (Chap. 14) Petr Urban (Czech Academy of Sciences, Czech Republic) draws attention to the urgent issue of the growing distrust in state and public sector institutions and offers a care ethical perspective on the role and modes of operating of public institutions in our societies and polities. He discusses the existing proposals for a care-oriented public administration and concentrates in particular on a recent debate about the possibility of merging caring and bureaucratic values within state and public sector institutions. Drawing on his fieldwork at the Ministry of Transport of the Czech Republic, he applies the theoretical framework of a care-oriented public administration to a concrete case and suggests an empirically grounded care approach to governmental institutions.

Together the chapters invite reflection on current political contexts and the analytic and conceptual value of care for democratic theory. As care ethics 'travels' it will inevitably and rightly generate dilemmas, contradictions and, we hope, productive conversations for scholars, researchers and teachers interested in the continuing potential of care ethics to advance theories and debate in democratic citizenship. Our hope is that in this collection readers find the inspiration and resources to confront the current challenges and further the possibilities and potential that emerge from putting care at the centre of our moral and political thinking.

Acknowledgements We are indebted to Joan Tronto and Sophie Bourgault for their valuable comments on a draft of this chapter. Petr Urban's work on this chapter as well as his co-editing of the entire volume was supported by the project 'Towards a New Ontology of Social Cohesion', grant number GA19-20031S of the Czech Science Agency (GA ČR), realised at the Institute of Philosophy of the Czech Academy of Sciences in Prague.

References

Baier, C. Annette. 1995. *Moral Prejudices. Essays on Ethics*. Cambridge, MA: Harvard University Press.

Barnes, Marian. 2006. *Caring and Social Justice*. Basingstoke: Palgrave Macmillan.

———. 2012. *Care in Everyday Life. An Ethic of Care in Practice*. Bristol: Policy Press.

Barnes, Marian, Tula Brannelly, Lizzie Ward, and Nicki Ward, eds. 2015. *Ethics of Care: Critical Advances in International Perspective*. Bristol: Policy Press.

Bartky, Sandra Lee. 1975. Toward a Phenomenology of Feminist Consciousness. *Social Theory and Practice* 3 (4): 425–439.

Bourgault, Sophie. 2017. Prolegomena to a Caring Bureaucracy. *European Journal of Women's Studies* 24 (3): 202–217.

Bourgault, Sophie, and Frans Vosman. 2020. Introduction. In *Care Ethics in Yet a Different Voice. Francophone Contributions*, ed. Sophie Bourgault and Frans Vosman, 5–26. Leuven: Peeters.

Bourgault, Sophie, Sophie Cloutier, and Stéphanie Gaudet, eds. 2020. *Éthiques de l'hospitalité, du don et du care: Actualité, regards croisés*. Ottawa: University of Ottawa Press.

Bozalek, Vivienne, Wendy MacMillan, Delia Marshall, Melvyn November, Andre Daniels, and Toni Sylvester. 2014. Analysing the Professional Development of Teaching and Learning from a Political Ethics of Care Perspective. *Teaching in Higher Education* 19 (5): 447–458.

Broughton, M. John. 1983. Women's Rationality and Men's Virtues: A Critique of Gender Dualism in Gilligan's Theory of Moral Development. *Social Research* 50 (3): 597–642.

Burnier, DeLysa. 2003. Other Voices/Other Rooms: Towards a Care-Centred Public Administration. *Administrative Theory and Praxis* 25 (4): 529–544.

Chodorow, Nancy. 1978. *The Reproduction of Mothering. Psychoanalysis and the Sociology of Gender*. Berkeley: University of California Press.

———. 1979. Feminism and Difference: Gender, Relation, and Difference in Psychoanalytic Perspective. *Socialist Review* 46: 42–64.

Clement, Grace. 1996. *Care, Autonomy, and Justice: Feminism and the Ethic of Care*. Boulder: Westview Press.

Conardi, Elisabeth, and Frans Vosman, eds. 2016. *Praxis der Achtsamkeit. Schlüsselbegriffe der Care-Ethik*. Frankfurt: Campus Verlag.

Davidson, Anneka. 1994. Gender Differences in Administrative Ethics. In *Handbook of Administrative Ethics*, ed. Terry L. Cooper, 415–433. New York: Marcel Dekker.

Dietz, G. Mary. 1985. Citizenship with a Feminist Face: The Problem with Maternal Thinking. *Political Theory* 13 (1): 19–37.

Dingler, Catrin. 2016. Relationale Subjektivität – Zur Theoriegeschichte der Care-Ethik. In *Praxis der Achtsamkeit. Schlüsselbegriffe der Care-Ethik*, ed. Elisabeth Conradi and Frans Vosman, 93–113. Frankfurt: Campus Verlag.

Donovan, Josephine, and Carol J. Adams, eds. 2007. *The Feminist Care Tradition in Animal Ethics: A Reader*. New York: Columbia University Press.

Engster, Daniel. 2015. *Justice, Care, and the Welfare State*. Oxford: Oxford University Press.

Engster, Daniel, and Maurice Hamington, eds. 2015a. *Care Ethics and Political Theory*. Oxford: Oxford University Press.

———. 2015b. Introduction. In *Care Ethics and Political Theory*, ed. Daniel Engster and Maurice Hamington, 1–16. Oxford: Oxford University Press.

Erikson, H. Erik. 1968. *Identity: Youth and Crisis*. New York: W. W. Norton.

Finch, Janet. 1984. Community Care: Developing Non-sexist Alternatives. *Critical Social Policy* 9: 6–18.

Finch, Janet, and Dulcie Groves. 1983. *A Labour of Love: Women, Work and Caring*. London: Routledge and Kegan Paul.

Fineman, Martha Albertson. 1991. *The Illusion of Equality. The Rhetoric and Reality of Divorce Reform*. Chicago: The University of Chicago Press.

Fisher, Berenice, and Joan C. Tronto. 1990. Toward a Feminist Theory of Caring. In *Circles of Care: Work and Identity in Women's Lives*, ed. Emily K. Abel and Margaret K. Nelson, 35–62. Albany: SUNY Press.

Fraser, Nancy. 1987. Women, Welfare and the Politics of Need Interpretation. *Hypatia* 2 (1): 103–121.

Friedman, Marilyn, ed. 2005. *Women and Citizenship*. Oxford: Oxford University Press.

Gilligan, Carol. 1982. *In a Different Voice. Psychological Theory and Women's Development*. 2003 ed. Cambridge, MA: Harvard University Press.

———. 1986. Reply (to the Critics). In "On *In a Different Voice*: An Interdisciplinary Forum". *Signs: Journal of Women in Culture and Society* 11 (2): 324–333.

Gilligan, Carol, and David A.J. Richards. 2009. *The Deepening Darkness: Patriarchy, Resistance, and Democracy's Future*. Cambridge: Cambridge University Press.

Gouws, Amanda, and Mikki van Zyl. 2015. Towards a Feminist Ethics of *Ubuntu*: Bridging Rights and *Ubuntu*. In *Care Ethics and Political Theory*, ed. Daniel Engster and Maurice Hamington, 165–186. Oxford: Oxford University Press.

Graham, Hilary. 1983. Caring: A Labour of Love. In *A Labour of Love: Women, Work and Caring*, ed. Janet Finch and Dulcie Groves, 13–30. London: Routledge and Kegan Paul.

Groenhout, E. Ruth. 2004. *Connected Lives. Human Nature and an Ethics of Care*. Lanham: Rowman and Littlefield.

———. 2019. *Care Ethics and Social Structures in Medicine*. New York: Routledge.

Hamington, Maurice, ed. 2010. *Feminism and Hospitality: Gender in the Host/Guest Relationship*. New York: Lexington Books.
Hamington, Maurice, and Dorothy C. Miller. 2006a. Introduction: A Modern Moral Imperative. In *Socializing Care: Feminist Ethics and Public Issues*, xi–xxii. Lanham: Rowman and Littlefield.
———, eds. 2006b. *Socializing Care: Feminist Ethics and Public Issues*. Lanham: Rowman and Littlefield.
Hamington, Maurice, and Maureen Sander-Staudt, eds. 2011. *Applying Care Ethics to Business*. Dordrecht: Springer.
Hankivsky, Olena. 2004. *Social Policy and the Ethic of Care*. Vancouver: UBC Press.
———. 2014. Rethinking Care Ethics: On the Promise and Potential of an Intersectional Analysis. *American Political Science Review* 108 (2): 252–264.
Hartsock, Nancy. 1984. The Feminist Standpoint: Developing the Ground for a Specifically Feminist Historical Materialism. In *Discovering Reality. Feminist Perspectives on Epistemology, Metaphysics, Methodology, and Philosophy of Science*, ed. Sandra Harding and Merrill B. Hintikka, 283–310. New York: Kluwer Academic Publishers.
Held, Virginia. 1983. The Obligations of Mothers and Fathers. In *Mothering: Essays in Feminist Theory*, ed. Joyce Treblicot, 9–20. Totowa, NJ: Rowman and Allanheld.
———. 1987. Non-contractual Society: A Feminist View. In *Science, Morality and Feminist Theory*, ed. Marsha Hanen and Kai Nielsen, 111–137. Canadian Journal of Philosophy (suppl. 13). Calgary: The University of Calgary Press.
———. 1990. Feminist Transformations of Moral Theory. *Philosophy and Phenomenological Research* 50: 321–344.
———. 1993. *Feminist Morality. Transforming Culture, Society, and Politics*. Chicago: The University of Chicago Press.
———. 2006. *The Ethics of Care. Personal, Political, and Global*. New York: Oxford University Press.
Kittay, Eva Feder. 1999. *Love's Labor. Essays on Women, Equality, and Dependency*. London: Routledge.
———. 2001a. A Feminist Public Ethic of Care Meets the New Communitarian Family Policy. *Ethics* 111 (3): 523–547.
———. 2001b. From Welfare to a Public Ethic of Care. In *Women and Welfare: Theory and Practice in the United States and Europe*, ed. Nancy J. Hirschmann and Ulrike Liebert, 38–64. New Brunswick, NJ: Rutgers University Press.
Koggel, Christine, and Joan Orme. 2010. Care Ethics: New Theories and Applications. *Ethics and Social Welfare* 4 (2): 109–114.
Kohlen, Helen. 2009. *Conflicts of Care. Hospital Ethics Committees in the US and in Germany*. Frankfurt: Campus Verlag.
Langford, Rachel, ed. 2019. *Theorizing Feminist Ethics of Care in Early Childhood Practice. Possibilities and Dangers*. London: Bloomsbury Academic.

Laugier, Sandra, ed. 2012. *Tous vulnérables? Le care, les animaux et l'environnement.* Paris: Payot.

Leget, J.W. Carlo. 2013. Analyzing Dignity: A Perspective from the Ethics of Care. *Medicine, Health Care and Philosophy* 16: 945–952.

Lever, Janet. 1976. Sex Differences in the Games Children Play. *Social Problems* 23: 478–487.

Mahon, Rianne, and Fiona Robinson, eds. 2011. *Feminist Ethics and Social Policy: Toward a New Global Political Economy of Care.* Vancouver: UBC Press.

McClelland, C. David. 1975. *Power: The Inner Experience.* New York: Irvington.

Miller, Jean Baker. 1976. *Toward a New Psychology of Women.* Boston: Beacon Press.

Mol, Annemarie. 2008. *Logic of Care. Health and the Problem of Patient Choice.* London: Routledge.

Molinier, Pascale, Sandra Laugier, and Patricia Paperman. 2009. *Qu'est-ce que le care? Souci des autres, sensibilité, responsabilité.* Paris: Payot.

Murdoch, Iris. 1970. *The Sovereignty of Good.* London: Routledge and Kegan Paul.

Nedelsky, Jennifer. 2011. *Law's Relations. A Relational Theory of Self, Autonomy, and Law.* Oxford: Oxford University Press.

Noddings, Nel. 1984. *Caring. A Feminine Approach to Ethics and Moral Education.* Berkeley: University of California Press.

———. 2002. *Starting at Home: Caring and Social Policy.* Berkeley: University of California Press.

———. 2003. *Happiness and Education.* Cambridge: Cambridge University Press.

Okin, Susan Moller. 1979. *Women in Western Political Philosophy.* Princeton, NJ: Princeton University Press.

Parker, Gillian. 1985. *With Due Care and Attention. A Review of Research on Informal Care.* London: Family Policy Studies Centre.

Pettersen, Tove. 2008. *Comprehending Care: Problems and Possibilities in the Ethics of Care.* Plymouth: Lexington Books.

Pulcini, Elena. 2009. *Care of the World. Fear, Responsibility and Justice in the Global Age.* Dordrecht: Springer.

Rauner, Diana Mendley. 2000. *They Still Pick Me Up When I Fall: The Role of Caring in Youth Development and Community Life.* New York: Columbia University Press.

Rich, Adrienne. 1976. *Of Woman Born: Motherhood as Experience and Institution.* New York: Norton.

Robinson, Fiona. 1999. *Globalizing Care. Ethics, Feminist Theory, and International Relations.* Boulder: Westview Press.

———. 2014. Discourses of Motherhood and Women's Health: *Maternal Thinking* as Feminist Politics. *Journal of International Political Theory* 10 (1): 94–108.

Rose, Hilary. 1971. The Myth of the Neutrality of Science. In *The Social Impact of Modern Biology*, ed. Watson Fuller, 215–224. London: Routledge and Kegan Paul.

———. 1983. Hand, Brain, and Heart: A Feminist Epistemology for the Natural Sciences. *Sings: Journal of Women in Culture and Society* 9: 73–90.

Ruddick, Sara. 1980. Maternal Thinking. *Feminist Studies* 6 (2): 342–367.

———. 1989. *Maternal Thinking: Toward a Politics of Peace*. Boston: Beacon Press.

Sander-Staudt, Maureen. 2015. Caring Reciprocity as a Relational and Political Ideal in Confucianism and Care Ethics. In *Care Ethics and Political Theory*, ed. Daniel Engster and Maurice Hamington, 187–207. Oxford: Oxford University Press.

Sevenhuijsen, Selma. 1988. Vrouwelijkheid als bron van politieke wijsheid. Amerikaanse politieke filosofen over het moederschap. *Amsterdams Sociologist Tijdschrift* 15 (2): 208–234.

———, ed. 1991. *Gender, Care and Justice in Feminist Political Theory*. Utrecht: Anna Maria van Schuurman Centrum.

———. 1998. *Citizenship and the Ethics of Care. Feminist Considerations on Justice, Morality and Politics*. Trans. Liz Savage. London: Routledge.

Slote, Michael. 2007. *The Ethics of Care and Empathy*. New York: Routledge.

Stensöta, Olofsdotter Helena. 2010. The Conditions of Care: Reframing the Debate About Public Sector Ethics. *Public Administration Review* 70 (2): 295–303.

Taylor, J. McLean, Carol Gilligan, and Amy M. Sullivan. 1995. *Between Voice and Silence. Women and Girls, Race and Relationship*. Cambridge, MA: Harvard University Press.

Timmerman, Guus, Andries Baart, and Frans Vosman. 2019. In Search of Good Care: The Methodology of Phenomenological, Theory-oriented 'N=N Case Studies' in Empirically Grounded Ethics of Care. *Medicine, Health Care and Philosophy* 22 (4): 573–582.

Tronto, C. Joan. 1987. Beyond Gender Difference to a Theory of Care. *Signs: Journal for Women in Culture and Society* 12 (4): 644–663.

———. 1993. *Moral Boundaries. A Political Argument for an Ethic of Care*. London: Routledge.

———. 1996. Care as a Political Concept. *Revisioning the Political: Feminist Reconstructions of Traditional Concepts in Western Political Theory*, ed. Nancy J. Hirschmann and Christine Di Stefano, 139–156. Boulder, CO: Westview Press.

———. 2001. Who Cares? Public and Private Caring and the Rethinking of Citizenship. In *Women and Welfare: Theory and Practice in the United States and Europe*, ed. Nancy J. Hirschmann and Ulrike Liebert, 65–83. New Brunswick, NJ: Rutgers University Press.

———. 2013. *Caring Democracy. Markets, Equality, and Justice*. New York: New York University Press.

———. 2017. There Is an Alternative: *Homines Curans* and the Limits of Neoliberalism. *International Journal of Care and Caring* 1 (1): 27–43.

Ungerson, Clare. 1983. Why Do Women Care? In *A Labour of Love: Women, Work and Caring*, ed. Janet Finch and Dulcie Groves, 31–49. London: Routledge and Kegan Paul.

Voet, Rian. 1998. *Feminism and Citizenship*. London: SAGE Publications.

Vosman, Frans. 2016. Kartographie einer Ethik der Achtsamkeit – Rezeption und Entwicklung in Europa. In *Praxis der Achtsamkeit. Schlüsselbegriffe der Care-Ethik*, ed. Elisabeth Conradi and Frans Vosman, 33–51. Frankfurt: Campus Verlag.

Waerness, Kari. 1984. Caring as Women's Work in the Welfare State. In *Patriarchy in a Welfare Society*, ed. Harriet Holter, 67–87. Oslo: Universitetsforlaget.

Weil, Simone. 1952. *Gravity and Grace*. Trans. E. Crawford and M. von der Ruhr. London: Routledge and Kegan Paul.

Wendel, Saskia. 2003. *Feministische Ethik zur Einführung*. Hamburg: Junius.

White, Anne Julie. 2000. *Democracy, Justice, and the Welfare State. Reconstructing Public Care*. University Park: The Pennsylvania State University Press.

PART I

Exploring Core Concepts

CHAPTER 2

Democratic Practice and 'Caring to Deliberate': A Gadamerian Account of Conversation and Listening

Sophie Bourgault

In *On Bullshit* (2005), Harry Frankfurt argues that contemporary socio-political life is characterized by an unprecedented amount of bullshit. Given the ubiquity of the phenomenon and the paucity of scholarship on the subject, Frankfurt sees great urgency in offering a detailed account of what bullshit is and how it differs from its closest, less dangerous kin—lying.[1] For Frankfurt, the chief attributes of the bullshitter are carelessness and inattentiveness (2005, 23–33). Indeed, the bullshitter embodies a radical "lack of care" (ibid., 31), an inattentiveness to truth, to details and to others. But if the bullshitter is unconcerned with an ideal of truth-seeking, he is wedded to what Frankfurt regards as the opposite ideal: a thoroughly *self-oriented* ideal of sincerity. The bullshitter seeks solely to be

[1]The bullshitter "does not reject the authority of the truth, as the liar does, and oppose himself to it. *He pays no attention to it at all.* By virtue of this, bullshit is a greater enemy of the truth than lies are" (61; emphasis added).

S. Bourgault (✉)
School of Political Studies, University of Ottawa, Ottawa, ON, Canada
e-mail: Sophie.bourgault@uottawa.ca

P. Urban, L. Ward (eds.), *Care Ethics, Democratic Citizenship and the State*, International Political Theory,
https://doi.org/10.1007/978-3-030-41437-5_2

'true to his own nature': "Rather than seeking primarily to arrive at accurate representations of a common world, the individual turns toward trying to provide honest representations of himself. [...] It is as though he decides that since it makes no sense to try to be true to the facts, he must therefore try instead to be true to himself" (ibid., 65–66).

Frankfurt's *On Bullshit* is extremely timely today. If anything, the Trump presidency will be remembered decades from now as defined by a carelessness for truth, a refusal to listen and engage with others (whether media, scientists or dissenting citizens). Like other populist leaders around the world, this president does not "care to know"—to use Vrinda Dalmiya's terms (2016). Or, phrased in terms that speak to this chapter, he simply does not 'care to deliberate'—if by 'deliberating' we mean, at a minimum, participating in mutual exchange with fellow citizens regarding matters of *shared concern*. The consequences of such carelessness are surely significant for political life, and will seem particularly worrisome to those who maintain that democratic citizenship must include inclusive/open conversations, concerned reciprocity, reason-giving and a modicum of listening to views that jar with our own—a position espoused by several deliberative democracy theorists. "Post-truth politics", observe Bächtiger et al. (2018, 2), "is the antithesis of deliberative democracy. Resurgent authoritarian and populist leaders in many countries have little interest in deliberation—except to suppress it. Even where deliberation is not repressed, we too often see levels of political polarization that *signal inabilities to listen to the other side and reflect upon what they may have to say*" (emphasis added).[2]

There is an urgency attached to reflecting on this growing legitimization and *normalization* of careless (and hateful) talk and inability to listen. The challenge this poses for democratic theory invites us to look anew at what matters for citizenship and deliberation, and particularly at listening. The latter has not been the subject of extensive study: political theorists have theorized political *speech* much more than listening (notable exceptions include Barber (1984/2003) and Bickford (1996)). Over the past five years, we have witnessed an increase in interest for listening (Lacey 2013; Dobson 2014), including among deliberative democrats (e.g. Mutz 2006; Hendriks et al. 2019). But Michael Morrell (2018) is still correct to

[2] This is not to suggest that all deliberation and listening *necessarily* decreases polarization; deliberation is highly context-dependent. For discussions of the complex and variable ties between public discussion and polarization, see, for example, Sunstein 2009; Mutz 2006; Mansbridge and Latura 2016; Hendriks et al. 2019.

observe that listening remains decidedly under-theorized—a surprising gap considering that for many, "the future of democracy lies in listening" (Mansbridge and Latura 2016, 29).

Still, one group of contemporary scholars stands out as the exception to this scanty theorization: namely care theorists. Well before the 'second generation' of deliberative democracy theorists (who sought to address the blind spots of earlier Habermesian accounts of deliberation),[3] care ethicists insisted on attentiveness and listening's significance for care work, ethical judgement and, more generally, political and institutional life. To be clear, feminist[4] care theorists did not dismiss the desirability of having a voice, but many made the crucial point that without attentive listening, there is really no such thing as 'voice' or meaningful conversation. One could think of Gilligan's relational account of voice (1993 [1982], 1995) or of Tronto's portrait (1993) of attentiveness as entailing a hyper-receptive *listening to others' needs* (see also Noddings 1984; Sevenhuijsen 1998; Hamington 2001; Bourgault 2016). In a paper fittingly titled 'Stop Talking and Listen', Fiona Robinson (2011) also proposed a care ethics critique of discourse ethics—insisting that the mere inclusion of excluded parties in deliberation is thoroughly inadequate without a genuine commitment to listen on the part of dominant groups. Elisabeth Conradi (2002) and Sandra Laugier (2009) have also both argued that care itself might come down largely to a matter of attentive listening.

This chapter's goal is not to recap these important insights. I wish rather to build upon them by turning to Hans-Georg Gadamer's work—an uncharted territory for care ethics.[5] I wish to indicate the resonances between feminist care ethics and Gadamerian hermeneutics, and to show how these might be informative for democratic theory. While Gadamer did not theorize at length democratic and political practice, he offered an account of attentive listening that is relevant for care theorists as they flesh

[3] Quite sharply underscored by Young (1996) and Sanders (1997). Many second-generation theorists have responded to these by acknowledging further the significance of listening, embodiment, emotions and rhetoric.

[4] As Julie Perreault and myself have argued (2015), care theory is, at its core, feminist. This is not to dismiss the important differences between various articulations of care theory; the fact that there are a great variety of feminisms will obviously be mirrored in care scholarship. Nonetheless, I do think that the great bulk of care theorists share (to varying degrees) a feminist commitment. Hence I use the terms 'feminist care theorists' and 'care theorists' interchangeably in this chapter.

[5] That is true at least for Anglo-Saxon and French scholarly circles. But see the fine work of Schuchter (2016) in German-speaking circles.

out their account of citizenship, plurality and solidarity (their account of 'caring with' (Tronto 2013)). Gadamer liked to define his entire hermeneutic philosophy as "the ability to listen to the other",[6] and he repeatedly affirmed the primacy of attentive listening. In a late essay, Gadamer argued that he considered the true mark of humanity to consist in the capacity to "become always capable of conversation—that is, to listen to the Other" (Gadamer 2006a, 358). Consider also his definition of hermeneutics as "a practice, the art of understanding and of making something understood to someone else. [...] what one has to exercise above all is the ear" (Gadamer 2007, 21). Walhof (2017, 9) as such is certainly correct to sum up Gadamer's account of practical philosophy as "the discipline of paying attention"—one centred on listening and attending to the other. As we shall see, Gadamer presented his hermeneutics chiefly (albeit not exclusively) via a consideration of individual character dispositions and dyadic relationships—of relationships that could be labelled pre-political. But Gadamer was deeply convinced that character and dyadic encounters were of utmost importance for socio-political life and, in particular, for fruitful cross-cultural exchanges (as Gadamerian theorists like Charles Taylor (2002) and Fred Dallmayr (2009) have both also convincingly argued).[7]

By turning to Gadamer, I wish to take up Tronto's invitation to take seriously citizenship as a matter not only of "caring for citizens" but also of caring "for democracy itself" (2013, x). To *care for democracy itself* partially entails what I would like to term 'caring to deliberate': a commitment to conversation Gadamer understood as a *commitment* to listening to another. As we shall see, Gadamerian 'caring to deliberate' resonates at once with Gilligan's "caring to hear" (1995) and Dalmiya's "caring to know" (2016). And like Dalmiya and Gilligan's thought, Gadamer's sits at the cross-roads of the ethical, epistemological and political.

The chapter proceeds as follows: the first two sections draw the contours of Gadamerian care-based deliberating/listening—focusing chiefly here on listening's situatedness, its relational and humble character, the priority it gives to questions and its embrace of indeterminacy. I argue that Gadamerian 'caring to deliberate'[8] is congruent with feminist aims, that it

[6] Cited in Grondin 2003, 250.

[7] See also deliberative democracy theorist Morrell (2018) for the crucial importance of individual character dispositions for public large-scale deliberations.

[8] One note on terminology: while Gadamer does not employ the term 'deliberate', his very frequently used 'dialogue' and 'conversation' are close (if imperfect) equivalents of what some deliberative democracy theorists today mean by deliberation (especially those theorists

is respectful of difference/plurality yet committed to truth-seeking. With Dalmiya, I suggest that we ought to "retain a basic commitment to truth" (2016, 23)—a commitment (*if anchored in humility*) vital for our populist age. In my conclusion, I briefly indicate what a Gadamerian 'caring to deliberate' and its commitment to listen to radically different views might disturbingly require—noting the ties between listening, solidarity and loss (ties too rarely underscored in democratic theory). In these concluding remarks, I also underscore the limitations of Gadamerian hermeneutics on the questions of power and domination.

Conversation, Situatedness and Relationality

Gadamer's *Truth and Method* (Gadamer 2004) is the most well known and controversial of his works—in part because of its defence of prejudice and tradition. The book's chief objective is to describe the phenomenon of human understanding—that which takes place in the humanities, social sciences and arts but also, more generally, in all human conversations and experiences. His is not a work that offers a methodology or rules/procedures; rather, it seeks to describe the characteristics of understanding. For Gadamer, whether we are trying to understand a text, a painting, a student or a fellow citizen, the characteristics of these encounters are basically the same: they are always situated (informed by particular historical/socio-cultural horizons), and they are always dialogical, relational and practical. We consider the practical and dialogical aspects later in the chapter, but let us first consider situatedness.

For Gadamer, there can be no understanding that is separate from 'subjectivity', from the traditions we belong to and the prejudices we hold (consciously or not). The positivist dichotomy between objectivity and subjectivity is simply not tenable. All human experience, truth-claims,

most concerned with small-scale deliberative forums and 'horizontal' deliberation, where a few citizens deliberate with one another). For one recent study in deliberative democracy scholarship that focuses on *horizontal* listening and dialogical encounters that partially speak to my discussion of Gadamerian hermeneutics, see Hendriks et al. 2019. (Note that my chapter does not consider 'vertical' dialogic encounters or 'vertical' listening [e.g. the listening of elected officials, political parties or media]). In short, in this chapter I follow the lead of Darren Walhof (2005) in moving quite freely from dialogue/conversation to deliberation. Moreover, since the heart of Gadamer's account of conversation is listening (as indicated in Gadamer 2006a), I also move freely between the expressions 'caring to deliberate' and 'caring to listen'.

conversations and listening are affected by our historicity, material reality and "real factors conditioning human life, such as hunger, love, labor and domination" (Gadamer 2007, 25). Alcoff (in Code 2003) describes this as Gadamer's "immanent realism" (251). Rather than impediments to reason and exchange, prejudices and traditions are treated by Gadamer as necessary *conditions for* understanding and conversation: texts or fellow beings *can only speak to us* (mean something to us) because we are located within horizons of significance and listen with some pre-judgements and anticipations. Gadamer's defence of prejudice is obviously dependent upon a particular definition of the latter: namely "a judgement that is rendered before all the elements that determine a situation have been finally examined" (Gadamer 2004, 273). Yet, despite this 'quasi-neutral' definition, Gadamer's account of prejudice/tradition has earned him a great deal of criticism (notably from Habermas and Derrida).

Some feminist theorists have, however, found much inspiration in Gadamer's account of the situated and dialogic nature of all understanding (e.g. Code 2003; Warnke 2012). Linda Alcoff even insists that *Truth and Method* proposes a "feminist epistemology" (in Code 2003, 231). These feminist scholars stress that Gadamer's defence of the *situatedness* of all understanding/listening cannot be read as conservative. We are historically shaped beings, but we *participate* in the transmission and evolution of tradition—we constantly reshape it, and we can object to its transmission (Gadamer 2004, 293–294). Overall Gadamer certainly tends to emphasize *continuity* more than change. Still, Gadamerian prejudices and horizons of significance can and *must* change (horizons are neither fixed nor closed). His hermeneutics underscores the ethico-political responsibility we have to test and go *beyond* "limited and local" prejudices (ibid., 298); there are *illegitimate* prejudices (and social practices) that are "the undeniable task of critical reason to overcome" (ibid., 278).

Indeed, if one genuinely wishes to understand (a book or another), one must 'foreground' one's prejudices, temporarily suspending 'their validity for us'. The goal is to separate "productive prejudices that enable understanding from the prejudices that hinder it and lead to misunderstandings" (ibid., 295). Gadamer argues that temporal distance—that is, the passage of time, a confrontation between past and present (ibid., 298)—will do part of this sorting: a view that might leave many unsatisfied (suggesting that 'time' will do its job, eventually, to eliminate racism or sexism seems overly naïve if not morally repulsive).[9] But he insists that the filtering out of illegitimate prejudices can also take place 'now', ***in deliberation with others***—especially ***different*** others. Indeed, the foregrounding of our prejudices can be sparked by an encounter with alterity, which can sometimes act as a 'provocation', a 'challenging' and 'disorienting', because one is exposed to the limitations of one's existing worldview (2006b, 16–19).[10] This important role played by the other in shedding limited/illegitimate prejudices is one reason for Gadamer's celebration of our interdependency. Like care scholars, Gadamer espouses a thoroughly relational ontology: an individual, he writes, is "never simply an individual because he is always in understanding *with others*" (Gadamer 2004, 303; emphasis added), following here in the footsteps of his teacher Martin Heidegger.[11] For Gadamer, it is thanks to others—*to relationships*—that we can acquire more robust accounts of reality, of the world: "We come closer to the truth because we do not exist by ourselves" (2001, 49) Fleming (in Code 2003) incorrectly sees here an 'instrumentalization' of the other. What Gadamer's treatment of therapeutic dialogue (tackled in his set of lectures on health and doctor-patient conversations (1996)) suggests is that if the conversation partner is treated only instrumentally, it is no conversation worthy of the name and the transformative power of dialogue is compromised.

Now, note that the 'foregrounding of prejudices'—an integral part of 'caring to deliberate'—doesn't entail a complete 'stepping aside' of our prejudices or personal concerns: it is not a perfectly reciprocal stepping into the shoes of someone else. It is not akin to Seyla Benhabib's 'reciprocal symmetry', to Barber's radical empathy (2003, 186–188) or to Simone Weil's radically compassionate attentiveness (an attentiveness often

[9] Another unsatisfying part of *Truth and Method* is its too rapid treatment of the distinction between illegitimate and legitimate prejudices—with Gadamer merely explaining, almost in passing, that the former type of prejudices are identifiable as those that are dogmatic, that are 'local and limited' and that hinder understanding between human beings (TM 298, 295). Legitimate ones would be, presumably, the very opposite. But the all-too-neat dichotomy proposed by Gadamer remains highly problematic.

[10] I unfortunately have no room here to enter into a detailed discussion of the slight changes/evolution in Gadamer's hermeneutics and especially in his position on alterity/difference. For a helpful treatment, see Karmis 2013.

[11] For discussions of the deep influence of Heidegger on Gadamer's hermeneutics, see for example, Grondin 2003; Dostal 2002.

discussed by care ethics scholars). There is no 'emptying of the self' or Weilian decreation possible or desirable; Gadamer offers us a distinct view of reciprocity and empathy. He insists that "a hermeneutically trained consciousness" must be sensitive to alterity, but notes that "this kind of sensitivity involves neither *'neutrality' with respect to content nor the extinction of one's self*, but the foregrounding and appropriation of one's own fore-meanings … [the awareness] of one's own bias, so that the text [or the other] can present itself in all its otherness and *thus assert its own truth against one's own fore-meanings*".[12] The point is relevant for care ethicists as they reflect on what 'caring about' and 'caring with' entail for plurality/difference. For Gadamer, the other *has to remain other* if conversation is to have any modest transformative power on *all* interlocutors. Hence, even if we could somehow 'empty' ourselves of pre-judgements and be 'detached' conversational partners, this would in fact eliminate our ability to appreciate alterity for what it is; it would *diminish* our respect for the other and compromise the possibility that our encounter with difference might lead to the enlarging of our cultural-political horizon.[13] Consider how Gadamer describes what 'transposing oneself' into another horizon entails:

> What do we mean by 'transposing ourselves'? Certainly not just disregarding ourselves. This is necessary of course, insofar as we must imagine the other situation. *But into this other situation we must bring, precisely, ourselves.* Only this is the full meaning of 'transposing ourselves' […] we will understand him—i.e. become aware of the otherness, the indissoluble individual of the other person—by putting ourselves in his position. […] Transposing ourselves *consists neither in the empathy of one individual for another nor in subordinating another person to our own standards.* (Gadamer 2004, 304; emphasis added)

Let me note two things about this passage: first, an apparent ambiguity/hesitation on the issue of 'disregarding' oneself (did we not just learn above that there can be no 'extinguishing of oneself'?).[14] But the ambiguity might not be one: Gadamer claims that while we cannot put aside our

[12] Gadamer 2004, 272 (emphasis added); also Gadamer 2004, 298–299. For a detailed study of the transformative impact of conversation, see Walhof 2005.

[13] Gadamer defined a horizon as "the range of vision that includes everything that can be seen from a particular vantage point" (Gadamer 2004, 301).

[14] See, for example, *Truth and Method*, Gadamer 2004, 319–321.

historicity, this does not relieve us of the ethico-political *responsibility* of "looking *away from oneself* and looking out toward the other" (1998, 35; emphasis added); both are reconcilable. That responsibility he considered critical for social encounters and solidarity, and as something *we owe to ourselves* if we wish to acquire more defensible accounts of things ethico-political. It is for this reason that Gadamer (1999, 12) insisted that part of what solidarity and citizenship as friendship require is friendship *with oneself*—which is no self-love, but self-knowledge and humble acknowledgement of one's limited perspective. Second, note the claim about empathy and the impossibility of perfect 'symmetrical reciprocity': one should never presume (either prior to, during or after a conversation) that one *can* really know the other or exchange positions. Gadamerian 'caring to listen' does not hang on radical empathy and it refuses the claim that one might *actually* truly know the other (her thoughts or feelings).[15] If one presupposes in advance to emphatically 'feel' or know the other, this is not conversation but domination, since by "claiming to know the other you rob him of his claim's legitimacy" (Gadamer 2004, 354). In a passage striking for its Buberian overtones, Gadamer adds: "in human relations the important is [...] to experience the Thou truly as a Thou—not to overlook his claim but to let him really say something to us" (Gadamer 2004, 355).[16] Gadamer would agree with the likes of Young (1997) and Bickford (1996), who both express concerns about insisting on radical empathy in deliberation. That radical empathy is not a condition for Gadamerian 'caring to deliberate' is worth noting partially because it 'lowers the bar' for what might be needed for listening to those whose views we find abhorrent (we return to this in the conclusion). In cases of severe political polarization, this is an important insight (Bächtiger et al. 2018).[17]

[15] Naturally, much could be said about the numerous treatments of empathy offered in the history of philosophy, and the many authors who have proposed nuanced treatments of the subject that are *not* anchored in the presupposition that one can ever fully understand the other (e.g. Edith Stein).

[16] For care scholarship drawing on Martin Buber (e.g. his treatment of receptivity and attentiveness)—albeit in a way that does not stress asymmetrical reciprocity, see Noddings 1984.

[17] But this is not to suggest that empathy cannot sometimes *help* improve deliberations. As Diana Mutz (2006) and Michael Morrell (2018) have indicated, for instance, an individual predisposition to empathy often translates into an open-mindedness and respect that can bolster listening (particularly to dissonant views).

In this section, we noted that if all conversations are necessarily situated, one of the goals of conversations is—somewhat paradoxically—to chip away at this situatedness, to enlarge it. Conversations are epistemic and political goods precisely because they have the power to take us out of the "narrow confines of our knowledge" (Gadamer 2001, 49) and to get a little closer to a defensible account of truth—which remains open, subject to contestation (Gadamer 2004, 298). For Gadamer, narrow vision is problematic because it tends to be false, dogmatic and the contrary of a life well lived, which he conceives as consisting of a wide-range, diverse series of experiences (with the many disappointments, losses and suffering these entail—not solely joys). For him, most encounters with difference entail rubbing against both one's limitations and anticipations: "Every experience worthy of the name thwarts an expectation" and entails suffering (ibid., 350). This is the reason why the "experienced" person might be the most undogmatic (ibid., 350) and the most likely to regard with hope rather than insular despair the possibilities offered by an age of "interrelated foreignness" (Gadamer 2001, 80). Gadamer's invitation to cross-cultural conversations is loud and clear—and has been heard by the likes of Charles Taylor (2002), Fred Dallmayr (2009), Cynthia Coe (2009) and Dimitrios Karmis (2013).[18] This call might also speak to care ethicists interested in comparative political theory and in 'decolonizing' ethics (for recent efforts in that direction, see e.g. Barnes et al. 2015; Brannelly 2016).

Practice, Questions and Humility

We noted earlier that *Truth and Method* challenges the dichotomy between subject and object, and deflates the positivist's faith in uncommitted/detached inquiry. Unsurprisingly, given his emphasis on the situated concern present in all research and conversations, Gadamer resolutely places hermeneutics in an 'in-between' position: an intermediate position between subjectivity and objectivity, between self and other. Largely for this reason, hermeneutics cannot be about procedures that a subject would 'apply' to an object. Similarly, decent listening and deliberation cannot be about rules (a claim that resonates with care ethics' challenge to neo-Kantian conceptions of moral or political judgement). Listening/deliberation are rather to be regarded as 'events' that entail a *participation* in

[18] Karmis correctly sums up Gadamerian hermeneutics as a "hermeneutics of difference" (2013, 217).

something—something that often "happens to us over and above our wanting and doing" (Gadamer 2004, xxvi). While there is often agency in a conversation's initiation and while Gadamer acknowledges the importance of certain pre-discursive conditions (whether they be temporal, economic or technological),[19] he insists that, ultimately, we cannot ever fully control where the dialogue will take us, what arguments (or refusals) will arise and *how* these will affect us. Gadamer's conviction about the need to regard conversations as events that 'happen *to us*' is tied to his critique of the modern desire to control and master others/the world. What he proposes in turn is partially an ethico-political posture grounded in the admission of a universal, *shared vulnerability*: this vulnerability flows from our human interdependency but also from the *unpredictable* nature of conversation, and the risk-taking and unsettling implications of conversation (discussed later in the chapter).

Now, if Gadamerian listening/deliberating is not about rules, it is most certainly about practice. Like ethics and moral knowledge more generally, listening is a *doing* and requires repeated engagement. This is a claim that speaks to care scholarship (e.g. Robinson's emphasis on caring practices as key for the cultivation of listening [2011]). However (and here is the challenge), this practice for Gadamer cannot be meaningful without a (prior) commitment—a *caring* for deliberating: "at the beginning of every effort to understand is a *concern* about something" (2001, 50; emphasis added). How are we to understand this commitment or concern? Without succumbing to the temptation to propose a 'method' for the 'art of conversation', can we put some flesh onto that concept of commitment? I think that much hangs here on two character dispositions: humility and courage.

Let us begin with humility. The close ties between commitment, humility and openness (the latter two are used quasi-interchangeably) are underscored at length in *Truth and Method*: "In order to be able to ask, one *must want to know*, which involves knowing that one does not know" (Gadamer 2004, 348; emphasis added). For him, both openness and humility have the 'structure of a question': they come down to a

[19] In certain late essays, for instance, he briefly acknowledges the importance of bettering living conditions, of having adequate temporal resources for dialogue (e.g. in pedagogical and medical situations), as well as the particular value of face-to-face encounters (contra encounters mediated by technology). See, for example, Gadamer 1996, 2001, 80–82; 2006a. But all these remain unfortunately quite underdeveloped claims in his work. For one recent discussion of the significance of reducing economic inequalities for improving listening, see Mansbridge and Latura 2016.

willingness to seriously consider opposites—that is, the possibility that 'this might be A or B'. To ask a question entails "to bring into the open. The openness of what is in question consists in the fact that the answer is not settled" (ibid., 356–357). As such, he insists, "only a person who has questions can have knowledge" (359), and it is for this reason that he insists that questions are most critical to deliberation. The 'primacy of questions' thesis runs through Gadamer's work; it is one he learnt from teaching and from his study of Plato's dialogues. It is also a thesis that evidently troubles 'classic' treatments of deliberative democracy as chiefly about *reason-giving* (more than question posing).

We saw earlier that a genuine conversation is about 'putting our prejudices' at risk; it demands that we "listen to the other *in the belief that he might be right*".[20] I stress the sentence's crucial end: one must be willing to entertain the (unsettling) possibility that the other might be correct and one misguided. Like Dalmiya (2016, 26), Gadamer is convinced that *relational humility* is 'the condition for successful inquiry' and all 'caring with'. But Gadamer's perspective on humility and questioning resonates also with feminist theorists like Young, who insist that "respectful listening involves attentive and *interested* questioning" (1997, 56). I underscore 'interested' because for Young (as much as for Gadamer), there can be empty, uninterested questions and more 'strategic' questions. While some of these can serve daily to facilitate relationships (as Young acknowledges) and are necessary for the information-gathering that administrative/political life requires, Gadamer's 'caring to listen' celebrates (in its highest aspirational register) questions that are genuinely *concerned*. But what Gadamer insufficiently acknowledged, in my view, is that there can be hardly ever a strict separation between more 'strategic' or rhetorical questioning and completely *concerned* ones; socio-political conversations typically exist on a continuum.

One more element needs to be considered about Gadamer's account of questioning: "To conduct a conversation [...] requires that *one does not try to argue the other person down but that one really considers the weight of the other's opinion*. Hence it is an art of testing. But the art of testing is the art of questioning. [...] As against the fixity of opinions, *questioning makes the object and all its possibilities fluid*" (Gadamer 2004, 361; emphasis added). Worth noting is, first, that the 'art of questioning' proposed by Gadamer must keep 'all possibilities fluid' and, second, that the 'finality' pursued by

[20] Grondin 2003, 250; emphasis added.

this questioning is not victory. Third, if many see in Gadamerian conversation excessive agreement and serenity, one ought to note his emphasis on 'testing' and his repeated mention of "critique" and "struggle" (2006b, 17). Most simply put, Gadamerian 'caring to deliberate' entails a type of questioning that will and must cause epistemic frictions.

We noted earlier that 'caring to deliberate' entails entertaining the unsettling possibility that one's interpretation/arguments might be wrong (including one's pre-judgements about what the other might *need*—an important point for care ethics). This is one reason why listening and deliberation requires courage and generosity[21]—an ability to embrace a certain loss: "Openness to the other, then, involves recognizing that I myself must accept some things that are against me" (Gadamer 2004, 355). While this passage might strike us as standard fare of democratic theory, elsewhere Gadamer insists on something slightly more radical: when we deliberate/listen, we must not only take the other's arguments seriously, we must also try to "make his arguments *even stronger*" than they are (ibid., 292). Put differently, Gadamerian 'caring to listen' requires a significant effort to *bolster* the other's views. This is partially reminiscent of philosopher Miranda Fricker's invitation (2007) to engage in 'credibility adjustments' when a privileged interlocutor enters into conversation with someone at the bottom of the socio-economic or epistemic credibility ladder. But unlike Fricker, Gadamer insists that credibility *excesses* are also problematic (as his discussion of a medical doctor's authority/expertise indicates). What Gadamer underscores is that what is required for inclusive political communication is, first, an increasing/boosting of the other's view (especially in cases of epistemic credibility inequalities) and, second, a *diminishment* in the credibility we assign to our *own* views (or those of our group). If epistemic credibility is a comparative and finite good (as Medina (2011) underscores), Gadamer is right to insist that decent listening requires both the boosting of the other's view and a *certain* effacement of our own—a sacrifice that is in line with the 'disregarding of ourselves' or 'looking away from oneself' we noted earlier. But here

[21]What we see in this section is that Gadamerian 'caring to deliberate' is chiefly about character dispositions/individual qualities; but as I emphasized above, Gadamer was convinced that one could not reflect on these without simultaneously considering larger societal/structural prerequisites and socio-epistemic conditions, as well as the importance of practice. For him, there was no tension between stressing the importance of the one or the other. As a convinced Platonist, he thought that soul (ethics) and city (institutions) were intimately intertwined.

is what Gadamer failed to truly tackle: what if the conversation entails responding to a highly bigoted or racist interlocutor? Do we have, in *that* case, an ethical responsibility to "make even stronger" our interlocutor's abhorrent views? We consider this 'toughest case' in our conclusion.

Humility not only defines the decent deliberator but also informs how Gadamer looks at *what conversation and philosophy can accomplish and what principles can inform it*: "Hermeneutic philosophy [...] does not understand itself as an 'absolute' position but as a path of experiencing. Its modesty consists in the fact that for it there is no higher principle than this: holding oneself open to the conversation" (2007, 34). Gadamer emphasizes modesty not only in terms of philosophy's manner of proceeding/principles but also in terms of 'outcomes' (truth's open-endedness). Witness his humble take on what might result from a conversation: "Understanding is not [...] understanding better [...] in the sense of superior knowledge of the subject. [...] it is enough to say that we understand in a different way" (Gadamer 2004, 296). It is also in that respect, then, that Gadamerian 'caring to deliberate' resonates with care ethics: it is comfortable with ambivalence. It is appreciative of the hesitant 'It depends' of the likes of Gilligan's Amy, and regards these not as signs of psychological or ethical immaturity, but as the opposite. It is a striking trait of Gadamer's work that while he was thoroughly wedded to Platonic dialectic, often used fairly 'thick' moral terms and invited us to *seek truth* (and denounced false, careless statements), he constantly emphasized the fluid, unstable and open-ended nature of truth. It is as such no surprise that Gadamer has been described as a "Post-modern Plato" (Zuckert 1996). Gadamer's ethics not only has affinities with post-modern thought, it is also one that can speak to feminist postcolonial projects (despite his limited, unsatisfying treatment of power, which partially flows from his focus on dyadic encounters). Gadamerian 'caring to deliberate' is non-colonizing in light of the extreme humility it is anchored in, but also because its 'art of questioning' entails that one will prevent that any question be "suppressed by the dominant opinion" (Gadamer 2004, 361). His is a political philosophy that invites us to pay attention to the margins, to "silent utterances" and discreet bodily gestures (Gadamer 2006a). Cynthia Coe is thus correct to suggest that Gadamer can offer some tools to condemn colonizers' epistemic arrogance and their "failure to reflect on their own historically effected consciousness" (2009, 931).

What Stands in the Way of a Caring Democracy?

In a recent text in honour of Benjamin Barber (which briefly indicates the influence of care ethics on Barber's 'strong democratic talk'), Carol Gilligan asks: "what stands in the way of knowing what we know"? (2016, 56). What stands in the way of 'strong democracy', of a non-patriarchal, caring democracy? Gilligan's answer unsurprisingly stresses better listening to 'the different voice', to what we already know. For Gilligan, *we already know* what makes for less violent relationships, and a more democratic polity: we already have within ourselves many of "the requisites for [...] democratic citizenship" (2016, 75). Gadamer is partially arguing something similar in his discussion of (democratic) solidarity: that we *always already have* some of the basic prerequisites for solidarities, but that the latter need uncovering (something consistent with his conception of philosophy as a practice that "consists in making what we all already know another step more conscious" (1996, 139)). There is no room to enter here into a detailed account of Gadamerian solidarity. I merely wish to note that the latter is largely (albeit not exclusively) dependent upon conversation, since the latter might reveal what we (already) share. Indeed, solidarities are not 'created' out of an identification of shared interests or characteristics, *but revealed through conversation* (Warnke 2012; Walhof 2006). Moreover, Gadamerian solidarities are not anchored in sameness but in the acknowledgement of a shared vulnerability and plurality: solidarity is "no unanimity" (Gadamer 2009, 8). Gadamer would, as such, have been sympathetic to Sevenhuijsen's call for a politics of solidarity that is respectful of difference rather than construed in terms of 'mutual exchange' or sameness (1998, 150).

Similarly to Gilligan, what stands in the way of better citizenship for Gadamer is in part a deeper commitment to listen/deliberate. Politics' main task is "to make us more generally aware of [the] deep solidarities" that already exist (2001, 80)—and here it is listening that mattered most. As such, we really ought to concern ourselves more with our growing "incapacity for conversation", particularly one that "refuses to admit itself "—a deliberative posture that typically ignores or mishears others (2006a, 357). The root cause of these two failures in listening was the same for him: "one who ignores or mishears is one who constantly listens to himself, whose ears are so filled from the encouragement that he constantly gives to himself [...] that he is unable to hear the Other" (ibid., 358). Gadamer's description is reminiscent of Frankfurt's description of the bullshitter: an individual caught up in his own (self-oriented) ideal of 'sincerity'. Like Frankfurt, Gadamer insists that we are all capable of conversational faults—of empty sophistry, of lying, ignoring and mishearing, of carelessness. But Gadamer still sought to find ways to partially address the particular incapacity for conversation he thought linked to hyper-specialized, 'anonymous' and advanced technological societies. The fact that we can all fail miserably in our attempts at listening according to Gadamer is worth noting, for many critics fault the philosopher for an overly optimist take on conversation (not unreasonably given his self-description as inherently optimistic).[22] Yet, genuinely caring conversations were not the norm in his view, but the exception: we rarely achieve mutual understanding and intense frictions are all too common. As Gadamer noted in his reply to Derrida: "we encounter limits again and again; we speak past each and are even at cross-purposes [but …] we could not do this at all if we had not traveled a long way together, perhaps without even acknowledging it to ourselves. All human solidarity, all social stability, presupposes this" (Michelfelder and Palmer 1989, 57).

In closing, I wish to return to the 'toughest' case mentioned earlier—the entering into a conversation with an individual who is not only careless about truth-seeking but who holds racist views. This case seems to disclose all the serious limitations of Gadamer: for instance, his insufficient (quasi-existent) treatment of power and of radical close-mindedness. Given these grave blind spots, we would do well to complement his account of deliberation with a finer analysis of power and also of the weight of prejudice and of cultural/linguistic capital inequalities on communication (in the manner of a Bourdieu, Foucault, Spivak or Medina). I would suggest that care ethics could here also offer healthy correctives.

Nonetheless, there is still something about Gadamerian 'caring to deliberate' that might remain pertinent (if depressingly so) for this 'toughest case'. Gadamer often insisted that small-scale dialogical encounters might be the most fruitful ones and that bodily presence was key for attentive listening and transformative dialogue (1996, 2006a). As such, faced with our 'tough case', Gadamer might have here underscored the desirability of organizing micro-deliberative forums or one-on-one, face-to-face encounters, with one deliberative ordinary hero changing one person

[22] For example, Gadamer 2001, 83; also 2007 (25): "Even the total breakdown of communication, even misunderstanding and the famous admission that one does not know, presuppose that understanding is possible."

at a time.[23] Allow me to illustrate this with the case of Daryl Davis. For the past decades, this African American blues musician purposefully sought conversations in bars with Ku Klux Klan (KKK) members, hoping to change their views, one at a time, over drinks and dinner (200 members are said to have given up their robes as a result). Davis's account of these conversations highlights three Gadamerian insights: first, one can initiate a (potentially) transformative dialogue with someone for whom one has no empathy (a point discussed earlier). Second, face-to-face conversation about apparently trivial matters might be capable of troubling someone's political view: "If you spend five minutes with your worst enemy—it doesn't have to be about race, it could be about anything … you will find that you both have something in common […] you're forming a relationship and as you build about that relationship, you're forming a friendship. […] I didn't convert anybody … [they] converted themselves."[24] That something (solidarity or a relationship) is 'revealed' by a *conversation* (an event one does not fully control, an event that might not at first have elaborate reason-giving) is something that Gadamer was convinced of. Moreover, this story indicates the impact that witnessing someone else's 'caring to know' can have on a closed-minded bigot. What Davis underscores repeatedly is that he was truly committed to learn about the KKK and its supporters—a commitment that provoked a certain openness in the other: "I knew as much about the Klan, if not more than many of the Klan people that I interviewed. When they see that you know about their organization, their belief system, they respect you. Whether they like you or not, they respect the fact that you've done your homework."[25]

But there is one very disturbing thing this story underscores and that Gadamer dramatically failed to see: that it tends to be the case that those who sacrifice and suffer most in deliberative exchanges like these are often not the privileged or powerful. Indeed, it is the non-racist, black American who *first* had to diminish his own argument's credibility and self-respect in order to initiate the conversation (and it is he who had to 'do his homework'). It is Davis who *first* accepted a loss for the sake of transforming the other's view and, possibly, of decreasing racism. If we hold up Davis as an

[23] For some recent theoretical and empirical discussions of the impact of micro-deliberative fora and of face-to-face encounters, see ch.18 and 20 of Bächtiger et al. 2018.

[24] https://www.npr.org/2017/08/20/544861933/how-one-man-convinced-200-ku-klux-klan-members-to-give-up-their-robes.

[25] Ibid. (NPR).

exemplar of the emancipatory potential of Gadamerian hermeneutics, we see immediately however the perversity of inviting racialized minorities or women to do some of the 'leg work' on conversations with racists or misogynists, to risk and sacrifice in order to breach these divides. And we unfortunately know all too well that in some cases, the risks entailed might include the possibility of suffering violence or death—indeed, concrete threats to one's physical safety.

Gadamer is to be lauded for underscoring (in a manner too few democratic theorists have) that loss and sacrifice are crucial for solidarity and transformative deliberations (recall that decent Gadamerian conversations entail making ourselves vulnerable and accepting that some things might be 'against us'). But we must certainly chastise him for never realizing the extent to which it is racialized minorities and epistemically marginalized groups who tend to have to make the greatest sacrifices.[26] Embracing Gadamerian hermeneutics as a resource for a caring democracy will thus require attending to the unequal sacrifices demanded of citizens. In a powerful work on friendship and democratic citizenship in the USA, Danielle Allen (2006) has drawn our attention to the place of sacrifice in maintaining and upholding civic friendship and, in particular, to the manner in which black Americans have borne the greatest burden. This is something to which democratic theorists of all stripes should attend as they pursue more inclusive, more caring political communities: namely we must think about ways to shift the burden of sacrifices from those who are the object of racist and sexist invectives to those in positions of power. To champion dialogue as a response to violent domination seems to the agonist like a straightforward category mistake. But common citizenship requires that such relationships be transformed—'caring democracy' requires of us that we face up to the reality of power and domination, without giving up on the potential of hermeneutics.

Acknowledgements I would like to thank Lizzie Ward and Petr Urban for their helpful feedback on this chapter, as well as Robert Sparling and my Canadian Political Science Association (CPSA) 2019 panellists in Vancouver (particularly Eleonor MacDonald).

[26] For a fine discussion of sacrifice in the field of care ethics, see van Nistelrooij 2015.

References

Allen, Danielle. 2006. *Talking to Strangers*. Chicago: University of Chicago Press.

Bächtiger, Andre, John S. Dryzek, Jane Mansbridge, and Mark Warren. 2018. *The Oxford Handbook of Deliberative Democracy*. Oxford: Oxford University Press.

Barber, Benjamin. 2003. *Strong Democracy*. 2nd ed. Berkeley: University of California Press.

Barnes, Marian, Tula Brannelly, Lizzie Ward, and Nicki Ward, eds. 2015. *Ethics of Care. Critical Advances in International Perspective*. Bristol: Policy Press.

Bickford, Susan. 1996. *The Dissonance of Democracy: Listening, Conflict and Citizenship*. Ithaca: Cornell University Press.

Bourgault, Sophie. 2016. Attentive Listening and Care in a Neoliberal Era: Weilian Insights for Hurried Times. *Ethics and Politics* XVIII (3): 311–377.

Bourgault, Sophie, and Julie Perreault, eds. 2015. *Le care: Éthique féministe actuelle*. Montréal: Éditions du Remue-Ménage.

Brannelly, Tula. 2016. Decolonising Research Practices with the Ethics of Care. *Nursing Ethics* 23 (1): 4–6.

Code, Lorraine, ed. 2003. *Feminist Interpretations of Hans-Georg Gadamer*. University Park: Penn State University Press.

Coe, Cynthia. 2009. Strangers and Natives: Gadamer, Colonial Discourse and the Politics of Understanding. *Philosophy & Social Criticism* 35 (8): 921–933.

Conradi, Elisabeth. 2002. *Take Care. Grundlagen einer Ethik der Achtsamkeit*. Frankfurt: Campus Verlag.

Dallmayr, Fred. 2009. Hermeneutics and Inter-cultural Dialog: Linking Theory and Practice. *Ethics and Global Politics* 2 (1): 23–39.

Dalmiya, Vrinda. 2016. *Caring to Know. Comparative Care Ethics, Feminist Epistemology, and the Mahābhārata*. Oxford: Oxford University Press.

Dobson, Andrew. 2014. *Listening for Democracy*. Oxford: Oxford University Press.

Dostal, Robert. 2002. *The Cambridge Companion to Gadamer*. Cambridge: Cambridge University Press.

Frankfurt, Harry. 2005. *On Bullshit*. Princeton: Princeton University Press.

Fricker, Miranda. 2007. *Epistemic Injustice. Power and the Ethics of Knowing*. Oxford: Oxford University Press.

Gadamer, Hans-Georg. 1996. *The Enigma of Health*. Stanford: Stanford University Press.

———. 1998. *Praise of Theory*. New Haven and London: Yale University Press.

———. 1999 [2009]. Friendship and Solidarity. *Research in Phenomenology* 39: 3–12.

———. 2001. *Gadamer in Conversation*. Trans. Palmer. New Haven: Yale University Press.

———. 2004. *Truth and Method*. London: Continuum.

———. 2006a. The Incapacity for Conversation. *Continental Philosophy Review* 39 (4): 351–359.

———. 2006b. Language and Understanding. *Theory, Culture & Society* 23 (1): 13–27.
———. 2007. Autobiographical Reflections. In *The Gadamer Reader*, ed. Richard Palmer. Northwestern University Press.
———. 2009 [1999]. Friendship and Solidarity. *Research in Phenomenology* 39: 3–12.
Gilligan, Carol. 1993 [1982]. *In a Different Voice*. Cambridge: Harvard University Press.
———. 1995. Hearing the Difference: Theorizing Connection. *Hypatia* 10 (2): 120–127.
———. 2016. Strong Democracy and a Different Voice. What Stands in the Way? In *Strong Democracy in Crisis: Promise or Peril?* ed. Trevor Norris. Lanham: Lexington Books.
Grondin, Jean. 2003. *Gadamer*. Yale: Yale University Press.
Hamington, Maurice. 2001. Jane Adams and a Politics of Embodied Care. *The Journal of Speculative Philosophy* 15 (2): 105–121.
Hendriks, M. Carolyn, Selen A. Ercan, and Sonya Duus. 2019. Listening in Polarized Communities. *Policy Sciences* 52 (1): 137–151.
Karmis, Dimitrios. 2013. Skinner contre Gadamer? Deux contributions à une herméneutique de la différence. In *Ceci n'est pas une idée politique. Réflexions sur les approches à l'étude des idées politiques*, ed. Dimitrios Karmis and Dalie Giroux. Laval: PUL.
Lacey, Kate. 2013. *Listening Publics*. Bristol: Polity Press.
Laugier, Sandra. 2009. Le sujet du care: vulnérabilité et expression ordinaire. In *Qu'est-ce que le care?* ed. Pascale Molinier, Sandra Laugier, and Patricia Paperman. Paris: Payot.
Mansbridge, Jane, and Audrey Latura. 2016. The Polarization Crisis in the United States and the Future of Listening. In *Strong Democracy in Crisis: Promise or Peril?* ed. Trevor Norris, 29–54. Lanham: Lexington Books.
Medina, José. 2011. The Relevance of Credibility Excess in a Proportional View of Epistemic Injustice. *Social Epistemology* 25 (1): 15–35.
Michelfelder, Diane, and Richard Palmer, eds. 1989. *Dialogue and Deconstruction*. SUNY.
Morrell, Michael. 2018. Listening and Deliberation. In *The Oxford Handbook of Deliberative Democracy*, ed. André Bächtige, John S. Dryzek, Jane Mansbridgem, and Mark E. Warren, 237–250. Oxford: Oxford University Press.
Mutz, Diana. 2006. *Hearing the Other Side*. Cambridge: Cambridge University Press.
Van Nistelrooij, Inge. 2015. *Sacrifice: A Care-Ethical Reappraisal of Sacrifice and Self-Sacrifice*. Leuven: Peeters.
Noddings, Nel. 1984. *Caring: A Feminine Approach to Ethics and Moral Education*. Berkeley: University of California Press.

Robinson, Fiona. 2011. Stop Talking and Listen. *Journal of International Studies* 39 (3): 845–860.
Sanders, Lynn M. 1997. Against Deliberation. *Political Theory* 25 (3): 347–376.
Schuchter, Patrick. 2016. *Sich einen Begriff vom Leiden Anderer machen. Eine praktische Philosophie der Sorge*. Transcript Verlag.
Sevenhuijsen, Selma. 1998 [2003]. *Citizenship and the Ethics of Care: Feminist Considerations on Justice, Morality and Politics*. London: Routledge.
Sunstein, Cass R. 2009. *Going to Extremes: How Like Minds Unite and Divide*. Reprint ed. New York: Oxford University Press.
Taylor, Charles. 2002. Understanding the Other: A Gadamerian View on Conceptual Schemes. In *Gadamer's Century. Essays in Honor of Hans-Georg Gadamer*, ed. J. Malpas, U. Arnswald, and J. Kertscher. Cambridge: MIT Press.
Tronto, Joan C. 1993. *Moral Boundaries*. New York: Routledge.
———. 2013. *Caring Democracy: Markets, Equality and Justice*. New York: New York University Press.
Walhof, Darren. 2005. Bringing the Deliberative Back In. *Contemporary Political Theory* 4: 154–174.
———. 2006. Friendship, Otherness, and Gadamer's Politics of Solidarity. *Political Theory* 34 (5): 569–593.
———. 2017. *The Democratic Theory of Hans-Georg Gadamer*. Basingstoke: Palgrave Macmillan.
Warnke, Georgia. 2012. Solidarity and Tradition in Gadamer's Hermeneutics. *History and Theory* 51: 6–22.
Young, Iris Marion 1996. Communication and the Other: Beyond Deliberative Democracy. In *Democracy and Difference: Contesting the Boundaries of the Political*, ed. Seyla Benhabib, 120–135. Princeton, NJ: Princeton University Press.
Young, Iris Marion. 1997. Asymmetrical Reciprocity: On Moral Respect, Wonder and Enlarged Thought. *Constellations* 3 (3): 340–363.
Zuckert, Catherine. 1996. *Postmodern Platos*. Chicago: University of Chicago Press.

CHAPTER 3

Democratic Inclusion Through Caring Together with Others

Jorma Heier

In *Caring Democracy* (2013), Joan Tronto argues that the current political ways of organizing human living together are wrought with a democracy deficit and a care deficit. As a result, many, if not most, people are excluded from the deliberations and responsibility-setting processes that most severely affect how well they will be able to live and participate in their polity. This chapter takes up Joan Tronto's suggestion to solve this grievance by dovetailing care and democracy in democratic 'caring with'. All citizens, Tronto argues, must be enabled to participate as fully as possible in the decision-making processes that distribute care responsibilities in their polities. To contextualize these broad claims, and to flesh out what shape the care deficit and the democracy deficit can take, consider the

J. Heier (✉)
University of Applied Sciences Flensburg, Flensburg, Germany
e-mail: Jorma.heier@hs-flensburg.de

P. Urban, L. Ward (eds.), *Care Ethics, Democratic Citizenship and the State*, International Political Theory,
https://doi.org/10.1007/978-3-030-41437-5_3

example of Markus Igel,[1] a German dis_ability[2] rights activist with tetraparesis.

To live a self-determined and socially integrated life, Markus Igel needs a variety of assistance on a daily basis. Igel uses a wheelchair for mobility and needs help with getting dressed, bathing and preparing food. To communicate with others verbally and by letter, Igel needs the support of others who are trained in understanding Igel's speech impairment. Falsely diagnosed with a learning difficulty as a child, Igel was placed in a special needs school where Igel's teachers did not deem it necessary to teach Igel sufficient speaking and writing to communicate without assistance. Markus Igel grew up in care homes, but did not like it there due to lack of personal freedom to decide even the basest of things like whom to live with, when to eat, whether or not to shave, when to go to the toilet or to get up. These all depended on when overwhelmed professional care workers would find the time. And Igel did not like the placement in a workshop for people with dis_abilities. In Germany, these workshops are supposed to prepare people with dis_abilities for their inclusion into the regular labor market. In reality, many workers never transfer to the general employment market. Wages at the workshops are below Germany's minimum wage, and some categories of workers only make €8.50 a day, while €8.50 is supposed to be the legal minimum wage per hour.

Then in the twenty-fifth year of life, Igel makes use of the neoliberal employer model in the *Federal Participation Act* and moves into a two-room apartment, assisted around the clock by three care workers paid for by Igel via social aid. Five years into Igel's newfound freedom to make decisions over daily life, the state of Saarland in which Igel lives revokes the employer model and decides that Igel only has a right to the assistance that costs the least. The state stops paying the social aid for the care

[1] I opted for not changing Markus Igel's name because Igel has openly fought politically for the democratic inclusion in care responsibility-setting processes affecting Igel's life for years. I would like to honor Igel's voice, activism and resilience.

[2] I use the underscore character in the term dis_ability to bring attention to the fact that in polities whose basic structures are designed with people considered to be able-bodied in mind, it is not only the faculties of human bodies deemed 'disabled' that render some people unable to fully participate in them, but the structures themselves that dis-able full participation in the polity. In this sense, it is not so much the fact of using a wheelchair to get around that disables the mobility of a person for whom mobility has the shape of wheeling, but buildings and public transport and parks that are not adequately designed with people using wheelchairs in mind.

workers' wages and suggests that Igel discharge the care workers who use Igel's wage to finance their livelihoods and university studies. Igel's polity leaves Igel with two choices: either to move back into a care home, or to employ two Polish or Romanian migrant care workers who would work below or for minimum wage while being at work twenty-four hours a day on standby for weeks on end. These care workers would have to live with Igel in the two-room apartment, and Igel would be responsible for financing the assistant's food and insurance. The migrant care workers would only get to go home to their families every two months. Even if Igel agreed to exploiting migrant workers at the behest of the German state, it is not clear if Igel could employ a care worker for minimum wage who speaks German sufficiently enough to understand Igel in the speaking impairment.

To my mind, it is obvious that the German state places Markus Igel in a situation in which neither option is acceptable because neither option fulfills the needs of the people involved. In democratic theory terms, there is a democracy deficit to the demands of the state of Saarland then, because it regards neither the needs and voice of Markus Igel nor the prospective migrant care workers in their decisions and directives. Traditionally, the branches in democratic theory which have centered this democracy deficit are participatory and deliberative democracy. The punchlines of these accounts can be put in a nutshell as follows: collective decisions should only be considered binding and legitimate if they have been arrived at by way of an inclusive process of deliberation in which all who will be affected by that decision have participated, and if all who will be affected can reasonably agree to it. From the outset, care ethics has committed itself to amplifying the voices that are oftentimes not heard in the dominant political discourse. In recent years, care theory has also taken on the democracy deficit illustrated by Markus Igel's case more decidedly (Robinson 2011; Tronto 2013; Barnes et al. 2015; Heier 2015). In no account is the democratic deficit more center stage than in Joan Tronto's *Caring Democracy* (2013). In some instances, this chapter argues, care theory has followed the path trodden by deliberative and participatory democracy; in others it adds its own distinct voice and perspective to the democracy deficit. With *Caring democracy*, Joan Tronto delivers care theory's very own punchline to the democracy deficit, claiming that the democracy deficit can only be solved if democracy becomes more caring, whereas the democracy deficit in care can only be solved if care becomes more democratic.

In this chapter, I will first situate 'caring democracy's' assertion that Markus Igel and Igel's care workers are harmed by a democracy deficit by outlining the bedrock claims of participatory and deliberative democracy as they pertain to Igel's case. Then I will highlight how Tronto's account of 'caring democracy' issues a much more radical claim pertaining to both our understanding of the democracy deficit and the possible ways to decrease it. I will end on a short appraisal of the 'moot' points of democracy that democratic caring opens up for renegotiation.

Participatory and Deliberative Democracy

The last three decades have seen an increasing awareness in polities in Europe and North America_Turtle Island[3] that said polities have their own unique histories of centering the perspectives of some groups on collective issues and flourishing over that of marginalized others, and the structural oppression this begot.[4] I read both participatory and deliberative accounts of democracy as attempts to respond to the issue of political exclusion of marginalized groups and voices in democracies. Democratic theory, in both the veins of deliberative and participatory democracy, is an academic debate that spans many decades and centuries and encompasses a myriad of authors. I am not capable of doing justice to the multivocality of these discourses between these few pages and will therefore resign myself to its cornerstones. The story of participatory democracy is commonly told with Aristotle's claim in the fourth century B.C. that a citizen is who partakes in government as a starting point and then progresses to Jean-Jacques Rousseau's (1762) assertion that all voices need to be counted to derive the public good, until it fans out with authors such as

[3] I use the terms North America_Turtle Island or United States_Turtle Island as a way to bring the history and continued influence and harm of colonialism in settler societies into focus. Turtle Island is an indigenous term, though not indigenous word, for North America that stems from Anishinaabe, Haudenosaunee and Lenape origin and creation stories. It is not representative of all the many different names that the North American continent has in the hundreds of languages of First Nations. And it is not a representation of an indigenous concept in an indigenous language, since English is a colonial language for First nations. I sincerely regret that I could not come up with a more inclusive approach to naming that does not repeat the harm of once more centering one language, and a European language at that.

[4] Some cases in question are a growing, if reluctant, debate about Germany's, the Netherland's and Belgium's colonial past and the atrocities committed therein and the harms reaching into the present; the increase of civil rights for queer, trans and intersex people, and affirmative action codes to include women in historically male-dominated professions.

Benjamin Barber (1985), who accentuates the transformative and intrinsic dimensions of political participation and its basis for negative and positive freedom, Ingeborg Maus (1994), who claims that democratic participation is a much needed corrective to the undemocratic elements of expertocracy and the neocorporatist state in representative democracy (see Weber 2012, 224–228), and Hannah Fenichel Pitkin's (2004) assertion that representative democracy is a *contradictio in adiecto*.

The history of deliberative democracy is usually told as starting with Jean-Jacques Rousseau (1762) and Immanuel Kant (1785), before it picks up pace when Joseph Bessette coins the term deliberative democracy in 1980 and Jürgen Habermas[5] publishes the first monography on the matter in 1994; it then fans out into works by Seyla Benhabib (1994), James Bohmann (1996), Amy Gutmann and Dennis Thompson (1996) and Iris Young (2000), to name a few. Since to me, the punchlines of both discourses on democracy intersect in the work of Iris Marion Young (1990, 2000), and since Young is considered to be a "fellow traveler" (Vosman 2017) by many care theorists, I will use Young's account to sketch a brief portrait of the taglines of deliberative and participatory democracy. Young's take on participatory and deliberative democracy is most fruitful for a care theoretical consideration because Young defends the importance of particularity and heterogeneity against the "Enlightenment republicanism" (Young 1990, 119) of many participatory and deliberative democracy proponents, who desire political unity and a single unified conception of the common good, and seek to relegate particular and bodily needs to the private realm.

In the seminal *Justice and the Politics of Difference* (1990), Iris Marion Young calls for a paradigm shift toward participatory democracy. Young understands participatory democracy as a project that seeks to repoliticize public life and, by implication, current representative democracy as constraining democratic participation. What is needed to overcome structural processes of political exclusion and marginalization, Young argues, are

> real participatory structures in which actual people, with their geographical, ethnic, gender, and occupational differences, assert their perspectives on social issues within institutions that encourage the representation of their distinct voices. (Young 1990, 116)

[5] See Landwehr 2012, 355–359.

Young identifies "five faces of oppression" (Young 1990, 40) that are in the way of effective democratic participation. Oppression is present where a structurally defined group is subjected either to "exploitation, marginalization, powerlessness, cultural imperialism or violence" (ibid.) or a combination thereof. To mitigate these forms of oppression, participatory democracy is needed as a tool and condition of "social justice" (Young 1990, 183). To include both privileged and oppressed groups in participatory democracy, Young suggests a specific group representation for oppressed groups in public decision-making processes (see Young 1990, 184). Markus Igel's audible protest against the compulsory placement of dis_abled people who cannot afford around the clock home care into care homes is not taken into account in the care responsibility-setting process conducted by the Saarland State that decides how Igel and other dis_abled people will be supported by their polity to lead self-determined lives. In Young's participatory understanding of democracy, this exclusion constitutes structural oppression. The same goes for the fact that Igel's prospective migrant care workers are not included in the decisions that structure the conditions of their work. This fact is exacerbated by the economic reality in which people who are placed in workshops for people with dis_abilities do not even make minimum wage and therefore cannot privately finance around-the-clock care outside of institutions for themselves. This problematization is echoed in Tronto's *Caring Democracy* (2013). There, Tronto argues that all citizens ought to participate as fully as possible in the care responsibility-setting processes that affect their well-being to mitigate the democracy deficit in care and the care deficit in democracy. The main two tasks of democratic politics should therefore be "assigning responsibilities for care, and [...] ensuring that democratic citizens are as capable as possible of participating in this assignment of responsibilities" (Tronto 2013, 7). But in order to enable Igel to participate in political processes as fully as possible, Igel's care needs must first be met sufficiently. But for Igel's care needs to be met sufficiently, Igel needs to enter the political stage and claim that the state of Saarland has a responsibility to include Igel in the care responsibility-setting processes that affect Igel. More on this care paradox in the subsequent section.

Young's *Inclusion and Democracy* (2000) is a follow-up in-depth exploration of the requirements that participatory democratic practices need to fulfill in order to overcome exclusion and oppression. This time, the account of democracy that Young centers is deliberative democracy as a tool to foster inclusive democratic participation and to tackle forms of exclusion oppressed groups face when they have "obtained a presence in the public" (Young 2000, 55). Young defines deliberative democracy as a process that consists primarily of "a discussion of problems, conflicts, and claims of need or interest" (Young 2000, 23). It is shaped by four normative, interrelated ideals, "inclusion, equality, reasonableness, and publicity" (ibid.). To render political decisions legitimate and just, all those who will be affected by these decisions need to be included in the decision-making processes and test each other's proposals for solutions and the arguments that back them. But those affected need not only be nominally included, they must be included "on equal terms" (ibid.). This means that all must have the "equal effective opportunity" to contribute their perspectives, to question and criticize one another, to speak and be heard "free from domination" (ibid.). The participants in deliberative discussions need to partake with a willingness to listening to others that they do not agree with. They need to be willing to understand positions and perspectives that are not their own and to be open to being moved by them to change their own preconceived ideas. "Reasonable people enter discussion to solve collective problems with the aim of reaching agreement" (Young 2000, 24), even though they acknowledge that reaching agreements is often not possible, and that valuable insights into problems can also be gained from disagreement. Publicity of the decision-making process enhances its transparency and inclusivity. It fosters holding one another accountable and increases the capacity for solutions to meet actual needs and for identifying harmful beliefs and idiosyncrasies such as racism or ableism, by bringing diverse epistemologies into the process.

In order for public deliberation to become truly open to the heterogeneous groups that make up the public of a polity, it needs to broaden the permitted styles of democratic participation and argumentation. Dominant norms regulating styles of expression or ways of making an argument constrain effective participation for marginalized groups. Young therefore suggests relying on "affirmative uses of rhetoric" (Young 2000, 63) that allow for affective and embodied uses of rhetoric. In deliberation, it is not necessary to rely solely on speech to get points across. Communicative traditions that center on sign language and bodily gestures are included. Protest, crying or shouting are not considered as unorderly disruptions, but as forms of contribution in their own right. "[F]igurative language" (Young 2000, 40) allows differently situated speakers to draw on their particular discursive traditions of story and parable telling and testimony. To make use of affirmative rhetoric, citizens must make recourse to "enlarged thought" (Young 2000, 76) to fathom the situation of the listeners, to orient their discursive vocabulary to what is understandable for the audience (see Young 2000, 67). This requires participants in democratic processes to have learned about their fellow citizens and to adapt their vocabulary and style, so that people who are not well educated, who do not share the speaker's lived experience, who have learning difficulties or who are not used to formal academic reasoning can still understand and respond to what is being said. Forms of narrative and situated knowledge (see Young 2000, 65), embodied in testimony, storytelling and narrative, make differently situated knowledge available for all members of the political community (see Young 1996, 132). The prudent intervention of Sophie Bourgault in this volume cautions us that even when diverse forms of articulation are admitted into political processes, an additional skill needs to be cultivated to make the voices of the disprivileged heard. That skill is 'attentive listening'. Without 'attentive listening', the mere inclusion of excluded groups in deliberations will not get the contributions of the formerly excluded across to the privileged.

The Elements of 'Democratic Caring with'

In *Moral Boundaries* (1993), Joan Tronto analytically intertwined human dependency on care and political exclusion. Tronto retraced the historic discoursive practices through which groups of people deemed 'autonomous' marked groups of people more visibly in need of care as 'dependent' and therefore unfit for democratic participation. The same political exclusion befell the gendered, classed and racialized groups of people within the polity who carry out disproportionate amounts of care work. Rendering care invisible as a political practice through which all life is maintained serves as a bedrock that cements "the inequitable distribution of power, resources, and privilege" (Tronto 1993, 111) in a given society.

In *Caring Democracy* (2013), Tronto takes this insight one radical step further. The process of democratic inclusion of the past three centuries, Tronto argues, has been "to presume that the previously excluded are simply the same as those included, no longer dependent and no longer weighed down by the burden of dependency" (Tronto 2013, 25–26). Since the formal inclusion of the excluded rests on "a performative proof of a now discarded dependency" (Heier 2015, 202), the varieties of needs that differently situated citizens have and bring to the democratic table have been exempted from discussion and renegotiation, along with the question of who is responsible to care for these needs. As a result, the fundamental institutions of current polities have not been designed to include all people in their specificities and to work for all people in their diversity, equally. Tronto traces this grievance back to a twofold issue: a "care deficit" of democracy that fails to "reflect the real values and ideas of citizens"; and a "democracy deficit" (Tronto 2013, 17) of care, which fails to provide all citizens equally with the care needed so that they can live in their polity "as well as possible" (Tronto 1993, 103). The analysis of the care deficit and democracy deficit of current politics is coupled with an in-depth look at the elements of the neoliberal narrative of the competent citizen that exacerbates both deficits. Tronto intends the account to hold for the context of the United States_Turtle Island, only. Still I think it provides a crucial explanation for the curious contemporaneity of a growing awareness of political exclusion and structural injustice within European and North American_Turtle Island democracies, and the failure to engage in even the most symbolic discussion of how to repair those deficits.

Equipped with Tronto's analysis, the story of Markus Igel undergoes a shift. The polity of which Igel is a citizen assumes that the market ought to provide for the care necessary within the polity. If the around-the-clock care that Igel needs for participation in society costs too much for Igel's means, they should use the market to employ Eastern European care workers for a fraction of the German costs. The state of Saarland employs the "bootstrap" (Tronto 2013, 115) frame of mind. It is as if it calls out to Igel "you got to pull yourself up by your own bootstraps, e.g. finance the care you find morally habitable on your own by making choices on the market. If you do not have the financial means to lift yourself up by your own bootstraps, it is because you are not a productive member of the political economy. In that case, surrender to the neoliberal austerity policy and the charity we throw the way of the least well-off". According to Tronto, the neoliberal narrative "results in an account of politics that misconceives citizens and their lives, overvaluing their lives as workers, devaluing their lives as people engaged in relationships of care" (Tronto 2013, 26). People and political institutions that subscribe to bootstrap mentality see no political need for collective care because they believe that they pull themselves out by their own bootstraps, and that it is everyone else's facility and responsibility to do so, as well. This omits a crucial fact about the human condition: for every single human life—bootstrap mentality subscribers included—to exist and continue it is dependent upon intimate and institutionalized networks of caring. What is more, bootstrap proponents are in an epistemically disprivileged position to perceive the structural constraints and historically accumulated hardships that hinder people differently positioned from them from pulling themselves up by their own bootstraps. As Martin Luther King Jr. put it so poignantly: "It is cruel jest to say to a bootless man that he ought to lift himself by his own bootstraps. It is even worse to tell a man to lift himself by his own bootstraps when somebody is standing on the boot" (King 2015, 243). As this quote suggests, bootstrap proponents do not see the boot that stands on disprivileged and disenfranchised people's foot.

It is painfully clear from the Markus Igel case that the claim "nothing about us without us" of the movement of people with dis_abilities is still blatantly disregarded by the democracy that Igel is a part of. Igel's polity excludes Igel from the process that decides how care is organized in the polity and what financial means are provided for it. Furthermore, the state of Saarland relegates care work to a specific ethnic and gendered group, making decisions for Polish and Romanian care workers who are also excluded from voicing whether or not and under which conditions they want to become migrant care workers, or if the German minimum wage for two months for twenty-four hours a day shifts is really as desirable to them as public German discourse makes it appear. Germany, Markus Igel's case illustrates, has both a care deficit and a democracy deficit then.

Following Tronto, this chapter argues that the care deficit and the democracy deficit are intertwined, both being based in structural carelessness to which 'democratic caring with' others is the proposed solution. For the purpose of this chapter, I shall take structural carelessness to describe the dominant institution of political relationships in a given polity in a way that renders a collective democratic practice of 'caring with' others a 'moot point'. 'Democratic caring with', in turn, is defined by Tronto as a "relational" (Tronto 2013, 36) and political practice, which aim is "to ensure that all of the members of the society can live as well as possible by making the society as democratic as possible. This is the essence of 'caring with'" (Tronto 2013, 30). To achieve genuine democracy through care, "democratic politics should center upon assigning responsibilities for care, and for ensuring that democratic citizens are as capable as possible of participating in this assignment of responsibilities" (ibid.). 'Democratic caring with' entails the collective discussion and distribution of political responsibilities to care for democracy, then. Tronto argues that 'caring with' others and democracy reinforce one another: as citizens "learn to renegotiate caring responsibilities, citizens' care for democracy solidifies and reinforces the democratic nature of society" (Tronto 2013, 13).

To fulfill one's "responsibility for democracy" (Tronto 2013, 62), citizens must ensure that political decisions are made collectively, that "the scope of the discussion is wide enough" and that "all are engaged in 'caring with' others" (Tronto 2013, 64). To center caring practices within democratic deliberation, what democracy means must be *renegotiated and redefined*. Historically, caring practices and care practitioners have largely been excluded from political discourse due to deeply ableistic, classed, gendered and racialized assumptions about who does what type of work pertaining to the supposed common good of a given polity. 'Democratic caring with' demonstrates "how social and political institutions permit some to bear the burdens (and joys) of care and allow others to escape them" (Tronto 2013, 33). Starting from this epistemic vantage point, dominant institutionalizations of democracy and care are problematized in their underlying exclusions and overburdens. 'Caring democracy' renders visible that in current European and North American_Turtle Island polities shaped to different degrees by neoliberalism, passes are doled out that free certain groups of people from care responsibilities. These passes are the "protection pass, production pass, taking-care-of-my-own pass, bootstrap pass, and charity pass" (ibid.). In neoliberal political economies, the holders of these passes qualify for political participation because monied employment is an important qualifier for political membership. As a consequence, political institutions and practices are disproportionately decided upon by those with passes out of care responsibilities, to the exclusion of most of the people who fulfill these responsibilities and whose lives depend most immediately on institutionalized care. In a 'caring democracy', all issues concerning collective flourishing and the responsibilities to fulfill collective needs need to be decided in processes of 'democratic caring with' to dismantle the structural boundaries to participation and flourishing. Dismantling the structural boundaries to living well in the polity requires a *centering of relationality*. This centering reveals that there would be no citizens and hence no polities without individual and collective care relationships. All human and many non-human beings are entangled in a web of structural and intimate relationships that enable the maintenance of human and other lives. The view "of the self as a [care, J.H.] receiver, and not only an actor, becomes normalized" (Tronto 2013, 151). As a result, "care recipients cease to be viewed as 'others'" (ibid.). This gives rise to an expansion of "empathy" (ibid.), as caring democratic citizens start to perceive differently positioned people as similar to them in their interrelatedness and interdependency.

Centering relationality also has an epistemic function. The bootstrap pass holders get to see that the judgments they used to make about the non-existing need for 'caring with' stems from faulty epistemic assumptions that did not factor their own vital dependence on intimate and remote others in. In post_modern polities based on division of labor, a potentially infinite number of people need to contribute caring actions in order for a single person to achieve their own ends and actions. In order for the well off to participate in democratic processes the way they would like to, they depend on the care of those very people who they wish to exclude from political participation. This validates the perspectives of the structurally oppressed who know the value of caring about and for care.

It becomes clear that 'democratic caring with' others requires knowledge about these other's lives. *Learning about* the lives and needs and responsibilities of and to others free of distortions and prejudices and misconceptions requires the presence of those very others. Presently, the homes, schools, workplaces and recreational places of people tend to be segregated, with the problematic outcome that people spend more time with and *learning about* the lives of people who are positioned similarly to them than they do with people differently positioned in the political fabric. Tronto grants that it will take a "large investment of time and energy" (Tronto 2013, 147) to foster the conditions beneficial to *learning about* our differently positioned fellow citizens. But if 'democratic caring with' is to disrupt epistemic misconceptions about the needs and situations and contributions of our fellow citizens and to arrive at more just distributions of caring responsibilities, *learning about* all people's lives through our democratic practices and incorporating that knowledge into our *democratic caring* is indispensable.

Finally, caring democracy requires *democratic equality in unequal care situations.* As Tronto reminds us, care is not "an entitlement [...] as if it were a good to be distributed. Instead, we have to see care as *caring with*, that is, as an activity in which citizens are constantly engaged" (2013, 154; Tronto's emphasis). If 'caring with' others is the political activity par excellence, then one's political equality is based on one's participation in that activity. Equality is not something that can be bestowed upon citizens by academics, politicians or judges. It must be claimed and enacted performatively through asserting oneself into political practices.[6] Care theory has long argued that receiving care is an active and valuable contribution to the caring practice as well, so depending on other people's care does not diminish one's political equality and should therefore not disqualify one from democratic participation. Those in need of care have the lived experience and epistemic authority to make judgments about what care practices will fulfill their needs best and how responsibility needs to be redistributed in the polity for them to live in their polity as well as possible. To care democratically with others will require

> more than simply passing laws against discrimination. Since equality looks different across the life cycle, at least three different steps are required. First, when people are young and in a state of dependency, they need equal access to adequate care in order to grow into fully capable adults. Second, when people are adults, they need to be able to exercise their voices equally and independently, and provisions need to be made to guarantee that their voices are not silenced or drowned out by others. Third, when people are ill, elderly, or disabled, institutional arrangements need to be made to ensure that their voices are also heard. (Tronto 2013, 108–109)

If one takes equality to be at the heart of a caring democracy, then there is no justification for ignoring Markus Igel's voicing of disagreement with how Igel's polity assigns responsibility and resources for Igel's flourishing.

Democratic Caring with's 'moot' Points

The Old English term *moot* has undergone significant shifts in meaning in its current incarnation of the modern English use of language. Today, when people refer to an issue as being a moot point, the dominant usage is that though the point might in principle be debatable, it is usually not worth any further consideration or revisiting, at least not at the time of speaking. A second contemporary use centers on mock trials held by law students to practice their skills in the field, a going through the motions without holding any actual decision-making powers. In Old English, however, nothing was mock or simulated about the cases and issues brought before and decided upon the moot. Moot signified a meeting place, an assembly of people coming together at a circular place or hill under the

[6] See Anne Phillips 2015, 44.

open sky to debate issues that concerned diverse groups and the wider community concertedly.[7] To some moots, delegates from the different communities would bring soil from their homelands that would form a part of the moot, a physical representation of commonness in difference still discernible 600 years later.

In what follows, I will employ the idea of a moot point to demonstrate that 'caring with' brings concepts to the democratic table that transform traditional notions of democratic politics. It does so by reADdressing[8] four issues that are considered 'moot' points in the sense of being perceived as mere academic endeavors without practical applicability, although their contestedness and the usefulness of the debate are not put into question. These issues are backgrounded in traditional accounts of democracy and to an extent even deliberative democracy, but foregrounded in 'democratic caring with'. I suggest to render them 'moot' points in the Old English sense, issues that need our coming together collectively to renegotiate their meaning to overcome care's democracy deficit and democracy's care deficit, so that 'democratic caring with' may become a genuine expression of a polity "composed of diversities [that] can nonetheless enjoy moments of commonality when, through public deliberations, collective power is used to promote or protect the wellbeing of the collectivity" (Wolin 1994, 11).

Bringing the Political and Contestedness Back Into Care Politics

One of the main structural obstacles to renegotiating responsibility, power and authoritative standards within a given polity is "that most matters pertaining to them seem to have been settled in the past" (Tronto 2013,

[7] I acknowledge that I incur the same issue of idealizing an exclusionary system from the past and centering only its inclusive side that Hannah Arendt does in referring to the ancient Greek polis as a model for radical democratic action. Historically, moot hills were feudal institutions and only free male citizens of a borough could speak before it. This excluded women, dis_abled people, migrants, poor people, artisans, peasants, workers and non-citizens. Many moot courts used drowning pits and hanging gallows as their tools to 'right wrongs' within the community, while I strongly advocate that neither states nor democratic institutions should have the right to take people's lives.

[8] I use the term reADdress to combine the terms re-address and redress. I argue that there are structural issues in the fabric of contemporary democracies that need to be brought before all members of the polity for renegotiation and repair.

59). Matters settled in the past were usually decided by the dominant group within the polity, without the participation of structurally oppressed and disenfranchised groups. It is part and parcel of the dominant group to have more power to begin with and then to accumulate even more power over time, while the excluded groups accumulate burdens and responsibilities. As a result, the former manage to naturalize both their vision of collective well-being and their authority in public matters. That polities and their institutions are shaped the way they presently are is then taken for granted and hardly ever revisited, let alone renegotiated. In fact, one can measure the greatness of the power of the dominant group precisely by the fact that matters pertaining to all have not been renegotiated with the advent of newcomers to democratic processes. That oftentimes makes it hard to see that all matters concerning public life and collective well-being have been decided in mostly exclusionary, but no less political, processes.

'Democratic caring with' renders the politicity of past settlements concerning responsibilities for care and rights to political participation visible. In doing so, it joins a political intervention started by political theorists commonly identified as belonging to the school of thought of the political difference, or post-foundationalism. Authors of the political difference draw a distinction between practices that are commonly understood as political, such as government, representative democracy, bureaucracy and policing, which they see as apolitical or even antipolitical, and practices that they understand to be genuinely political. The political, in these accounts, is the moment of instituting the polity, but this moment is a contingent and fleeting grounding, one that occurs as a supplement in the absence of an ultimate grounding, as a "plurality of partial grounds" (Marchart 2007, 8). In order to be political, these grounds must always be contingent and tentative. If democratic, they are tentative because they are a snapshot of what the participating citizens of a polity think will foster the collective well-being best at a given time. The quality of democracy can be measured by whether or not past settlements come into dispute when the presence and participation of newly included groups bring the adequacy of the settled political care responsibilities into question. 'Democratic caring with' brings the political back in by demonstrating that for every presently authoritative grounding of the polity, such as the neoliberal political economy, there are other partial groundings that have not been heeded, but that could possibly be used to reconstitute the polity to enhance collective well-being. A 'caring democracy' opens up a space for alternative groundings that are more caring and more democratic and less excluding and harmful. The renegotiations of what the political means that care seeks to reground democracy in is an attempt to politically remedy the gap between the promise of the democratic polity that all members of a polity ought to be equally involved in its communal life and be equally protected by the authoritative standards governing their living together, and the factual practiced, exclusion- and inequality-begetting politics. Just as the proponents of the political difference do, Tronto's 'caring democracy' brings the wrongs of exclusion and inequality onto the political stage to renegotiate what living in the polity as well as possible means for each and every one.

With that, Tronto's 'democratic caring with' takes up a unique intermediary position between deliberative democracy and the political difference. As my last section illustrated, proponents of deliberative democracy are usually occupied with overcoming structural exclusions from and within deliberative processes. They are thusly concerned with renegotiating and reshaping the terms of the debate and the accepted forms of communicative participation. With the exception of Iris Young (1990), who looks for ways to end structural oppression and economic exploitation in deliberation, deliberative processes are not usually conceived as part of a broader project to restructure polities. The transformative potential of deliberative democracy is usually located within more inclusive debates, from which a more just distribution of power, resources and responsibilities is said to follow. With the exception of Jacques Rancière (1999), thinkers of the political difference usually shun grounding the political in a specific quality or practice for the obvious reason that this would violate post-foundationalism. Rancière suggests equality as the genuinely political quality for its "improper" (Rancière 1999, 13) or empty political property, thus still partially adhering to the function of non-ground.[9] What I find remarkable in Tronto's account—which granted is nowhere near based in post-foundationalism—is that Tronto dares to tackle bringing the political back in and making space for contestedness and contingency via a grounding practice, that of 'caring with'. 'Democratic caring with' becomes the gauge to measure whether or not the more inclusive responsibility-setting

[9]According to Rancière, equality is a non-ground founding of the polity because the demos is "simply free like the rest" (Rancière 1999, 8), the wealthy and the noble. Partaking in the polity neither through wealth nor through status, the "demos attributes to itself as its proper lot the equality that belongs to all citizens" (ibid.).

processes that Tronto suggests as a remedy to unpoliticalness function well by being both democratic and caring. This includes more than revised norms of political debate and better dialogical skills; to guarantee that all members of a polity can live in it as well as possible, concrete material and structural redistributions of power, resources, political standing and voice, care, responsibility and time are necessary. While Tronto's *Caring Democracy* may not have all the final answers as to how we might get there, it ponders all these questions intertwined and stitched together. That in itself is a highly unique contribution.

Bringing Epistemology to the Table

Joan Tronto has famously argued that the world will "look very different if we put care at the center of our political lives" (Tronto 2013, xi). Viewed through the care lens, the world will not be populated by autonomous, autopoietic, rational monads that pull themselves up by their own bootstraps, but by interdependent, interrelated beings with embodied knowledge that need each other for the maintenance of their biological, psychological and political lives. But even this world that care makes visible will look different from diverging positions within the political fabric. The care needs and democracy deficit that can be seen from Markus Igel's position within the political fabric will vary greatly from those that are seeable from the bootstrap pass holder's position. 'Democratic caring with' brings the epistemic dimension of responsibility-setting processes to the table. Because the world looks different from various positions within the political fabric, it is crucial for political care responsibility-setting processes that as many people with as many perspectives as are haveable are present. Without every haveable perspective, the knowledge basis of decision-making processes will at best be incomplete and at worst be faulty and distorted, resulting in incomplete and faulty decisions and solutions. Moreover, due to epistemic ignorance,[10] the more privileged members of the polity have misconceived notions about the hardships disadvantaged and oppressed members of the polity face. Since 'democratic caring with's'

[10] While I use the term epistemic ignorance to refer to a form of harmdoing that is based in the way humans perceive the world through gendered, racialized, classed, ableistic, ageistic, lookistic and sexualized lenses from which they construct distorted knowledge about the world, Tronto uses the term "epistemological ignorance" (Tronto 2013, 59) that Tronto borrows from Charles Wade Mills seminal *The Racial Contract* (1997, 18).

objective is to organize the polity so that all can live in it as well as possible, the situated knowledge of all who dwell in it is required to realize well-being for all. Democratic inclusion enhances epistemic accuracy of perceptions of differently situated people's situations and challenges epistemic ignorance of injustices pertaining to the political organizing of care and democracy.

Bringing questions of epistemic injustice to the political table is not entirely new. Recent years have seen important works that analyze the part that epistemic ignorance and epistemic injustice have in upholding structural inequality and oppression (e.g., Mills 1997; Fricker 2007; Sullivan and Tuana 2007; Dotson 2014; Pohlhaus 2012; Kidd and Carel 2017). What is a new approach, however, is to factor epistemic ignorance and injustice into thinking about care and caring democracy. This statement may seem surprising given that most care theorists would probably agree to trace the beginning of care scholarship back to Gilligan's *In A Different Voice* (1982), wherein it is argued that perceptions of and judgments about ethical issues have gendered lenses, which are routinely ignored. While I would agree that epistemic injustice has never been far from the minds of care theorists and practitioners, to my knowledge, it has not usually been at the center of theoretical considerations of what caring democracies entails, so far. If the critical transformation of political processes that 'democratic caring with' seeks to realize depend on a more inclusive and careful knowledge base to redistribute societal care responsibilities, then it is time to foreground the epistemic dimension of political debates.

Tackling In_Equality[11] *and the 'Care Paradox'*

Above, I have unfolded that to become an equal one must insert oneself into politics as an equal. In order to enable all people to participate, we must first tackle what I would like to call the 'care paradox' of democratic participation. To include all citizens in the deliberation and distribution of political care needs and responsibilities, their care needs must first be met more comprehensively than they presently are. At this point, most theories of participatory or deliberative democracy content themselves with the indication that to have genuinely inclusive political deliberations, citizens

[11] I use the underscore in In_Equality to illustrate the tension between formally and legally granted equality of citizens within democracies and the factually existing inequality that still prevails among different groups of citizens; let alone non-citizens.

would need to have more time to engage politically than they have under the present neoliberal need to earn a living, and then they give up the ghost.[12] Not so 'democratic caring with', as it picks up were deliberative democracy left off and suggests a feasible way to dissolve the care paradox in democracy.

Jennifer Nedelsky and Tom Malleson suggest a concrete way out of the care paradox with their model *(Part) Time for All (PTfA)*. In it, Nedelsky and Malleson advocate a "structural change in the form of part time paid work and part time unpaid care that would become the new norms for everyone" (Nedelsky 2018, 1). Nedelsky and Malleson propose that all adults who are capable of working should do so "no less than 12 and no more than 30 hours a week" and in addition do "unpaid care work part time—also somewhere between 12 and 30 hours a week" (ibid.). For the work, all workers shall receive a wage high enough to meet one's needs and participate in social activities. Part-time work and living wage in this context will come to mean not struggling at the subsistence minimum but to lead a decent, fulfilling and included life. The living wage that Nedelsky proposes is one by which "one adult should be able to earn enough to support [themselves] and a child by working 20 hours a week" (Nedelsky 2014, 27).[13] The part-time care work can be done to maintain oneself, one's family and_or one's political community.

Nedelsky and Malleson envision a change in norms in which the non-compliance of part-time work and part-time care will be met with the same indignation that stay-at-home dads or welfare recipients are met with today. Those who try to eschew their care responsibilities or work more than thirty hours a week shall be discredited as amoral, money-hungry careerists. Norms around care and work are reframed and renegotiated to solve three pressing issues: "unsustainable stress on families, persistent inequality for women and others who do care work, and policy makers who are ignorant about the care that life requires—because most high level policy makers have virtually no experience of providing care" (Nedelsky 2018, 1). This will enable people to participate actively in their families, neighborhoods and communities. Overworked and undercared for adults cannot care sufficiently for dependent children, sick or dying loved ones. And overwhelming care arrangements undermine democracy

[12] See, among others, David Plotke 1997; Hanna Fenichel Pitkin 2004.

[13] I will leave the discussion about why one adult providing for only one child is a problematic Eurocentric notion for another day.

because they obstruct political participation. According to Nedelsky, *Part Time for All* also solves the gap between care and policy in which those in the highest ranks determining public policies generally have the least lived experience with the meaningfulness, requirements and fulfillments of care.

Since care is a central source of human relationships and fulfilling relationships the central point of a fulfilling life, care is an existential part of living in the political world as well as possible. When all people who can start to care part-time for their political communities, this will certainly not abolish political conflict. But political conflicts will then be solved by people who are better cared for, who have more practice and competencies in care, who will make less harried and qualitatively better decisions and who can fulfill their democratic caring responsibilities more attentively.

Renegotiating Relationships of Dissociation

Care theory contributes a relational understanding of the political to 'democratic caring with'. Structural and intimate relationships relate people to one another and to different positions in the fabric of relationships, and human lives are maintained entangled in relationships. But the bootstrap-pass holders negate these life-sustaining relationships. Through the lens of 'democratic caring with', it becomes seeable that it is not simply that the bootstrap-pass holders do not see their entanglements in relationships with others that sustain their lives. They actively dis-solidarize themselves with their fellow citizens. With those positioned similarly to themselves, as well as with those positioned differently. Stuart Hall famously argues that "it is because their history and ours is so deeply and profoundly and inextricably intertwined that racism [and we might insert, all other forms of harmful—isms] exists. For otherwise, how could they keep us apart?" (Hall 1997, 99). A relational theory of the political relays that the relatedness with a group is prior to the move to distance oneself from it. All subjects are engendered in relationships. Group identity, then, is an effect of a specific form of relationship.

In the case of the bootstrap-pass holders, their group identity is maintained by dissociating themselves from their fellow citizens who contribute to the maintenance of their lives. 'Democratic caring with' asks about the politico-structural dissociations within the polity. According to Bini Adamczak, there is a relation between relationship and dissociation. Specific "kinds of relationships are born out of concrete dissociations", and certain "relationships can only be maintained through dissociation"

(Adamczak 2017, 246–247; transl. J.H). 'Democratic caring with' problematizes relationships founded on dissociation. It does not condone dissociative relationship as a form of empirical diagnosis. Instead, it highlights that dissociative relationships need to be stitched together with "relationship's own thread", as Carol Gilligan (1982, 31) calls it. 'Democratic caring with' locates a revolutionary potential in this practice of trying to re-stitch relationships back together. Following Bini Adamczak, 'democratic caring with' suggests to reserve the term 'revolution' for political processes in which "the most reified and ossified ways of relating to one another, those that hardly ever appear as relationships any more, are put up for renegotiation. [Revolutions seek] neither to transform the individual, nor the totality, but the relationships that make up the sociality of society" (Adamczak 2017, 245–246; transl. J.H.). The prevalence of dissociative ways of relating to their fellow citizens that the bootstrap-pass holders demonstrate underlines the need to renegotiate these relationships. Dissociative relationships are not only based on epistemically faulty accounts of the human condition, they also hinder the lives of those they exclude from being held by the political fabric, threatening the maintenance of their lives. Those who style themselves as pulling themselves up by their own bootstraps may be moved to understand that they have actually one-sidedly dissociated with and abandoned relationships of mutual dependency.

Conclusion

This chapter has taken up Joan Tronto's suggestion that there is a democracy deficit in care and a care deficit in democracy, underlined by the example of Markus Igel's fight against compulsory admission into a care home or state-prescribed employment of precarious migrant care. Both deficits, it was argued, can only be resolved if they are dovetailed in practices of 'democratic caring with'. I have tried to specify both the practices that this claim would require by carving out the elements of 'democratic caring' with and the structural obstacles to perceiving a need for 'democratic caring with' as I have found them in Tronto's *Caring Democracy*. I suggest that 'democratic caring with' comprises (1) responsibility as a political practice; (2) responsibility for democracy; (3) renegotiating and redefining democracy; (4) centering relationality; (5) learning about others; and (6) democratic equality in unequal care situations. The structural obstacle that stands in the way of epistemically perceiving the need for 'democratic caring with' is, for the matter of this chapter, the bootstrap mentality.

My second part of the chapter was dedicated to identifying the ways in which 'democratic caring with' shifts the focus of more traditional debates about democratic participation as they are currently held in deliberative and participatory accounts of democracy. I argued that 'democratic caring with' (1) brings the political and contestedness back into care politics; (2) brings epistemology to the table; (3) tackles in_equality and the care paradox; and (4) renegotiates relationships of dissociation. Relating these elements back to Markus Igel's case, I am now in a position to claim that the harm done to Igel lies not solely in the exclusion from the deliberative process. Instead, 'democratic caring with' highlights that even with the equality formally granted to citizens in current democracies, not all citizens are allowed to insert themselves into politics on equal terms. Not admitting Igel to the responsibility-setting processes of Igel's polity constitutes a rejection of Igel's politicity, one that undermines the basic principle of democracy. What is more, this exclusion also leads to a faulty epistemic foundation of Igel's polity. I am hopeful to have shown that 'democratic caring with' paints a richer picture of both the harms associated with factual democratic exclusion of people on the grounds of human diversity and the practices that will assist us in overcoming democratic exclusion than deliberative and participatory democracy accounts generally do. Only dovetailed with care will democracy ever genuinely become democratic, that is, equipped to tackle the paradox in the democratic paradigm that keeps democratic polities from truly fostering and heeding the contributions and voices of everyone.

Acknowledgments I would like to thank Petr Urban and Lizzie Ward for putting their heads, hands and hearts into feedback on this chapter.

References

Adamczak, Bini. 2017. *Beziehungsweise Revolution – 1917, 1968 und kommende.* Frankfurt a.M.: Suhrkamp.

Barber, Benjamin. 1985. How Swiss is Rousseau? *Political Theory* 13(4): 475–495.

Barnes, Marian et al. 2015. *Ethics of Care. Critical Advances in International Perspective.* Bristol: Polity Press.

Benhabib, Seyla. 1994. *Democracy and Difference. Contesting the Boundaries of the Political.* Princeton: Princeton University Press.

Bohman, James. 1996. *Public Deliberation. Pluralism, Complexity, and Democracy.* Cambridge: MIT Press.

Dotson, Kristie. 2014. Conceptualizing Epistemic Oppression. *Social Epistemology* 28(2): 115–138. http://dx.doi.org/10.1080/02691728.2013.782585. Accessed 10 May 2018.

Fricker, Miranda. 2007. *Epistemic Injustice. Power and the Ethics of Knowing.* Oxford: Oxford University Press.

Gilligan, Carol. 1982. *In a Different Voice.* Cambridge: Harvard University Press.

Gutman, Amy, and Dennis Thompson. 1996. *Democracy and Disagreement.* Cambridge: Belknap Press.

Hall, Stuart. 1997. Subjects in History: Making Diasporic Identities. In *The House That Race Built*, ed. Wahneema Lubiano, 289–300. New York: Random House.

Heier, Jorma. 2015. Disabling Contraints on Democratic Participation. *Ethics and Social Welfare* 9(2): 201–208.

Kant, Immanuel. [1785] 1999. *Grundlegung zur Metaphysik der Sitten.* Hamburg: Meiner.

Kidd, Ian. J., and Havi Carel. 2017. Epistemic Injustice and Illness. *Journal of Applied Philosophy* 34(2): 172–190.

King, Martin Luther, Jr. 2015. *The Radical King.* Edited and Introduced by Cornell West. Boston: Beacon Press.

Landwehr, Claudia. 2012. Demokratische Legitimation durch rationale Kommunikation. Theorien deliberativer Demokratie. In *Zeitgenössische Demokratietheorie. Band 1: Normative Demokratietheorien*, ed. Oliver W. Lembcke et al., 355–386. Springer.

Marchart, Oliver. 2007. *Post-foundational Political Thought.* Edinburgh: Edinburgh University Press.

Maus, Ingeborg. 1994. *Zur Aufklärung der Demokratietheorie.* Frankfurt am Main: Suhrkamp.

Mills, Charles Wade. 1997. *The Racial Contract.* Ithaca: Cornell University Press.

Nedelsky, Jennifer. 2014. *Part Time for All. In Support of Families, Equality and Good Governance.* http://d3n8a8pro7vhmx.cloudfront.net/bicn/legacy_url/66/BIEN2014_Nedelsky.pdf?1439837502. Accessed 10 January 2018.

———. 2018. *What Will It Take to Revalue Care?* http://www.wpsanet.org/papers/docs/nedelsky2018.pdf. Accessed 30 December 2018.

Phillips, Anne. 2015. *The Politics of the Human.* Cambridge: Cambridge University Press.

Pitkin, Hannah Fenichel. 2004. Representation and Democracy: Uneasy Alliance. *Scandinavian Political Studies* 27: 335–342.

Plotke, David. 1997. Representation is Democracy. *Constellations* 4(1): 19–34.

Pohlhaus, Gaile. 2012. Relational Knowing and Epistemic Injustice: Toward a Theory of Willful Hermeneutical Ignorance. *Hypatia* 27(4): 715–735.

Rancière, Jacques. 1999 [1995]. *Disagreement: Politics and Philosophy.* Trans. Julie Rose. Minneapolis: University of Minnesota Press.

Robinson, Fiona. 2011. Stop Talking and Listen: Discourse Ethics and Feminist Care Ethics in International Political Theory Millennium. *Journal of International Studies* 39(3): 845–860.

Rousseau, Jean-Jacques. [1762] 1977. *Vom Gesellschaftsvertrag oder Grundsätze des Staatsrechtes*. Stuttgart: Reclam.

Sullivan, Shannon, and Nancy Tuana (eds.). 2007. *Race and Epistemologies of Ignorance*. Albany: SUNY Press.

Tronto, Joan C. 1993. *Moral Boundaries. A Political Argument for an Ethic of Care*. New York: Routledge.

———. 2013. *Caring Democracy. Markets, Equality, and Justice*. New York: New York University Press.

Vosman, Frans. 2017. *We Should Look for Fellow Travelers*. https://ethicsofcare.org/look-fellow-travelers/#more-7022. Accessed 10 May 2019.

Weber, Florian. 2012. Selbstbestimmung durch Teilhabe. Theorie der partizipativen Demokratie. In *Zeitgenössische Demokratietherie*, Band 1: Normative Demokratietheorien, ed. Oliver W. Lembcke et al., 224–228. Springer.

Wolin, Sheldon. 1994. Fugitive Democracy. *Constellations* 1(1): 11–25.

Young, Iris Marion. 1990. *Justice and the Politics of Difference*. Princeton: Princeton University Press.

———. 1996. Communication and the Other. Beyond Deliberative Democracy. In *Democracy and Difference. Contesting the Boundaries of the Political*, ed. Sheila Benhabib, 120–135. Princeton: Princeton University Press.

———. 2000. *Inclusion and Democracy*. Oxford: Oxford University Press.

CHAPTER 4

Why the Publicly Funded Solution Is Better Equipped to Provide Democratic Care 'For All'

Helena Olofsdotter Stensöta

Within care ethics debates, two separate enquiries can be distinguished: on the one hand, the enquiry into the favourable circumstances of particular treatment and flexible care for the individual (Noddings 2006; Held 2006) and, on the other hand, the exploration of more general terms of care ethics, such as citizenship (Sevenhuijsen 1998) and social policy (Hankivsky 2004), which moves us into the wider public realm where institutions and policies serve to establish and promote "the conditions under which caring-for can flourish" (Noddings 2006, 22–23).

Based on a paper originally published in *International Journal for Care and Caring* [Sophie Bourgault and Fiona Robinson (eds.)], pp. 1–15. https://doi.org/10.1332/239788219X15688541168071, Policy Press 2019. Parts of the original paper are republished here with permission of Bristol University Press, UK.

H. O. Stensöta (✉)
Political Science Department, University of Gothenburg, Gothenburg, Sweden
e-mail: Helena.stensota@pol.gu.se

P. Urban, L. Ward (eds.), *Care Ethics, Democratic Citizenship and the State*, International Political Theory,
https://doi.org/10.1007/978-3-030-41437-5_4

This chapter engages specifically with the intersection between care and democratic theory as it is discussed by Tronto in her book *Caring Democracy* (2013, building on Tronto 1993). The reading of Tronto's book, that the chapter builds on, emphasises the problem of access to and coverage of care for all citizens. Even though the theory presented by Tronto is broader than simply the problem of access to care, the chapter argues that the problem of access is a necessary component if the ambition is to include 'all' citizens. The chapter argues that it is doubtful as to whether one can discuss care 'for all' without touching upon the question of accessibility to care. Thus, the way Tronto frames the problem of democratic care brings up to date the problem of coverage of care.

The particular argument put forward here is that the publicly funded solution, or the 'state' solution, of access to care is an important facilitator of the goal of access to care for all. The chapter forwards the general impression that ethics of care scholars often have treated publicly provided and financed care in a somewhat step-motherly way, assuming that this type of care cannot meet the demands as outlined by care ethics scholars, where flexibility with respect to the care recipient is emphasised. Indeed, the state often operates through general solutions which are held in opposition to care ethics ideals. This is in line with how previous discussions on how to provide care along the ideals of ethics of care have considered the question of democratic care chiefly in terms of the dichotomy between particularised and standardised solutions and have suggested that the logic of civil society may be most in line with ethical care ideals. This is, however, likely to change, if we reformulate the problem as democratic access to care *for all.* Using notions of citizenship, the state has a unique capacity to reach 'all', which the market or civil society does not. Thus, if we discuss democratic care as access to care 'for all', the publicly funded alternative seems better aligned with the ideals of care ethics and the state- or the publicly funded solutions seem more suitable.

A contributing reason for the direction of previous research is, this chapter further suggests, that considerable care ethics discussion takes the American context as its point of departure, which is the case of the 2013 book by Tronto and its critique of neoliberalism. From a Scandinavian perspective, several circumstances seem to be taken for granted in this discussion which are not applicable everywhere. For example, the social insurance schemes of Scandinavian countries include everyone who has performed paid work; the public school systems and health care services are further examples of how care is accessible *to all*, and where solutions are publicly funded, that is, provided as policy through 'the state'.

The chapter elaborates in greater detail on how the goal of providing democratic care 'to all' meets with the logics of three societal spheres: the civil society, the market and the public solution or the state (cf. Marshall 1964). The analysis can be seen as applying a birds-eye perspective on the implementation of care 'for all'. Generally, implementation refers to the processes whereby policies are translated from goals and ambitions into policy outcomes that actually meet the needs of citizens (Pressman and Wildavsky 1984). Here, the chapter discusses implementation as logics pertaining to the particular spheres. There has been a lot of discussion within care ethics debates on how the logics of the market are at odds with care ethics; there has, however, been less on state or publicly funded care. The chief objective is to consider distinct trade-offs associated with the particular societal sphere in which care provision takes place, with regard to aims of democratic care. The chapter argues that when it comes to the goal of providing access to care 'for all', care provided through the public alternative, or the state, seems to reach a broader range of people than the other two alternatives.

By the public solution or 'the state' the chapter refers to *publicly funded* policies. This definition is in line with how the state is discussed in the governance literature (Pierre 2011), as it incorporates the multifaceted way that public services are produced in today's society. This definition points to the importance of how the policy is financed and distributed. As long as the services are funded by taxes and outlined through government decisions as public policies, they count as the public alternative, regardless of whether they are contracted out to service providers in civil society or the market. The question of whether publicly funded service varies depending on whether it is produced 'in house' or contracted out is of course also an interesting topic, and which has been researched a lot, but this is not the question discussed here.

Care as a Finite Resource?

In defining care, the chapter builds on Tronto's notion of care as a practice and a process, but considers specifically how public policies can address the needs of citizens. A particularly important problem to address when discussing democratic care as equal access to care *for all* is the complex issue that care is a finite resource. An underlying ambition of much care ethics scholarship is to re-evaluate care and increase its societal importance, which includes increasing our participation in care in terms of attention, skills in actual caregiving and, most importantly, ensuring that more people start to care in deeper ways. But will this mean that care no longer will be a scarcity? In a related discussion, Clare Ungerson (1997) has argued that care is not a commodity, as a commodity is something that you can possess; when you give it away, you no longer have it. In contrast, when care is provided, something is given away, but something also stays with the carer. These insights into the nature of care are, however, mostly directed at the personal or individual level of the relationship between carer and care-receiver, the face-to-face problem.

If we discuss democratic access to care at the societal level, it seems that there will most likely be moments when actual caregiving to a particular person, or alternatively, the depth of the care responsibility assumed, will become limited, even if only temporarily, because it conflicts with other assignments, possibly other caring assignments. The simplest illustration of this situation is that a care provider can only actively care for one person at a time. This is true, for example, with regard to professional homecare where carers move from one care recipient to another, and thus, obviously cannot be in two places at the same time.

Building on street-level bureaucracy literature, one could further argue that the process of caring involves new care needs emerging, so that there is a certain non-limitation built in that needs to be taken into account. In the work of Lipsky (1980/2010), the central idea is that street-level workers identify more with their clients than with their supervisors, which is an illustration of such limitlessness. Further, in the work of Maynard-Moody and Musheno (2000), it is suggested that an ideal street-level worker be personally (morally) engaged with his/her clients in order to help him/her in the best way. They give examples of street-level workers who 'go out of their way' to help clients, which most likely is not possible to do with all clients without stretching the budget, in both time and money, to unforeseen levels.

In addition, one could argue that for many care activities, there is an inherent ambition that the person in need may learn how to care more for him/herself. This is true for care of children who are growing up and for persons receiving care as a part of their recovery, for example, from a broken bone. It might also be true for older people where a new situation with more limited possibilities to care for oneself, for example, after a stroke, may still involve a learning process of absorbing new skills of coping, based on this new situation. Thus, in providing care, there is a balance between providing care extensively and limiting this provision for the sake of the person in need.

Thus, the chapter argues that the problem of limitation is inherent in the processes of care. Further, this problem is intensified when the ambition of providing democratic care, in a flexible and particular way directed to a particular client, needs to be weighed against the ambition to provide democratic care *for all* as coverage. This is the basis for enquiring into trade-offs. If we agree on the finite nature of care, the next step of the argument is that it leads to trade-offs in the access to care. These trade-offs, however, are not fixed, but are likely to vary between societal spheres as a consequence of the respective logics dominating in each sphere. Thus, it becomes crucial to address the question of how to discern more carefully how these trade-offs play out depending on the sphere in which care is provided.

Access to Care and the Encompassing Welfare State

In the book *Caring Democracy*, Tronto continues her elaboration of ethics of care theory, and raises an argument against market forces. She argues that real people's needs will never be satisfied when the market rules. Instead, we need to take care back from the market and anchor it firmly in democracy. But what society and state is she referring to?

From a Scandinavian perspective, the vision that Tronto outlines bears clear resemblance to the encompassing welfare state, as it aims at redistributing resources, both material and immaterial. The social insurance schemes give people monetary reimbursements when they cannot provide for themselves, and the public healthcare and school systems are accessible to 'all' funded through the tax system. Even though scholars have argued that we have witnessed a retrenchment of the encompassing welfare state (Jessop 1996), most researchers insist there is still a distinct Scandinavian welfare state type that differs from the liberal welfare state model in terms of policy (Bradley et al. 2003; Korpi and Palme 1998; Lundberg et al. 2008; Pierson 1994) and implementation (Møller and Stensöta 2017). This distinctiveness remains, even though there has been an increase in contracting out solutions, involving the production of public services being partly performed by market or civil society actors, as there has been no change in the authority of the duties or the financing system. Thus, using a definition of public from the governance literature, the term *public* can be grounded in *the authority of the duties* that agencies or institutions fulfil (Pierre 2011), meaning that all agencies or institutions performing governmental—thus, publicly agreed upon—tasks should be included in the definition of public, regardless of whether the task is performed in a public organisation or contracted out to market agents. In the care ethics literature, the importance of funding through taxes has been emphasised earlier by Engster (2007) and by Stensöta (2015).

In previous care ethics literature, there has further been a discussion on whether care ethics points in the same direction as social democracy. Sevenhuijsen (2000) has discussed Giddens's third way of social democracy, arguing that an ethics of care serves a better framework for forwarding Giddens's ideals, as ethics of care puts responsibility and not duties at the centre of the analysis. Sevenhuijsen's work here seems to underscore the degree to which an encompassing welfare state and care ethics may target the same goals, albeit through different routes. Tronto refers to Sevenhuijsen (2000) but argues that "questions about allocation of care responsibilities do not follow the traditional division of 'left' and 'right' in predictable ways" (Tronto 2013, 57).

There are several topics included in the earlier discussion. One is that social democracy evolves its system for protection around paid work, while care and care ethics evolve around care that is often not paid. The most central question is, however, the question of responsibility and whether the encompassing welfare state can be thought of as a construct that emphasises responsibility.

Care as Responsibility or Resource

In the care ethics literature, there is a further discussion on care as a responsibility versus a resource, which touches upon the above-mentioned discussion on care as a commodity. Is the discussion about the public solution and the role of the state dependent on whether care is discussed as a responsibility or as a resource?

Professional care work could be seen as providing care as a resource, if it refers to the setting up of care provision. Then the role of the state could lie in governing and regulating the distribution of this resource. Policy, however, is about much more than providing care as a resource. Deciding on a policy of care means to take some responsibility for the care need to be met. Further, these policies could be set up in a way that actually makes room for professional flexibility, and in that case, responsibility for the care need has been assumed to some extent, which is elaborated later.

Responsibility is central to care ethics and was one of the initial notions of Gilligan's definition of care ethics (1993). Responsibility emphasises how people stand in relation to each other. In Sevenhuijsen's definition, responsibility is, however, also a concept that may apply to policies: "Because it [an ethic of care] starts from a relational ontology, it focuses primarily on the question of what politics could mean for the safeguarding of responsibility and relationship in human interactions" (Sevenhuijsen 1998, 12). And further:

> It would also proceed by taking different perspectives of needs into account—those of care-providers and care-receivers, as well as those of policy-makers. Social policies should, accordingly, be framed by being responsive to the needs of those with whom they are concerned. In this approach the caring attitude is not confined to private interactions, but should count also as a 'public virtue' which should enter the considerations of policy-makers. (Sevenhuijsen 1998, 19)

It is quite possible to comprehend care as a public responsibility and thus put the emphasis on the public solution.

Going back to the argument of social insurance schemes and public care and public education as powerful tools for providing care *for all*, these are clearly both responsibilities and resources. The state has a responsibility to provide these resources. By responsibility, the chapter refers to how the state may need to be flexible in how care is provided in order to reach all.

The fine line here is between seeing the state as the primary coordinator of citizens' responsibility in areas of care and seeing it as a solution for situations where 'nothing else works'. In recent governance theory, the state is advanced in its coordinating capacity, which means coordinating initiatives from various spheres: family, market and civil society. For such coordination to work well, though, it needs to have considerable capacity. It is not possible to develop such capacity when the public solution is thought of as a last resort when nothing else works, which is often the case in societies with more limited states and lower levels of tax-funded care. It is much more likely to work in a society where the public solution has considerable resources, based on revenues, to successfully coordinate care to be accessible to all in democratic ways.

The Public Solution or 'the State'

Some objections can be made to the above: first, it could be argued that the public solution, connected to the state, is a realm of power and coercion and thus less democratic than the market and civil society, which are instead based on individual choice and voluntariness. As such, how can the debate on 'democratic care' coincide with the force of the state?

This depends, of course, on the definition of democracy that is applied. Definitions that give greater room for voluntariness might emphasise the ways in which the state is a coercive power, whereas definitions that give greater room to the capacity of the state to enforce public policy give greater room to, for example, the rule of law. In the definition of democracy by Diamond and Morlino (2016), four key elements are mentioned: a system for choosing and replacing governments through fair elections, the active participation of citizens in politics and civic life, the protection of human rights of all citizens and the rule of law in which laws and procedures apply equally to all citizens. Thus, in three of these four, the equality between citizens is emphasised. Hence, the basic idea as to why the public solution is an attractive option if the goal is expanded to include the democratic access to care to 'all', is the capacity of the state to reach 'all' in an equal manner. Thus, all states have a certain basic level of coercion, without which external and internal peace would not be secured. Without a basic level of coercion, democracy would most likely not be possible at all.

Programmes that are funded through the state have the capacity to reach all in ways that the market and civil society do not. There is an inherent logic in the public solution, or 'the state', of reaching 'all', which is not present in the market or in the civil society. In neither of the latter is there an obligation to treat citizens equally. Nor is there a demand to cover the nation as a whole. As the market discriminates on the basis of capacity to pay, and the civil society is geographically and locally anchored, the state, or the public solution, is in fact the only way that 'all' can be reached. The goal of providing care in a way that is compatible with 'justice, equality, and freedom *for all*' is thus better defended through the public solution.

Democratic Access to Care 'For All': Spheres and Trade-Offs

The aim of this chapter is to discuss trade-offs in providing care democratically for *all*. On this question, Trudie Knijn's research (2000) is an early attempt to describe how the three institutional pillars of welfare provision—the state, the market and civil society—can affect care in distinctive ways. One of her conclusions is that the state, as the public alternative for providing care, is probably the most desirable route, for it makes the care recipient into a citizen with rights and duties, while the market and family work through other logics that might be less beneficial to the person in need. Thus, Knijn explicitly names the logics of different societal spheres in relation to care—inviting us to consider more closely the advantages and difficulties of each. In an earlier work, Berenice Fisher and Joan Tronto also discussed what they describe as "primary social modes of caring in our society" (1990, 37), where they distinguished the household, the market and the bureaucracy in terms of care production and their ideas are discussed as part of the following discussion where each sphere is considered in turn.

The Market

If there is one societal sphere or logic that has been the object of a wide range of concerns, objections and criticisms in the care ethics literature, it is most definitely the market. As early as 1980, Kari Waerness proposed the concept of a 'caring rationality' (Waerness 1980). Her example was that of homecare workers who often did extra work for their clients, even though it might, for example, mean working overtime without compensation. She also considered the problem that arises when technical rationalities and demands for efficiency collide with care provision. Waerness argued that when care is paid for, it risks being industrialised, which happens at the expense of several features that distinguish good care, such as personalisation and flexibility. She argued that care goes against both efficiency (the market) and technical rationalities (the bureaucracy). She placed the ideal of care in the family and/or non-reimbursed caregiving, even though she also acknowledged the problems that this raises for carers, who are mostly women.

Other scholars have expanded upon why market rationality should be regarded as contrary to care ethics. Fisher and Tronto (1990) have discussed how care production in the market means that people in need of care often need someone to pursue their interest in order to receive care which means that the satisfaction of their needs becomes hampered. In later work, Tronto also has emphasised the strong contrast between market rationality and the ethics of care (2010, 2017). She criticises the resort to notions of 'customer satisfaction' as a basis for evaluation of good care delivery and interrogates the view that competition should improve care. In Tronto's elaboration (2017) of her concept of 'caring with' she argues that understanding people as originally caring, as *homines curans*, poses a forceful challenge to neoliberalism. She writes: "What if we were to argue *against* neoliberalism from the standpoint of care, understood within a democratic society's frame that care must be adequately and equally provided for all, and that all must contribute their fair share to care?" (Tronto 2017, 28).

Further, Held has indentified how "questions about what we ought to do [should] be answered by rational deduction from abstract rule to particular case, or rational calculation of costs and benefits" (Held 2015, 19), are contrary to care ethics. White (2015) similarly argued that both privatisation and commodification are troubling for ethical ideals of care and that much in neoliberalism hinders a meaningful or robust commitment to care.

In sum, the market alternative seems to have quite severe trade-offs when it comes to access to care, which does not seem to favour equality. It is above all the logic of the ability to pay which ought to concern us, since it heavily informs the mechanisms for distribution of care on the market. As economic resources are unevenly distributed, this obviously affects the extent to which care is accessible 'to all': those with abundant financial resources can likely buy as much good quality care as they need and will hence receive more care than people with fewer resources. Financial resources also, in theory at least, affect the abilities that we have to give care to those to whom we are close and wish to care for; an individual with greater economic resources may have less pressure to perform paid work and may thus have more time for other tasks, such as caring. The market seems to favour the most well off, which goes against goals forwarded by ethics of care research.

Civil Society

Civil society may seem a good alternative for providing care if one argues that what makes up the core of care ethics is the ability to be responsive to the particular context. It is therefore not surprising that several care scholars seem to understand civil society as an appropriate site for good care outside of the family. For instance, Allison Weir (2005) describes how a feminist vision of caring may be realised in circumstances where care is reprivatised, not via the traditional family model but in community care spaces, where parents could at times leave their children in the care of trusted others and at other times provide care for other children. Weir is convinced that an expanded sphere of civil society, in which parents could share care with other people in the community, would eliminate the enforced isolation of caregivers and children in the domestic sphere, and would make the work of care much more fulfilling and much more attractive (Weir 2005, 326). Further, she proposes that in this vision, men would be more likely to take advantage of parental leave policies, and the care sphere might expand as a focus of community social activity.

However, civil society also seems to have discriminatory features. For instance, civil society is likely to be more developed in some geographical areas than others, with variations that may well correlate with the level of economic resources. In economically affluent areas, people have the opportunity to respond more generously to fundraising, and family structures may be built so that one partner has more time to invest in charity work or local participative organisations.

The logics of civil society regarding access to care for specific individuals may also show discriminatory patterns. An individual's likability varies and affects how deeply that person can tap into the resources, including care resources, offered by civil society. For example, the increasingly common method of fundraising through social media for otherwise unaffordable surgery or treatment might be affected by a number of discriminatory patterns: people who are conventionally attractive or traditionally vulnerable (especially women, girls or those suffering non-self-inflicted conditions) may be more likely to receive support by stirring sympathies provoked by common social prejudices or reactions against stigmatisation (Corrigan 2004).

Diagnoses or situations that are new to the public are also more likely to receive funding, as our capacity to be upset over a person's tragic situation seems to wear down the more often we are confronted with it. Thus, we can suspect that people who are considered ugly, angry, not thankful enough or lacking in other important social cues are less likely to receive care through civil society, as are people suffering from ordinary problems or self-inflicted problems. In the literature that discusses why state-funded social welfare is preferable to the help of local or charitable organisations, there is abundant evidence of these negative consequences of civil society serving as the chief provider of care. We can demand justice, but we must beg for charity or forgiveness (Piven and Cloward 2012; Morris 2009).

Publicly Funded Care or the State

Publicly funded care is financed fully or considerably through taxes. It is important to distinguish between the funding of public policy and its implementation. Publicly funded policies, such as care policies, may be implemented directly by the state or contracted out to market actors or civil society. For our purpose here, which is to discuss the distinctive logics of access to care, it is the financial aspect that is important. Care and other services funded through taxes may be regarded as accessible to all citizens, but accessibility of care 'for all' remains important and uncertain.

Among critics of publicly funded care and proponents of the view that public institutions can meaningfully 'care' in the same way as individuals is Nel Noddings (2015) who argues that organisations can provide food or building material after a catastrophe, and they may establish "conditions under which caring-for can take place" (Noddings 2015, 75) but they cannot provide the actual person-to-person relationship between carer and cared for.

Fisher and Tronto discussed the option of the state as care provider in their 1990 work, in the form of "bureaucracy", defined as large-scale hierarchical organisations. This definition is of course unproblematic, building on Weber, and their discussion on how these organisations work through routine and standardisation is in line with this and also taken up later by other scholars. For an argument that takes up this question of whether big organisations are necessarily less caring than small ones, see Bourgault (2017).

However, in the further discussion Fisher and Tronto discuss both policy and the organisational form of its implementation, and while the latter relates to bureaucracy, the former does not. They argue that the main difference between the two are the mechanisms by which it is decided what to care for (1990, 48). Here, they disclose how their perspective is anchored in a liberal limited state as they claim that "the government allocates caring tasks to public sector bureaucracies when other major institutions fail to meet certain socially defined caring needs" (1990, 48). A more encompassing view of the state, which is elaborated further later, would instead point at how certain collective problems are more efficiently handled through common (public) solutions.

As indicated earlier, the option of publicly/state-funded care seems absolutely critical when the ambition is to provide care democratically to all citizens. A basic notion of the state is its universal characteristics pertaining to citizens. This is most clearly manifested through the right to vote, where each eligible person has one vote, no more, no less. The principle of equality before the law is manifested in the notion that citizens all are included and on equal footing. Neither of the other two spheres entails a similar encompassing logic of who is included and who is not.

It could be argued that there is a difference between formal and informal equality in the democratic state. We may have a formal right to vote, but informally the political influence of citizens is unequal. The argument against this objection is that inequality results from interfering spheres and logics rather than the state. Using an analogy of Michael Walzer (2008), we can argue that different spheres in society may have different logics, and this is acceptable so long they do not spill over. The example of unequal political influence is likely to be due to other logics, for example, monetary resources, spilling over to the political sphere. As such this is no argument against the idea of the state providing equal rights, but an argument against spillovers between spheres.

If our aim as care ethicists is to make sure that care is provided democratically 'to all', it seems that the state has much more capacity than have the other societal spheres to handle the democratic access to care. Indeed, the state has the capacity to reach 'all', including the more vulnerable and marginalised, who would not be entitled to equal care according to a market logic. Also, civil society seems more arbitrary than the public/state solution. As noted earlier, the right to benefits in the welfare state seems superior to civil society/charity solutions, in part because right is a more dignified way to provide benefits than unregularised civil society solutions, which may be arbitrary.

However, we ought to acknowledge that the public alternative also discriminates. First, there are commonly qualifications for citizenship that can be more or less restrictive and can also be passed on generationally in different ways. For example, ex-Soviet citizens were allowed to apply for German citizenship through reference to their German ancestors after the fall of the Berlin Wall, when historical biological relationships were strongly emphasised, while other countries' regulations do not allow citizenship to be passed through parental relationships. Second, groups who reside in a nation but lack citizenship are in no position to demand citizenship rights, which often include rights to tax-funded welfare as part of public policy. This affects refugees or immigrants who reside without legal status in a country. Hence, the publicly funded care alternative could be said to discriminate along national borders. And certainly, the problem of national borders and care ethics has been considered by many (Robinson 2006; Hochschild 2000). Are there ways to alleviate this problem? Federal solutions or solutions now current in the European Union might represent some modest ways to provide rights on a supranational level. However, membership of states in this super-level mirrors citizen membership in nations, so it uses the same principle, only on a higher level of analysis.

Conclusion

This chapter has highlighted the importance of considering the public alternative, when the problem of democratic access 'for all' is included in the discussion and argued that the public solution, and the state as an apparatus with capacity to reach 'all', is superior to market or civil society solutions in this respect. The important thing is that policies are formulated and that they are funded through taxes. In sum, different spheres meet the ethical care demands along the two dimensions discussed in the beginning: first, between particularised and standardised solutions, where we may comprehend civil society as better able to meet ethical care demands than the state or the market. Second, between high and low democratic access to care, where it seems that the state, or the publicly funded solution, provides a better alternative than either the civil society or the market.

Finally, the chapter has aimed to move the discussion in the ethics of care debate closer to the problem of how to provide access to care 'for all', and it indicates that the question of how the two dimensions, discussed earlier, may be integrated is a problem that we have just started to explore. There are a number of interesting problems related to how care ethics regards democratic care as access to care that remains to be explored; this chapter has only scratched on the surface of this interesting field.

References

Bourgault, Sophie. 2017. Prolegomena to a Caring Bureaucracy. *European Journal of Women's Studies* 24 (3): 202–217.

Bradley, David, et al. 2003. Distribution and Redistribution in Postindustrial Democracies. *World Politics* 55 (2): 193–228.

Corrigan, Patrick. 2004. How Stigma Interferes with Mental Health Care. *American Psychologist* 59 (7): 614.

Diamond, Larry, and Leonardo Morlino. 2016. The Quality of Democracy. In *In Search of Democracy*, ed. Larry Diamond, 33–45. London: Routledge.

Engster, Daniel. 2007. *The Heart of Justice: Care Ethics and Political Theory.* Oxford: Oxford University Press.

Fisher, Berenice, and Joan C. Tronto. 1990. Toward a Feminist Theory of Caring. In *Circles of Care*, ed. Emily K. Able and Margaret Nelson. Albany, NY: SUNY Press.

Gilligan, Carol. 1993. *In a Different Voice.* Cambridge, MA: Cambridge University Press.

Hankivsky, Olena. 2004. *Social Policy and the Ethic of Care.* Vancouver, BC: UBC Press.

Held, Virginia. 2006. *The Ethics of Care: Personal, Political and Global.* New York: Oxford University Press.

———. 2015. Care and Justice, Still. In *Care Ethics and Political Theory*, ed. Daniel Engster and Maurice Hamington, 208–226. Oxford: Oxford University Press.

Hochschild, Arlie R. 2000. Global Care Chains and Emotional Surplus Value. In *On the Edge: Living with Global Capitalism*, ed. W. Hutton, A. Giddens, and N. Myers, 130–146. London: Jonathan Cape.

Jessop, Bob. 1996. Post-Fordism and the State. In *Comparative Welfare Systems*, ed. Bent Greve, 165–183. Basingstoke: Palgrave Macmillan.

Knijn, Trude. 2000. Marketization and the Struggling Logic of (Home) Care in The Netherlands. In *Care Work: Gender, Labor and the Welfare State*, ed. M.M. Harrington, 232–248. New York: Routledge.

Korpi, Walter, and Joakim Palme. 1998. The Paradox of Redistribution and Strategies of Equality: Welfare State Institutions, Inequality, and Poverty in the Western Countries. *American Sociological Review* 63 (5): 661–687.

Lipsky, Michael. 1980/2010. *Street-level Bureaucracy: Dilemmas of the Individual in Public Service.* New York: Russell Sage Foundation.

Lundberg, Olle, et al. 2008. The Role of Welfare State Principles and Generosity in Social Policy Programmes for Public Health: An International Comparative Study. *The Lancet* 372 (9650): 1633–1640.

Marshall, Thomas H. 1964. Class, Citizenship and Social Development. In *Democracy a Reader*, ed. R. Blaug. Edinburgh: Edinburg University Press.

Maynard-Moody, Steven, and Michael Musheno. 2000. State Agent or Citizen Agent: Two Narratives of Discretion. *Journal of Public Administration Research and Theory* 10 (2): 329–358.

Møller, Marie Ø., and O. Helena Stensöta. 2017. Welfare State Regimes and Caseworkers' Problem Explanation. *Administration & Society.* https://doi.org/10.1177/0095399717700224.

Morris, J. Andrew. 2009. *The Limits of Voluntarism: Charity and Welfare from the New Deal Through the Great Society.* Cambridge: Cambridge University Press.

Noddings, Nel. 2006. *Starting at Home: Caring and Social Policy.* Berkeley, CA: University of California Press.

———. 2015. Care Ethics and "Caring" Organizations. In *Care Ethics and Political Theory*, ed. Daniel Engster and Maurice Hamington, 208–226. Oxford: Oxford University Press.

Pierre, Jon. 2011. Stealth Economy? Economic Theory and the Politics of Administrative Reform. *Administration and Society* 43: 672–692. https://doi.org/10.1177/0095399711412928.

Pierson, Paul. 1994. *Dismantling the Welfare State? Reagan, Thatcher and the Politics of Retrenchment.* Cambridge: Cambridge University Press.

Piven, Frances Fox, and Richard Cloward. 2012. *Regulating the Poor: The Functions of Public Welfare.* New York: Vintage.

Pressman, L. Jeffrey, and Aron Wildavsky. 1984. *Implementation: How Great Expectations in Washington Are Dashed in Oakland; Or, Why It's Amazing that Federal Programs Work At All, This Being a Saga of the Economic Development Administration as Told by Two Sympathetic Observers Who Seek to Build Morals on a Foundation.* Berkeley: University of California Press.

Robinson, Fiona. 2006. Care, Gender and Global Social Justice: Rethinking "Ethical Globalization". *Journal of Global Ethics* 2 (1): 5–25.

Sevenhuijsen, Selma. 1998. *Citizenship and the Ethics of Care: Feminist Considerations on Justice, Morality and Care.* New York: Routledge.

———. 2000. Caring in the Third Way: The Relation Between Obligation, Responsibility and Care in Third Way Discourse. *Critical Social Policy* 20 (1): 5–37.

Stensöta, O. Helena. 2015. A Public Ethics of Care: A General Public Ethics. *Ethics and Social Welfare* 9 (2): 183–200.

Tronto, C. Joan. 1993. *Moral Boundaries: A Political Argument for an Ethic of Care.* New York: Routledge.

———. 2010. Creating Caring Institutions: Politics, Plurality and Purpose. *Ethics and Social Welfare* 4 (2): 158–171.

———. 2013. *Caring Democracy: Markets, Equality, and Justice.* New York: New York University Press.

———. 2017. There Is an Alternative: Homines Curans and the Limits of Neoliberalism. *International Journal of Care and Caring* 1 (1): 27–43.

Ungerson, Clare. 1997. Social Politics and the Commodification of Care. *Social Politics* 4 (3): 362–381.

Waerness, Kari. 1980. Omsorgsarbete – en begreppsdiskussion. *Tidskrift för genus-vetenskap TGV* 3: 6–17.

Walzer, Michael. 2008. *Spheres of Justice: A Defense of Pluralism and Equality.* New York: Basic books.

Weir, Allison. 2005. The Global Universal Caregiver: Imagining Women's Liberation in the New Millennium. *Constellations* 12 (3): 308–330.

White, Julie Ann. 2015. Practicing Care at the Margins: Other-mothering as a Public Care. In *Care Ethics and Political Theory*, ed. Daniel Engster and Maurice Hamington, 208–226. Oxford: Oxford University Press.

CHAPTER 5

Re-thinking 'Paternalism' for a Democratic Theory of Care

Marion Smiley

In recent years, feminists and social democrats alike have been inspired by Joan Tronto's pathbreaking work on the ethics of care to develop a welfare state that is both caring and democratic (Tronto 1993, 2013). Moreover, in doing so, they have frequently referred to the kind of care associated with such a state as non-paternalistic (White 2010). But they have not made fully clear how—within what kind of state—such care is possible. Nor have they made fully clear how—in what respects—paternalism is a threat to democracy. I set out to remedy this situation later in the chapter. I show what it is about paternalism that threatens democracy in general and a democratic welfare state in particular. I then specify the conditions of non-paternalism. In both contexts, I find it necessary to re-think paternalism itself.

I begin by arguing that we need to take paternalism seriously in discussions of democracy—and democratic care in particular—and that we cannot do so without replacing the concept of paternalism that now prevails among philosophers, political theorists and legal scholars. I go on to

M. Smiley (✉)
Philosophy Department, Brandeis University, Waltham, MA, USA
e-mail: smiley@bradeis.edu

P. Urban, L. Ward (eds.), *Care Ethics, Democratic Citizenship and the State*, International Political Theory,
https://doi.org/10.1007/978-3-030-41437-5_5

critically analyze the prevailing concept of paternalism and to draw out its negative consequences in practice. I reformulate the concept by treating paternalism as a distinctly paternal kind of hierarchical governance and then use the concept as so reformulated to suggest how we might develop a non-paternalistic, democratic, system of state care.

Democracy and the Question of Paternalism

Two points about democracy become key here. The first is that while democracy requires us to take distributive justice seriously, it is not, as Iris Young, Ian Shapiro and others have pointed out, a system of distributive justice per se. Instead, it is a system of governance in which individuals exercise power together as equals when making collective decisions (Young 1990; Shapiro 2001, 2003, 2011). The second is that democracy understood, as such, requires individuals not only to participate as equals when making collective decisions but to *relate* to each other as equals in governing particular spheres of life. In other words, it requires democratic *relationships* as well as democratic institutions.[1]

While democratic relationships take their meaning from an important aspect of democracy, namely co-governance, they are not simply relationships between those who share a belief in democracy. Nor are they relationships between those who acknowledge each other as abstract moral equals. Instead, they are relationships between those who acknowledge each other as co-governors in a particular sphere of life and who feel comfortable governing there together. In other words, they are relationships between those who share an identity—co-governor—and who interact with one another according to that identity as it is understood in a particular sphere of life.

Since what renders these relationships democratic is the fact that those in them relate to each other as co-governors rather than as, say, citizens, they are not tied exclusively to a public sphere. Nor do they require individuals to leave their particular identities and/or social roles behind. Instead, they can, as democratic relationships, exist in the family, marriage, organized religion, the workplace, clubs, social and political movements,

[1] Feminist philosophers have in recent years argued strenuously for the importance of taking relationships seriously in ethical and political life. For an example of how we might do so in the context of democratic equality, see Anderson (1999). H. O. Stensöta stresses the importance of taking relationships seriously when talking about democratic practices of care (Stensöta 2015).

and public life. Likewise, they can, as democratic relationships, be between individuals who, in acknowledging each other as co-governors, do so as spouses, worshippers, workers, club members, activists and citizens.

While democratic relationships are potentially at home in all of these spheres of life, they will be hard to develop in many of them. For, as things now stand, the social roles that ground these spheres of life are often configured hierarchically, that is, in such a way that individuals in them are led to relate to each other as governors and governed rather than as co-governors. Moreover, these roles, as well as the spheres of life of which they are a part and the relationships that they sustain, are not only grounded in systems of power over which we have little control, but are frequently thought to be necessary to either individuals or the community as a whole.

How far can we expect to get here? Since hierarchical governance appears to be necessary in at least some spheres of life, for example, child-rearing and the military, and since individuals cannot leave their socialization in one sphere of life behind completely when they enter into others, we cannot expect democratic relationships to be feasible or even desirable everywhere. Nor can we expect them to exist in a pure form anywhere. But we can, at the very least, ask ourselves whether particular modes of hierarchical governance are as necessary as we now assume them to be and whether they might be replaced in particular spheres of life with democratic alternatives.

In our efforts to democratize state care, we might do well to place the system of hierarchical governance called *paternalism* at the center of our attention. But we cannot do so without re-thinking paternalism itself. For, the concept of paternalism that now prevails among philosophers, political theorists and legal scholars does not understand paternalism as a kind of hierarchical governance or treat it as a political practice of any kind. Nor—surprisingly—does it make reference to things distinctly paternal: paternal authority, paternalistic relationships, a paternalistic model of care and so on. Instead, it treats paternalism as a discrete moral act, namely the act of making personal (read: self-regarding) choices for individuals understood as the restriction and/or violation of an individual's right to free choice in the private sphere. (I document this treatment later in the chapter.)

Not surprisingly, this way of thinking about paternalism is very helpful to libertarians, since it reinforces the importance of individual rights to free choice in a tightly bounded private sphere. But it does not help those who are concerned to grasp the anti-democratic (as distinct from anti-liberal) aspects of paternalism or those whose goal is to sketch the contours of a non-paternalistic, democratic, system of state care. Indeed, as I suggest in the next two sections, it holds those who use it back from pursuing both of these projects. What is the concept of paternalism that now prevails among philosophers, political theorists and legal scholars?

The Prevailing Concept of Paternalism

Gerald Dworkin offers what is perhaps the most widely accepted definition of paternalism among contemporary philosophers, political theorists and legal scholars. According to Dworkin, paternalism is

> roughly the interference with a person's liberty of action justified by reasons referring exclusively to the welfare, good, happiness, needs, interests or values of those being coerced. (Dworkin 1971, 120)

A large majority of those writing on paternalism agree with Dworkin here that paternalism entails the coercive interference with an individual's liberty for the sake of her own well-being. According to Rosemary Carter, "a paternalistic act is one in which the protection or promotion of a subject's welfare is the primary reason for attempted or successful coercive interference with an action or state of that person" (Carter 1977, 138). Joel Feinberg, John Hodson, Donald VanDeVeer, John Kleinig, Jeffrie Murphy agree with Carter here (Feinberg 1971, 113; Hodson 1977, 61–62; Murphy 1964; VanDeVeer 1986; Kleinig 1984), as does John Young, Mark Strasser and many others who characterize paternalism not only as the making of personal choices for individuals on the basis of our sense of their own good but as a kind of 'intervention', a 'restriction of individual liberty' and the 'violation of an individual's right to free choice in the private sphere' (Young 1982, 47; Strasser 1988, 103; Scoccia 2008, 351–381).

Mark Strasser captures all of these attributes when he writes of paternalism:

> Paternalism is roughly the interference with, limitation of, or usurpation of individual autonomy justified by reasons of the person whose autonomy is being interfered with, limited, or usurped in her private sphere of free choice. (Strasser 1988, 104)

Dworkin, in his later work, drops the term 'coercion' from the definition of paternalism and replaces it with the 'restriction of autonomy'. In *Paternalism: Second Thoughts*, he associates paternalism with intervention into *autonomy*, rather than with intervention into *actions*, and concedes that paternalism is as such not necessarily coercive. But, like Simon Clarke and others who make the same move in their own work, Dworkin continues to view paternalism as a restriction of individual liberty and an intervention into an individual's sphere of self-regarding choices associated with the making of choices for the individual on the basis of her own good (Dworkin 1983, 105–111; Clarke 2002, 2009, 25–46).

Dworkin's definition of paternalism continues to hold forth. While those writing on paternalism in the last few years have sometimes chosen to reinterpret particular aspects of the subject matter, for example, 'an individual's own good' or 'a paternalistic reason' (Bullock 2018; Raibley 2013; Grill 2018),[2] they have not rejected the above way of thinking about paternalism itself. Indeed, they have frequently cited Dworkin's definition as foundational and, in doing so, made clear that paternalism is for them still a matter of violating (or at least intervening into) an individual's sphere of personal choice making for her own good—a violation that occurs when others make her personal choices for her.

In his 2018 essay on the concept of paternalism, Danny Scoccia presents what he takes to be the 'standard version' of paternalism. His emphasis here, once again, is on the violation of individual liberty in personal choice making. According to Scoccia:

A large number—the majority—of moral and political theorists assume a definition of paternalism according to which paternalism exists when:

1. P limits Q's liberty or interferes with Q's decision-making,
2. against Q's will, without his consent, or contrary to his preferences and
3. for Q's own good (Scoccia 2018).

The 'standard version' of paternalism also continues to view paternalism as something that takes place exclusively in an individual's own sphere

[2] Emma Bullock focuses on the meaning of "an individual's own good" in discussions of paternalism (Bullock 2018). Jason Raibley asks how we should interpret "individual well-being" in discussions of paternalism (Raibley 2013). Kalle Grill explores the importance of paternalistic reasons in 'The Normative Core of Paternalism' (Grill 2018).

of personal choice making and that is morally wrong (in most cases) because it violates individual autonomy. Christian Coons and Michael Weber underscore both trends in their own overview of the subject matter (Coons and Weber 2013, 2–3). Seanna Shiffrin, in her very influential piece on paternalism, demonstrates the continued association of paternalism with an individual's right to make personal choices in a sphere of personal life that, Shiffrin contends, the individual herself controls. According to Shiffrin, "[p]aternalistic acts by definition intrude on areas that the target legitimately controls" (Shiffrin 2000, 12).

Interestingly enough, this highly individualistic version of paternalism prevails in discussions of paternalism even when the paternalism is associated with realms of life that we do not normally think about in purely individualistic terms. I refer here to realms in which the choices in question, while personal, are collectively organized. Daniel Haybron and Anna Alexandrova focus on paternalism in the economic realm and, in doing so, conceive of paternalism, not in the systematic way that we might expect, but with reference to individual autonomy. According to Haybron and Alexandrova, paternalism in economics is a matter of "taking control over an individual's own affairs" and "managing them in some cases over time". Likewise, the 'wrong of paternalism' is that it "involves usurping an agent's authority to manage her own affairs" (Haybron and Alexandrova 2013, 157–177).

Sarah Conly brings this way of thinking about paternalism into her work on paternalism in the realm of public health. Since her examples, for example, banning trans-fats and cigarettes, are, along with other public health policies, part of collective action, we might expect Conly to develop a notion of paternalism that is at home in contexts of collective choice making. But she does not. Instead, she views paternalism as a matter of restricting individual autonomy for an individual's own good. The twist is that she is willing to accept paternalism in many public health cases. "In these cases", she writes, "we are restoring individuals' personal choices for their own good" and "limiting their freedom of action and their autonomy in the interests of better living" (Conly 2013, 17).

Three things about this way of formulating paternalism are worth underscoring. First of all, it does not understand paternalism as a system of care, a mode of governance, an ideology or any other kind of 'ism'. Nor does it pick up on the relationships of domination and subordination—or any other kinds of relationship—that exist between paternalists and their wards. Instead, it makes paternalism out to be a discrete moral act—the act of making personal choices for individuals on the basis of a sense of their own good—and, in doing so, focuses, not on the agent making these choices or on his place in the community, but rather on the fact that the individual for whom he is making these choices is not being allowed to make these choices herself.

Second, while the concept as so formulated retains the root term 'paternalism', it does not make paternalism out to be a distinctly paternal phenomenon by, say, referring to a paternalist and his wards, to the roles of father and child, to a paternalistic model of authority or to a paternalistic belief system. Nor does it characterize the act of making personal choices for individuals with reference to any of these things—or, for that matter, with reference to the very acts of care (by a paternalist) that it assumes. Instead, it zeroes in on the reason given for the act—an individual's own good—and expresses this reason (inappropriately) in the language of paternalism.

Third, while those who articulate the prevailing concept of paternalism profess to be simply describing paternalism, they do not simply record the nature of paternalism per se. Nor do they construe paternalism in a socially and politically neutral fashion. Instead, they construe it from a traditional liberal/libertarian perspective by, among other things, interpreting the act of making personal choices for an individual as both an intervention into the individual's private sphere and a restriction and/or violation of the individual's right to free choice. Moreover, they do so, not as a normative critique of the subject matter, but as part of the definition of paternalism itself.

Not surprisingly, the traditional liberal/libertarian norms embedded in the concept of paternalism as so formulated get reinforced whenever we use the concept as so formulated in practice. Since these norms are assumed, rather than made explicit, they are not always obvious. But they become visible once we grasp how particular aspects of paternalism get interpreted in the way that they do within the prevailing concept of paternalism itself. Take, for instance, the way in which 'personal choices' become 'self-regarding' and 'private' choices.

As things now stand, those who define paternalism in the way cited earlier use the terms 'personal', 'self-regarding' and 'purely private' interchangeably. Likewise, they go back and forth between the terms 'purely personal conduct', 'self-regarding activities' and 'private behavior'. Rolf Sartorius stresses that only certain kinds of well-being are relevant to state paternalism, namely 'personal conduct' or 'purely personal conduct', and it refers to such conduct as 'self-regarding' (Sartorius 1983, xi–xii). Joel Feinberg refers to paternalism as that involving 'private activities' and insists that the term 'state paternalism' be restricted to 'primarily self-regarding affairs' or 'self-regarding harmful conduct' (Feinberg 1971, 5).

Since the terms 'personal', 'self-regarding' and 'private' are used interchangeably here without pause, they might be taken to be natural or logical equivalents. (Indeed, that is how they were originally presented.) But they are not equivalents of a natural or logical kind. Nor can they be treated as such. For, even though personal choices are by definition choices that we make about our personal well-being and are hence choices that require us to think about ourselves, they do not have to be purely self-regarding. Nor do they have to be made by us alone. Instead, they can be other-regarding (as well as self-regarding) choices and they can be made together in a group.

Examples of such choice making already abound. Parents and domestic partners make choices about how to live their lives in ways that involve thinking about, say, what is good for their loved ones or their relationships to these others, and they sometimes make these choices together. So, too, do citizens who are confronted with personal choices that involve collective decision-making about, say, health care, consumer protection or financial security in retirement. In these cases, we not only make personal choices together and/or with others' well-being in mind, but we do so in ways that are arguably both necessary and psychologically healthy.

I do not mean to suggest here that we should construe all of our personal choices as other-regarding and collective or dismiss the claims of those who worry about the loss of privacy. (Clearly, we should retain a right to make many of our personal choices ourselves.) Instead, I mean to suggest only that when we construe personal choices as purely self-regarding and private, we do so, not because personal choices are *naturally* or *by definition* self-regarding and private. Instead, we do so because we think that these personal choices *should* be construed as purely self-regarding and private or because we have unselfconsciously accepted others' beliefs to this effect.

How, though, do we get from paternalism as the making of self-regarding choices for individuals to paternalism as a kind of intervention, a form of coercion, a restriction of individual liberty and a violation of individual rights to free choice in the private sphere? Two further normative, traditional liberal/libertarian, assumptions—both of which get incorporated into the prevailing concept of paternalism without acknowledgment—have to be made in order to make sense of such a move. The first is that individuals have an absolute right to make personal choices for themselves without the involvement of others. The other is that they make these choices in a tightly bounded private sphere that is both prior to and independent of collective action.

Since the prevailing concept of paternalism rests on these two controversial normative assumptions, as well as on a tendency to go back and forth between two different notions of 'the private',[3] we do not have to accept it if we do not want to do so. Indeed, we might want to reject it on the grounds that its traditional liberal/libertarian norms are not acceptable to us or because it is conceptually muddled. (I reject it on both grounds discussed later.) But we cannot—and should not—simply ignore it. For, it has a series of negative consequences in practice that will persist if others continue to use the concept as so formulated.

Consequences in Practice

Let me simply gesture here to several of the most important of these consequences.

The Privileging of a Normative Project

Since the concept of paternalism as formulated earlier reinforces the traditional liberal/libertarian norms on which it is grounded, it reinforces the traditional liberal/libertarian project of which it is part. Moreover, in doing so, it displaces and/or brings into question ethical perspectives that, while valuing individual rights, do not treat individual rights as the centerpiece of ethical life, for example, those that place care at the center of our attention, that emphasize the primacy of relationships and that take non-domination to be key. Likewise, it hinders projects that depend on these other ethical perspectives—projects such as the development of collective modes of personal decision-making in both public and private life.

[3] One of these notions refers to a particular kind of choice, namely a personal choice. The other refers to the place where individuals are now thought to have a right to make such a choice on their own, namely what we have come to call the private sphere.

The Narrowing of Focus and the Restriction of Attention

Since the prevailing concept of paternalism not only defines its subject matter with reference to the violation of individual rights but omits any reference to things distinctly paternal, for example, paternal authority, it significantly narrows our focus and, in doing so, restricts our attention in three important respects. First of all, it steers us away from cases of paternalism that do not involve the violation of individual rights to free choice. Second, it restricts us from grasping the way in which many groups now experience paternalism in their lives. Third, it obscures both the systems of power in which paternalism takes place and the anti-democratic nature of paternalism itself (Soss et al. 2011).

The association of paternalism with the violation of an individual's rights to free choice here is key. Take, for instance, the case of personal choices made in the family. In some families, husbands make personal choices for the family as a whole. In these cases, we might want to talk about paternalism as in play because a paternalist is making personal choices for others. But we cannot do so without leaving the traditional liberal/libertarian concept of paternalism behind. For, in these cases, we cannot say that a wife's individual right to free choice—as distinct from, say, her right to participate in collective decision-making—has been violated.

I do not mean to suggest here that we cannot talk about paternalism in cases where individuals do not have the kind of right that the prevailing concept of paternalism requires. (Indeed, I set out to show later that we can talk about paternalism in these cases very easily if we re-think paternalism in the way I suggest.) Instead, I mean to suggest only that the concept of paternalism sketched earlier gets in our way of doing so.

So, too, does the highly individualistic model of personal choice making that it assumes. Take, again, the case of the family. In the family, mother's choices, along with the choices of fathers who are primary parents, are rarely as self-regarding as those deemed relevant to paternalism by the earlier formulation of paternalism. Indeed, these choices, while personal, are often made with the well-being of others, for example, their children, in mind. Hence, even when a paternal authority, say her husband or the state, makes these choices for her, we are—if we accept the individualistic model of paternalism sketched earlier—unable to analyze them as paternalism.

The inability of the individualistic model to take into consideration cases of paternalism in collective contexts is also evident when it comes to matters of state care. Take, for example, the case of individuals who receive Federal welfare assistance. Here the state makes personal choices for individuals. But since these choices are collective by virtue of both their group-based nature and the fact that they require public funding, they are not generally associated with an individual right to free choice—other than to accept or reject assistance. Hence, while these choices may be made at the state level by a paternalist, they do not fit the prevailing model of paternalism and as such get left behind by those who employ this model.

Since financially poor individuals are more likely than others to depend on state care, we should not be surprised to discover that they generally experience paternalism not-analyzable-as-such more frequently than their financially better-off fellows. But financially better-off members of the community also have personal choices made for them by a public body, for example, choices associated with health care, safety, sanitation, home mortgages or financial well-being in retirement. Hence, they, too, can experience paternalism-not-analyzable-as-such—and indeed do so, I argue later, whenever the state makes decisions for them on the basis of a model of paternal authority.

The Distortion of an Experience

By ignoring the model of paternal authority and the hierarchical relationships in which paternalistic choice making takes place, the prevailing concept of paternalism not only limits our view of paternalism but distorts the way in which those who are subject to paternalism actually experience it. In particular, it obscures the domination and subordination, as well as lowered status in the community, that recipients of paternalism experience in their roles as child-like incompetents. Moreover, it suggests that the only way that we experience paternalism is as a restriction of individual liberty or as a violation of rights.

A Disconnect from Democracy

Since the prevailing concept obscures the domination and subordination associated with paternalism from us, it prevents us from grasping the anti-democratic nature of paternalism. I have in mind the relationships of domination and subordination that exist between paternalists (governors) and their wards (those being governed) in practices of care. Since these relationships are by definition undemocratic, we should be able to talk about paternalism itself as undemocratic and to treat non-paternalism as a condition of democratic care. But the prevailing concept of paternalism does not allow us to do so, since it leaves these relationships, as well as everything else distinctly paternal, out of paternalism.

Silence on Gender

By keeping things distinctly paternal out of its definition of paternalism, as well as by treating paternalism as a discrete moral act rather than as a system of any kind, the traditional liberal/libertarian concept of paternalism obscures the gendered nature of paternalism. In particular, it leads us to ignore the way in which the roles of paternalist and ward, as well as the kind of care associated with them, are shaped by a model of paternal authority that privileges those who fit that model. Likewise, it obscures the possibility that paternal care is part of a larger system of patriarchy that both shapes and anchors it.

The De-politicization of a Subject Matter

By doing all of these things, the concept de-politicizes what is clearly a political, as well as a moral, practice. The de-politicization that I have in mind here takes two forms. The first is what we might talk about as de-institutionalization, or, in other words, the treatment of institutionalized acts of paternalism—acts that are shaped by the larger system of which they are a part—as if they are isolated acts performed by an agent whose relationship to those whom he is governing does not matter. The second is the assumption that one's status as competent or incompetent in this context is a purely individual matter that has nothing to do with one's group identity or one's place in the larger community.

A Dilemma in Practice

Since personal well-being might be enhanced by particular kinds of state care, and since many of us do not want to retain paternalism as a mode of governance or, for that matter, violate individual rights, we might want to develop modes of state care that are non-paternalistic and that do not violate the rights of individuals. I suggest later that we should. But—and herein lies the dilemma—we cannot do so as long as the traditional liberal/libertarian concept of paternalism remains in place since, according to it, any mode of collective protection by the state that involves making personal choices for (or even with) individuals appears to be paternalistic and a violation of an individual's right to free choice.

This dilemma—created for us by the traditional liberal/libertarian concept of paternalism—can become especially painful in practice, since it treats as mutually exclusive two things that many of us value very highly, namely the provision of personal well-being by a caring state and the value of anti-paternalism. Not surprisingly, the dilemma has not gone unnoticed by those who value both state care and anti-paternalism. But the preferred ways for getting around it—either justifying paternalism in these cases as exceptional with reference to individuals' 'real wills'(Hodson 1977, 61–69)[4] or translating state paternalism into the language of 'nudging'[5]—leave us with paternalism, as well as the earlier dilemma, in place. The former turns the expert on an individual's 'real will' into a paternalist. The latter shifts the identity of paternalist from individual decision-makers to institution builders.

[4] According to Hodson:

> [P]aternalism is not justified in most cases. But there are exceptions. When an individual's will is not rational, we cannot assume that it is his real will, and if it is not his real will, then we cannot associate it with autonomy. (p. 67)

The invocation of a 'real will' or a 'rational will' or an individual's 'own will' in this context has resurfaced over the years in a variety of works on paternalism. Robert Goodin develops a set of criteria for discovering an individual's 'own will' in his efforts to show that the state is justified in going against individuals' stated choices to pursue a (supposed) self-regarding activity that is harmful if those choices are not reflections of their 'own will'. Goodin uses the case of smoking to make his point. According to Goodin, if we look at a smoker's 'deep preferences' we can see that his 'own will' is to quit smoking rather than to smoke, and that when the state prohibits smoking it is respecting his 'own will' (Goodin 2002).

[5] Cass Sunstein and R. H. Thaler develop this approach (Sunstein and Thaler 2008). So, too, does Sigal Ben-Porath (Ben-Porath 2010). Sunstein, Thaler and Ben-Porath all justify limited paternalism by, among other things, moving the paternalism that they find justifiable into the realm of institution building. Sunstein and Thaler zero in on the practice of 'nudging'. For a very helpful discussion of what kind of paternalism, if any, 'nudging' is, see Muireann Quigley (Quigley 2018).

Re-thinking Paternalism

What are we to do here? Presumably, there is not much that we can do if we are forced to retain the traditional liberal/libertarian concept of paternalism. But we are not. Nor do we have to accept the dilemma that it creates for us. Instead, we can re-think paternalism in a way that enables us to avoid the dilemma, as well as to do the other things that we need to do in order to sketch the contours of a non-paternalistic, democratic, caring state—for example, talk about paternalism in all spheres of life, zero in on paternalistic relationships, grasp the anti-democratic nature of paternalism and so on. Moreover, we can do so without distorting reality or simply making a subject matter up. How so?

Three general conceptual moves become necessary. The first requires us to shift our focus away from discrete acts of personal choice making for individuals by an undisclosed moral agent to a distinctly paternal system of hierarchical governance or, in other words, to bring both 'the paternal' and the 'ism' back into paternalism. The second requires us to open our eyes up to all of the distinctly paternal things associated with this system of governance. The third requires us to think about them all together in such a way that we can understand paternalism as a threat to democracy and its removal as a necessary condition for the development of a democratic caring state.

I suggest that we can meet all of these requirements by formulating paternalism as a distinctly paternal mode of governance that is organized around:

- paternalists and those who are deemed in need of care by them;
- a hierarchical relationship between the two groups akin to that between father and child;
- a distinctly paternal kind of care associated with this relationship;
- a model of paternal authority that sustains both this relationship and the care itself;
- a set of norms for deciding who gets to be a paternalist and who gets to be a ward; and
- a belief system to legitimate all of the above.

All of these things are, of course, manifested differently in particular cases of paternalism. So, too, is the distinctly paternal system of care of which they are a part. Paternal authority is always present. But it rests on various kinds of paternal imagery, ranging from explicit father images in the church to images of the strong disciplinarian and the trusted guardian in educational and medical establishments, respectively. Superior knowledge and strength of will is always presumed. But it takes on different forms depending on whether we are talking about the superior religious knowledge of the cleric over his flock, the superior technical knowledge of the doctor over his patients or the superior knowledge of those legislating Federal welfare assistance.

In the case of a state, paternalism is organized around a model of political authority that places the image of a caring father at the center of our attention, that views particular citizens as in need of paternal care and that understands the relationship between governors (caregivers) and governed (those in need of care) in familial terms. Paternalism of this kind is found among legislators who characterize the poor as in need of 'tough love' on the grounds that they are supposedly incapable of making care-based judgments for themselves, as well as among political leaders who hide the threat of a nuclear disaster from all citizens because the latter are supposedly not strong or knowledgeable enough to act rationally under pressure.

Since all of these phenomena partake in a distinctly paternal mode of care giving, we might do well in this context to bring all of them together into a concept of paternalism that takes such a paternal mode of caregiving as its over-arching referent. In other words, we might do well to construe paternalism as a distinctly paternal mode of caregiving, where paternal caregiving is itself understood as involving care that is provided by a person or group who/which wields paternal authority within relationships that are hierarchical and that assume distinct roles of guardian and ward that are themselves interpreted with images of father and child in mind.

Since this way of thinking about paternalism treats paternalism as an organized system of governance, rather than as a discrete act, it is understandably not as precise as its prevailing counterpart. Nor is it as well suited as its prevailing counterpart is to the reinforcement of the value of individual rights to free choice as now construed. But it does not undermine the value of individual rights to free choice either. Indeed, by allowing us to distinguish between care that empowers individuals and care that disempowers them, it might well provide us with just the basis that we need for legitimating the importance of particular rights to individual free choice.

Moreover, there are clear advantages of this way of thinking about paternalism. First of all, since it focuses our attention on things paternal rather than on the intervention into an individual's private sphere of personal choice making, it does not force us to think about paternalism as something that takes place in an individual's private sphere of self-regarding actions only or that requires a pre-existing right to free choice. Instead, it enables us to think about paternalism in all spheres of life where paternalists govern those supposedly in need of their care.

Second, since it places relationships of domination and subordination at the center of our attention, it does not, like its prevailing counterpart, trivialize the experiences of those who are treated paternalistically in practice. Nor does it isolate paternalism from the social and political institutions that designate particular groups worthy of being paternalists. Instead, it allows us to grasp the domination, inequality and condescension that those who are treated paternalistically in practice experience and to understand paternalism itself in a systematic fashion that is both reflective of a particular moral worldview and grounded in a particular distribution of power.

Third, it does not, like its prevailing counterpart, refer to all of the state's making of personal choices for (or with) individuals as paternalistic. Instead, it picks up only those that take place within paternalistic relationships on the basis of a paternal model of authority and care. Hence, unlike its prevailing counterpart, it enables us to distinguish between paternalistic and non-paternalistic modes of personal choice making for (and with) individuals and, in doing so, to establish the conditions necessary to the development of a non-paternalistic, democratic, mode of collective protection. In other words, it enables us to do what many of those now writing about state care are themselves concerned to do, namely democratize state care as much as possible by moving beyond existing hierarchical relationships.

As things now stand, many of those who are concerned to democratize state care refer to—and treat as problematic—paternalistic attitudes, paternalistic relationships and the paternalistic treatment of the poor in particular (White 2010; Sevenhuijsen 1998; Stensöta 2015, 183–200). Likewise, when they use the term *paternalism*, they clearly have distinctly paternal things in mind rather than a violation of individual rights, and are almost always fully aware of the importance of power relations.[6] But they do not have available to them a concept of paternalism that brings these things together systematically and that underscores what exactly is undemocratic about paternalism. Hence, they are not able to go all the way in using their claims against paternalism to sketch a model of democratic state care.

How might we use the concept of paternalism as I have reformulated it about to sketch the contours of such a model of state care?

Beyond Paternalism in a Democratic Welfare State

Since non-paternalism here signifies the absence of things paternal in a system of care, it is at least at the outset both negative and relatively empty. But a non-paternalistic system of state care does not have to remain a negation in our minds forever or be identified without reference to positive attributes. For, presumably, it would be possible only within particular kinds of states, that is, those that keep paternalism at bay and as such is associated with particular conditions—structural rather than logical—that have a positive content. What are these conditions? How can they provide us with a more positive—or content-laden—picture of non-paternalism?

Three particular conditions come to mind here. First of all, in order for state care to exist without the hierarchical relationships associated with paternalism, it has to be construed as applying to all individuals rather than only to a particular group of incompetents. Second, in order for it not to degenerate into care based on the roles of father and child, it has to be formulated and distributed within relationships that are based on norms of mutuality and co-governance. Third, in order for it to maintain these relationships, as well as the norms of mutuality and co-governance, it has to be construed as part of both citizenship and communal membership itself.[7]

In the end, all of these conditions of non-paternalism, which I have expressed here as positive attributes—recipience associated with all members of the community rather than with a group of incompetents,

[6] Joe Soss, Sanford Schramm and Richard Fording make explicit that they are departing from what they call the "neo-liberal definition of paternalism" and focusing instead on authority relationships. They write: "In referring to paternalistic governance, our use of the term departs from the liberal definition. … We begin with political relations rather than with unencumbered individuals, emphasizing that paternalism is an authority relationship based on unequal status and power" (Soss et al. 2011).

[7] Selma Sevenhuijsen underscores the need to think about public care as organized around citizenship throughout her *Citizenship and the Ethics of Care* (Sevenhuijsen 1998).

formulation and distribution within relationships of mutuality and equal membership on the basis of full participation, and association with community membership itself—will be part of almost all non-paternalistic systems of state care. But they are not part of the definition of non-paternalism itself. Instead, they are institutional—and hence contingent—conditions necessary for the non-re-emergence of paternalism, conditions that assume the resilience of paternalism as a system of power that continues to be deeply entrenched.

Since non-paternalism is construed here in terms of non-hierarchical relationships, inclusiveness and participation by individuals who are considered equal members of a community, it might be taken to be the same thing as democracy. But it is not. For, even though the concepts of non-paternalism and democracy have much in common and overlap in important ways, they place different, albeit related, phenomena at the center of our attention. While the concept of democracy focuses our attention on co-governance in particular spheres of life, the concept of non-paternalism refers to the absence of a distinctly paternal system of power in practices of care.

Interestingly enough, democracy and non-paternalism turn out to be conditions of each other in practice. Democracy turns out to be a condition of non-paternalism in that without those practices associated with it, for example, the participation of all citizens in the articulation of needs, the setting of priorities and the shaping of practices of state care, neither paternalism nor any other hierarchical system of governance (whether it is class, race or gender based) can be kept at bay.[8] Non-paternalism turns out to be a condition of democracy in that as long as paternal authority is in place, hierarchies of power, as well as rule by a few, will prevail and undermine the possibility of democratic relationships between those who acknowledge each other as co-governors.

How can we hope to meet these conditions in practice? At the very least, we will have to dispel the view of state care as associated with weakness, bad citizenship and the absence of personal responsibility in the lives

[8] While Joan Tronto does not bring democracy and non-paternalism together explicitly in *Caring Democracy*, she does underscore those aspects of democracy that would appear to be most powerful in keeping paternalism at bay. According to Tronto (2013), if care is to be democratic, it must be "aimed at reducing power differentials and their effects on people" (33); it must "break hierarchies" (151); it must be inclusive with respect to the definition and location of needs (141); and it must ensure that those who participate in it think about themselves as both caregivers and caretakers (146).

of those deemed in need of paternal care.[9] Likewise, we will have to get ourselves to think about state care as something that can be based on principles of mutuality and equal membership, as well as capable of enhancing, rather than undermining, personal responsibility and citizenship.[10] In other words, we will have to re-think state care itself, as well as make sure that care is taken to be an important part of the state overall.[11]

How can we get ourselves to give up our association of state care with weakness, the absence of personal responsibility, less than full citizenship and the need for paternal care? While various theoretical works that explicitly associate state care with, say, autonomy, dignity and communal membership will surely be helpful here, we will also have to hammer home that state care as now instituted does not, contrary to our use of the term 'welfare', include only programs designed for the benefit of individuals deemed incompetent and in need of paternal care, that is, children, the mentally challenged and the poor, but instead include programs that are both designed to benefit all citizens and attached to citizenship per se, for example, social security, home mortgage supports, consumer protection programs, unemployment insurance and even the military and the police.[12]

[9] The view of state care as associated with weakness, bad citizenship and the absence of personal responsibility is frequently bolstered by the (mis)characterization of state care as 'welfare dependence' and the (mis)construal of 'welfare dependence' as the absence of autonomy and personal responsibility, weakness, low social status and bad citizenship. I make this point more fully in "'Welfare Dependence': The Power of a Concept" (Smiley 2001).

Not surprisingly, the association in question is lent further credence by the sense that state care is for 'the vulnerable' and 'the vulnerable' are not only weak but failing in autonomy. Catriona MacKenzie brings this way of thinking about vulnerability into question (MacKenzie 2014, 33–59).

[10] Michael Walzer presents such a view of the welfare state in *Spheres of Justice* (Walzer 1983).

[11] The struggle to get care acknowledged as an important part, not only of the state in practice but of the very idea of the state itself, is in a sense the hallmark of much recent work on the ethics of state care. Joan Tronto got things rolling in *Moral Boundaries: A Political Argument for an Ethic of Care* (Tronto 1993). Stensöta reinforces the importance of maintaining a focus on both care and relationships in public ethics in 'Public Ethics of Care' (Stensöta 2015).

[12] Linda Gordon's definition of the welfare state is frequently cited by those who want to expand our sense of the welfare state's reach. According to Gordon "'Welfare' could accurately refer to all of a government's contributions to its citizens' well-being. These include paved streets and sidewalks; highways; public transportation systems; schools; parks; tree maintenance; policing; firefighting; public water; sewerage and sewerage treatment; garbage collection; food and drug regulation; pollution regulation; building inspection; and driving testing and licensing" (Gordon 1994, 2).

At the very least, by hammering home that most members of contemporary liberal democracies, including many of those who now profess to oppose the 'welfare state', already accept the possibility of non-paternalistic state care and even value such care in cases where, say, it is designed to help the middle class, we can provide ourselves with an image of state care that is neither paternalistic nor a violation of individual rights. Moreover, we can do so without leaving existing practice behind completely. (In other words, we can do so in a way that avoids utopianism.) But, of course, re-imagining the welfare state—which is an important first step in democratizing state care—has to be coupled with more purely institutional measures if we have any hope of meeting the three conditions of non-paternalistic, democratic, state care cited earlier.

Two such measures come to mind here. Both are advocated by social democrats in their efforts to develop a democratic welfare state. The first requires us to replace existing two-tier welfare systems, which distinguish poor people's aid (associated with bad citizenship) from middle class programs (associated with good citizenship) with a universal system of state care of the sort assumed, although not always carried out, by the states of Western and Northern Europe. The second requires organizing these particular welfare policies together into an all-encompassing system of care designed to enhance the lives of all citizens rather than just 'the incompetent'.

Both measures are clearly important. But they are not, as many social democrats now assume, the end of the story. For, as feminists throughout Scandinavia and Germany have been keen to point out over the years, universal state care can easily be paternalistic, either by treating all citizens as children/wives in need of paternal authority (the concern in Sweden) or by differentiating on a gender basis between different kinds of state care, for example, worker's compensation and aid to stay-at-home mothers (the concern in Germany). Moreover, as Norwegian feminists such as Helga Hernes have made clear, universalism can easily become part of a state that is itself construed in familial terms (Hernes 1984, 26–45). How are we to prevent these things from happening?

In the end, three things beyond the universalization of state care will become necessary if we are to prevent the re-emergence of paternalistic hierarchies at the level of governance, sustain the association of state care with citizenship rather than with weakness and keep paternal authority out of state politics. First of all, the universalism of recipience will have to be coupled with the universalism of participation in the formulation and legitimation of particular welfare policies. Second, policies will have to be scrutinized to ensure that, while taking different needs into consideration, they do not inadvertently create subordinate groups within a universal system of state care, for example mothers and members of immigrant populations in need of 'special protections'. Third, universalism will have to be accompanied by vigilant efforts to guarantee that paternal authority in the family, religion or elsewhere is not transferred to the state.[13]

All of these measures will require a great deal of knowledge on our part about how particular communities are organized. In this chapter, I have concentrated on making three more preliminary—and largely conceptual—points. The first is that if we want to develop democratic modes of care at the state level, we will have to challenge paternalism in both theory and practice. The second is that we cannot do so without replacing the liberal/libertarian concept of paternalism that now prevails among philosophers, legal scholars and political theorists with one that views paternalism as a hierarchical system of care and governance. The third is that by viewing paternalism in this way, we are able both to grasp the interdependence of democracy and non-paternalism and to hone the conditions of a non-paternalistic, democratic, welfare state.

References

Anderson, Elizabeth. 1999. What Is the Point of Equality? *Ethics* 109: 287–337.

Ben-Porath, Sigal. 2010. *Tough Choices, Structured Paternalism, and the Landscape of Choice*. Princeton, NJ: Princeton University Press.

Bullock, Emma. 2018. A Normatively Neutral Definition of Paternalism. In *Routledge Handbook of the Philosophy of Paternalism*, ed. Kalle Grill and Jason Hanna. Abingdon: Routledge Press.

Carter, Rosemary. 1977. Justifying Paternalism. *Canadian Journal of Philosophy* 7: 133–145.

Clarke, Simon. 2002. A Definition of Paternalism. *Critical Review of International Social and Political Philosophy* 5 (1): 81–91.

———. 2009. Principle of Paternalism. *Journal of Applied Ethics and Philosophy* 1: 25–46.

[13] I do not mean to suggest here that we should tolerate paternal authority in all aspects of the family or in any part of religion. Indeed, there are good arguments for being vigilant on these fronts. But bringing the state into these matters is controversial. Hence, we might want to concentrate on making sure that, at the very least, paternal authority in these other spheres of life does not translate into special powers, rights or privileges at the state level.

Conly, Sarah. 2013. *Against Autonomy: Justifying Coercive Paternalism*. New York: Cambridge University Press.

Coons, Christian, and Michael Weber, eds. 2013. *Paternalism: Theory and Practice*. Cambridge: Cambridge University Press.

Dworkin, Gerald. 1971. Paternalism. In *Morality and the Law*, ed. Richard Wasserstrom. Belmont: Wadsworth Publishing Co.

———. 1983. Paternalism: Second Thoughts. In *Paternalism*, ed. Rolf Sartorius. Minneapolis: University of Minnesota Press.

Feinberg, Joel. 1971. Legal Paternalism. *Canadian Journal of Philosophy* 1 (1): 105–124.

Goodin, Robert. 2002. Permissible Paternalism: Saving Smokers from Themselves. In *Ethics in Practice*, ed. Hugh LaFollette, 301–312. Oxford: Blackwell.

Gordon, Linda. 1994. *Pitied But Not Entitled. Single Mothers and the History of Welfare*. New York: Free Press.

Grill, Kalle. 2018. The Normative Core of Paternalism. In *Routledge Handbook of the Philosophy of Paternalism*, ed. Kalle Grill and Jason Hanna. London: Routledge.

Haybron, Daniel, and Anna Alexandrova. 2013. Paternalism in Economics. In *Paternalism: Theory and Practice*, ed. Christian Coons and Michael Weber, 157–177. Cambridge: Cambridge University Press.

Hernes, Helga. 1984. Women and the Welfare State: The Transition from Private to Public Dependency. In *Patriarchy in a Welfare Society*, ed. Harriet Holter, 26–45. Oslo: Universitetsforlaget.

Hodson, John. 1977. The Principle of Paternalism. *American Philosophical Quarterly* 14 (1): 61–69.

Kleinig, John. 1984. *Paternalism*. Totowa: Rowman & Allanheld.

MacKenzie, Catriona. 2014. The Importance of Relational Autonomy and Capabilities for an Ethics of Vulnerability. In *Vulnerability. New Essays in Ethics and Feminist Philosophy*, ed. Catriona MacKenzie, Wendy Rogers, and Susan Dodds, 33–59. New York: Oxford University Press.

Murphy, Jeffrie. 1964. Incompetence and Paternalism. *Archiv für Rechts-und Sozialphilosophie* 60: 465–486.

Quigley, Muireann. 2018. Libertarian Paternalism, Nudging, and Public Policy. In *Routledge Handbook of the Philosophy of Paternalism*, ed. Kalle Grill and Jason Hanna. London: Routledge.

Raibley, Jason. 2013. *Paternalism: Theory and Practice*. Eds. Christian Coons and Michael Weber. Cambridge: Cambridge University Press.

Sartorius, Rolf. 1983. Introduction. In *Paternalism*, ed. R. Sartorius, xi–xii. Minneapolis: University of Minnesota Press.

Scoccia, Danny. 2008. In Defense of Hard Paternalism. *Law and Philosophy* 27: 351–381.

———. 2018. The Concept of Paternalism. *Routledge Handbook in the Philosophy of Paternalism*. Eds. Kalle Grill and Jason Hanna, 11–23. New York: Routledge Press.

Sevenhuijsen, Selma. 1998. *Citizenship and the Ethics of Care*. London: Routledge.

Shapiro, Ian. 2001. *Democratic Justice*. New Haven: Yale University Press.

———. 2003. *The State of Democratic Theory*. Princeton University Press.

———. 2011. *The Real World of Democratic Theory*. Princeton University Press/ebook.

Shiffrin, V. Seana. 2000. Paternalism, Unconscionability Doctrine, and Accommodation. *Philosophy and Public Affairs* 29 (3): 205–250.

Smiley, Marion. 2001. 'Welfare Dependence': The Power of a Concept. *Thesis Eleven* 64: 21–38.

Soss, Joe, Richard Fording, and Sanford Schram. 2011. *Disciplining the Poor: Neoliberalism and the Persistent Power of Race*. Chicago: University of Chicago Press.

Stensöta, O. Helena. 2015. Public Ethics of Care - A General Public Ethics. *Ethics and Social Welfare* 9 (2): 183–200.

Strasser, Mark. 1988. The New Paternalism. *Bioethics* 2 (2): 103–117.

Sunstein, Cass, and Richard Thaler. 2008. *Improving Decisions about Health, Wealth, and Happiness*. New Haven: Yale University Press.

Tronto, C. Joan. 1993. *Moral Boundaries: A Political Argument for an Ethics of Care*. London: Routledge.

———. 2013. *Caring Democracy: Markets, Equality, and Justice*. New York: New York University Press.

VanDeVeer, Donald. 1986. *Paternalistic Intervention*. Princeton: Princeton University Press.

Walzer, Michael. 1983. *Spheres of Justice, A Defense of Pluralism and Equality*. New York: Basic Books.

White, Julie. 2010. *Democracy, Justice, and the Welfare State: Reconstructing Public Care*. University Park: Penn State Press.

Young, John. 1982. Autonomy and Paternalism. *Canadian Journal of Philosophy, Supplementary Volume* 8: 47–66.

Young, Iris Marion. 1990. *Justice and the Politics of Difference*. Princeton: Princeton University Press.

CHAPTER 6

The Nurturing Language of Care Ethics and of Other Related Feminist Approaches: Opposing Contemporary Neoliberal Politics

Brunella Casalini

Introduction

In the social sciences and political and moral philosophy, some approaches are available which seem to share a language aimed at recasting sociality and strengthening democracy and the social fabric, against the rise of neoliberalism, populism, and their strange alliance—the 'new nightmare' to paraphrase Wendy Brown (2006)—which, in some ways, continues the former alliance between neoliberalism and neoconservatism. The reason for stressing the role of language lays in the importance of framing in politics (Lakoff 2014): changing the frame can contribute significantly to changing the world we live in. The words we use make it possible to tell new stories, stories that can challenge the way we see and care for others, and what and who really matters, what we mind and care to know (Butler 2006; Molinier 2018; Featherstone 2017). The feminist approaches I

B. Casalini (✉)
Department of Political and Social Science, University of Florence, Florence, Italy
e-mail: brunella.casalini@unifi.it

P. Urban, L. Ward (eds.), *Care Ethics, Democratic Citizenship and the State*, International Political Theory,
https://doi.org/10.1007/978-3-030-41437-5_6

analyze in this chapter[1] and the language they use are all aimed at reframing our view of politics.

Their language offers a nurturing view of politics in opposition to the 'autonomy myth' (Fineman 2004) and the current trend to be not only indifferent to the environment and the dismantling of the commons but also to show outright contempt toward disabled people, poor people, migrants, and asylum seekers. This dangerous, almost universal, tendency is now fueled by a combination of right-wing populism and neoliberal incitement to precarity and extreme individualist self-reliance. Against the neoliberal and neopopulist devaluation of social projectuality and collective responsibility, the vocabularies used by the feminist approaches considered here stress the role of bodily interdependence, cooperation, and relationality.

Care ethics is a primary example of the attempt to conceptualize a responsive connectedness among people in their concrete social relations. The word 'care' is being increasingly used on a wide scale and became even more popular after the publication of the most recent book by Naomi Klein, *No Is Not Enough: Defeating the New Shock Politics* (2017), where 'care' is described as 'the revolution,' namely, the 'yes' we have to say if we want to build a genuine political alternative to the populist right. Its success can even be measured by the attempt to make an instrumental use of the language of care by the market, from the marketing of green products to the marketing of cosmetic products for self-care (Puig de la Bellacasa 2017).

In the literature on care ethics, there is still no unanimous agreement on what 'care' means and how the term is conceptually formed. For example, there is a clear semantic shift in its meaning as we move from moral philosophy to a public care ethics, political economy, or epistemology. We easily proceed from care as motivation to care as labor or work to care as a concern. As Maurice Hamington has underlined, notwithstanding this "lack of articulated precision, the growth in care ethics scholarship persists, in part, because care thinking fills a moral, epistemological and political lacuna that cannot be met by today's dominant social-theoretical framework: liberalism" (Hamington 2018, 309). Care ethics has been very influential in the last few years, and it has been expanded in very

[1] The works of Beasley and Bacchi have inspired me in confronting these different vocabularies. Nevertheless, my comparison goes beyond their intent and extends the contrast to other theoretical languages, defending the value of care ethics.

creative ways (e.g., Barnes et al. 2015; Engster and Hamington 2015; Dalmiya 2016; Bourgault and Perrault 2015; Bourgault and Pulcini 2018; Molinier 2018). Given the widispread use of this concept with many different meanings, it might be interesting to analyze how it is used in care ethics, comparing the different lexical choices that have been proposed by other feminit approaches I analyze here as alternatives—sometimes with the clear intention of going beyond the limits of the language of care.

The notion of care ethics lacks a clear definition. However, this might be the very reason why this notion is sufficiently flexible to be easily compared with other approaches. Therefore, I argue that care ethics is a promising language, which might contribute even more substantially to democratic discourse and the creation of care arrangements if it is compared with different ideas and vocabularies. Here, I focus on those represented by 'affective equality,' the 'ethics of social flesh,' and 'social reproduction,' which are closely related to the vocabulary of 'care' and not always clearly distinguishable from it.

It is my contention here that Joan Tronto's broad definition of care (Tronto 1993, 2013) has had a deep impact on contemporary literature because of its capacity to include almost all ideas and concerns that are also shared by these alternative approaches. Comparing care ethics with these other related vocabularies, we shall be able to better appreciate the strengths of Tronto's theory and contemporary care ethics, develop some relatively unexplored topics, and address some criticisms against care ethics.

Common Ground Between Care Ethics, Social Flesh, Affective Equality, and Social Reproduction

The theoretical approaches considered here share a common ground first in their assessment of individualism and the modern sovereign subject. Care ethics, affective equality, social flesh, and social reproduction all criticize the modern idea of the rational, atomistic, self-reliant, and independent individual. Their assessment of social reality is based on a relational as well as embodied view of the individual, which stresses the role of noncontractual and sometimes even unchosen relationships, being at the same time more open to change and to challenging traditional norms than the communitarian analysis of liberalism (e.g., Sandel 1982).

A second common trait is that they all explore our everyday, intimate lives, carefully considering the micro, meso, and macro levels of social interaction in their close interrelationships, and in the way they influence each other and social change.

Their third shared feature lies in a language of resistance and the capacity to offer an alternative social imaginary, a counter-discourse, to the hegemonic paradigm of the *homo oeconomicus* and its contemporary incarnation in neoliberalism. The languages of social flesh, care, affective equality, and social reproduction make it possible to express a powerful assessment of the increasing trend toward the commodification, corporatization, and managerialization of schools, universities, health care, and long-term care systems, as well as general social and public services (e.g., Bakker 2007; Lynch 2010; Tronto 2013; Beasley 2017a, b). They all see the dangers that neoliberalism, with its policies of austerity and dismantling of the welfare state, poses to individual, societal, and environmental life, creating conditions of systematic negligence and carelessness, which are dangerous for individual and social resilience, erode the bonds of communitarian relationships, and degrade the environment.

The analyses of individualization processes in late modernity (e.g., Giddens 1991; Beck 1992; Beck and Beck-Gernsheim 1995) presume that they are "experienced in a disembodied gender-neutral fashion" and are now based mostly on individual decisions. In contrast, a fourth important common aspect of these vocabularies is that they all presuppose a feminist perspective and adopt a gender-sensitive framework, without indulging in any kind of essentialism or any form of nostalgia for women's past traditional roles in the family and community (e.g., Beasley 2017a, 375). They all contain this image against a narrative of late modernity in an epoch of individualization, in which gender hierarchy has been overcome because, in modernity, individuals rule (e.g., McRobbie 2009).

If the feminist approaches I analyze here share common grounds, they also differ in important ways. Only in the social flesh approach, it is possible to find an explicit attempt to move away from care ethics and challenge its perspective, even if, as we shall see, the criticism is mostly based on a partial understanding of contemporary care ethics. In the three following sections, I present a brief summary of the main elements of the social flesh approach, the affective equality theory, and the social reproduction theory. In the last section, I then analyze care ethics, in particular Tronto's version of care ethics.

The Ethic of Social Flesh

Chris Beasley and Carol Bacchi coined their 'ethic of social flesh' after closely examining how the notion of 'body' has been addressed in the contemporary liberal literature on citizenship, in which the body has been mostly neglected and the citizen has been typically imagined as a rational, autonomous actor (see Bacchi and Beasley 2002, 2005a, b; Beasley and Bacchi 2005, 2007, 2012; Beasley 2017a, b). According to Beasley and Bacchi, in the few instances in which it has been considered—outside of the feminist literature on citizenship, and of the literature following Foucault's analysis of biopolitics and of few other cases—it has been addressed in terms of "something people 'had,' and 'owned' and 'controlled'" (Beasley and Bacchi 2012, 103). In the mainstream liberal literature on citizenship, real citizens are those "having control of their bodies" and "in command of their bodies (hypo-embodied)" (Beasley and Bacchi 2007, 291), that is, having normal cognitive and behavioral capacities and, thus, being able to cooperate with others. A more uncertain position within citizenship is occupied by those "deemed to be controlled by their bodies (hyper-embodied)" (Beasley and Bacchi 2007, 291). The former are conceived as autonomous, decision-making subjects in line with the idea of modern sovereign subjectivity. In a neoliberal political context, their bodies are at best a piece of capital in which to invest through a variety of possible interventions, from aesthetic surgery to diets. Instead, those who are considered as controlled by their bodies are seen as needing special surveillance and/or protection. Their bodies are a heavy burden with which they are identified, a burden that limits their possibility to be who they want, in turn affecting their autonomy and decision-making capability.

From this point of view, care ethics offers a more positive theoretical stance based on the work of Beasley and Bacchi, who pay special attention to the body. According to these two Australian feminist authors, care ethics is a promising perspective when it moves from moral philosophy to a public care ethics. With the second generation of care ethicists (in particular authors such as Selma Sevenhuijsen and Joan Tronto), care has come to be viewed as a crucial social practice for social institutions. It is no longer just the moral motivation and character that lie at the center of political philosophy's critique of liberal atomistic individualism but also the body with its need for care.

However, some important limits must be emphasized, according to Beasley and Bacchi. Care ethics sees the body only in terms of its corporeal needs: "The body tends to enter the room only in relation to certain aspects of childhood, older age and ill-health" (Beasley 2017a, 379). Care ethics implicitly legitimizes the attention paid to the embodied character of the subject exclusively in an asymmetrical caring relationship. This leads to a limited conception of embodied sociality, in which the very distinction between caregivers and care-receivers ends up reproducing the separation between active citizens and dependent others. Thus, the caregiver's obligation to care for dependent others ends up colliding with the neoliberal rhetoric of individual accountability.

Beasley and Bacchi's metaphor of social flesh is thought to overcome the limits of care ethics, establishing a vocabulary capable of prefiguring a social imaginary alternative to neoliberalism in so far as "fleshly sociality is profoundly levelling" (Beasley and Bacchi 2007, 292). Furthermore, "A political ethic of embodied intersubjectivity requires us to consider fleshly interconnection as the basis of a democratic sociality, demanding a rather more far-reaching reassessment of national and international institutional arrangements than political vocabularies that rest upon extending altruism," such as they think is care ethics (ibid.).

For the social flesh approach, it is important to abandon every form of distinction between those who are in control of their bodies and can be generous and provide care to those who are not as lucky. Everyone is a giver as well as a receiver of "socially generated goods and services," and lives in social spaces that are practicable and accessible thanks to social infrastructures (Beasley and Bacchi 2007, 280, 293). In other words, our moral obligations toward others do not come from dependency but from interdependency. In this sense, according to Beasley and Bacchi, the vocabulary of social flesh has greater, radical democratic potential than care ethics, which has a "limited conception of embodied sociality" and whose altruism is tinged with patronizing moralism. As Beasley explains:

> [...] the moralist asymmetry at the heart of care as altruism not only functions to disable those who receive care as the 'needy,' but also constitutes their need in relation to only certain kinds of embodiments that are apparently deemed appropriate to provoke altruism. (Beasley 2017b)

Many scholars of disability studies have underlined, especially in the 1990s (e.g., Finkelstein 1991; Morris 1997; Shakespeare 2000), that if bodily nurturance and maintenance receive proper attention and consideration in care ethics, then it risks in some cases reproducing an idea of disabled people as vulnerable, passive, and suffering subjects that can never have true access to independent living, whose bodies can never be imagined as desiring and pleasingly sexual. In this sense, care ethics ends up depicting "care as a sexless moral respectability; care is not good for the bedroom" (Beasley 2017b), in the sense that care ethics does not seem to be useful in a sexual relationship, where desire rather than need is at the center of the relationship.

Beasley and Bacchi's theory of social flesh wants to give an active role to the body and considers the role of pleasure and play—not only that of suffering. Bodies can be seen as passive recipients of altruistic care or social responsibility, but can also play a more active role as desiring and challenging bodies, even when naked and vulnerable, such as in Spencer Tunich's flesh photography mentioned by Beasley and Bacchi (2012). Tronto's broad definition of care—which I address later—can provide a response to most of Beasley and Bacchi's criticisms of care ethics. However, in so far as it excludes the ludic dimension of care (which includes not only play but also the desiring and sexual body in general), it is still open to their criticism.

Affective Equality

The intention of going beyond the asymmetrical relationship between caregiver and care-receiver that in the literature is often attributed to care ethics also characterizes the concept of 'affective equality' theorized by Kathleen Lynch, John Baker, and Maureen Lyons in a book by the same title, published in 2009 (Lynch et al. 2009b) and developed especially by Lynch in her other works. Affective equality includes—and distinguishes between—love work, care work, and solidarity work. At the same time, affective equality considers its role in society, which ought to reflect social justice. The idea is that affective equality should, in a theory of justice, play a different but equally important role as resources, recognition, and representation—the three main components of social justice indicated by Nancy Fraser in her more recent works (see Cantillon and Lynch 2017, 2). In contrast to some versions of care ethics, the issue of affectivity is posed here in terms of justice: the unequal distribution of the conditions for receiving love, care, and solidarity is a problem of justice, strictly interconnected with other forms of injustice (in particular with economic, cultural, and political injustice).

Life would be void and meaningless without affective bonds and attachments. We usually consider the roles of economic, social, and cultural capital in an individual's life, but, according to Lynch, there is another type of capital we should focus on, the "nurturing capital." "The amount of nurturing capital available impacts on people's ability not only to relate to others at an intimate level, but also to flourish and contribute in other spheres of life" (Lynch 2007, 554). The basic idea of "affective equality" is the importance of affective bonds in every society and each individual's life, in the workplace, in all organizations, in educational and social relationships in general, and inside as well as outside the domestic sphere. This significance has been downplayed by the fact that "love and care have, for the most part, been treated as private matters, personal affairs, not subjects of sufficient importance to be mainstreamed in egalitarian theory or empirical investigations, while the subject of solidarity is given limited research attention" (Lynch et al. 2009a, 12).

The discourse on affective equality prompted by Lynch and others has acquired increasing urgency given a series of contemporary trends analyzed in social and political theories. For example, the commodification of the so-called emotional labor (Hochschild Russell 2003, 2013) that has characterized the world of labor has radically changed with the shift from Fordism to post-Fordism to cognitive capitalism. Another example is the managerialization of many public services, from social services to educational institutions, and from childcare to academia. Other examples could be made as well, such as the discourse on the so-called affective economies that accompanies social and political decisions—particularly with the advent of right-wing populism—or the commodification and embarkations of care work, which according to some authors is already going in the direction of corporatization (Marchetti and Farris 2017).

When affective equality is included in the analysis of the way in which schools (from kindergarten to universities), the workplace, or social services take care of their users, it offers a valid instrument for criticizing the degenerative effects produced by the welfare state's contemporary neoliberal reforms (also in terms of increased social inequality). This is a problem recognized in the second generation of care ethics literature, not only with regard to health and long-term care services but also educational institutions, as Tronto (2013) shows.

For example, the new public management (NPM) perspective has dramatically altered the way in which research is performed in academia; not only professional and private lives need to be conciliated but also the different tasks required by the job. Some academic activities (such as research, publication, fundraising, and public engagements) provide access to a greater academic capital, career chances, and recognition than other tasks (such as teaching, tutoring students, or administrative work), and in today's universities there is a lack of time that affects everyone. At the same time, there is a gendered distribution of labor, in which organizational housework is mostly carried out by women researchers, reproducing the traditional division of labor between females and males even in academia. The necessity to keep pace with the quantity of research work required by current assessment criteria, well summarized by the slogan 'publish or perish,' affects the level of attention and care that academic professionals dedicate to their students or to broaching new areas of investigation, as claimed by the slow-academia movement (see Mountz et al. 2015; Berg and Seeber 2016).

Likewise, precarity and quantification also affect the tasks of other care professionals, such as social workers. How can precarious social workers maintain the expectations of their caring roles when they do not know how long their contracts are going to last, and what and where their new jobs will be? It is not surprising that one consequence of this new context is an increased stress and burnout among social workers, and the tendency to develop indifference as a way of coping with a situation in which there is very little that can be actively controlled by the social worker.

In a recent article, Cantillon and Lynch wrote: "To create socially just and gender-just societies, public policies need to be directed by norms of love, care, and solidarity rather than norms of capital accumulation" (Cantillon and Lynch 2017, 3). This statement raises an issue that is implicit in much contemporary work in care ethics, namely the criticism of neoliberal capitalism and the relationship between capitalism and care. Clearly, there is a tension between neoliberal capitalist reform and human caring and affective needs.

The Social Reproduction Theory

The relationship between care and capitalism is the core of the social reproduction theory, which somehow results from an updated reappraisal of the old debate on domestic work inaugurated in the 1980s by Marxist and materialist feminists. Both the old domestic labor discourse and the new social reproduction approach see the cost of the reproduction of the species, of workers and communities, as mostly hidden, invisible, or underpaid and unrecognized work. Beyond the productive sphere, labor falls on women's shoulders, and even among women it is unequally distributed: poorer and racialized women pay the highest price in social reproduction,[2] doing most of the tasks necessary to meet fundamental human needs on a daily and generational basis (see Okano and Maruyama this volume). Nevertheless, according to the social reproduction perspective, we cannot limit our analysis of the complex set of activities necessary to reproduce labor power to the domestic space and unpaid domestic labor. We must tackle at least three major, broader problems that have found varied solutions in different societies and times: (1) the reproduction of the species, which concerns the factors that influence the decision whether to have children or not, as well as the social construction of gender and motherhood; (2) the reproduction of the labor force (the subsistence, socialization, and training of workers); and (3) the reproduction of social and communitarian boundaries and the provision of care (Bakker and Gill 2003; Bakker and Silvey 2008; Bakker 2007). In Brenner and Laslett's definition, social reproduction indicates:

> the activities and attitudes, behaviors and emotions, and responsibilities and relationships directly involved in maintaining life, on a daily basis and intergenerationally. It involves various kinds of socially necessary work—mental, physical, and emotional—aimed at providing the historically and socially, as well as biologically, defined means for maintaining and reproducing population. Among other things, social reproduction includes how food, clothing, and shelter are made available for immediate consumption, how the maintenance and socialization of children is accomplished, how care of the elderly and infirm is provided, and how sexuality is socially constructed. (Brenner and Laslett 1991, 314)

The three problems mentioned earlier show how "social reproduction entails much more than literal procreation" (Ginsburg and Rapp 1995, 2) or care work for dependent others. The naturalization of gender, sexuality, and reproduction has tended to veil the fact that these areas of life are not reducible to the effect and production of natural drives. Rather, they are

[2] On social reproduction, see Bezanson and Luxton 2006; Ferguson 2008; Ferguson and McNally 2013, 2015; Ferguson et al. 2016; Casalini 2017; Bhattacharya 2017).

influenced by non-deterministic factors, as well as facilitated or inhibited by social norms, including laws (such as family law, health and school legislation, and reproduction techniques and legislation). The solutions applied to the above-mentioned problems of social reproduction have, in fact, undergone profound transformations with the advent of capitalism and its different phases to facilitate the "processes of capital dispossession and accumulation" (McNally and Ferguson 2015). Social reproduction in particular has been organized in various ways according to how its burden and responsibility have been shouldered within the state, over time, and through welfare, the market, the community, or households (Gill and Bakker 2003; Bakker 2007).

Social reproduction theory, like the second generation of care ethics, has many points of convergence with intersectionality feminism, a heuristic tool widely used in contemporary feminist scholarship, which has been fundamental in overcoming a simple reductive economic view of social reality. The fundamental difference between social reproduction and intersectionality concerns how they conceptualize the relationship between different axes of oppression. Intersectionality theory can take two different directions. According to the first, different axes of power may be considered as the expression of distinct, pre-existing ontological social dimensions. For example:

> Patriarchy and colonialism may intersect, and even affect each other at their points of intersection, but they are conceived as ontologically distinct systems. They combine to create a wider reality, but they are not themselves constitutive of and constituted by that reality. The social whole thus retreats from view significant only as a vessel or neutral field containing the sum of its distinct, intersecting parts. (Ferguson 2016, 42)

The second theoretical direction, instead, "gestures towards an integrative logic," but, according to Ferguson, never clearly identifies "the actual unifying social forces involved" (Ferguson 2016, 45). Social reproduction aspires to offer an "integrative logic" that is missing:

> those formulations of social reproduction feminism[,] which view the social through the lens of the daily and generational labor undertaken to (re)produce it[,] provide a promising way to theorise the integral unity of the diverse, differentiated social relations that intersectionality feminism foregrounds. (Ferguson 2016, 48)

Care ethics seems closer to the first version of intersectionality, as revealed, for instance, considering the criticism of some cultural forms of masculinity (e.g., Tronto 2013, 2017). This assessment does not insist on the possible existence of a unifying logic underlying the maintenance of a certain idea of gender relationships, such as that found in the evaluation of the so-called 'ideology of gender,' neither on the present alliance between the state and neoliberal capitalism, an alliance in which the state does not simply leave the market to its own devices, in the old laissez faire spirit, but rather helps and sustains its development—even in the care sector. This is particularly evident in Europe, as an effect of the cash-for-care policies adopted by most contemporary European welfare states.

Opening a Conversation

The broad concept of care proposed by Tronto in *Moral Boundaries*, and even more openly in *Caring Democracy*, is immune to many of the criticisms moved against it by the social flesh approach. Care ethics is well aware of the importance of care, not only outside of the family but also outside of the relationship between the caregiver and care-receiver. It not only encompasses (as affective equality also suggests) nurses, paid caregivers, and relatives but also teachers and professors, and many maintenance professionals, including farmers (see Mol et al. 2010). It includes love work, care work, and solidarity work and even more. In Tronto and Fisher's definition, it goes beyond personal relationships; it regards the care of the self as well as the care of the environment (intended as maintenance and reparation) and our world. According to this perspective, care is directed not only at reducing suffering but also at giving us the possibility "to live as well as possible" (Tronto 1993, 2013, but see also Held 2006).

Overall, if we consider the criticisms moved by the social flesh approach toward care ethics, they seem to address some of the uses of care ethics in the literature on care work rather than the complexity of care ethics in itself. Here, the body has always been included in a very substantial way (see, e.g., Hamington 2004) and it has always been very clear that the rhetoric of individual accountability and privatization of care had to be contrasted and opposed, stressing the vulnerability, and the risk of precarity, not only of the care-receiver but also of the caregiver. Beasley and Bacchi seem to deal with earlier care ethics works, but cannot apply to all care ethics perspectives, also when they describe what they call care ethics' paternalistic altruism. In fact, altruism has long been considered something from which 'care' has to distance itself, and care ethicists typically agree that it is impossible to have a good caring relationship without a sound care of the self (e.g., Gilligan 1982). Because of the limits of altruism, many versions of care ethics recognize the role of collective responsibility and the necessity of the welfare state (see Kittay 1999; Tronto 1993, 2013; Engster 2015). Marian Barnes (2012, 7) admits that "'care' has been and remains associated with practices that are anything but 'caring,'" as argued by Beasley and Bacchi. However, it is also true that care ethics literature has identified as one of its critical aims that of distinguishing between bad and good care, avoiding any temptation of idealizing and romanticizing over care relationships, and taking into consideration how caring labor still remains often associated with oppressive practices (Barnes 2012, 7).

There are, though, two aspects of the social flesh approach that need careful attention in a care ethics perspective. First, the idea that we should include 'play' as part of care practice and activities (on this see Urban and Koubová 2019) and, second, the proposal to consider our sex lives too as part of care activities. In both cases the suggestion seems to be that care should not only be about needs but also desires.

Starting from the second issue, there are some good reasons to include sex within the purview of care, for "queering the imaginary of care" (Roseneil 2004) at least more clearly than it has been done until now. As emphasized by the concept of 'sex-affective production,' used by Ann Ferguson and Nancy Folbre (1981), care is involved not only "in caring for the dependent but also includes the providing of affection and the nurturing of relationships" (Held 2006, 35). Sex work itself might be considered as care work, as stated by Maria Laura Augustin (2012), and sexuality is a topic worth exploring in care work professions as some recent works have emphasized (e.g., Dunk-West and Hafford-Letchfield 2018; Raithby and Willis 2017, 148–161).

As for the first issue concerning play, it is clear that if care has to do with maintenance and reparation of oneself and the relationships in which one is involved, play can be a fundamental part of it, and it certainly shares with the idea of care a criticism to our excessive contemporary stress on productivity, economics, and utility. The image of the *homo ludens* may be opposed to that of the *homo curans* because many people tend to associate the *homines curantes* with the idea of an attention that needs sacrifice. However, if we want to understand care in all its forms and manifestations, it is plausible to say that the *homo ludens* shares many features with the *homo curans*, and its real opposite are the *homo faber* and the *homo oeconomicus* (Caruso 2012).

A public care ethics needs an analysis of the present based on a critical feminist political economy, like the one proposed by the social reproduction theory (see Hamrouni 2015). Joan Tronto in *Caring Democracy*, and other care ethicists, such as Barnes (see, e.g., 2012; Barnes et al. 2015), have longer emphasized the negative role of neoliberal capitalism. Like the social reproduction theory, they have come to emphasize the characteristics of the present phase of capitalist accumulation and the effects it generates in terms of the precarization of life conditions. In other words, care ethics seems now much more focused on the destabilizing consequences produced for social reproduction by the penetration of market forces and capital in basic social and human institutions. There seems to be a close link between contemporary neoliberal precarization (which in most cases means exploitation) and oppression; this connection is becoming increasingly clear due to the shift of many care activities from the unremunerated private and domestic spheres to the care market, a change that contributes to making even more visible the fact that care is collocated between production and reproduction. Care relationships need certain conditions, not only in terms of subjective motivation, attention, and competence but also in terms of material conditions; not only regarding economic and social infrastructural resources but also pertaining to time (e.g., Baraister 2017) (see White this volume) (stability, length, the possibility of establishing relationships based on reciprocal trust, and nurturing the legitimate expectations and planning that social interventions require). Therefore, care ethics cannot avoid a serious assessment of the constraints which *homines curantes* must confront within modern social and economic structures. In comparison to social reproduction, care ethics has nevertheless the advantage of considering the dual nature of care: care as work or labor but also care as disposition (see Tronto 2018, 22). It has also a clearer commitment toward a reform of the welfare state, while social reproduction literature sometimes seems more focused on the possibility of re-inventing the common and spontaneous ways of living outside the state, in order to find an alternative option not only to the market but also to the state. Furthermore, Tronto's care ethics seems more attentive to and conscious of the fact that changing the ideological framework, narrating a different story with a different vocabulary, and, thus, disrupting common sense is crucial to enlarge our sense of collective responsibility toward social groups previously excluded, marginalized, and treated carelessly.

Conclusion

Contemporary neoliberal capitalism represents a huge challenge for those who care for society, the environment, and our everyday lives. In this context, I have shown here how care ethics and the other feminist approaches offer promising theoretical frameworks. They all express the need for an alternative description of life and give us a language in which to imagine a different society, in which economic growth and productivity are not seen as the only priorities, and public concern and citizens are prioritized, whose interests are not limited to work. They all give us the possibility to imagine different social futures, a real alternative opposing neoliberalism and right-wing populism. Among the vocabularies offered by the approaches I have examined here, nevertheless 'care' seems to be the more successful. Many contemporary contributions in care ethics, starting from Joan Tronto's contribution, aim at giving an account of all the complex aspects involved in the notion of care, not confining it only to a problem concerning a dyadic relationship, such as raising children and caring for the elderly, nor limiting it to its moral or economic dimension, but enlarging its relevance and making it a central issue in a political theory of democracy that gives attention to "the qualities necessary for democratic citizens to live together well in a pluralistic society" (Tronto 1993, 161). To reach this aim, care ethics has shown the historically constructed nature, and thus the contingency, of the boundaries that have separated morality and politics, the private from the public sphere, relegating care to the margins of political discourse. The capacity of contemporary care ethics to question boundaries and discuss the justifications given by hegemonic discourses for the distribution of care and the meaning of care has allowed it to move from the responsibilities toward others in the domestic field, mostly women, to institutional responsibility at the local, national, and global level, opening new theoretical and political spaces of debate.

References

Augustin, Laura Marìa. 2012. *Sex at the Margins: Migration, Labour Markets and the Rescue Industry*. New York: Zed Books.

Bacchi, Carol, and Chris Beasley. 2002. Citizen Bodies: Is Embodied Citizenship a Contradiction in Terms? *Critical Social Policy* 22 (2): 324–352.

———. 2005a. Reproductive Technology and the Political Limits of Care. In *Ethics of the Body: Postconventional Challenges*, ed. Margrit Shildrick and Roxanne Mykitiuk, 175–194. Cambridge, MA: MIT Press.

———. 2005b. The Limits of Trust and Respect: Rethinking Dependency. *Social Alternatives* 24 (4): 55–61.

Bakker, Isabella. 2007. Social Reproduction and the Constitution of a Gendered Political Economy. *New Political Economy* 12 (4): 541–556.

Bakker, Isabella, and Stephan Gill, eds. 2003. *Power, Production and Social Reproduction. Human In/security in the Global Political Economy*. Basingstoke: Palgrave Macmillan.

Bakker, Isabella, and Rachel Silvey, eds. 2008. *Beyond States and Markets: The Challenges of Social Reproduction*. New York: Routledge.

Baraister, Lisa. 2017. *Enduring Time*. New York: Bloomsbury Academic.

Barnes, Marian. 2012. *Care in Everyday Life. An Ethic of Care in Practice*. Bristol: Policy Press.

Barnes, Marian, Tula Brannelly, Lizzie Ward, and Nicki Ward, eds. 2015. *Ethics of Care: Critical Advances in International Perspective*. Bristol: Polity Press.

Beasley, Chris. 2017a. Care Is Not Enough. Beyond Care and the Vocabularies of Altruism. In *Mending the World?: Possibilities and Obstacles for Religion, Church, and Theology*, ed. Niklas Blåder and Kristina Helgesson Kjellin. Eugen: Pickwick Publications.

———. 2017b. Beyond Care and Vocabularies of Altruism. Considering Sexuality and Older People. In *ReValuing Care in Theory, Law and Policy. Cycles and Connections*, ed. Rosied Harding, Ruth Fletcher, and Chris Beasley. London: Routledge.

Beasley, Chris, and Carol Bacchi. 2005. The Political Limits of 'Care' in Re-imagining Interconnection/Community and an Ethical Future. *Australian Feminist Studies* 20 (46): 49–64.

———. 2007. Envisaging a New Politics for an Ethical Future Beyond Trust, Care and Generosity – Towards an Ethic of 'Social Flesh'. *Feminist Theory* 8 (3): 279–298.

———. 2012. Making Politics Fleshy: The Ethics of Social Flesh. In *Engaging with Carol Bacchi. Strategic Interventions and Exchanges*, ed. Angelique Bletsas and Chris Beasley. North Terrace: The University of Adelaide.

Beck, Ulrich. 1992. *Risk Society: Towards a New Modernity*. London: Sage.

Beck, Ulrich, and Elisabeth Beck-Gernsheim. 1995. *The Normal Chaos of Love*. Bristol: Polity Press.

Puig de la Bellacasa, Maria. 2017. *Matters of Care: Speculative Ethics in More than Human Worlds*. Minneapolis: University of Minnesota Press.

Berg, Maggie, and Barbara K. Seeber. 2016. *The Slow Professor: Challenging the Culture of Speed in the Academy*. Toronto: University of Toronto Press.

Bezanson, Kate, and Meg Luxton, eds. 2006. *Social Reproduction. Feminist Political Economy Challenges Neo-Liberalism*. Toronto: McGill University Press.

Bhattacharya, Tithi, ed. 2017. *Social Reproduction. Remapping Class, Recentering Oppression*. London: Pluto Press.

Bourgault, Sophie, and Julie Perrault, eds. 2015. *Le care. Ethique féministe actuelle*. Montréal: Les éditions du remue-ménage.

Bourgault, Sophie, and Elena Pulcini, eds. 2018. *Emotions and Care. Interdisciplinary Perspectives*. Leuven: Peeters.

Brenner, Johanna, and Barbara Laslett. 1991. Gender, Social Reproduction and Women's Political Self-Organization: Considering the U.S. Welfare State. *Gender and Society* 5 (3): 311–333.

Brown, Wendy. 2006. American Nightmare: Neoliberalism, Neoconservatism, and De-Democratization. *Political Theory* 34 (6): 690–714.

Butler, Judith. 2006. *Precarious Life: The Powers of Mourning and Violence*. London: Verso.

Cantillon, Sara, and Kathleen Lynch. 2017. Affective Equality: Love Matters. *Hypathia* 32 (1): 169–186.

Caruso, Sergio. 2012. *Homo Oeconomicus. Paradigma, Critiche, Revisioni*. Florence: Firenze University Press.

Casalini, Brunella. 2017. A Materialist Analysis of Contemporary Feminist Movements. *Anthropological Theory* 17: 497–517.

Dalmiya, Vrinda. 2016. *Caring to Know. Comparative Care Ethics, Feminist Epistemology, and the Mahabhārāta*. Oxford: Oxford University Press.

Dunk-West, Priscilla, and Trish Hafford-Letchfield. 2018. *Sexuality, Sexual and Gender Identities and Intimacy Research in Social Work and Social Care: A Lifecourse Epistemology*. London: Routledge.

Engster, Daniel. 2015. *Justice, Care, and the Welfare State*. Oxford: Oxford University Press.

Engster, Daniel, and Maurice Hamington, eds. 2015. *Care Ethics and Political Theory*. Oxford: Oxford University Press.

Featherstone, Brid. 2017. Foreword. In *Critical Ethics of Care in Social Work. Transforming the Politics and Practices of Caring*, ed. Bob Pease, Anthea Vreugdenhil, and Sonya Stanford, xv–xvii. London: Routledge.

Ferguson, Susan. 2008. Canadian Contributions to Social Reproduction, Race and Embodied Labor. *Race, Gender & Class* 15 (1–2): 42–57.

———. 2016. Intersectionality and Social-Reproduction Feminisms. *Historical Materialism* 24 (2): 38–60.

Ferguson, Ann, and Nancy Folbre. 1981. The Unhappy Marriage of Patriarchy and Capitalism. In *Women and Revolution: A Discussion of the Unhappy Marriage of Marxism and Feminism*, ed. Lydia Sargent. Boston: South End Press.

Ferguson, Susan, and David McNally. 2013. Capital, Labour-Power, and Gender-Relations: Introduction to the Historical Materialism Edition of Marxism and the Oppression of Women. In *Lisa Vogel, Marxism and the Oppression of Women: Toward a Unitary Theory*. Chicago: Haymarket Books.

———. 2015. Social Reproduction Beyond Intersectionality: An Interview. *Viewpoint*, October 31. https://www.viewpointmag.com/2015/10/31/social-reproduction-beyond-intersectionality-an-interview-with-sue-ferguson-and-david-mcnally/.

Ferguson, Susan, Genevieve Lebaron, Angela Dimitrakaki, and Sara Farris. 2016. Special Issue on Social Reproduction. *Historical Materialism* 24 (2): 25–37.

Fineman, Martha. 2004. *The Autonomy Myth: A Theory of Dependency*. New York: The New York Press.

Finkelstein, Vic. 1991. Disability: An Administrative Challenge? In *Social Work: Disabled People and Disabling Environments*, ed. M. Oliver. London: Jessica Kingsley.

Giddens, Anthony. 1991. *Modernity and Self-Identity. Self and Society in the Late Modern Age*. Stanford: Stanford University Press.

Gilligan, Carol. 1982. *In a Different Voice: Psychological Theory and Women's Development*. Cambridge: Harvard University Press.

Ginsburg, Faye D., and Rayna Rapp, eds. 1995. *Conceiving the New World Order: The Global Politics of Reproduction*. Berkeley: University of California Press.

Hamington, Maurice. 2004. *Embodied Care: Jane Addams, Maurice Merleau-Ponty, and Feminist Ethics*. Chicago: University of Illinois Press.

———. 2018. The Care Ethics Moment: International Innovations. *Journal of Care and Caring* 2 (3): 309–318.

Hamrouni, Naïma. 2015. Vers une théorie politique du care. In *Le care. Éthique féministe actuelle*, ed. Sophie Bourgault and Julie Perreault. Montréal: Les editions du Remue Ménage.

Held, Virginia. 2006. *The Ethics of Care: Personal, Political, Global*. New York: Oxford University Press.

Hochschild Russell, Arlie. 2003. *The Managed Heart: Commercialization of Human Feeling*. Berkeley: University of California Press.

———. 2013. *The Outsourced Self. What Happens When We Pay Others to Live Our Lives for Us*. New York: Picador.

Kittay, Eva Feder. 1999. *Love's Labor: Essays on Women, Equality and Dependency*. New York: Routledge.

Klein, Naomi. 2017. *No Is Not Enough: Defeating the New Shock Politics*. Toronto: Allen Lane.

Lakoff, George. 2014. *The All New Don't Think of an Elephant!: Know Your Values and Frame the Debate*. Chelsea Green: Chelsea Green Publishing.

Lynch, Kathleen. 2007. Love Labour as a Distinct and Non-Commodifiable form of Care Labour. *The Sociological Review* 55 (3): 550–570.

———. 2010. Carelessness: A Hidden Doxa of Higher Education. *Arts and Humanities in Higher Education* 9 (1): 54–67.

———. 2014. Why Love, Care and Solidarity are Political Matters: Affective Equality and Fraser Model of Social Justice. In *Love. A Question for Feminism*

in the Twenty-First Century, ed. Anna G. Jónasdóttir and Ann Ferguson, 173–192. New York and London: Routledge.
Lynch, Kathleen, John Baker, Sara Cantillon, and Judy Walsh. 2009a. Which Equality Matter? The Place of Affective Equality in Egalitarian Thinking. In *Affective Equality: Love, Care and Injustice*, ed. Kathleen Lynch, John Baker, and Maureen Lyons, 12–34. Basingstoke: Palgrave Macmillan.
Lynch, Kathleen, John Baker, and Maureen Lyons, eds. 2009b. *Affective Equality: Love, Care and Injustice*. Basingstoke: Palgrave Macmillan.
Marchetti, Sabrina, and Sara Farris. 2017. From the Commodification to the Corporatization of Care: European Perspectives and Debates. *Social Politics* 24 (2): 109–131.
McRobbie, Angela. 2009. *The Aftermath of Feminism: Gender, Culture and Social Change*. London: Sage.
Mol, Annemarie, Ingunn Moser, and Jeannette Pols, eds. 2010. *Care in Practice: On Tinkering in Clinics, Homes and Farms*. Bielefeld: Transcript Verlag.
Molinier, Pascale. 2018. *Le care monde: Trois essais de psychologie sociale*. Paris: ENS Éditions.
Morris, Jenny. 1997. Care of Empowerment? A Disability Rights Perspective. *Social Policy Administration. An International Journal of Policy and Research* 31 (1): 54–60.
Mountz, Alison, Anne Bonds, Becky Mansfield, Jenny Loyd, Jennifer Hyndman, Margaret Walton-Roberts, Ranu Basu, et al. 2015. For Slow Scholarship: A Feminist Politics of Resistance Through Collective Action in the Neoliberal University. *ACME: An International E-Journal for Critical Geographies* 14 (4): 1235–1259.
Raithby, Michele, and Paul P. Willis. 2017. 'No Sex, Please…'. Applying a Critical Ethics of Care Perspective to Social Care Provision for Older Lesbian, Gay and Bisexual Adult. In *Critical Ethics of Care in Social Work. Transforming the Politics and Practices of Caring*, ed. Bob Pease, Anthea Vreugdenhil, and Sonya Stanford. London: Routledge.
Robinson, Fiona. 2011. *The Ethics of Care: A Feminist Approach to Human Security*. Philadelphia: Temple University Press.
Roseneil, Sasha. 2004. Why We Should Care About Friends: An Argument for Queering the Care Imaginary. *Social Policy and Society* 3 (4): 409–419.
Sandel, Michael. 1982. *Liberalism and the Limits of Justice*. Cambridge: Cambridge University Press.
Sevenhuijsen, Selma. 1998. *Citizenship and the Ethics of Care. Feminist Considerations on Justice, Morality, and Politics*. London: Routledge.
Shakespeare, Tom. 2000. *Help*. Birmingham: British Association of Social Workers.
Tronto, C. Joan. 1993. *Moral Boundaries. A Political Argument for an Ethic of Care*. London; Routledge.

———. 2013. *Caring Democracy. Markets, Equality, and Justice*. New York: New York University Press.

Tronto, Joan C. 2017. There Is an Alternative: Homines Curans and the Limits of Neoliberalism. *International Journal of Care and Caring* 1 (1): 27–43.

Urban, Petr, and Alice Koubová. 2019. Beyond the Individualistic Paradigm of the Self with Donald Winnicott and Carol Gilligan. HUMANA.MENTE *Journal of Philosophical Studies* 12 (36): Beyond the Self: Crisis of Disembodied and Individualistic Paradigms, ed. by Benjamino Cianferoni and Lanfredini Roberta. https://www.humanamente.eu/index.php/HM/article/view/300.

CHAPTER 7

Caring Democracy as a Solution Against Neoliberalism and Populism

Fabienne Brugère

Many countries around the world are experiencing a crisis of care because the value of health care or social care seems less important than the global market and all sorts of investments. This means that activities of care are not recognized as important and that needs are left unanswered. The most notable consequence is a care deficit: people who work are caught in a circle of working harder to earn more money, which demands more of their time and energy, and spending less time caring for their families and friends or for vulnerable others. Is an ethics of care a solution to the care crisis affecting countries North and South? Is morality strong enough to play a part in politics at a time when economic enterprise and success hold so much weight? This chapter seeks to address these questions through a discussion of the current challenges facing the realization of 'caring democracy' presented by neoliberalism and populism.

Neoliberalism and populism are two very different forms of government, yet they both claim to address the crisis of care by introducing a government of human conducts. We consider these two solutions and describe how they

F. Brugère (✉)
Department of Philosophy, Paris 8 University, Vincennes-Saint-Denis, France
e-mail: fa.brugere@orange.fr

P. Urban, L. Ward (eds.), *Care Ethics, Democratic Citizenship and the State*, International Political Theory,
https://doi.org/10.1007/978-3-030-41437-5_7

define individuals. Neoliberalism strives to orient behavior in a society of risk: care becomes a question of service. Populism turns care into a matter of paternalistic protection based on a divide between nationals and foreigners, men and women, heterosexuals and homosexuals. On the one hand, care is included in a market ideology. On the other, care is carried out in the name of patriarchy. Neoliberal and populist forms of governmentality are important to analyze for care ethicists because of their attraction and their discourses of care. These discourses are political and appear to provide an ideological framework for resolving the care crisis.

Care, however, is not central to these contemporary forms of government consistently devoted to a vertical concept of society according to which care dispositions and practices are put to use. An ethics of care, and more specifically a democratic way of life, must be taken into account. In a "caring society," according to Joan Tronto, an ethics of care is defined by its skepticism toward authoritarian systems of government and by taking into consideration the value of personal, interpersonal, and institutional relationships. It is important not only to define the meaning of "good care" but also to "care with others." Only then, Tronto argues, do democratic commitments to justice, equality, and freedom have a chance of becoming effective (Tronto 2013). This chapter asks: is the normativity of care enough to guide us, or should we think beyond this approach?

The Crisis of Care

Care is a central part of human life: human beings, from the very beginning of their lives, cannot live without care. As 'care-giving,' care is a kind of practice. We care for the sick, for the young, for the elderly, and for poor and excluded people but also for each and every individual, for the environment, and for institutions: care affects both living and inanimate beings, as well as objects. In the human realm, it refers to an activity of support that seeks to maintain, continue, or restore one's capacity to be, speak or act with respect to Fisher and Tronto's definition; care is "a species activity that includes everything that we do to maintain, continue, and repair our 'world' so that we can live in it as well as possible" (Fisher and Tronto 1990, 40). But activities of care are not well regarded, supported, or respected in contemporary societies, especially in the Global North because they are considered as not productive. Care is an invisible condition of the labor market. Yet, the entry of some into economic competition is possible only because others assume responsibility for everything else that falls within a given society's category of care: raising children, taking care of the sick and elderly people, doing social work and volunteering. A division thus forms between the valued world of the highly productive and the marginalized world of caregivers and care recipients—with gender and social lines intersecting in the category of vulnerability (Tronto 1993; Fraser 2013).

When we turn to hospitals, nursing homes, nurseries, and hospices, we realize that workers are very often demoralized. In a way, they are prevented from properly doing their jobs. They have to act in the name of budgetary austerity and are forced to face different sorts of tax cuts; public services are no longer adequately funded because they are not attractive for a market society. Hence the diagnosis of a 'crisis of care.'

Alison Holt, a journalist at the BBC, has shown how the adult social care system in the UK is on the brink of collapse and in dire need of reform after years of austerity (Holt 2019) (cf. Ward et al. this volume). In Somerset, home to one of the UK's fastest aging populations, she describes the perspective of four families in desperate need of support and of those charged with providing it. On the one hand, pain, exhaustion, and dependence have become ways of life. On the other hand, social workers are desperate and underline the sheer impossibility of cutting taxes and slashing funding while poverty and vulnerability increase.

The crisis of emergency services in France during the spring of 2019 is also symptomatic of the present situation in Northern countries: the social movement, which lasted three months, demanded more human and material resources to cope with overcrowded care units. The annual number of patients has increased by an average of 3.5%. The decrease in the number of general practitioners in the context of an aging population can serve as an explanation. But, more generally, as sociologist François Dubet already showed in 2002, a more general crisis of care is at work and one affecting caring institutions in particular (Dubet 2002). The French institutional model of working for/with others is no longer efficient. This model adhered to a principle by which caregivers participated in the transformation of values and principles into action through professional and organized work. But how might we keep personal work for others from dissolving into a mere assortment of services? Have we forgotten the importance of care in its connection with ethics?

The crisis of care—principally of health care—was an important diagnosis made by Obama when he became President of the United States: he offered a new health policy, the Affordable Care Act, approved by the

Democrats. Undoubtedly, the new health policy offers crucial and tangible benefits. As the law's full name makes clear, one of its fundamental accomplishments is to protect patients from mistreatment by health insurance companies. For example, so-called Obamacare guards against arbitrary loss or denial of insurance coverage. Alondra Nelson, an American sociologist, explains that it improves access to medical services through a public-private regime: in 2013, she argued that, as a result, the numbers of underinsured and uninsured people in the United States was expected to shrink from its then current level of 50 million persons to about 20 million (Nelson 2013). This means a salient reduction in human need and suffering. But the assessment of a care crisis hinges on political assessments of the role of individuals.

Yet, the crisis of care is not only an issue in the Global North, an aftereffect of the demise of the welfare state which began in the 1980s. Globalization means that practices of care have become global rather than merely local issues. Globalization implies the proliferation of care crises. One of the key features of globalization is the movement of workers within and across national borders. Care workers are affected by these flows and largely exploited, especially when they come from poorer regions of the world. The exploitation of low-wage and immigrant labor (especially women) merits attention, as in the case of migrant domestic workers from the Philippines, Madagascar, or India (Zimmerman et al. 2006). As Parvati Raghuram explains, the way the forces and processes of economic globalization have played out has shrunken the scope of women's lives in the Global South, leaving them to pursue alternative survival strategies, especially through emigration (Raghuram 2016). The increase in two-wage families, combined with the personalization of care arrangements in the Global North, has created a care deficit for households in the North. The Global North, therefore, has increasingly come to depend on care workers from the Global South. These workers are very often women from poor countries. New globalized domestic workers, who benefit from fewer rights because they arrive illegally, often experience long and complicated regularization processes (cf. Mahadevan this volume).

The crisis of care refers to a deficit of care for people who work a lot, to a widening gap between the private and the public sphere, and to new sorts of exploitation often in connection with migrations in this age of globalization. Of course, there are different dimensions of 'crisis.' Two aspects are important. On the one hand, the public care system is considered too expensive and can be replaced by private care. The care crisis is due to a crisis of the welfare state in a logic of state debt reduction. On the other hand, the care crisis concerns any domestic work in the Global North that few people want to do because it is poorly paid and recognized. In these circumstances, care is not a value and it doesn't matter how well it is done. We are very far from the possibility of good care or a care ethics. It seems that we have forgotten how to care and that caring is no longer an important set of practices capable of expressing our situation as interconnected human beings affected by the lives of others.

Furthermore, care relations should be considered within a globalized world where competition, deepening hierarchies, and patterns of exclusion are very present, increasing the importance of nationalist emotions and sovereignty in contrast with the perception of an interdependence rooted in the necessity of ethical and political responses to situations of suffering (Robinson 1999, 99–104).

Care ethics[1] should not only be understood in terms of interpersonal relationships. Care calls into question the separation between morality and politics and between the private and the public realm, just as it challenges the distributions between center and periphery and North and South defined by these divisions. The ethic of care is also defined by the notion of 'crisis': it must expose the processes through which caring for the most vulnerable has become marginalized and through which the recognition of care-related practices, people, and institutions has been undermined. While those who provide care help to preserve a bond of mutual assistance, solidarity, and concern, they are also condemned to silence, little involved in public spheres of decision-making, poorly compensated, or relegated to unpaid and solitary dedication in the private realm.

In fact, the crisis of care is symptomatic of hierarchical relationships. According to Tronto, authority in caring relationships does not lie with care workers, but with those who, without exercising care, define how needs will be met: "it is the physician who 'takes care of' the patient, even if the care-giving nurse notices something that the doctor does not notice or consider significant" (Tronto 1993, 109). It is symptomatic to notice that the more care departs from 'taking care of'—according to the highly valued model of the doctor in charge of a patient's recovery—the more it is linked to care for local bodily concerns (as in the case of the nurse who cleans up patients) and the more it is abandoned by the powerful and

[1] The term "care ethics" includes not only the theoretical dimension of care but all the practices that are invested by the possibility of good care.

depreciated by societies devoted to an encompassing and seemingly dematerialized market. This is especially true if we consider the history of bodily cleaning tasks, which are central to the care given to the most dependent (young children, the elderly, the seriously ill, etc.). It should be stressed that these tasks have been mainly assigned to women within the private, family, or professional sphere, as well as to immigrants or to the working class.

Care is socially distributed across lines of gender, race, and class. It then becomes the object of poorly paid work (the work of the dominated or the weak at the service of the powerful) and is depreciated, however essential it may be to the workings of the market society. While care is an important part of our daily lives, we do not recognize its value and do not grant this dimension the attention it merits. While it aims at coping with vulnerability, it often only generates patterns of vulnerability making up as many patterns of exploitation of the individuals in charge of care. To elaborate on Tronto's analyses, we may add that bad care is not only marginalized care, lessened care, or care whose institutional existence is at risk (Tronto 1993, 111–122). It is also a form of care won over to market demands of economic profitability. Caring for a singular vulnerable being becomes a nearly impossible task, weighed down by relations that leave no time for personal or psychological availability.

All sorts of care crises suggest we have trouble acknowledging practices of care. Caring work is achieved by exploiting individuals and their supposedly humane dispositions. The systematic undermining of care stems from the current globalized political system's incapacity to take care into account. How can capitalistic societies organize activities, practices, or occupations which, from their perspectives, fall outside the narrow sphere of financial profitability? Among the privileged, devolving care tasks to others prevents a deeper reflection on the question of what we should collectively be doing to further care. Our understanding of care is fragmented: caring activities are scattered and described as trivial concerns. The mission of the ethics of care is to produce a systematic reflection and to turn the very concept of care into a central category for the analysis of society.

The difficulty of unifying care lies in the lack of recognition of its activities, grounded in turn in the notion that talking about care is unnecessary because it lies at the border between the private and the public, the body and the mind, or in the nebulous realm of the "heart" (Folbre 2001, xi–xii). It is grounded in the fact that care is consistently associated with intimacy, affectivity, and proximity—care is hence naturalized and feminized, hindering its identification as a type of work. The fragmentation of care activities prevents any unified perception of care. How may we then grasp the structurally central part it plays in social life? The unequal allocation of power, resources, and social distinctions affects caring activities in particular, because they take place in a fragile world governed by individuals who only have to care about themselves and their own self-interests.

Neoliberalism and Populism: Two Ways of Resolving the Crisis of Care?

Engaging in a reflection on 'good care' and advocating a solution to the care crisis suggests reorganizing the activities pertaining to health care, education, social work, and all the fields that express a form of concern for others. Neoliberalism and populism are appealing or efficient because they are aware of the care crisis; they know how to exploit it politically and propose solutions that inexorably separate those who are entitled to care from those who are not. In this context, analyzing the importance given to care practices seems key. On the one hand, neoliberalism brings care into the slogan "business as usual." Care activities are services like any other service and depend on the standard of living of individuals. On the other hand, populism separates care recipients and non-recipients. Caring protection exists but not for everybody. In both systems, the crisis of care is solved, but only for a part of the population.

Neoliberalism and populism are forms of government that claim to address the crisis of care by introducing a government of human conducts by a standardization of human behavior. They are regimes of subject formation. They develop and promote codes of conducts and ensure compliance with these codes. Drawing on Foucault, Thomas Lemke defines government as conduct or, more precisely, as "the conduct of conduct," and thus as a term which ranges from "governing the self" to "governing others" (Lemke 2002). Power, and more specifically political power, is defined as guidance. Coercion and consensus are reformulated as means of government among others. Neoliberalism and populism offer propositions to solve the crisis of care that begin with the possibility of governing others. Practices of care are carried out in a hierarchical world implying specific forms of dominance and the exclusion of certain parts of the population from care practices.

Neoliberalism and Care

Let us begin with neoliberalism. Neoliberalism is a transformation of politics that negates the universality of care by relinquishing social securities and political rights. My aim is not to provide a full-fledged definition of neoliberalism but to explain how neoliberalism considers care activities and tries to render them compatible with a market society. As Joan Tronto writes: "Like every political theory or ideology, neoliberalism contains a concept of care within it" (Tronto 2017, 30). Care becomes a set of practices for people who can afford such "services." In addition, care is viewed as a matter of individual responsibility rather than as a collective issue. The neoliberal world sees people as workers and consumers. The logic of consumption is individualistic: personal responsibility is the solution to the problem of care. Tronto has described how the Bush administration policies cast care as a personal matter: "If you cannot care for your own children, your own community, then there is a problem in your family or community, the problem is your inadequate sacrifice" (Tronto 2013, 42).

Today, caring activities and the motives behind them cannot be properly assessed without first describing neoliberal mechanisms and the role played by activities that exploit care from others while promoting care as a personal matter. Wendy Brown's *Neo-liberalism and the End of Liberal Democracy* (2003) shows how world politics and American politics in the first place have been shaped by a globalizing and all-encompassing market rationale. Neoliberalism does not only consist in the implementation of a generally masculine world of oligarchic finance. It is expansionist, and employs political tactics which, following the inexorable reasoning of the market, add the further element of an authoritarian statism fed by conservative values imposed as behavioral norms on ordinary citizens. Wendy Brown argues that this suggests the construction of a non-democratic global regime, an authoritarian government of conducts. This new governmentality does not only adopt the economic reasoning that developed in the market economy and whose intellectual flag-bearer is Adam Smith's *The Wealth of Nations*, it also includes a contagious political reasoning permeating every sphere of reality. This reasoning consists in extending and disseminating market values to social politics and institutions. It absorbs the state through the influence of oligarchic privatization, but its subversion of the people's power does not stop there. It pervades individuals' bodies and minds and produces subjects, modes of citizenship, and behaviors, as well as a new way of organizing society. In fact, individual subjects are permeable and experience difficulties in constructing their inner psychic landscape. Extending Foucault's analysis, Wendy Brown understands neoliberalism as a globalized structure originating in various well-identified parts of the world but aimed at subjecting politics and every aspect of contemporary life to an economic rationale. Humans should be able to see themselves as *homo oeconomicus*. They should know deep down that a viable existence presently requires acquiring entrepreneurial habits, thanks to the figure of the high-performing and ever-calculating individual. The characteristic thereby constructed is rooted in norms which infiltrate people to turn them into creatures wholly dedicated to economic rationalism.

The matter of 'taking care' has been appropriated and reconstructed as the hidden but necessary work of care providers. Further, the neoliberal construct thrives on the notion of 'taking care' of oneself, repurposed by neoconservatism's eagerness to extend the realm of individual responsibility in the face of any collective project striving to reintroduce solidarity, mutual aid, or freedom within social ties. It is very clear, in this neoliberal and conservative society permeating through the channels of human life around the world, that care is construed as a matter of health where human beings are dedicated to deploying their human capital. In *The Birth of Biopolitics*, Michel Foucault clearly showed this restriction of caring activities to the protection of productive subjects, always available and willing to accept and spread a narrative that links together human capital, well-being, the morality of individual responsibility, and a return to a homogeneous social order. Michel Foucault notes how the liberal mentality at play in this narrative aims to capture human beings from birth by harnessing their abilities. That human capital bears fruit is the essential condition of the market. By this account, it is necessary to invest in one's human capital and put it to work. The logic of the market implies a total mobilization of mankind. Care becomes a valuable asset in the service of capitalism. It is at best an accessory and at worst an ideology serving a universal and all-encompassing idea of government which promotes exchange as a real value not only of things but of people themselves. Care for others is hence described as an investment, like the love or education parents invest in their children: these more or less voluntary investments made in the service of a deployable human capital generate, according to Foucault, "kinds of ability-machines which will produce income" (Foucault 2008, 229). The new liberalism described by Foucault focuses on the manufacturing of competent individuals. Subjects of care fit in more easily with the modern circuitry of economic and political calculation. Consequently, in this system, the question of 'taking care' is the object of a reappropriation. It loses track of its ethical project but gains the possibility that certain care practices will be valued because they are considered productive: they are "marketized" and "privatized" (Held 2006, 107–124). These practices often become "services": personal services, home services (household tasks, childcare, help for elderly people, as well as health care). The notion of "service" helps to underscore what Geneviève Fraisse calls "the house in reverse" ("*la maison à l'envers*") (Fraisse 1979), in reference to domestic workers, equally ignored in the present and in the past. Service verges on servitude when people find themselves bound to other people for work that is often infinite and all the less remunerated for being infinite. Neoliberal care "services" are privatized and presented as perfectly adjusted to the needs of those who cannot or will not perform certain care tasks. The world is shared between those who have the choice (to care or not to care) and those for whom care is their livelihood.

Populism and Care

Populism is constituted in reaction to an omnipresent market society that creates many outsiders. It claims to solve the care crisis by giving protection to nationals (cf. Okano and Maruyama this volume). What kind of protection is it? Why are some sorts of vulnerability more legitimate than others?

New forms of populism (as a form of government) have claimed to solve the care crisis. First, 'care-giving' and 'care-receiving' depart from globalization (in stark contrast with neoliberalism) by reintroducing the importance of nationality and sovereignty. Populists claim to act for the people, using phrases such as "we the people." In this context, it can be tempting to set this "us" against another group. This is what populists do, paving the way for the confrontation of "us" versus "them," national subjects versus strangers. Populists tend to marginalize anyone who is not considered part of the "real" people: the others are "corrupt" and "crooked" (Müller 2017). This distinction is totally constructed and requires borders (and borders need policing). Populists develop forms of government based on heavy-handed security policies because they govern conducts by implementing and fostering fear. When emotions are reduced to fear, this "us" requires borders. As Martha Nussbaum writes in an effort to account for Trump's victory in the United States, what we are currently experiencing is "a monarchy of fear" as opposed to democratic reciprocity (Nussbaum 2018). Fear is not only the first emotion we experience in our human lives (when we are babies), it is also the most broadly shared within the animal kingdom. Nussbaum's argument is that fear is less complex than compassion. All that fear requires is an awareness of the looming danger. In many cases, people experience fear without ever being aware of it. It is practical to be governed by fear: it is easy, in a complex world, to base this "us" upon fear. All sorts of populists resort to fear: it is easy to appeal to popular emotion with the notion of thousands of refugees invading "our" democracies. Altruism, love, and gratitude are more complicated than fear because they require the ability to think about the other person as a separate (yet connected) individual and to imagine what this other person feels and wants. When we experience fear, we do not imagine anything about the other person. It is harder to govern with altruism. It is harder to govern with values of plurality and inclusion than those based on exclusion and violence.

If we assume that care practices have connections with altruism and love as norms for good care, populist governments are incapable of solving the care crisis. Populism promotes care practices structured by hierarchies of power and dominance. Such hierarchies would be rooted in a natural difference between male and female, manhood and womanhood. Care practices are a priority for women, the model of the mother playing a fundamental part in re-justifying the ancient divide between the private and the public space. Masculinity is considered superior, while femininity features as a natural way of practicing care. When women assume their "natural" role, populists consider the care crisis to be nonexistent: men are breadwinners, women are homemakers. The government of conducts by fear renders these roles essential thanks to the proliferation of a certain sexual anxiety: the fear of not entirely being a man or a woman. Populism has ties with fascism in its promotion of sexism and misogyny, and because it defines care in connection with patriarchal protection. As Jason Stanley writes in *How Fascism Works*, fascism (and Donald Trump represents a new fascism in Stanley's view) employs a politics of sexual anxiety by which the political leader is a father protecting the people, particularly women and children who are more vulnerable than men (Stanley 2018). Freedom and equality are attacked in the name of safety. Moreover, populism or neopopulism has to be connected with a protectionist discourse of care (Tronto 2017). The notion of the leader—the father of the nation—does not only suggest a natural and sexual basis for care. Care tasks are for women because they are more connected to birth and sex. These practices take place in a hierarchical world where the masculine world of production is of greater value than the feminine world of social reproduction. Care is not defined by services but by activities which follow a natural and hierarchical order. As Carol Gilligan and Naomi Snider explain in *Why Does Patriarchy Persist?* patriarchy, with its gender binary and hierarchy, forces girls and women to silence. It is important to depart from patriarchy if we aim to hear the human voice of men and women and to experience their real connection (Gilligan and Snider 2018).

But this account of care activities is not convincing from an ethical point of view. In *In a Different Voice*, Carol Gilligan develops an ethics of care drawing on the experience of women and their role in care. Gilligan does not seek to promote a feminine morality and the assignment of women to maternity (see Urban and Ward, this volume). Her point is not to think of women's morality as different from men's and as stemming from the sphere of the finer feelings. As she writes very clearly today, her goal has always been to question well-established certainties on morality to reveal practices rooted in care for others—practices which have been underestimated because they have mostly been carried out by women. And care practices assigned to women are underestimated.

Gilligan introduced a feminism rooted in the will to make feminine and inaudible voices heard and designed to establish an ethics of equal voices against male dominance as well as the moral standard which serves and confirms it. To do so, Gilligan initially denounced a recurring methodological problem in Kohlberg's theory of moral development: the exclusion of women. According to Kohlberg, because women are less suited for abstraction, they fail to reach the standards of moral perfection, namely individual autonomy and the capacity to justify one's behavior rationally.

What neoliberalism fails to take into account is the possibility of an equality of voices. It considers that money and power constitute the value of individuals who have to be adapted to financial capitalism. What populism fails to take into account is the notion of an ethical feminism: a feminism in which the allocation of care practices to women is accounted for by cultural reasons rather natural ones. Gilligan's aim is to make women's voices, forgotten voices, finally heard.

Care implies attending to everyone's lives with a certain number of attitudes, with a capacity to take responsibility, to care for bodies, or to satisfy needs. When caring attitudes become a part of a society of financialized production or when they are assigned in priority to nationals, they divide the society in insiders and outsiders. These forms of government do not recognize the plurality of human lifestyles, the different sorts of needs, or of degrees of vulnerability.

From Good Care to Caring Democracy

The notion of a normative care in contrast to a descriptive care deserves to be examined in resolving the crisis of care. Eva Feder Kittay and Licia Carlson's analysis of the crisis of care from the angle of cognitive disability highlights the limits of a medical model and helped to develop a perspective rooted in the emergence of "moral personhood" (Kittay and Carlson 2010). Have we forgotten how to care ethically? Can there be alternative care practices? With neoliberalism and populism, ethical care becomes counter-cultural.

First, it is important to maintain the possibility of 'good care.' This suggests a different way of organizing activities pertaining to care, education, social work, and all the fields expressing a form of concern for others. It also means advocating a role for subjective dispositions for caring, which can be understood as a certain availability of caregivers, expressing the conciliation of capacity and activity. The attentive availability of caregivers is built on a form of respect for the specificity of care work, which implies a relation to time structured by the uncertainties of human lives rather than by the reign of objects. Deciding to reflect on good care suggests that we consider "when both the activity and disposition of care are present" (Tronto 1993, 105).

The aim is to explain the interplay of disposition and activity by describing in concrete terms the various phases of good care. Tronto's book *Moral Boundaries* is extremely clear with regard to this analytical project: "We noted that, as an ongoing process, care consists of four analytically separate, but interconnected, phases. They are: caring about, taking care of, care-giving, and care-receiving" (Tronto 1993, 105f.). The first phase engages the caring process, defined as 'caring about': it consists in the disposition for attentiveness, a readiness to recognize unmet needs. This accounts for the dimension of moral disposition. The second phase, 'taking care of,' implies seeing that the need can indeed be met and determining the adequate means to do so—it involves taking charge and assuming responsibility. We are still at a dispositional stage, that of a moral disposition for responsibility. The third phase, 'care-giving,' emphasizes the actual care work and the 'competence' provided in one's response to a need. Finally, good care involves "care-receiving," which implies the care-receiver's responsiveness. This last step consists in an assessment of good care: the care-receiver is asked if the care provided was adequate to his or her need (Garrau 2006). We may then define a role for the disposition to understand, as a disposition for receptiveness.

Attentiveness, responsibility, competence, and responsiveness constitute an ethical grammar of care in which disposition continues to play a part (Tronto 1993, 105–108; Brugère 2009). What it shows is the difficulty of describing care's ethical aim as 'good care' by doing completely without the notion of 'disposition.' Instead, the indivisibility of disposition and activity needs to be examined, bearing in mind the necessity of identifying the specific kind of work and practices required by others' needs (Tronto 1993, 105–108).

If an ethic of care has more to do with practice than with a set of rules and principles, we may then, following Tronto, draw on the four steps of good care to define the four steps of an ethics of care: attentiveness, responsibility, competence, and responsiveness (ibid., 127). Being inattentive to the needs of others is a moral failure from the standpoint of the ethic of care. Attentiveness must be brought to the fore, as the vehicle of genuine human interaction. Attention to others goes hand in hand with listening. Listening suggests the composition of a non-authoritarian society that takes differences into account and includes them within a democratic model of government. Responsibility follows from attentiveness, as a moment of 'taking care of.' Responsibility is not only a formal moral category considered as an obligation to be carried out: it also bears a political meaning that requires examining its allocation within society, and hence acknowledging needs for care. The third step, that of competence, is to be understood in the framework of a moral consequentialism that calls for the concrete expression of concern: it hinges on the tangible success of one's actions. Caring implies caring about consequences and the final outcome. The care's adequacy to the situation expresses the competence of the practice itself. Finally, the responsiveness of the care-receiver is a key factor: it reminds us of the fact that the response is often difficult, indirect, or comes in the form of a denial of care, since relationships often play out in situations of vulnerability and inequality. Care offers a critique of autonomy understood as a position everyone may occupy at all times. This is not to say that autonomy does not exist or to refuse to acknowledge the life ideal it may convey. But the practice of care "is concerned with conditions of vulnerability and inequality" (ibid., 134). Having to resort to care means being in a position of vulnerability whose scope is both moral and political. Enabling care-receivers to respond means recognizing their vulnerability, against the imperatives of individual autonomy. An ethical care implies a critique of individual responsibility.

Second, an ethical care must take into consideration relationships between women and men. Women's voices are no different from men's, but male domination has made them inaudible by creating a correlation between moral feelings, the private or family arena, and a supposed female nature (particularly in the eighteenth century, when the notion of the public sphere was tied to contracts and excluded dependent individuals—primarily women but also slaves, domestic servants, and poor workers). Gilligan argues that women's voices must be valued in order to establish equality between two moralities: one referencing subjects of rights capable of distancing themselves from their activities, which Gilligan calls an ethic of justice based on the ideal of a neutral public sphere, and one referencing subjects of need who must be "taken care of," and requires subjects acting in favor of others and on behalf of an ethics of responsibility. Of course, such an ethics—of responsibility or 'care'—must account for the forgotten experiences of women, which have been poorly assessed in male-centered moral psychologies (such as Kohlberg's, cited by Gilligan 1982, 19–20). But above all, it must transform gender relationships and abolish the inequalities that lead to a social positioning of men and women that minimizes the activities involving concern for others which women perform. In short, a feminist ethics is needed in order to democratize society and promote equality between voices, thereby shifting the barriers (too hastily erected in the name of a normalizing rational identity of individuals) between reason and feeling, the public and the private, the moral and the political. A similar ethic must make women aware of the need to depart from the imposed conventional goodness of 'care' as self-sacrifice, in favor of a relational morality that combines concern for the self and concern for others, all the while remaining aware of situations and chains of vulnerability (between caregivers and recipients, women, the poor, migrants, etc.). A care ethical criticism of neoliberalist and populist "solutions" of the care crisis has to consider the power of gender. But as Joan Tronto explains, shifting the barriers of care does not only concern gender but class and race (Tronto 1993). Poor care workers are not only women.

Restoring equality in the area of care thus means considering vulnerability within the framework of an ethics that, instead of expressing the moral weakness of women, expresses a relational maturity, a sense of collective responsibility (with respect to all forms of need): an ethics which, having deconstructed gender inequalities, could be applied to humankind and enable us to relate to others in a way that reflects a concrete, rather than a generalized, other (Benhabib 1986). This involves accepting a particularistic, as opposed to a universalistic, morality, or even calling for an "interactive" universality that takes into account the plurality of human lifestyles.

One major difficulty in the topic of 'care' is knowing to which extent vulnerable beings are marked by the actions of others and the ways in which they might respond (favorably or unfavorably). Tronto insists on our duty to "protect the vulnerable," but she is critical of the way care is dispensed to the most vulnerable so long as those who protect them are presented as defenders. There is therefore the danger that care providers will abuse their power, granting themselves the right to define the needs of the vulnerable (Tronto 1993, 145; cf. Smiley this volume). Vulnerability always enables the potential abuse of power because the ability to respond to it does not stem from reciprocity between equals. Knowing how to relate morally to vulnerability involves considering the position of the other as she herself expresses it, rather than assuming the other to be identical to oneself. When vulnerability needs to be protected, taken charge of, or attended to, it highlights alterity, that is, a situation that is not interchangeable and deserves an appropriate response.

We are all vulnerable. As Tronto writes, throughout our lives, we all experience varying degrees of dependence and independence, autonomy, and vulnerability (Tronto 1993, 146). However, depending on our position—rich or poor, in the center or on the margins of power relationships—we may, to a greater or lesser extent, forget the vulnerability of others as we come to believe in our own power or invincibility (Butler 2004). We forget that some people experience more vulnerability than others, and we leave responding to their needs to the less powerful, the less recognized, thus creating chains of vulnerability in our society that also compose chains of social precarity: care practices create inequalities not only along gender lines but also along lines of class and race. Resolving the crisis of care demands that we acknowledge human vulnerability, as well as the vulnerability of animals and of the world. Neoliberalism and populism focus on the rationality of individuals or on the strength of people: they consider that vulnerability only exists for outsiders or undesirable foreigners undeserving of care.

In fact, 'caring' for the vulnerable is a form of interpersonal support and should be given a greater role in social policies regarding non-autonomous individuals. However, this support cannot be achieved without respect for the recipient's capacity to act, be, or speak. Addressing vulnerability means not losing sight of the care recipient's ability to be productive: assistance should not be confused with charity. Moreover, in the area of gender inequality, the issue of care clearly marks a shift from industrial to post-industrial capitalism, from classical liberalism to neoliberalism. One could argue that the naturalization movement, which tied the future of women to feelings and solicitude within the sphere of the family, was replaced with the need for a certain number of women to consider care as work and accept poorly paid, invisible jobs that turn their dependence into exploitation at precarious jobs.

If care becomes more democratic when it is based on an ethics, feminism, and the consideration of vulnerability, is this enough to solve the care crisis? Tronto advocates a caring democracy as a solution against the care deficit. She describes a fifth phase of care (following the four phases of good care): 'caring with,' which conveys the moral dimensions of solidarity and trust. These dimensions exemplify moral qualities referring to humans in constant relations with others: "To make sense of human life requires a relational perspective" (Tronto 2013, 36). Tronto explains this fifth phase of care with the help of Selma Sevenhuijsen's book, *Citizenship and the Ethics of Care* (1998):

> Sevenhuijsen argues, care also requires commitments to 'plurality, communication, trust and respect.' These qualities pinpointed by Sevenhuijsen help to identify which critical moral qualities will enable people to assume collective responsibility, to consider citizens as both receivers and givers of care, and to seriously think about the nature of caring needs in society. (Tronto 2013, 35)

On the one hand, collective responsibility implies the definition of a common good. Equality and freedom are democratic values for all. Responsibility is collective and must be used to develop practices and institutions designed to organize people's interdependence. Tronto calls this perspective of solidarity between individuals 'caring with': we are all relational human beings. Care is ethical and can be understood as a democratic connection between people because the issues it addresses focus on relationships and the meeting of needs rather than on the perfection of the virtuous individual. On the other hand, receivers and givers of care are equal and interdependent. Care relations are reciprocal and a caring society is a caring democracy: relations are more horizontal than vertical. A caring society produces trust and solidarity: "Caring with occurs when a group of people (from a family to a state) can rely upon an ongoing cycle of care to continue to meet their caring needs. When such patterns become established and reliable, they produce the virtues of trust and solidarity" (Tronto 2017, 31).

For Tronto, "democratic" means that responsibility is not personal. A primary task of democratic societies is to allocate caring responsibilities, to consider human cooperation and conflict resolution. Relations have to be not inhabited by status and hierarchy. A caring society is a society of inclusion considering the possibility for all vulnerable or dependent people to participate in political discussions and decision-making. Under-represented groups have to be included and it is important to deliver them care and to make them participate in a caring society (Tronto 2017; Young 2010).

Public Policies and Social Work

But the project of a caring democracy as Tronto describes could be the focus of a closer investigation into the crisis of the welfare state. Caring people or *homines curans* as developed by Tronto can be understood as a resurgence of the solidarity of working-class parties in the first half of the twentieth century. It is important to convoke this moment of the history of Northern Europe when systems of social security, income support, social rights, and health care were created (Tronto 2017). Now we experience a crisis of the welfare state and it becomes difficult to consider policies of inclusion. In situations of extreme vulnerability and exclusion, care is highly relevant. It becomes important to consider a new welfare state with a new definition of social rights and new practices of support (Engster 2015). Care has to do with support. If a caring society turns to new support policies, it must focus on supporting the most vulnerable, the most dependent, all those left out by neoliberalism and populism. Care is not only about health care, it must change social work for the benefit of an inclusive society.

In this view, social work may be examined from the angle of the ethics of care and a caring society. Many people are currently demanding that care become a full-blown instrument of social policymaking, paving the way for a caring democracy capable of reintroducing the most vulnerable lives into the social bond and of resolving the crisis of the welfare state—lives which the excessive difficulty of social integration has led to depend on social benefits.

Social workers are expected to protect individuals from marginalization, primarily by improving their well-being: they take care of adults, children, or entire families and act on their behalf when they cannot or can no longer take care of themselves, or when they do not enjoy decent living conditions. Caring, assisting, and supporting are actions meant to express a benevolent care in support of those who caregivers help to achieve a better life, or simply to survive in a social world that has become incomprehensible and from which these individuals have in some way departed. Care is always practiced in connection with vulnerability and life situations ranging from precarity and unemployment to exclusion and the bare necessity of survival.

Now more than ever, the loss of social bearings resulting from exclusion calls for an ethics of care. It can be combined with analyses on social suffering to examine the increasing exposure of the intimacy of people whose subjectivity is confronted with impossibilities to speak or act. It leads to a vision of social work based on the distress and the unmet needs of these subjects, all the while protecting them from abuses of power or the manipulation of their life stories. At the same time, in its proximity with a clinical approach, care denounces the inadequacy of contractual, procedural, and often bureaucratic assistance, which acknowledges people's dependence on social action and on the disappearance of social ties without trying to grasp the singularity of these paths in life and how they can be repaired.

Introducing singularity and taking into account narratives and experiences is only relevant if we take the necessary steps to implement adequate forms of support, helping to restore individuals' capacity to act and speak freely. As opposed to an impersonal social approach, unmindful of individuals and of their life journeys, care is a type of support that allows individuals to restore a connection with themselves and with others by letting them reacquire self-esteem, a desire to act and to be. Care partakes of what Didier Vrancken calls a "new protectional order" (Vrancken 2010) pertaining both to outside support and to individuals' own capacities, vulnerability, and performativity.

By this account, social workers are not the agents of a state using them to maintain the social bond by sprinkling on various types of aid, they are neither representatives of a "humanitarian reason" nor benevolent actors in a troubled social world (Fassin 2012). They are not here to monitor every misstep committed by recipients of social assistance. They are professionals who, throughout their professional experience and training, develop competences, promote values, and act to improve the social well-being of vulnerable populations largely left in their care. Social workers work to strengthen the social bond and strive to establish relations of trust with those in their charge.

Social workers' competence lies in an "art of the relation" (Vrancken 2010, 237–239) made up of a combination of techniques (cleaning, conducting group activities, etc.) and social skills (finding the proper distance: neither too close nor too far). This competence must yield a form of freedom for the care-receiver (if only the minimal freedom of resisting or continuing to position oneself on the fringes of society). Promoting this form of interdependence and this mediated form of reciprocity, which takes into account patterns of vulnerability and dignity, means instituting an ethics of care. The ethics of care involves a project for a decent society similar to that envisioned by Avishai Margalit: "A decent society is one whose institutions do not humiliate people" (Margalit 1992, 1). Margalit argues that, whereas a civilized society rests on pacified relationships between individuals, attaching great importance to interpersonal relationships, a decent society mobilizes a more archaic level of social reality: that of institutions. The idea is not to promote a social model grounded in a humanitarian and compassionate notion of the other, but to structure the social bond so that each human being may consider every other person as a human being rather than as inferior (colonialism) or invisible (migrants, illegal workers) (Brugère 2019, 93–94).

While the ethic of care can help us to reflect on social work through concrete care for human lives, it should not let us forget that the objective of the welfare state is to open the way for the possibility of non-humiliating lives in general: this includes learning to read and write as well as acquiring fundamental technical skills, having access to health care, to an income, to decent housing, and to common goods. The ethics of care can serve as a basis for public policies, provided that it is not confined to moral sentiment and to the glorification of proximity as opposed to distance (Engster 2007, 2015; Barnes 2012). Why should we introduce care in the social field? It helps to promote the notion of vulnerable social individuals possessing their own agency. While the welfare state relies on service-provider individuals whose identity depends on their belonging to the professional world, a state inspired by care takes every individual into account, including the most invisible populations who currently fall outside of standard welfare provisions. A politics of care starts by making the infra-political political. Social work is an adequate angle from which the resolution of the care crisis may be approached: there is no caring democracy without consideration for people who are excluded from all social bonds. Caring means enhancing practices of social inclusion.

With neoliberalism or populism, citizens are confronted with an increasingly vertical and authoritarian state. More than ever, they require public policies attentive to the expression of their agency, both collectively and individually. Public services must reinstate a form of proximity in their various practices rather than be consumed by top-down diktats and expensive organizational modes resulting from a perpetual deconstruction and reconstruction contrary to the interests of its very agents (Bonelli and Pelletier 2010). A caring state cannot do without the civil society understood in all its diversity. Acknowledging our differences without giving up on the construction of a common world means putting creative power back in society to avoid the risks of a standardized society stifled by norms and rules of social reproduction (White 2001).

The ethics of care aims at transforming the social world, at inventing a pluralistic society as opposed to a status-based society. It strives to promote, in these times of crisis and segregation, real emancipation.

References

Barnes, Marian. 2012. *Care in Everyday Life: An Ethic of Care in Practice*. Bristol: The Policy Press.

Benhabib, Seyla. 1986. The Generalized and the Concrete Other. In *Feminism as Critique: Essays on the Politics of Gender in Late-Capitalist Societies*, ed. Seyla Benhabib and Drucilla Cornell. Minneapolis: University of Minnesota Press.

Bonelli, Laurent, and Willy Pelletier, eds. 2010. *L'État démantelé*. Paris: La Découverte.

Brown, Wendy. 2003. Neo-liberalism and the End of Liberal Democracy. *Theory and Event* 7 (1): 1–25.

Brugère, Fabienne. 2009. Pour une théorie générale du *care*. http://www.laviedesidees.fr/Pour-une-theorie-generale-du-care.html. Accessed 8 May 2009.

———. 2019. *Care Ethics. The Introduction of Care as a Political Category*. Leuven: Peeters.

Butler, Judith. 2004. *Precarious Life: The Powers of Mourning and Violence*. New York: Verso.

Dubet, François. 2002. *Le déclin de l'institution*. Paris: Seuil.

Engster, Daniel. 2007. *The Heart of Justice: Care Ethics and Political Theory.* New York: Oxford University Press.

———. 2015. *Justice, Care, and the Welfare State.* Oxford: Oxford University Press.

Fassin, Didier. 2012. *Humanitarian Reason: A Moral History of the Present.* Berkeley, Los Angeles, and London: University of California Press.

Fisher, Berenice, and Joan C. Tronto. 1990. Toward a Feminist Theory of Caring. In *Circles of Care: Work and Identity in Women's Lives*, ed. Emily Abel and Margaret Nelson. Albany: SUNY Press.

Folbre, Nancy. 2001. *The Invisible Heart: Economics and Family Values.* New York: The New Press.

Foucault, Michel. 2008. *The Birth of Biopolitics.* New York: Palgrave Macmillan.

Fraisse, Geneviève. 1979. *Femmes toutes mains. Essai sur le service domestique.* Paris: Seuil.

Fraser, Nancy. 2013. *Fortunes of Feminism: From State-Managed Capitalism to Neoliberal Crisis.* London and New York: Verso.

Garrau, Marie. 2006. La théorie politique à l'épreuve de la vulnérabilité. *Intersections philosophiques. Cahiers de l'ED* 139: 25–40.

Gilligan, Carol. 1982. *In a Different Voice: Psychological Theory and Women's Development.* Cambridge: Harvard University Press.

Gilligan, Carol, and Naomi Snider. 2018. *Why Does Patriarchy Persist?* New York: Polity Press.

Held, Virginia. 2006. *The Ethics of Care. Personal, Political, and Global.* New York: Oxford University Press.

Holt, Alison. 2019. The Crisis in Care. *BBC.*

Kittay, Eva Feder, and Licia Carlson, eds. 2010. *Cognitive Disability and Its Challenge to Moral Philosophy.* New York: Wiley-Blackwell.

Lemke, Thomas. 2002. Foucault, Governmentality, and Critique. *Rethinking Marxism* 14 (3): 49–64.

Margalit, Avishai. 1992. *The Decent Society.* Cambridge, MA: Harvard University Press.

Müller, Jan-Werner. 2017. *What Is Populism?* Philadelphia: University of Pennsylvania Press.

Nelson, Alondra. 2013. After Obamacare: The New Stakes of US Healthcare Policy. In *La Clé des Langues*, 25–32. Lyon: ENS de LYON/DGESCO.

Nussbaum, Martha. 2018. *The Monarchy of Fear: A Philosopher Looks at Our Political Crisis.* New York: Simon and Schuster.

Raghuram, Parvati. 2016. Locating Care Ethics Beyond the Global North. *ACME, An International Journal for Critical Geography* 15 (3): 511–533.

Robinson, Fiona. 1999. *Globalizing Care: Ethics, Feminist Theory, and International Relations.* Colorado: Westview Press.

Sevenhuijsen, Selma. 1998. *Citizenship and the Ethics of Care: Feminist Considerations on Justice, Morality, and Politics.* London: Routledge.

Stanley, Jason. 2018. *How Fascism Works: The Politics of Us and Them*. New York: Penguin Random House.

Tronto, Joan C. 1993. *Moral Boundaries: A Political Argument for an Ethic of Care*. New York: Routledge.

———. 2013. *Caring Democracy. Market, Equality, and Justice*. New York: New York University Press.

———. 2017. There Is an Alternative: *Homines Curans* and the Limits of Neoliberalism. *International Journal of Care and Caring* 1 (1): 27–43.

Vrancken, Didier. 2010. *Le Nouvel ordre protectionnel*. Lyon: Parangon/Vs.

White, Anne Julie. 2001. *Democracy, Justice, and the Welfare State*. University Park: The Pennsylvania State University Press.

Young, Iris Marion. 2010 [2000]. *Inclusion and Democracy*. New York: Oxford University Press.

Zimmerman, Mary K., Jacquelyn S. Litt, and Christine E. Bose. 2006. *Global Dimensions of Gender and Carework*. Stanford: Stanford University Press.

CHAPTER 8

Time for Caring Democracy: Resisting the Temporal Regimes of Neoliberalism

Julie Anne White

Introduction

Democracy 'takes time.' So does care. This has not gone unnoticed in the literatures. This chapter draws on the work of Joan Tronto (1993, 2013) in elaborating the conditions of 'caring democracy,' arguing specifically that making time for democracy requires making time for care; that a shift from 'productive time' to 'care time' is critical to efforts to democratize care and that care work is a standpoint from which the contradictions of neoliberal logics become apparent as well as a position from which we can imagine a temporal regime more consistent with 'caring democracy.'

Tronto's work with Berenice Fisher outlines four "phases of caring" central to an ethic and politics of care (Fisher and Tronto 1990). Care work so conceived is temporally out of synch with the accelerationist and futurist tendencies of neoliberal democracies. More specifically, I argue that the temporal problem is not one of straightforward displacement; it is not simply the rise of a "new economy favoring speed and flexibility over

J. A. White (✉)
Department of Political Science, Ohio University, Athens, OH, USA
e-mail: whitej@ohio.edu

P. Urban, L. Ward (eds.), *Care Ethics, Democratic Citizenship and the State*, International Political Theory,
https://doi.org/10.1007/978-3-030-41437-5_8

loyalty and long-term temporal commitments" (Sennett 1998 in Scheuerman 2005, 470). Rather it is one of coexisting but incompatible temporal regimes that ensure that care work and care workers can never 'keep up.'

'Caring democracy' must confront the ways care work requires a different temporal regime, one incompatible with the regimes of productive work. (Ehrenreich 2014; Fraser 2016) 'A woman's work is never done,' begins to capture the ways traditionally feminine care work exceeds the boundaries of measurable time and commodified outcomes. This is particularly true when care is unpaid. But even in paid work there is often the expectation that the affective labor of care work exceeds the boundaries of the workday and workspace. Teachers, social workers, elder care and childcare providers often have unscripted job expectations that shape these patterns of excess. 'Good' care workers are 'generous' with their time and attention in ways that are driven by situational needs rather than by predetermined script. When we describe this kind of care as 'generous' we are actually capturing work that is not just 'more' but recognizing that it is qualitatively different. It is excessive in the sense that it cannot be contained by or measured within the categories of productive time and value through which our economic order is sustained.

Productive time depends on, while simultaneously marginalizing, the value of care work (Folbre 2009). This marginalization cannot be addressed exclusively through reallocating productive time so that care work is given its fair share of hours in the day and is more adequately compensated. This is in part because the marginalization of care work can still be maintained in a context that tries to convert the measure of the value of care to productive time. Care work is slow work and its marginalization is in part about being subject to deceleration in an economy and politics that are oriented to acceleration as the aesthetic of efficient production. Care is dyssynchronous with the dominant temporal regimes.

Care work is thus generative of a different temporal regime and a regime that we should not seek to convert to the efficiency logics of productive time. Rather we should recognize care time as more adequate to a range of distinctly human tasks and more specifically a temporal regime more adequate to deep democracy. 'Caring democracy' is slow democracy. If 'caring democracy' is to avoid the plight of care work within neoliberalism—the exploitive working conditions, the inegalitarian distribution of care from caring attention to caring work and the "privileged irresponsibility" (Tronto 2013) of some to avoid or neglect care work entirely, it must resist the neoliberal temporal regime that commodifies time and reduces the value of work to productive efficiencies. This process of reclaiming 'care time' has potentially egalitarian redistributional consequences for care work and constitutive consequences for care workers. Both are important to accomplishing 'caring democracy.'

Neoliberal Time

Critical work on time typically turns to Marx's *Grundrisse* in which he famously argues that capitalism "compresses" both time and space in its desire for new efficiencies and endless markets. This work is a foundation for much of the more recent focus on acceleration as a tendency that begins with industrialization and takes on new extremes in the digital age. Rebecca Solnit captures this orientation to productive time in a description of the 1870s' milieu in which photographer Edward Muybridge produced his work. "Time," she writes, "had not yet become a scarce commodity to be measured out in ever-smaller increments as clocks acquired second hands, as watches became more affordable mass-market commodities, as exacting schedules began to intrude into more and more activities. … The new age, with its factories and mobilities, its industrial scale, was to be impersonal as nothing had been before" (Solnit 2003, 14).

This conception of time structures both our economics and our politics. It makes time unaffordable ('who can afford the time?') as it reduces time to its relation to productive output. Industrial time parsed and measured in relation to production is then accelerated and compressed in a digital age. 'Big data' is celebrated as a guide to efficient decision-making, where efficiency is accomplished by reducing all questions ultimately to questions about economic growth. Wendy Brown (2015) argues this is because the logics of neoliberalism have displaced what were at one point distinctly political logics. We now operate in the political arena as though citizens are "investors or consumers, not members of a democratic polity who share power and certain common goods, spaces, and experiences." She continues, "democracy itself has been radically transformed by the dissemination of neoliberal rationality to every sphere, including politics and law. Thus distinctly political meanings of 'equality,' 'autonomy' and 'freedom' are giving way to economic valences of these terms, and the distinctive value of popular sovereignty is receding" (Brown 2015, 177).

Neoliberalism then produces the kind of citizen-subjects required for such a democracy: "technically skilled human capital not educated participants in public life and common rule" (Brown 2015, 177). And this then drives the shape of public education in ways that define knowledge exclusively in terms of its contribution to capital enhancement. Education in this context is a form of private investment (of individual energy and capital in the case of higher education) in future earning capacity rather than a collective investment in a social and public good. And efficient public education, as we shall see in a moment, leaves no time to waste.

The Time Deficit

Dan Schulman, the founder and CEO of PayPal, is fond of saying, "it's expensive to be poor." And to understand just how expensive, Schulman says, you have to walk in their shoes. After his own month-long experiment doing just that, standing in lines at check-cashing operations, listening to the conversations going on around him, he comes to see the costs of poverty both in time and in money: "Without doing that, you don't understand that managing and moving money is not just about the cost element—it's also the time element. It's practically a part-time job to go and do it" (Mangalingdan 2017, online).

While there has been a significant literature on the culture of efficiency and its companion 'acceleration' much of this literature homogenizes the impact of acceleration. But the organization of time is a critical way in which privilege is organized and this is particularly and differently true in the context of care work.

Arlie Hochschild (2012) outlines the practice of 'outsourcing' care work—that is moving what was once unpaid care work, often gendered, but also the care work that was communally supported, into the marketplace. She contrasts the traditional role of 'the villager' and that of the 'outsourcer' as a way of capturing the new organization of care made necessary by changes in the family and the simultaneous decline or absence of significant public systems of care support. In such conditions a burgeoning market for care services has developed. But as Hochschild observes, commodified care immediately becomes subject to the pressures of the market to be efficient care, to be exchangeable care and to be productive care. Her opening chapter on courtship is entitled "You Have Three Seconds"—a reference to speed dating and the logics of rapid 'exchange' that seem to dominate the culture surrounding dating websites. And later, by contrast and with the help of a friend "who had brought with her the wisdom, patience, and authority of a village elder" Hochschild contrasts this with a chapter, "For as Long as You Both Shall Live" depicting a 32-year marriage (Hochschild 2012, 63).

It is too easy to dismiss Hochschild as simply a sentimentalist. Her work is sensitive to all the ways in which markets for care can do important work in the absence of broader public commitments, work that makes at least middle-class family life possible for women who do wage work outside the home. But she notices the ways that commodifying care work ultimately means some people can afford to purchase it while others cannot. And configured as a commodity care must be abstracted from more enduring bonds in order to become a discrete and therefore, exchangeable, good for purchase.

If affective labor requires affective bonds to be 'good care' this commodification is inconsistent with the maintenance of such relationships. Surrogates as birth parents, nannies as co-parents, therapists as wise elders—many might well wonder if paying birth parents or co-parents or wise elders would undermine their relational authority. Yet one of the most disturbing findings in *The Outsourced Self* is that the value we attach to care work seems to be directly related to what we pay for that work—therapists are more 'valued' than friends, life coaches more valued than family—value is determined by the price we pay rather than the relationships we have. Echoing Brown, the technical expertise of the credentialed therapist is recognizably 'valuable,' while also for many, not readily affordable.

This commodification of care is made to appear efficient/valuable because of the culture of acceleration (Folbre 2001, 2009). Those who worry about 'not having enough time' to practice care are right to worry. And the mutuality of caring relationships, like friendships that might have been the context for mutual emotional support, require more time and more fluid time than a one-hour appointment with a therapist. But it is *both* the lack of time and our habituation to a model of accelerated time that is a problem; a problem that requires thinking about *the practices of care time* and not only about the amount of care time: mutuality is displaced by exchange in Hochschild's model of outsourcing. And friendship is eclipsed by the status of client or consumers. Simultaneously this culture of neoliberal outsourcing and acceleration is one in which privilege is maintained in part through unequal access to acceleration. "The elderly, the poor, the sick live deceleration ... dissynchronization can aggravate the problem of ghettoization" (Sennett 1998, 19).

Moreover, care work very often occurs in temporal spaces of deceleration. And this puts care workers at particular risk occupying the space in between (Eckenwiler 2020). When the needs of others are neither well bounded by time or space—a primary schoolteacher concerned about a child's safety at home, a hospice worker navigating the needs of both patient and family or an elder care worker navigating a client's desire for independence while trying to provide a safe space—this kind of affective labor is leaky labor. It is labor that defies commodification.

Making Time for Care Versus Caring Time

One way to approach this problem is to try to recognize the centrality of affective ties and then build an infrastructure that allows us to care for those to whom we are tied. Jennifer Nedelsky's work *Part-Time for All* (forthcoming) takes making the time to care seriously. Responsible use of time is the lens through which she reconfigures the relationship between 'time spent' working and 'time spent' caring. *Part-Time for All* tries to put the responsibility for care work on parity with the responsibility to earn wages. Her work persuasively decenters wage work in ways that have important implications for de-gendering the work of care. And she has an expansive understanding of care work that anticipates volunteerism and the work of maintaining public life through public participation as part of care work. Nedelsky's approach is an excellent place to begin.

But in her own account of the temporal context of care, Tronto (2013) recognizes some of the limits of this approach when she outlines the way the time deficit and the care deficit are linked but also suggests an uncoupling would make visible a qualitative difference between care work and productive work. While Marxists and market fundamentalists alike see the spread of market logics to all forms of life as inevitable, Tronto resists that claim, arguing that a 'caring democracy' would consist in democratic political institutions that would limit the expansion of this logic. She acknowledges the temporal dimension of neoliberal logics presents a particular challenge: "Nevertheless, there is one important vector along which the spread of market thinking poses real problems from the standpoint of care, that is time" (Tronto 2013, 121). She continues: "no greater time efficiencies can be achieved in intimate caring, where spending time itself is a part of the activity. … (A)n important aspect of care is simply spending time with another, listening to stories, observing care receivers" (Tronto 2013, 121). Caring attention is exactly the space of attending rather than producing, of being rather than doing. 'Spending(time) without producing' has neither discursive nor material space within neoliberalism.

Care like democracy is a relational process not a discrete commodity (Sevenhuijsen 2014). And folding care into neoliberal logics by commodifying it has real risks. Commodified care participates in a market of exchange for other commodities in which it is then configured as one among many other possible goods in an environment of scarce resources. "The usual view that arises from thinking of care as a commodity is to see any increase in caring time as a cut in time for another activity" (Tronto 2013, 164). And where this other activity is productive, care can't compete for our attention.

A second aspect of time that is out of synch with neoliberal temporal regimes is historical time. Tronto argues that without a sense of history "only proximity and family remain to ground responsibility. The enlarged sense of responsibility cannot emerge under these circumstances" (Tronto 2013, 126).

Market thinking focuses us on the move from the present to the future; the future orientation of neoliberalism centers us on the question of worthwhile investments, future yields, rather than present needs. It accelerates our attention, collapsing it into production, as only instrumentally valuable, something on the way to the future commodity. Care work can't keep up. Neither can democracy. As William Scheuerman suggests, "One of the immediate off-shoots of social acceleration is that we are becoming more likely to avoid activities that require patience, learning and total commitment" (Scheuerman 2005, 448–449). Both care work and democratic practice require such activities.

Making Time for Democracy Versus Democratic Time

Sheldon Wolin's (1997) work on democracy recognizes the tensions between productive time and democratic time and these tensions parallel the tensions between productive time and care time. "Political time" as Wolin understands it requires a "leisurely pace"—"This is owing to the needs of political action to be preceded by deliberation and deliberation, as its 'deliberate' part suggests, takes time because, typically, it occurs in a setting of competing or conflicting but legitimate considerations" (Wolin 1997, online).[1]

[1] See also Bourgault, this volume.

Access to leisure—the leisure time to care for self and other, or to care about politics—is radically unevenly distributed (Shippen 2014). This is perhaps not surprising as we frame 'leisure' largely as the absence/the outside of wage work. By contrast Wolin describes the temporalities of the economy, what I have called neoliberal time as "dictated by innovation, change and replacement through obsolescence" rather than the needs of deliberation. He goes on to note that this has not always been the case:

> At one time the meaning of "culture" was reflective of an agricultural understanding: *cultivating, taking care of, nurturing*. And when one referred to someone as "a person of culture" or "a cultivated person," the implied *reference was to the care and attention* which a person, or his or her teachers and parents, had given to selecting certain knowledge and encouraging certain tastes so as eventually to create a sensibility. (Wolin 1997, online; emphasis added)

Much democratic theorizing recognizes that deliberative democracy, broadly participatory democracy, is slow democracy (Polletta 2002; White 2000). Iris Young offers case studies that suggest that inequality of resources and status can sometimes make up for that with organization and time; here slow and careful deliberation, "sustained public discussion," provides openings for more egalitarian processes and outcomes (Young 2000, 3).

Young recognized that this democratic work is out of synch with the speed of the economy and culture and could be boring. And as William Scheuerman puts it: "In a society obsessed at all levels with speed, even the basic rudiments of citizenship are likely to seem temporally wasteful and even self-indulgent" (Scheuerman 2005, 458). By itself slow democracy carries risks. While deceleration might well favor status quo institutional interests, it might "reproduce the worst elements of every static and unchanging order" (Scheuerman 2005, 458). Historically it has been progressives who discursively embraced acceleration and conservatives who resisted it. But an intentional social deceleration in order to make possible 'caring democracy' would have to be committed to a changed order.

If we think about care work as the productive work of citizens—that is the work done by and in order to produce flourishing citizens—we must think about it quite differently. The kind of care it takes to produce workers is quite different from the kind of work it takes to produce citizens. It is itself 'slow'—this accounts for its neglect in neoliberal regimes. Both democracy and the creation of democratic citizens are marginalized or entirely neglected in neoliberal temporal regimes. By this I mean more than that they are privatized; that the discourse of 'citizenship' as a justification for public education or more broadly a discourse of citizenly responsibility for the care and well-being of the very young, the elderly or the sick is absent from public life. I mean that they are largely absent because they are out of synch with the temporal regimes that create the conditions of value. Not only is care not a commodity and therefore not properly understood in terms of exchange value. But also care is outside the social relational organization of capital—the spatial, temporal disembedding that capitalism requires is incompatible with care work and also with the robust democracy.

Education as Deferred Investment

Neoliberal logics are not only accelerating, they are financialized (Harvey 2005). And there is perhaps nowhere where these logics play out more clearly than in the educational context. The kind of cultivation Wolin describes finds little parallel in mainstream educational pedagogy and practice. But education produces not just common citizenship through the common core—a process usefully understood in the languages of acceleration and financialization. Education also sorts. And increasingly the practice of sorting is about reproducing the expectation of leisure for some and disciplining 'others' to the culture of acceleration, and financialization as deferred gratification.

Democracy cannot be a deferred investment and neither can democratic subjects. Yet in a recent *New Yorker* article, Adam Gopnik suggests that deferred investment is exactly the framework that shapes most of our reflections on education and parenting. He reviews several recent works on child-rearing, sketching out parenting practices from Germany and France to little Norwich Vermont, and tracing the process of producing Olympic athletes and child prodigies. Gopnik notes that in the area of prodigies, Ann Hulbert finds that with a few exceptions, "exactly the kind of hover parenting that we rightly deplore does seem to be essential to the kind of hyper-achievement that we admire" (Gopnik 2018, 66). To draw what at first seems to be a contrast, he turns to the story of Norwich—a place where "no parent presses, no bar is set, and after a kids scores two goals in a soccer game he is sat down so that some other kid has a chance to score. Yet Norwich continually sends athletes to the Olympics in numbers and other competitions in numbers ridiculously disproportional to its size" (Gopnik 2018, 67). But Gopnik argues that despite what might appear to be significant differences in the practices of parenting in each of these accounts, they ultimately share something much more significant in common, they are deferred investments in the same future, they are different strategies for achieving the same 'victories.' As Gopnik puts it, "If Norwich values matter, it's because they're good, not because they're shortcuts to victory. The point of a non-competitive attitude can't be that it makes us better able to compete" (Gopnik 2018, 67).

Gopnik is doing more than objecting to consequentialist logics shaping parenting practice. He is illustrating the way that they crowd out the space to understand and experience parenting (and for that matter child-ing) as anything more than an investment with deferred returns. It seems unlikely that helicopter parents actually have the relationship to their children wholly structured by this philosophy of investment. There are surely moments of mutual joy in the process of a parenting relationship that have little to do with achievement. Yet it also seems undeniable that the framework for so much of the way we talk about parenting and education circulates around 'strategies' for producing high achievers. In reflecting on this Gopnik cites Alexander Herzen: "Because children grow up, we think a child's purpose is to grow up. But a child's purpose is to be a child. Nature doesn't disdain what only lives for a day. It pours the whole of itself into each moment. … Life's bounty is in the flow, later is too late" (Gopnik 2018, 68).

This idea of 'flow' is a concept getting a lot of attention in some circles—circles that highlight practices of 'unschooling,' of 'free-range' parenting or building educational contexts that facilitate unstructured play where time is held at bay to facilitate a fully immersive experience. In critical organizational theory as well as critical pedagogy there is increasing interest in 'timeless time'—"the experience of transcending time and one's self by becoming immersed in a captivating present-moment activity or event" (Mainemelis in Berg and Seeber 2016, 26). Timelessness is a space of creativity, say Berg and Seeber, where 'engrossment' in the present is made possible. And then here, in a way that parrots the parenting manuals, they note that the availability of timeless time paradoxically increases the productivity of organizations inviting us to examine the conditions that foster or impede it—critical among those conditions that impede it is simply the stress of having too much to do; a stress they argue we must relieve so that people can get more done (Berg and Seeber 2016, 55).

Education has for so long now been defended as employment training that it is perhaps not surprising that discourses of 'productivity' and 'efficiency' rather than 'creativity' dominate the justification for institutional schooling. In these contexts, disciplining students, and specifically disciplining them to be productive with their time, is a critical mission of the school. In poorer school districts the mission of disciplining students becomes even more central. In one Appalachian high school where over 40% of the students live below the poverty line, there is a particularly vigilant approach to time management: a three-minute passing time between classes, bathroom 'privileges' must be exercised during that time, tardiness policies are strictly enforced and lunch periods are 22 minutes. When one school administrator was asked about the possibility of extending the passing time to five minutes to facilitate bathroom access, she dismissed the possibility outright, suggesting it would just be more time for "kids to get into trouble." As Joe Soss, Richard Fording and Sanford Schram have argued, in their work *Disciplining the Poor: Neoliberal Paternalism and the Persistent Power of Race* (2011), citizenship is differently operationalized for the poor, and particularly for poor adolescents the centrality of temporal discipline is evident in the schools. Disciplining in schools is about training people for an accelerated society even when they will be part of the decelerated ghetto or holler. No one familiar with Foucault will find the idea of schools as a site of disciplining at all novel. But here the relevance is the contrast with many of the cases for elite education that seem to work from the assumption that this kind of disciplining is at odds with critical aims of education for citizenship: where accomplishing these aims requires escaping such discipline.

So, while at one end of the socioeconomic spectrum we worry about providing discipline, at the other end, we worry about burnout. Both are concerns about prescribed futures. For example, a group of Harvard researchers studying college transitions assert that a gap year could be "an answer to the burnout faced by ultra-ambitious students who have competed to get into the right schools and colleges, and at 18 are already feeling the pressure to think about the right professional schools and the right careers. The increasing popularity of gap years in the U.S. could signal increased efforts to combat the workaholic culture that has proliferated at elite American higher-education institutions" (Green 2016). But, the increasing willingness of high-performing students to take time off stands in contrast with the recent push to get 'at risk' high-school students straight into college after graduation. This push is borne out of the fear that the longer these students, who typically come from underserved backgrounds, wait, the less likely they are to enroll in college as time passes. Surveys consistently note that there is a positive relationship between estimated parental income and student gap years. A 2015 survey indicated that 71% of students taking a gap year received financial support for it from their parents (Green 2016). Choosing to slow down appears to be a privilege.

Timeless Time and Caring Democracy

Clearly having 'too much to do' sets us up for personal and professional failure. But in ways that parallel Gopnik's concerns, there are also risks to arguing that having 'less to do' is valuable because we can ultimately still get more done. Instead of defending 'timeless time' as more productive, I want to defend it as critical to deliberative democratic practice and the development of caring attention.

Martha Nussbaum argues that democratic citizenship requires the development of narrative imagination, imagining what it might be like to be in the shoes of a different person. She sees engagement with literatures in the humanities as a critical part of this. She also argues, drawing on the work of Donald Winnicott, that "play has an important role in shaping democratic citizenship." She cites his work, arguing that democratic equality brings vulnerability and play teaches people "to be capable of living with others without control; it connects the experiences of vulnerability and surprise to curiosity and wonder, rather than to crippling anxiety" (Nussbaum 2010, 100–101). Winnicott and Nussbaum make a persuasive case for the role of literature and the arts—adult forms of play!—to nurturing our capacities to relate well to others. And yet, despite their critical role in the development of democratic capacities, they are often understood as 'wastes of time.' After the first several years of elementary education, schools struggle to create the time for play, college students and parents confront the question of majors: "what do I do with an English degree?" and a Saturday spent reading is a day when "I got nothing done." We both reveal and reinforce the priority of work over citizenship, productive over deliberative skills.

Tronto recognizes that democratic caring is about relationships and relationships require time and space; fostering democratic caring will require asking the question not how do I fit care in around my work, but how do I fit work in around my caring responsibilities. Yet if we are to go beyond the zero-sum model of time scarcity this is not only a question of prioritizing the value of care but recognizing the way the temporal regimes of productive work create the kinds of subjects ill adapted to the temporal regimes consistent with caring relationships. The irony may be that democratic caring requires going slow while the precarity of care work makes the risks of slowing down untenable. 'Slow food' and 'slow professors,' 'slow classrooms' and 'slow yoga' are consistent with the temporal regimes of the relatively privileged.

Meanwhile, the emphasis on speed, efficiency and measurable individual outcomes shapes the temporal orientation of the relatively more vulnerable—from students in impoverished school districts to care workers who—despite often having less reliable access to the resources of an accelerated world, resources like reliable transportation or reliable communication—are expected to 'keep up.' The housekeeper or childcare provider who faces a two-hour commute from affordable housing to work each day is still expected to be on time. The rural hospice nurse with a 45-minute drive on unpredictable back roads is still expected to get to work. A defining feature of their vulnerability is that they are expected to participate in accelerated culture even while they often inhabit spaces of isolation—rural 'hollers' and urban 'ghettos'—that are being left behind. More often than not, life in these spaces is not leisurely or slow but rather governed by the anxiety to keep up and get out.

Under neoliberalism we naturalize the market as an institution that is both inevitable and moral. Markets are seen to produce 'fair compensation' and 'fair distribution' through the wealth that is a consequence of 'efficient production of goods.' These are bound up with a labor theory of value and very specifically capitalist temporalities that clearly undermine our ability to care well, our ability to deliberate well and ultimately, as the work of Moishe Postone (1993) demonstrates, capitalism's temporalities undermine labor as the source of value. It is here that the possibilities for an alternative temporality, one compatible with prioritizing both care and democracy, become an imaginative possibility.

This imaginative act is an ambitious one. Neoliberalism's productive impulses and competitive efficiencies create subjects who are "anxious, ashamed, resentful, and exhausted" (Kotsko 2018, 125). This anxious, perpetually insecure and readily fearful subject is the constitutive work of neoliberal time. Such subjects don't have time to waste on a deliberative politics within which we might share the "recognition that the world we inhabit is something we made collectively, as a society, and therefore, that we could also have made differently" (Graeber 2018, 238).

Engaging in this process of remaking requires a confrontation with a central paradox of work. While many workers see their work as meaningless "bullshit," employment is also a primary source of "self-worth" (Graeber 2018, 241). That we derive our 'self-worth' from jobs many of us think are 'bullshit' would seem to make no sense. But this merely illustrates the perversity of neoliberalism as a comprehensive account of social, political and moral order. Meaningful work requires a break with, a challenge to, market logics, in Adam Kotsko's terms, an alternative 'political theological' space for taking collective responsibility for directing production and distribution of economic goods. And it is constructing this slow space of deliberation that is ultimately critical on his account:

> it does not matter whether the forms of collective action that direct production are conceived as belonging to the 'state' or the 'economy'—in fact the practice of collective deliberation about production would represent the most durable possible break with that foundational binary of the modern world. (Kotsko 2018, 142)

Because neoliberalism here rejects the binary between economic and political, Kotsko also rejects Wendy Brown's account that it is marked by the infiltration of economic logics into the political; those logics have always already been political and ultimately theological. But Kotsko shares with Brown the concern that neoliberal ideology undermines particular political practices, ones I have argued are central to meaningful democracy: "Neoliberal ideology has conditioned us all to be suspicious of any prospect for deliberate, conscious social change" (Kotsko 2018, 143).

When we naturalize the market and the neoliberal orientation to time that it produces it might seem that there is nothing to deliberate about. But there is good reason to believe that neoliberal time is neither necessary to nor good for our collective lives. The vast majority of us—the global 99%—have plenty of incentive to imagine and enact an alternative. We might start by drawing on traditions of critical political economy. Postone (1993), for example, pushes us to think about the possibilities of historicizing the category of labor and thinking about its possibilities beyond capitalism. We have reached the point where the productive potential of advanced capitalist societies means:

that 'extra time' for the many potentially emerges, reducing socially necessary labor time and transforming the structure of labor and the relationship of work to social life. Indeed, the possibility exists for society to transform the social meaning of time, according to which there would still be an 'economy of time' but the form of wealth would not be temporal; rather, people would control the economy of time for their own benefit (Miller 2004, 220).

The realization of these possibilities depends on deliberation—a collective process of purposefully distinguishing practices of care that should be maintained and other practices that should be created and fostered in ways consistent with flourishing. As Tronto admonishes:

> We have got things backwards now. The key to living well, for all people, is to live a care-filled life, a life in which one is well cared for by others when one needs it, cares well for oneself, and has room to provide for the caring—for other people, animals, institutions, and ideals—that gives one's life its particular meaning. … The purpose of economic life is to support care, not the other way around. (Tronto 2013, 170)

'Caring democracy' requires not just more time for care and more time for caring deliberation, it requires sustaining an alternative temporal regime, one that resists the commodification of care and care workers and notions of 'productive' democracy. Hours spent keeping the lonely company or holding hands with the dying are not hours "wasted." Similarly, hours spent deliberating are not 'wasted' when we fail to accomplish agreement. Democracy as a process of relating, educating and caring for one another is slow. But it is this kind of pace and space that generates both citizen-subjects and citizen relationships critical to robust democracy. And if our democratic concerns are to be at the center rather than the margins of our collective lives, we will have to insist on the time to care.

References

Berg, Maggie, and Barbara K. Seeber. 2016. *The Slow Professor: Challenging the Culture of Speed in the Academy*. Toronto: University of Toronto Press.

Brown, Wendy. 2015. *Undoing the Demos: Neoliberalism's Stealth Revolution*. New York: Zone Books.

Eckenwiler, Lisa. 2020. Ethics and Careworker Migration. *International Encyclopedia of Philosophy*. https://www.iep.utm.edu/cw-migra/. Accessed 25 March 2020.

Ehrenreich, Barbara. 2014. Its Expensive to Be Poor. *The Atlantic*. https://www.theatlantic.com/business/archive/2014/01/it-is-expensive-to-be-poor/282979/. Accessed 10 September 2019.

Fisher, Berenice, and Joan C. Tronto. 1990. Toward a Feminist Theory of Caring. In *Circles of Care: Work and Identity in Women's Lives*, ed. Emily Abel and Margaret Nelson. Albany: SUNY Press.

Folbre, Nancy. 2001. *The Invisible Heart: Economics and Family Values*. New York: New Press.

———. 2009. *Greed, Lust and Gender: A History of Economic Ideas*. Oxford: Oxford University Press.

Fraser, Nancy. 2016. Contradictions of Capital and Care. *New Left Review* 100: 99–117.

Gopnik, Adam. 2018. The Parenting Paradox. *The New Yorker*, January 29, 65–67.

Graeber, David. 2018. *Bullshit Jobs: A Theory*. New York: Simon & Schuster.

Green, Adrienne. 2016. How Common Is a Gap Year? *The Atlantic*. https://www.theatlantic.com/education/archive/2016/05/how-common-is-a-gap-year/480921/. Accessed 11 September 2019.

Harvey, David. 2005. *Neoliberalism: A Brief History*. New York: Oxford University Press.

Hochschild, Arlie. 2012. *The Outsourced Self: Intimate Life in Market Times*. New York: Metropolitan Books.

Kotsko, Adam. 2018. *Neoliberalism's Demons: On the Political Theology of Late Capital*. Stanford: Stanford University Press.

Mainemelis, Charalampos. 2001. When the Muse Takes It All: A Model for the Experience of Timelessness in Organisations. *The Academy of Management Review* 26 (4): 548–565.

Mangalingdan, J.P. 2017. PayPal CEO: Its Expensive to Be Poor. *Yahoo Finance*, September 25. https://finance.yahoo.com/news/paypal-ceo-expensive-poor-221202508.html. Accessed 11 September 2019.

Miller, Karen. 2004. The Question of Time in Postone's Time, Labor and Social Domination. *Historical Materialism* 12 (3): 209–237.

Nedelsky, Jennifer. Forthcoming. *Part-Time for All: A Care Manifesto*. New York: Oxford University Press.

Nussbaum, Martha C. 2010. *Not for Profit: Why Democracy Needs the Humanities*. Princeton: Princeton University Press.

Polletta, Francesca. 2002. *Freedom Is an Endless Meeting*. Chicago: University of Chicago.

Postone, Moishe. 1993. *Time, Labor and Social Domination*. Cambridge: Cambridge University Press.

Scheuerman, William E. 2005. Busyness and Citizenship. *Social Research* 72 (2): 447–470.

Sennett, Richard. 1998. *The Corrosion of Character: The Personal Consequences of Work in the New Capitalism*. New York: Norton Publishing.

Sevenhuijsen, Selma. 2014. Care and Attention. https://ethicsofcare.org/wp-content/uploads/2014/02/AandachtHUU2014SLS.pdf. Accessed 11 September 2019.

Shippen, Nicole Marie. 2014. *Decolonizing Time: Work, Leisure and Freedom*. New York: Palgrave.

Solnit, Rebecca. 2003. The Annihilation of Time and Space. *New England Review* 24 (1): 5–19.

Soss, Joe, Richard Fording, and Sanford Schram. 2011. *Disciplining the Poor: Neoliberal Paternalism and the Persistent Power of Race*. Chicago: University of Chicago.

Tronto, C. Joan. 1993. *Moral Boundaries: A Political Argument for the Ethic of Care*. New York: Routledge.

———. 2013. *Caring Democracy: Markets, Equality and Justice*. New York: New York University Press.

White, Julie Anne. 2000. *Democracy, Justice and the Welfare State: Reconstructing Public Care*. University Park: Pennsylvania State University Press.

Wolin, Sheldon. 1997. What Time Is It? *Theory and Event* 1 (1). Project MUSE. https://doi.org/10.1353/tae.1991.0003.

Young, Iris. 2000. *Inclusion and Democracy*. New York: Oxford University Press.

PART II

Applications in Different Contexts

CHAPTER 9

Caring Democracy: How Should Concepts Travel?

Joan C. Tronto

Introduction

Can the conceptual framework of 'caring democracy' be applied beyond the time and place where it first emerged? On the one hand, the chapters in this volume, inspired by the concept, attest to its ability to stimulate intellectual work elsewhere. On the other hand, though, the issue is more problematic. After all, every intellectual endeavor starts in a particular place and time. In *Caring Democracy* (Tronto 2013), I began with an acknowledgment that the book is primarily about the case I know best, which is the United States. This is not because I believe American experience is more universal or more valuable, but that this is the only case I really know well enough to describe.[1]

[1] And, of course, I have had the privilege of an academic position in a country in the Global North which has allowed me to become a scholar of these questions. It is important to keep always in mind the power dimensions that create such privileges and who benefits.

J. C. Tronto (✉)
University of Minnesota, Minneapolis, MN, USA

The City University of New York, New York, NY, USA
e-mail: jctronto@umn.edu

P. Urban, L. Ward (eds.), *Care Ethics, Democratic Citizenship and the State*, International Political Theory,
https://doi.org/10.1007/978-3-030-41437-5_9

As many have observed, there is a danger that as theories and ideas travel, even under the best of circumstances and with the best of intentions, they bring a widespread and often unacknowledged set of assumptions with them. In many circumstances, traveling theories and ideas are not only curiously out of place, more seriously, they may also operate as a form of dominating power, as a wide range of scholars concerned with postcolonial and decolonizing thinking have observed.[2]

Is it possible for scholars committed to making claims for more justice and more caring futures to avoid, or to mitigate against, these power-imbalanced effects? Is there any reason to expect that care ethics theories (which ironically grow, in part, out of a desire to avoid overly abstract and universalizing categories that distort human reality) can avoid committing a similar form of epistemic injustice (Fricker 2007) or inflicting both epistemic and other forms of violence? Indeed, even if we can take some refuge in the ways that care operates as local practices, theorists of care ethics must also recognize that 'care ethics' and all theories of care also operate as discursive practices, and thus can enhance ideologies committed to dominating ends. Good intentions are no defense if the end result of one's intellectual work is to create forms of domination.

That care ethics, in particular, has some explaining to do in this regard has long been established. More than twenty years ago, Uma Narayan noted how discourses of care in the nineteenth-century UK were deliberately meant to buttress imperialist practices, especially in persuading women to join forces with imperialism. She concluded:

> While aspects of care discourse have the potential virtue of calling attention to vulnerabilities that mark relationships between differently situated persons, care discourse also runs the risk of being used to ideological ends where these 'differences' are defined in self-serving ways by the dominant and powerful. (Narayan 1995, 136)[3]

Although it is not usually framed this way, if we look more broadly we will also see many harmful care discourses explicated. Spivak's account of "white men saving brown women from brown men" (1987) is a

[2] Among writers who consider postcolonial and decolonial thoughts who have been helpful in structuring the arguments here are Spivak (1987, 1988), Shilliam (2011a, b), Connell (2007), Comaroff and Comaroff (2012), as well as texts cited elsewhere in this chapter. See also Raghuram et. al. (2009).

[3] Compare Marion Smiley's critique of paternalism in this volume.

protectionist care discourse, as is the neopopulist refrain of protection against migrants and dangerous others.[4]

But one need not even leave home to have practiced care ethics in a narrowed frame. While White feminist scholars of care have been somewhat attentive to concerns of race and class,[5] there is still much work to do here. For example, most discussions of the origins of the term 'ethics of care' do not include a citation to Patricia Hill Collins in *Black Feminist Thought* (Collins 1990, 262–266). Collins noted the similarity between African epistemological assumptions and three central components of an 'ethic of caring': an emphasis on individual uniqueness, on the appropriateness of emotion in dialogues, and on the capacity for empathy (264). Collins also argued that this ethics of caring gained institutional support in the Black Church, and it applied to the thinking of Black men as well as women. This different path into ethics of caring thus already situated care ethics differently vis-à-vis both gender and power, which were to be issues in feminist accounts of care ethics as well. Much writing about care from African-American perspectives has failed to make it into American scholars' reading lists. Surely, though, such work as Vanessa Siddle Walker's and John R. Snarey's work on *Race-ing Moral Formation: African American Perspectives on Care and Justice* (Siddle Walker and Snarey 2004), Christina Sharpe's *In the Wake: On Blackness and Being* (Sharpe 2016)[6] and Freeden Blume Oeur's *Black Boys Apart* (Oeur 2018) are examples of this literature. In 2014, Olena Hankivsky offered a critique of care ethics that drew upon intersectional analyses to challenge the focus exclusively upon gender. Hankivsky raised the concern that by focusing primarily on gender, scholars of care ethics missed many dimensions of the power issues. She thus argued that "an important but largely under-investigated theoretical resource for further developing care ethics is intersectionality." Nevertheless, Hankivsky also observed that the obverse claim is also true; scholars of intersectionality "have not paid much attention to care as a practice that shape human lives." Thus, her conclusion that "care theory

[4] On the harmful nature of protectionist care discourses, see Young (2003).

[5] Among exceptions, see, for example, Mignon Duffy (2011).

[6] "Living as I have argued we do in the wake of slavery, in spaces where we were never meant to survive, or have been punished for surviving and for daring to claim or make spaces of something like freedom, we yet reimagine and transform spaces for an practices of an ethics of care (as in repair, maintenance, attention), an ethics of seeing, and of *being* in the wake as consciousness; as a way of remembering and observance that started with the door of no return, continued in the hold of the ship and on the shore" (Sharpe 2016, 130–131).

would benefit from developing more complex analyses of diversity and cross-cutting relations of power" (Hankivsky 2014, 262).

Will the distorting dangers of such oversights now be compounded? As care ethics travels beyond its originary cultures to other locations, the dangers of misreading care elsewhere as if it were care at home is compounded. Scholars such as the geographer Parvati Raghuram have already noted the importance of *place* for care ethics, and the usual assumption of a denatured western place as the origin of care ethics (Raghuram 2016).

From an ethical perspective, many early critiques of care ethics were concerned to disrupt the close connection of care with relationships, because, critics observed, to speak of maintaining relationships is not yet to discern which relationships are worth preserving, and which ones not. Hankivsky (2004) observed that so-called second-generation care ethics helped to solve this problem arguing that care always had to be placed in the larger contexts of power relationships in which care relations were a part.

More recently, a number of scholars have criticized care ethics for its provincialism. Kanchana Mahadevan notes in her book *Between Femininity and Feminism* that western feminists often ignore the work of bodies in care because their privilege keeps them above such concerns. She writes, "Since Western feminists have been similarly privileged with respect to women from poorer nations, they need to apply their critique of patriarchy to themselves. Self-criticism on the part of Western feminism and non-Western feminism's activist criticism can allow for greater egalitarian intersections between them" (Mahadevan 2014, 229). For Mahadevan and others, the attachment of feminist ideals to autonomy and liberal individualism are sometimes problematic.

Olena Hankivsky, also following such thinkers as Rita Kaur Dhamoon, has argued that care would benefit from a more intersectional analysis (Hankivsky 2014; Dhamoon 2011). Hankivsky endorses Patricia Hill Collins's idea of a 'domination matrix' that complicates a binary account of being powerful/powerless. When feminists emphasize their relative powerlessness, they provide themselves with an opportunity to avoid being reflexive about their own practices of 'privileged irresponsibility.' It was such concerns that animated Tronto's turn to democratic care as a way to broaden questions of power and the intersections of class, race, and other grounds for domination with relationships of care. The next step, though, is to recognize how 'Northern' forms of care presume an association of care ethics with western forms of feminism that might not be the primary entry point for engagement with ideas about care elsewhere in the world.

Consider, as another example, Stephanie Collins's succinct argument that the 'core of care ethics' involves this claim: "dependency relationships generate responsibilities" (Collins 2015). At first glance, this approach is to some extent a helpful way to escape the too-close connection of care ethics to feminism. After all, not all dependency relationships are gendered, though most are. But the problem with this framework is that 'relationships' can be cast too narrowly and follow other lines of power in any given society. Further, dependency is also inherent in structures of domination and oppression (Young 1990; Plumwood 1993) As a result, an outcome of this framework is that it is likely to reify relationships, and especially to see relationships that historically track as 'care,' such as those in families, to be overvalued. Further, Collins's account puts too much emphasis on a form of incapacity as a starting point for care. But much care begins or ends in forms of mutual life. Vulnerability is important, but it is not the only grounds for care.

The significance of these problems is that this account of care takes us away from noting that care ethics is always about power. Neocolonialism as a discourse of care is a form of power relations. As people with disabilities often note, assuming that care is about dependency already puts people with disabilities into a separate category of lacking something. That is, the very assumption of dependency already creates a dynamic of power. Insofar as care is seen as meeting people's needs, it already assumes that some people are needy. Tronto and others have argued that, indeed, all people are needy. But this construction in a liberal democratic society has a different valence than might other assumptions. To what extent, then, does this backgrounded set of assumptions already create a power dynamic that requires, and the least self-reflective practices?

What is required, then, is to step back to a more theoretical level and consider the meta-theoretical issues involved in asking: what kind of theory is 'care ethics?' From there, the issue of addressing how to avoid, or to mitigate, over-reaching and possibly colonialist or imperialist forms of analysis are possible. The argument in this chapter proceeds by beginning with a short account of the historical emergence of some 'mainstream care ethics' in order to locate it before it can be dislocated. From there, the chapter considers how alternative framings might be possible.

Provincializing Feminist Care Ethics

The first step to take in eschewing a false universalism to any set of ideas is to 'provincialize' those ideas, that is, to show how they are not universal (Chakrabarty 2000). What distinguishes feminist care ethics up to this point from other approaches are two key sets of assumptions. First, obviously, feminist care ethics made feminist assumptions and, second, feminist care ethics in the Global North made liberal democratic assumptions as well.

Care Ethics as a Feminist Ethics

The first question to consider is whether care ethics is necessarily feminist; after all, non-feminist scholars have also written about care (inter alia, see) (Foucault 1986; Frankfurt 1982; Amoore 2006; Moore 1992; Mayeroff 1990). Olena Hankivsky's extremely useful separation of care ethics into two generations might allow us to stage the debate (Hankivsky 2004). For thinkers who consider themselves part of the 'first generation,' where care is taken to be about specific dyadic relations of care, they might argue that they do not have to think more broadly about these questions, since at the level of individual caring, one for another, these problems of power do not disappear but they are not so broad as to reach cultural dimensions. But there are two arguments against this view. First, the idea that care is only limited to dyads is a culturally specific way to think about care relations. Second, to separate care relations from their larger social context[7] is to leave too much to 'unintended consequences,' which is often an argument to limit responsibility.

Expanding care beyond individualized care practices, what this so-called second generation of feminist care ethicists brought to light, made concerns about the nature of power relationships central to care ethics. Tronto had argued as early as 1987 that care ethics was akin to a 'power of the weak' in that, not only gendered, but other marginalized groups as well were more likely to think in less universal frames for morality. In that essay, she drew upon work by Sandra Harding to show that some African philosophies, among others, were focused on moral concerns that did not grow out of individualistic and universalized ways of framing moral questions.

[7] Of course, this is not to assert that all second- and perhaps third-generation care ethics writings address this issue.

Different versions of dynamics of power were also noted elsewhere. For example, Nordic scholars (e.g., Waerness 1990; Leira 1994) had noted that care burdens in households in the welfare state reflected other assumptions about the nature of the family that were deeply patriarchal. In Nordic countries, care was not far away from the ways in which assumptions about how women's exclusion from the labor market shaped their participation in public life and argued that greater attachment to the workforce for women would solve many of these problems.

Thus, Virginia Held explicitly excluded a variety of arguments that seemed to be close to ethics of care in her 2006 book:

> My own view is that to include nonfeminist versions of valuing care among the moral approaches called the ethics of care is to unduly disregard the history of how this ethics has developed and come to be a candidate for serious consideration among contemporary moral theories. The history of the development of the contemporary ethics of care is the history of recent feminist progress. (Held 2006, 22)

But Held's exclusion failed to note that, among the elements she labeled as non-feminist in this passage were religious traditions that are not so much non-feminist as they are non-liberal.

Care Ethics and Its Liberal Origins

A second 'local condition' of care ethics is its connection with liberal theory. From the beginning of so-called second-wave feminism, there have been differences about how 'liberal democratic' feminist theory would be. Western feminist theorists were not always explicit about the ways in which liberal democratic values continued to inform their writings. Nevertheless, such assumptions clearly inform the work of many theorists of care ethics. Consider, for example, Eva Kittay (1999), who frames her work within liberal political theory and aims to use the ethic of care to correct Rawls's assumptions in his original position (Kittay 1999, 78–79 and passim), and for Held, for whom care is meant to operate alongside legal systems that are liberal and democratic. Similarly Nel Noddings (Noddings 2002, 2015) seems to assume the continuing structure of institutions in her social and political writings, Nedelsky (2011) assumes a liberal state, and Tronto (2013), though arguing for a more radically democratic form, nonetheless endorses liberal democratic practices of rights.

Not all feminist scholars agreed to honor all liberal democratic values. An illustration of this conflict within feminist thoughts concerns the difference in value placed upon, and different accounts of, autonomy as a goal. Feminist scholars have devoted a great deal of thought in recent decades to the critique of autonomy as it is manifested and about its value as a key goal for political life (Barvosa-Carter 2007; Koggel 1998; Layton 2004; Mackenzie and Stoljar 2000a, b; Nedelsky 2012; Verkerk 2001). In more recent years, this discussion has returned within care ethics itself as a discussion of the centrality of vulnerability and dependency within care ethics (see Casalini, this volume). Once again, the context of liberal thought shapes how these questions are shaped within feminist theory.

Perhaps most seriously, though, is another dividing line that separates liberal thought from more radical approaches and which speaks to basic ideas in liberal feminist thought. In a more radical tradition, to draw upon Iris Young's framing of the issue (Young 1990), the matter of injustice is not a matter of the maldistribution of resources but of the existence of forces of domination and oppression. So, too, one can understand the problems of care in liberal democratic societies as a distributive problem (think of Kittay's solution) or as a deeper problem of forms of domination that shape social institutions from the family to schools to workplaces, and so on. This point is made more explicit in the chapters in the volume by Yayo Okano and Satomi Manuyana and Adriana Jesenková. The extent to which theories of care need to be attentive to distinctions about wealth that are reflected in family structure are therefore more or less important to particular feminist scholars of care.

Other assumptions that somehow came along with liberal assumptions in political theory also worked their way into feminist political thought. Among these was a presumption that looked upon religious traditions with some degree of skepticism. Some feminist critiques of multiculturalism are roundly criticized for their inattentiveness to religion. Indeed, many world religious traditions posit care (and other forms of) relations between deities and humans and ground their cultural practices of, and commitments to, care in religious frames. The secularism that is part of the western separation of public and private, church and state, actually mark liberal and western forms of care, but often are taken to be more universal. Care ethics has already been compared to a number of other global intellectual traditions over the past thirty years. Consider scholars have spoken about the connection between care and Confucian thought (Herr 2003), care and Ubuntu (Waghid 2010, 2019), care and Jewish thought

(Batnitzky 2003), care and Hindu texts (see especially Dalmiya 2016), care and Islamic thought (Munawar 2019), and others. Obvious connections could also be made to Buddhist traditions and to various Native American traditions.

To conclude this section, then, while Held also discussed ways that feminist care ethics needed to be broadened to be more attentive to difference, for example, by including issues of race, she did not entirely acknowledge how much all that she counted as 'contemporary moral theories' began and ended in liberal democratic frames (Mahadevan 2014). Because this fissure exists (as do others) within western feminist theory, it is no surprise that it manifests itself in the ways that western feminist theory can travel.[8] Since our concern in this chapter is with care ethics, the larger questions about the purposes and practices of feminist theory cannot be fully explored here.

As many others, including Mahadevan (2014), have argued, assuming that one's local conditions prevail everywhere else accords a kind of epistemic privilege that quickly translates into forms of power, privilege, and disregard for others. From here it is more likely that the kinds of harms discussed earlier will occur. Once we recognize, then, that care ethics in its western feminist forms might suffer from the problem of making its provincial claims into more universal ones, the next question arises about whether such provincialisms can be overcome.

How to Travel and Leave Domination Behind

So far we have established that care ethics may fall into the same problems as other approaches that try to be universal; they can end up being harmful or counterproductive if they give in to categories that appear universal or neutral but are not so.[9] If not all care grows out of feminist or liberal feminist assumptions, we might well ask, is there anything that distinguishes care as a concept? After all, right-wing authoritarians also assert that they are engaged in practices of care.

[8] To demonstrate this point thoroughly would go beyond the limits of this short chapter; indeed, it would require a retelling of much of recent feminist thought about disputes between more universalistic thinkers such as Martha Nussbaum and critics of that approach, including, for example, Mahadevan (also in this volume).

[9] Another example of this problem is the treatment of worthy refugees in Europe.

A key way to allay such concerns is to clarify that feminist care ethics is a kind of critical care ethics (Barnes 2012, 2015; Barnes et al. 2015). Critical theory, as Iris Young succinctly described it, starts from the gap between human suffering and the desire to end that suffering (Young 1990). Rather than trying to come up with any universal answer, Young's suggestion that the way to justice is through an exploration of the nature of injustice should guide us here; uncaring care may teach us a lot about how to proceed. Indeed, let's use Narayan's example of care as a discourse of colonialism, measure it against what has been said about the nature of care ethics, and use that starting point as a way to try to winnow down what we might want to say care is and is not, should and should not, be included in it. Narayan's example begins from the standpoint that British women especially became convinced of the value of imperialism because they were helping to 'civilize' and 'Christianize' the people of India. She also notes how this starting point blocked women from seeing the harm that their 'care' was causing as it disrupted society and people's daily lives.

Several points come into view from this example of uncaring care. First, Daniel Engster's profound suggestion that care should avoid doing harm is a good starting point (Engster 2007). Although this premise does not make clear how one knows when one is or is not doing harm, it provides a baseline. A second obvious point is that Narayan's uncaring carers simply imposed their worldview and assumed that the colonized needed to be civilized and Christianized. So another possible solution is to try to make certain that 'the politics of needs interpretation' (Fraser 1989) happens as fairly and as openly as possible. Third, scholars of care need to be deeply attentive to the scope of claims that they make about the nature of care. For example, virtually everyone in the globe now seems caught up in neoliberal economic orders, and so a care critique that focuses on these more universal elements might be able to presume it has more universal application. Ironically, of course, neoliberalism is a traveling concept itself. But those who wish to envelope the entire world in its framework are not dismayed by the ways in which it flattens and destroys local customs, habits, and ways of being—that is part of the logic of neoliberalism. Insofar as care does stand as a critique of neoliberal economics, it may be able to make some universal appeal. Nevertheless, what a care critique of neoliberal policies looks like in one place will be different from similar concerns elsewhere. For example, the ways that families are disrupted when thrown back on themselves and told to be 'resilient' looks different in different global settings. The injunctions to do no harm, to be sensitive to needs, and to be attentive to context even when it seems that one has not made any untoward assumptions are obvious.

Others have suggested several more ways to begin to think about a critical ethics of care. Parvati Raghuram has proposed another dimension to the solution: location, dislocation, and relocation. Observing that most care ethics has arisen in the Global North, she argues that "dislocation is crucial if we are to have a care ethics which is attuned to the difference that place makes" (Raghuram 2016, 513). Thus, recognizing that one is engaged in a process of travel is a first step. Farah Godrej has suggested ways in which cosmopolitan ideas might travel, by the traveler being more cognizant of their position. In this way she reframes cosmopolitanism, which she views "rather than being attached to a particular set of normative or institutional assumptions, becomes an ongoing set of practices by scholars themselves. It is a series of methodological interventions involving the *disciplined* carrying out of dislocative and relocative practices, which leads to a shift in *disciplinary* self-understanding" (Godrej 2011, 143). She writes, "Certain self-conscious positionalities and self-reflexive engagements with one's own location are crucial modalities of a cosmopolitan theorizing," including "self-dislocation" and then "self-relocation" (ibid., 17–18).

There is also an epistemic dimension to this switch from imperious observer or caregiver to accepting traveler. In her beautiful meditation on care in the context of Hindu teachings contained in the Mahābāratha, Vrinda Dalmiya proposes that a key element of the ethic of care is the capacity to exercise the virtue of 'relational humility': "The relinquishing of epistemic power oneself while empowering the other comes with relational humility—the intellectual virtue that actively limits our own cognitive achievements while establishing the knower-hood of others—is thus a necessary condition for a truly *interactive* caring/knowing relation" (Dalmiya 2016, 260). Sophie Bourgault (this volume) makes a similar analysis by turning to the thought of Hans Georg Gadamer to urge us to make listening central to care.

One of the limitations of this approach, though, is that it depends in part upon the competence of the self in these practices of location and dislocation.

But why should scholars of care engage in such difficult reconsiderations of their positions? Cannot that not be the work of others who wish to join into the conversation? While Dalmiya makes the argument that virtue requires 'relational humility,' we may well wonder whether virtue is the goal of scholars, or whether a commitment to virtue is sufficient to change people's perceptions of their own power and privilege. On the other hand, there are also a number of approaches to addressing this issue that go beyond individuals and require practices of solidarity and responsibility to address these possible dangers.

First, some scholars call upon solidarity. Given the harm that occurs from western women assuming various forms of privilege, Mahadevan begins from what she perceives to be "in a spirit of solidarity with global feminisms" (Mahadevan 2014, xxii). She thus follows Chandra Mohanty and argues that only *solidarity* with the situations of others—more than imagining oneself in the other's position but accepting and acting from that position—can adequately escape from models of being the tourist or an explorer in search of victimized others (Mahadevan 2014, 232–233). Such solidarity begins, she writes, in self-criticism:

> The system of privilege among women cannot be remedied merely through cultural reform, as Western feminists such as Okin suggest. Rather, it requires a critical intervention in tune with the democratic outlook of Western feminism. The latter questioned the very notion of a singular human subject as grounded on male freedom that presupposes feminine carework. Since Western feminists have been similarly privileged with respect to women from poorer nations, they need to apply their critique of patriarchy to themselves. Self-criticism on the part of Western feminism and non-Western feminism's activist criticism can allow for greater egalitarian intersections between them. (Mahadevan 2014, 229)

A second way to put this question is to frame it as a question of *responsibility*; indeed, the ideas of an ethic of care and an ethic of responsibility have been connected since Gilligan's (1982) original work. One of the key innovations of caring democracy is to think about the political dimension of caring practices from the standpoint of responsibility. Unlike the concepts of obligation and duty, which start from an individual and consider an abstract answer to the question, 'what do I owe,' responsibility is grounded in a response—it necessarily requires several parties who are in active negotiation and renegotiation about who should do what. As Margaret Walker eloquently put it, "An 'ethics of responsibility' as a normative view would try to put people and responsibilities in the right places with respect to each other" (Walker 2007, 84). As Iris

Young demonstrated in her description of a 'social connection model' of responsibility, not all responsibilities are equally felt, and it is possible to make judgments about responsibilities with others even if they are at a distance (Young 2006). Responsibility combats privilege by placing the more powerful party in a relationship in which the less powerful is still able to contest and to reject expectations of care that are improper. And the negotiation about what constitutes proper care is thus at the heart of the matter. In this manner, concerns such as the hierarchical nature of too many social institutions, or defining needs, and of self-reflective practices, become central to negotiating responsibilities across time and space (cf. Tronto 2010).

That care responsibilities have to be negotiated is no necessary guarantee that such negotiations will turn out well. As Walker suggests, the capacity to accept, reject, deflect, assignments of responsibility are always processes in which the relative power positions of those engaged in the negotiations shape the discussion as well as its outcome. For scholars, this realization creates a strong responsibility to engage in research practices that allow such negotiations to be visible and to include everyone. In a recent essay, Brannelly (Brannelly 2018), (in line with the discussion in this volume by Ward, Ray, and Tanner) has proposed that scholars pursuing topics in care ethics need to adopt forms of research practices that guarantee that the needs, concerns, and issues of people whose lives are being investigated, rather than the starting questions of researchers, are foremost. This approach provides another check upon the danger that researchers will use their own judgments in the place of others. So will the commitments that were mentioned earlier, to virtuous pursuit of one's goals, as Dalmiya suggested in describing 'relational humility,' as Mahadevan describes in a kind of 'solidarity' that will draw upon democratic values, and as Godrej describes in 'cosmopolitanism.'

Thus, a commitment to doing no harm, but recognizing the danger of the harms that can be done, point the way for future research in care ethics to proceed in ways that exemplify, in themselves, practices of caring. This description of a kind of democratic caring practice beyond the normal institutions of states is possible, and it might even provide new and innovative ways to think about caring democratic practices within states (compare the chapters by Urban and Stensöta in this volume for such examples). Such a possibility should provide some hope to those of us who would like to join in a struggle to fashion a more just and caring world.

References

Amoore, Louise. 2006. Invisible Subject(s): Work and Workers in the Global Political Economy. In *Poverty and the Production of World Politics: Unprotected Workers in the Global Political Economy*, ed. Matt Davies and Magnus Ryner, 13–37. New York: Palgrave Macmillan.

Barnes, Marian. 2012. *Care in Everyday Life: An Ethic of Care in Practice*. Bristol: Policy Press.

———. 2015. Beyond the Dyad: Exploring the Multidimensionality of Care. In *Ethics of Care: Critical Advances in International Perspective*, ed. Marian Barnes, Tula Brannelly, Lizzie Ward, and Nicki Ward, 31–43. Bristol: Policy Press.

Barnes, Marian, Tula Brannelly, Lizzie Ward, and Nicki Ward, eds. 2015. *Ethics of Care: Critical Advances in International Perspective*. Bristol: Policy Press.

Barvosa-Carter, E. 2007. Mestiza Autonomy as Relational Autonomy: Ambivalence the Social Character of Free Will. *Journal of Political Philosophy* 15 (1): 1–21.

Batnitzky, Leora. 2003. Dependency and Vulnerability: Jewish and Feminist Existentialist Constructions of the Human. In *Women and Gender in Jewish Philosophy*, ed. Hava Tirsosh-Samuelson. Indianapolis: Indiana University Press.

Brannelly, Tula. 2018. An Ethics of Care Research Manifesto. *International Journal of Care and Caring* 2 (3): 367–378.

Chakrabarty, Dipesh. 2000. *Provincializing Europe Postcolonial Thought and Historical Difference*. Princeton, NJ: Princeton University Press.

Collins, Patricia Hill. 1990. *Black Feminist Thought*. New York: Routledge.

Collins, Stephanie. 2015. *The Core of Care Ethics*. Basingstoke: Palgrave.

Comaroff, Jean, and John L. Comaroff. 2012. *Theory from the South: Or, How Euro-America Is Evolving Toward Africa*. Boulder: Paradigm.

Connell, Raewyn. 2007. *Southern Theory*. Malden, MA: Polity.

Dalmiya, Vrinda. 2016. *Caring to Know: Comparative Care Ethics, Feminist Epistemology, and the Mahābhārata*. New Delhi: Oxford University Press.

Dhamoon, Rita Kaur. 2011. Considerations on Mainstreaming Intersectionality. *Political Research Quarterly* 64 (1): 230–243.

Duffy, Mignon. 2011. *Making Care Count: A Century of Gender, Race, and Paid Care Work*. New Brunswick, NJ: Rutgers University Press.

Engster, Daniel. 2007. *The Heart of Justice: Care Ethics and Political Theory*. New York: Oxford University Press.

Foucault, Michel. 1986. *The History of Sexuality Volume 3: Care of the Self*. New York: Vintage.

Frankfurt, Harry. 1982. The Importance of What We Care About. *Synthese* 53: 257–272.

Fraser, Nancy. 1989. *Unruly Practices: Power, Discourse, and Gender in Contemporary Social Theory*. Minneapolis: University of Minnesota Press.

Fricker, Miranda. 2007. *Epistemic Injustice*. New York: Oxford.
Gilligan, Carol. 1982. *In a Different Voice: Psychological Theory and Women's Development*. Cambridge: Harvard University Press.
Godrej, Farah. 2011. *Cosmopolitan Political Thought: Method, Practice, Discipline*. New York: Oxford University Press.
Hankivsky, Olena. 2004. *Social Policy and the Ethic of Care*. Vancouver: University of British Columbia Press.
———. 2014. Rethinking Care Ethics: On the Promise and Potential of an Intersectional Analysis. *American Political Science Review* 108 (2): 252–264.
Held, Virginia. 2006. *The Ethics of Care: Personal, Political, and Global*. New York: Oxford University Press.
Herr, Ranjoo Seodu. 2003. Is Confucianism Compatible with Care Ethics? A Critique. *Philosophy East and West* 53 (4): 471–489.
Kittay, Eva Feder. 1999. *Love's Labor: Essays on Women, Equality and Dependency*. New York: Routledge.
Koggel, Christine M. 1998. *Perspectives on Equality: Constructing a Relational Theory*. Lanham, MD: Rowman and Littlefield.
Layton, Lynne. 2004. Relational No More. *Annual of Psychoanalysis* 32: 29–42.
Leira, Arnlaug. 1994. Concepts of Care: Loving, Thinking and Doing. *Social Science Review* 68 (2): 185–201.
Mackenzie, Catriona, and Natalie Stoljar. 2000a. Introduction: Autonomy Refigured. In *Relational Autonomy: Feminist Perspectives on Autonomy, Agency, and the Social Self*, ed. Catriona Mackenzie and Natalie Stoljar, 3–34. New York: Oxford University Press.
———, eds. 2000b. *Relational Autonomy: Feminist Perspectives on Autonomy, Agency, and the Social Self*. New York: Oxford University Press.
Mahadevan, Kanchana. 2014. *Between Femininity and Feminism: Colonial and Postcolonial Perspectives on Care*. New Delhi: Indian Council of Philosophical Research.
Mayeroff, Milton. 1990. *On Caring*. New York: Harper.
Moore, Thomas. 1992. *Care of the Soul: A Guide for Cultivating Depth and Sacredness in Everyday Life*. New York: Harper Collins.
Munawar, Sarah. 2019. *In Hajar's Footsteps: A De-Colonial and Islamic Ethic of Care*. University of British Columbia.
Narayan, Uma. 1995. Colonialism and Its Others: Considerations on Rights and Care Discourses. *Hypatia* 10 (2): 133–140.
Nedelsky, Jennifer. 2011. *Law's Relations*. New York: Oxford University Press.
———. 2012. The Reciprocal Relation of Judgment and Autonomy: Walking in Another's Shoes and Which Shoes to Walk In. In *Being Relational: Reflections on Relational Theory and Health Law*, ed. Jocelyn Downie and Jennifer J. Llewellyn, 35–62. Vancouver, Toronto: UBC Press.

Noddings, Nel. 2002. *Starting at Home: Caring and Social Policy*. Berkeley: University of California Press.

———. 2015. Care Ethics and "Caring" Organizations. In *Care Ethics and Political Theory*, ed. Daniel Engster and Maurice Hamington, 72–84. New York: Oxford.

Oeur, Freeden Blume. 2018. *Black Boys Apart: Racial Uplift and Respectability in All-Male Public Schools*. Minneapolis: University of Minnesota Press.

Plumwood, Val. 1993. *Feminism and the Mastery of Nature*. New York: Routledge.

Raghuram, Parvati. 2016. Locating Care Ethics Beyond the Global North. *ACME: An International Journal for Critical Geographies* 15 (3): 511–533.

Raghuram, Parvati, Clare Madge, and Pat Noxolo. 2009. Rethinking Responsibility and Care for a Postcolonial World. *Geoforum* 40 (1): 5–13.

Sharpe, Christina. 2016. *In the Wake: On Blackness and Being*. Durham, NC: Duke University Press.

Shilliam, Robbie. 2011a. Non-Western Thought and International Relations. In *International Relations and Non-Western Thought: Imperialism, Colonialism, and Investigations of Global Modernity*, ed. Robbie Shilliam, 1–11. London: Routledge.

———. 2011b. The Perilous but Unavoidable Terrain of the Non-West. In *International Relations and Non-Western Thought: Imperialism, Colonialism, and Investigations of Global Modernity*, ed. Robbie Shilliam, 12–26. London: Routledge.

Siddle Walker, Vanessa, and John R. Snarey. 2004. *Race-ing Moral Formation: African American Perspectives on Care and Justice*. New York: Teachers College Press.

Spivak, Gayatri. 1987. *In Other Worlds: Essays in Cultural Politics*. New York: Methuen.

———. 1988. Can the Subaltern Speak? In *Marxism and the Interpretation of Culture*, ed. C. Nelson and L. Grossberg. London: Macmillan.

Tronto, Joan C. 2010. Creating Caring Institutions: Politics, Plurality, and Purpose. *Ethics and Social Welfare* 4 (2): 158–171.

———. 2013. *Caring Democracy: Markets, Equality and Justice*. New York: NYU Press.

Verkerk, Marian. 2001. The Care Perspective and Autonomy. *Medicine, Health Care and Philosophy* 4 (3): 289–294. https://doi.org/10.1023/a:1012048907443.

Waerness, Kari. 1990. Informal and Formal Care in Old Age: What Is Wrong with the New Ideology in Scandinavia Today? In *Gender and Caring: Work and Welfare in Britain and Scandinavia*, ed. Claire Ungerson, 110–132. London: Harvester, Wheatsheaf.

Waghid, Yusef. 2010. *Education, Democracy and Citizenship Revised*. Stellenbosch: Sun MeDIA.

———. 2019. *Ubuntu* Caring: Cultivating Moral, Compassionate, and Restorative Justice in University Education. In *Towards a Philosophy of Caring in Higher Education: Pedagogy and Nuances of Care*, 89–96. Basingstoke: Palgrave Macmillan.

Walker, Margaret Urban. 2007. *Moral Understandings: A Feminist Study in Ethics.* 2nd ed. New York: Oxford University Press.

Young, Iris Marion. 1990. *Justice and the Politics of Difference.* Princeton, NJ: Princeton University Press.

———. 2003. The Logic of Masculinist Protection: Reflections on the Current Security State. *Signs: Journal of Women in Culture & Society* 29 (1): 1–24.

———. 2006. Responsibility and Global Justice: A Social Connection Model. *Social Philosophy and Policy* 23 (1): 102–130.

CHAPTER 10

Cosmopolitanism, Care Ethics and Health Care Worker Migration

Kanchana Mahadevan

Health Care as a Global Commodity

The "international commodification of care work" (Tronto 2005, 131) is also a visible Indian phenomenon. An integral factor in India's health care crisis is the paradox of a shortage of health care personnel, despite being a prominent destination for medical tourism and an exporter of health care workers. Health care is perceived as a commodity in continuation with India's colonial past. Public health in contemporary India continues to harbor a deep-rooted colonial assumption, namely that health is a commodity owned by individuals.[1] The opposing camps of British

[1] See Qadeer quoted in Soman and Dasgupta (2003, 4942). Yet, there were also exceptions to such institutionalized regimentation under colonization. For instance, Deepak Kumar notes that W.M. Haffkine had a deep knowledge of Indians and did not regard them all as superstitious. He did not endorse bureaucracy that prevented access to health institutions and felt that in such cases "men" should intervene (see Soman and Dasgupta 2003, 4943).

K. Mahadevan (✉)
Department of Philosophy, University of Mumbai, Mumbai, India

P. Urban, L. Ward (eds.), *Care Ethics, Democratic Citizenship and the State*, International Political Theory,
https://doi.org/10.1007/978-3-030-41437-5_10

administration and Indian nationalism paid scant attention to public health during the colonial period.[2] The post-independence context addressed this vacuum through a focus on planned public health with delivery of services and technology. However, over the years the state responsibility for public health has eroded through neoliberal measures of cost-cutting and privatization.

With its independence from British rule in 1947, the public health care sector in India provided only for 5–10% of care (Sengupta 2005). Although it increased in the decades that followed,[3] investment in the public health care sector in India is much worse than other countries in Asia.[4] It is also marred by rampant absenteeism, indifference and corruption (Baru et al. 2010, 56; Gupta 2005; Sengupta 2005). Thus, most Indians—even those without purchasing power—prefer to pay for private health care rather than avail of subsidized public health institutions (Baru et al. 2010, 52). The explicit neoliberal turn is further emphasized in the *National Health Policy* document of 2017 (National Health Policy 2017)[5] in its orientation toward universal and affordable health care through a collaboration between public and private sectors. Consequently, rather than a fundamental right or a subsidized service, health care is a purchasable good (Qadeer and Chakravarthi 2010, 51).[6]

These shifting policies reveal that the health crisis in India is one of increasing global commodification of health care. On the one hand, India is globally promoted as a "Medical Value Travel"[7] (MVT) (Bhargava 2018) destination.[8] On the other hand, it faces a shortage of health care

[2] See Kabita Ray's discussion in Soman and Dasgupta (2003, 4943). Also see Rao et al. 2011; Palriwala and Neetha, 2012.

[3] In 2005 it rose to 82% for outpatient visits, 58% of inpatient expenditure and 40% of births in institutions.

[4] Between 1950 and 1951, the average expenditure of the annual budget on health was 0.22%, while it has improved to approximately 1% at present.

[5] Henceforth, NHP 2017 and documented as National Health Policy, 2017. It proposes to increase health expenditure to 2.5% over a period of time by 2025 (Bhuyan 2017).

[6] Its declaration of change through Yoga also reveals its commitment to alternative medicine—particularly those coming from a specific cultural-religious context. It also does not propose a system of health taxation in order to address the burgeoning health issues confronting India. The shift in responsibility is also from comprehensive to primary health care (Qadeer and Chakravarthi 2010, 56).

[7] Henceforth, MVT.

[8] India currently controls about 18% of the global market in medical tourism (Bhargava 2018). During the year 2017, there were about 4.95 million medical visitors to India, a figure that is steadily growing (Bhargava 2018).

experts because it exports them. Foreigners who come to India for MVT do so because it is cost-effective and allows procedures not permitted in the West (Sengupta 2005; Gupta 2008).[9] However, the revenues earned through MVT are not necessarily directed to the masses of Indian poor in need of health care.[10] India also faces an alarming shortage of nurses in both rural and urban areas due to nurse migration (IndiaSpend 2017).[11] The "push factors" (Hooper 2008, 684) include lack of employment opportunities within India accompanied by access to English education, training in institutions and the social prestige of working overseas.[12] "Pull factors" (Hooper 2008, 684) comprise a surging demand for nurses, midwives and physicians' assistants (Groenhout 2012, 16).[13] Given this demand, India has joined other home countries in introducing special training facilities for nurses with a Western-oriented curriculum (Crozier 2010, 133; IndiaSpend 2017).

Prima facie, migrating nurses benefit with improved salaries, while scant health care services reach host countries (Hooper 2008, 685). The home countries are also projected as gaining financially with remittances (Hooper 2008, 685). These remittances, along with the finance gained with MVT, can in principle be channeled to resolving deficits—such as those described with reference to India above—making health care widely available in the home country as well. Yet, this triadic system of benefit is not quite played out in a balanced manner. For the most part, the migrant care worker is often alienated in a foreign culture, while home countries struggle for want of health care professionals. The notion of health care as a purchasable commodity hinders its accessibility across class divides. Moreover, the

[9] As Sengupta notes, a shoulder operation would cost £10,000 in the United Kingdom under private care or would require a long wait under the National Health Service (NHS); in India, it can be done within ten days for £1700 (2005). The economy has linked private hospitals in India with firms and public institutions in the West (Apollo with the NHS in the United Kingdom) (Reddy and Qadeer 2010).

[10] See Block (2018).

[11] India is short of 1.94 million nurses. In 2006, the WHO regarded India as facing an impending crisis as the figures for public health workers fell way below the standard limits (Walton-Roberts et al. 2017). There were heavy waves of migration in 1993 and between 2003 and 2009 (Walton-Roberts et al. 2017). This is due to low recruitment in India, migration and dropouts in nursing schools.

[12] Groenhout has articulated an analogical set of push factors with reference to Ghana.

[13] India, along with Philippines, is the largest exporter of nurses to Organisation for Economic Co-operation and Development (OECD) countries (Laguipo 2016). Quality concerns have been raised regarding Philippines (Crozier 2010, 128) and India as well.

care worker's and home country's dependence on the needs of the host country makes their relationship unstable and hierarchical (Hooper 2008, 685).[14] The absence of the projected triadic balance is visible in the reluctance of privileged citizens in host countries to perform care work compelling as Tronto notes, migrants, people of color and women to do so (2013, 2). Further, much of the care work is hidden from the public domain or not acknowledged as meaningful. Citing Harvey, Tronto argues that the neoliberal context in the host countries leads to volatile and ephemeral commodities and capital (2005, 133). It produces flexible and available labor to replace the "industrial working class" with "service" (Tronto 2005, 133). There are greater demands on the physical labor of the service class. As the example of knowledge workers shows, this leads to organizations investing more in their workplace and reducing the distance between work and life. In the resultant "care crisis", there is a deficit of workers in traditional care tasks of teaching, nursing and day-care. This in turn mandates what Tronto terms as "labor mobility" (2005, 134). She addresses the problem on a transnational scale as that of care work being "the new basic raw material imported from the developing world to the developed" (Tronto 2005, 134). Care workers often do not have security of nationhood and have a weak immigration status.[15] Thus for example those who become pregnant often face the danger of deportation.

This shows that the problem of care worker migration and deficit cannot be adequately comprehended by regarding its players as free and equal contracting individuals with prior entitlements. Nor can one think about it in terms of the relationship between abstract individuals and an abstract state/recruitment agency (Groenhout 2012, 11). Groenhout has enlisted libertarian responses within a liberal framework to the problem of deficit called by migration of care workers (6–11). The crisis of care is often perceived as one of apportionment of scant reserves (Tronto 2005, 134). However, these responses assume that the individual has a freedom to choose migration as an alternative overlooking the strong role played by circumstances in such choice. It also assumes that the economy benefits

[14] See Sharma (2011) for a general account of female migration from India, with nurses topping the list. Also see Percot and Irudaya Rajan (2007).

[15] Tronto observes that the care worker's plight in the West is analogous to those of foreigners in Moore's *Utopia* (2005, 131–132). For Moore slaves—both criminals from within the nation and foreigners—perform tasks that require cleaning and nurture. In his blueprint, such slaves are treated well by the citizens of *Utopia*, but then they have to perform arduous labor to be a part of the *Utopia*, which they could leave, if they wanted to.

with remittances; yet the latter do not impact the rural or urban poor in a constructive way, since those who have access to remittances are families that are not abjectly poor. Thus, the extent to which an individualistic approach based on remittances affects health care workers in the public health system is debatable as Groenhout (2012) notes. The privatization of care work makes it a commodity that is only available to those who can afford it. A person with buying power determines the care services that are received.

Migrant Care Workers and Citizenship

Tronto argues that since care is an inevitable dimension of the social environment,[16] it can be regarded as a political norm establishing citizenship. She upholds the institutionalization of care so that it is accessible to the disadvantaged (Tronto 2010). Moreover, it is also a recourse to ensuring care for caregivers (Tronto 2010). Responding to the global migration of care workers, Tronto suggests that migrant care workers in the Western world should be regarded as full citizens rather than partial (Tronto 2013, 10). Caring for infants, ailing or elderly people is not a personal problem, but a public social one. One can extend Tronto's suggestion for citizenship to migrant health care workers. It would address the needs of the population needing care, as well as the workers who give care. With citizenship rights, migrant health care workers would be cared for to make democracy more inclusive. Their sense of belonging will also infuse them with a greater dedication to offer care to those who want it. Democratic citizenship entails a sense of belonging to a larger polity through membership criteria connected to the values of justice and fairness (Tronto 2005, 139).[17] Globalization blurs the divisions between nations with employment mobility across the borders, but nation-states continue to retain borders at the political level. It is in this dual context that the European nations and the United States introduced legal rights for immigrants—who were in dire need of such rights—in the 1960s and 1970s. Tronto

[16] The social encompasses both the private and the public sphere.

[17] Tronto notes that property does not ground contemporary citizenship (2005, 139) Rather, the simultaneous notion of the welfare state has led to envisaging citizenship along the lines of the worker with "support staff" (139), the latter being feminine household labor for the most part. However, this in turn has become redundant with the gains of feminism that has led to women's participation in public work.

notes that these rights have diminished in the contemporary climate of increasing xenophobia, whereby migrants find it difficult to acquire citizenship. In advocating citizenship for migrant care workers, Tronto translates the notion of entitlement and belonging from the Western context to the "others" who have not been similarly entitled. She exposes what Butler terms as the failure of the universal norm (Butler 2002, 22), in this case that of citizenship rights, to all those who contribute to the nation. This allows for opening the "site of enunciation" (Butler 2002, 22) for the excluded as one where they are authorized despite being deauthorized. Yet it is precisely their care work that makes citizenship possible, Tronto suggests that the criteria of citizenship be reassessed in the current moment on the basis of care work. The latter's political recognition requires a solidarity among care workers, along with their visible presence in the public domain (Tronto 2005, 141).[18]

Tronto's argument for citizenship highlights the problem of migrant work by proposing their integration in an egalitarian democratic society. She engages with migrant care workers without nationalistic overtones and advocates a pioneering perspective on their integration. However, she confines herself to the Western context where there is a need for health care workers. Tronto neglects discussing the home countries of care workers who suffer from care deficit due their absence. Citizenship in Western countries cannot address the deprivation of care giving in so-called underdeveloped countries that are often the outcome of migration (Crozier 2010, 114). Care workers choose migration as recourse to increased income and well-being (Crozier 2010, 114). Many of those training to be nurses in India, Ghana and Philippines choose migration as a path without coercion, but their choice is not abstract. As argued earlier, they are impacted by the pull factors of the West but also by the push factors in their own countries. Advocating citizenship rights to migrants could have the consequence of serving as a "pull factor" to the host countries; a consequence that could lead to a greater loss of care workers in the home countries. The ethical responsibility that arises in the triadic context of care giving and receiving in home and host countries via the migrant worker has to address all three dimensions of the context. As Crozier

[18] Tronto revises her earlier position which analyzed care as devalued by politics as banal and as too profound for politics, given that it requires benevolence which is not available in politics (2005, 41). This assumes a realist and masculinist notion of politics which she rethinks.

notes, "the most vulnerable people in this entire set of considerations" (2010, 127) are care-receivers in the migrant workers' home countries, which Tronto's analysis has overlooked.

Obligations to potential care-receivers in global intersections of regimes of care cannot only be resolved by conferring citizenship to migrant care-givers, despite this act being well intentioned. Global human interdependence and what Butler terms as "precariousness" (2010, 2–3) of life reveals that care-receivers in the poorer home countries of care workers also matter. Moreover, it also reveals that citizenship in the richer host countries might lead to care-receivers at home being further deprived of help. Hence, rather than citizenship, a cosmopolitan perspective would bring together migrant caregivers and care-receivers in the host and home countries. It would more effectively supplement Tronto's ideal of a "caring democracy" (2013).

Cosmopolitanism and the Duty to Care

Cosmopolitanism emphasizes human beings as belonging to the world per se rather than any specific nation (Kleingeld 2013).[19] It is normatively committed to accommodating (and appreciating) difference, as well as engaging politically beyond the borders of the nation-state (Beck and Grande 2007, 12). It understands society at the local level as the outcome of global interdependence to advocate non-hierarchical global relations (Beck and Grande 2007, 13). The appreciation of difference is integral to cosmopolitanism from both the internal and external perspectives of the nation.[20] On this view, the normative claims do not arise from any singular location or national context, but at the intersection of diverse locations. This is revealed in the global commodification of care. In the latter con-

[19] Cosmopolitanism is an old notion going back to the Cynic Diogenes who proclaimed himself to be a world citizen (Kleingeld 2013; Beck and Grande 2007, 11). However, as Beck and Grande note the idea of cosmopolitanism is marshaled every time Europe is in a crisis with coping with difference. In the contemporary context, cosmopolitanism is seen as an alternative to the hegemony of the capitalist economy and the nation-state (Beck and Grande 2007, 11–12). See Deleixhe and Raillard, 2014 for grounding residence in cosmopolitanism.

[20] Beck and Grande note cosmopolitanism does not follow the post-modern route of advocating absolute otherness, despite its suspicion of pre-modern hierarchical responses to difference (15). However, their argument overlooks Derrida's claim that cosmopolitanism has the challenge of acknowledging the radically other. This challenge also confronts Razavi's transnational institutionalised care (2015).

text, the responsibilities of all the players toward each other can be better addressed from a cosmopolitan rather than a citizenship perspective. It posits the global need for care to address the intersection of vulnerability, need and dependency (Miller 2011, 399). Cosmopolitanism is particularly significant in this context because it rejects basing moral responsibility on homogeneous cultural identities and nationalisms (Kleingeld 2013). It acknowledges moral obligations despite the distance between human beings—who are often strangers—rather than limit it to one's immediate familiar circle of friends and family. Thus, cosmopolitanism, rather than citizenship, addresses the "precariousness" in which diverse agents are entangled.

The choice of cosmopolitan model compatible with the notion of care in contexts of "precariousness" (Butler 2010, 1) is not easy. There are many approaches to cosmopolitan ethics that attempt to accommodate the global commitment to humanity at large, given the interrelated nature of the world (Miller 2011, 392–394). In its liberal individualistic avatar—defended by Nussbaum and Appiah—cosmopolitanism is committed to the equal worth of individuals and to progressive versions of patriotism grounded in freedom and equality. However, such liberal cosmopolitanism is not suitable for a care ethical orientation that takes the non-Western world into consideration.

Appiah combines citizenship with cosmopolitanism toward a "cosmopolitan patriotism" (2002, 22) where rooted individuals are appreciative of differences to even acknowledge how such heterogeneity has shaped their homes. Moreover, since each life is interconnected with everyone else's, each individual has an obligation to create a world in which everyone gets an opportunity for self-development. Appiah maintains that each individual has the freedom and responsibility to develop his or her own life without intrusion. This also has an accompanying duty of building community. Appiah locates the obligation to care for others in reason, rather than feeling, which he regards as both irrational and ephemeral (2007, 155–176). The well-off should intervene in the plight of the lesser-off not because of the guilt of wealth causing poverty. They should instead do so because reasoning reveals that those with privilege have the obligation of developing themselves morally through a conscience that goes beyond the self. Thus, concern for strangers is linked to self-development. On this view, cosmopolitanism attempts to build connections on the basis of difference rather than identity (Appiah 2007, 135).

Nussbaum improves upon Appiah's rationalism, in adding the dimension of compassion to cosmopolitanism (Nussbaum 2002a, b). She defends global/cosmopolitan compassion as a response to the increasing racism and intolerance that has come to dominate the world. She cites Stoic philosophy as an inspiration for engaging compassionately for those who suffer in distant places. She enlists compassion as acknowledging that suffering for which the individual is not necessarily responsible due to vulnerability (Nussbaum 2002a, xi). Against Appiah, Nussbaum regards compassion as reflective in keeping with her perspective on emotions. Compassion forms a link between one's own self-interest and that of the other. She upholds that compassion develops at the local level and goes beyond this to the national and global. Nussbaum is critical of the sense of self-sufficiency and invulnerability that America's powerful status generates in its citizens. She acknowledges that such a sense of power underlies its collaboration with other nations—in a spirit of interconnectedness—to resist terrorism. Nussbaum suggests that such interconnectedness is best channelized in funding civilian and humanitarian projects (Nussbaum 2002a, xiii). Thus, she upholds that the interconnectedness of the world requires compassion to expand beyond the local domain to the rest of the world.

Both Appiah's and Nussbaum's positions are significant in the context of migrant care workers for they engage with the fraught subject of obligation to the non-Western world from the perspective of the privileged. They improve upon typically liberal conceptions of cosmopolitanism that prescribes abstract obligations to abstract humanity. Neither offer a non-contextual, idealized or abstract version of cosmopolitanism whose critique from the perspective of care is spelled out by Miller (2011, 396–397). Both Appiah and Nussbaum value differences and also foreground the duty to intervene in the suffering of those who are totally distant. They focus on the embeddedness of individuals in concrete situations and identities. They even suggest that one tries to comprehend the reasons for the person being in a situation of need (Appiah 2007, 168). They bring together engagement and reflection. In this respect they resonate with care ethics that reflects in very concrete ways with those in need of care (Miller 2010, 149). This is particularly so with Nussbaum who introduces the dimension of affect that is missing in Appiah. Thus, the stranger—a poor care-receiver in India in the context of this chapter—is for both Appiah and Nussbaum a concrete individual with a specific life-history. On the grounds of Nussbaum's compassion one can, for instance, defend the need to offer Western assistance for developing India's public hospitals.

However, despite discerning a global responsibility to concrete strangers both Appiah's and Nussbaum's versions of cosmopolitanism are problematic. They assume that human beings are separate individuals who are interconnected and motivated by pain (and difference) to mitigate suffering. Since they assume separate individuals as their starting point, they do not comprehend individual lives as equally interdependent and vulnerable. Consequently, there is the danger of those who intervene in the suffering of others assuming patronage and power over them. The care perspective has over the years argued that human interdependence requires abandoning the liberal assumption of the self as a separate individual to which Appiah and Nussbaum subscribe. Against the individualism of liberal theory, care focuses on relationships, relationships of nurture in affective contexts, which generate moral agents capable of exercising their freedom (Miller 2010, 148). Care assumes the human being to be dependent, vulnerable and with needs (Miller 2010, 150); the connectedness between persons does not arise from their mutual autonomy but on the contrary through mutual dependence. Against Appiah's and Nussbaum's idealized individualistic human being, care ethics takes dependencies, finitudes and vulnerabilities that bind human beings together.

In this context, following Miller, interdependence leads to acknowledging that care cannot be restricted to a specific group or set of individuals. Caring is not just the meeting of another's needs, it is rather the support that is given to the abilities of the other so that they can in turn meet the needs of others that surround them. Such an "obligation to support persons' abilities to meet others' needs" is to "ensure that they can care" (Miller 2010, 148). Miller connects cosmopolitan care with global responsibility to women who are oppressed by gender violence. She turns to the instance of the conflict in Sudan and rape inflicted on women from Darfur. Global responsibility to care requires that there is a focus not just on the needs generated by such violence, but on restoring agency to those who are victims. Further one needs to focus on local practices of care in a context-sensitive way to repair the situation. Caring across cultures involves engaging with the communities so that they too can care for rape-survivors. This entails solidarity that goes beyond the routine duty of aid. For it requires caregivers to interrogate their own position of power within North-South international relations and the obligation that this generates. There is a manner in which caregivers are complicit in patterns of oppression, which needs to be understood critically—as the Western world tends to be deeply advantaged by wars such as those in Sudan.

Although Miller improves upon the Appiah's and Nussbaum's individualism, her perspective focuses on rendering the care-receiver as autonomous. The duty of care does not lead to a deepening interdependency, but to self-determination. The notion of "duty to care" (Miller 2010, 150) also assumes that the caregiver is in a position of privilege with reference to the receiver. Although the "duty to care" does not imply that others are rendered as helpless and permanently needy, it does not entail the process of becoming autonomous as a one-off process, initiated by the caregiver. As Hamington notes, caring is not the same as altruism, since the caregiver also cultivates the self (2012, 55). On the contrary, such a duty brings together the mutual dependence of the caregiver and receiver in ways that result in new communities. Hamington upholds care as a disposition and practice in which the caregiver is oriented toward being open to the care-receiver. It is an "other-directed disposition" (Hamington 2015, 280). There is a back and forth active interaction between the caregiver and receiver, which remains unexplored in Miller's cosmopolitan proposal. Miller argues that when care ethics is placed in consonance with the Kantian model, it generates a "duty to care" (2010, 150). It has a "wide" (Miller 2010, 120) range of application and cannot be limited to just friends and family. Thus, caring does not confine itself to what is naturally given or for that matter socially conditioned (Miller 2010, 120). Further by following the Kantian route, Miller's "duty to care" emphasizes care as a rational principle. Miller notes that while emotions restrict caring to the intimate circle of family and friends, they cannot motivate care for strangers (2010, 151). In this respect, she upholds a point analogous to Appiah that reason enables obligation to strangers. However, this overlooks a complex array of emotions, which are not necessarily confined to the proximate. Miller's proposal also overlooks the performative dimension of care, which brings the relationship between caregiver and receiver into existence (Hamington 2015, 281). Thus, care is much more than a principle or a "duty" in bringing an empathetic interdependent mode of being into existence. It is an existential notion rather than just a principle.

Decolonizing Cosmopolitan Care

Returning to the context of migrant care workers whose absence has generated a deficit for care-receivers in their home countries, there are concrete suggestions for engaging with their global intersections in keeping with Tronto's concept of "caring with" (2013, 23). Crozier explores the proposal that the demand for care workers in host countries be reduced so that care workers can stay back in their own country to provide care. This can be done through trade and through self-sufficiency in care (Crozier 2010, 130). Crozier acknowledges that the possibility of trade through strict immigration laws is problematic as it could lead to human rights violation. It could also result in encouraging the trafficking of care workers.[21] On the other hand, if there is self-sufficiency in care this problem could be addressed in a better way. Care work could be acknowledged as a civic virtue and a public good so that all human beings can participate in it (Crozier 2010, 130–131). If this is worked on adequately, the "pull" of richer nations could be weakened, as they would have their own care workers. However, such a proposal for self-sufficiency overlooks the inevitability of migration and interdependence of diverse contexts. It also tends toward a strictly juridical solution that has the risk of violating freedom of movement.

However, as the circulation of care workers suggests, such self-sufficiency is perhaps neither possible nor attainable considering the inevitability of interdependent, vulnerable and boundless bodies. Care workers in richer countries could be cared for with citizenship in the manner argued for by Tronto. However, one also needs to adopt a decolonizing tone by addressing the other side of the phenomenon, namely the neglect of care-receivers in poorer countries. An engagement with the burgeoning field of medical tourism could allow for articulating a system of responsibilities to care-receivers in poor countries. A system of taxation could be channelized toward strengthening the structures of care in public hospitals. Further, medical tourists (and their relatives) could be encouraged to volunteer in public health institutions so that the process of commodification of health is mitigated and interdependencies are acknowledged. But if the "push" factors of migration remain the problem of migration would persist anyway. The problems in the countries of origin would have to be addressed in more primordial ways.

With reference to the shortage of Ghanaian medical workers in their home country, Groenhout notes that their exit should be construed as a problem rather than an achievement (2012, 13). She suggests that those who leave the country be called out for actively bringing down welfare structures to deter others from leaving. This suggestion is deeply problematic as Groenhout ignores how the problem of care work migration in

[21] It could also force women to do tasks that they were not doing earlier.

both Ghana and India is hardly voluntary, but is structurally governed by the "push" factors in the home country and "pull" factors in the host. It disregards the loneliness and alienation that nurses experience—often living away from their families or living singly. It overlooks their nostalgia for a home and their desire to engage substantially with its institutions. Gita Hariharan's short story *Nursing God's countries* (2014) portrays a nurse's nostalgia for her home and village in Kerala, India, as she goes from Bahrain to Canada to pursue her profession under the "push" and "pulls" factors.[22] Yet her desire to return to India is:

> Not to grow old, or die in my ancestral village, but to be a sister among sisters, hold up placards like them, or shout slogans, demanding my rights. I have never shouted a slogan in my life, but maybe I could do that in Kerala, make up for all the things I can be in Bahrain or Canada but not at home". (Hariharan 2014, 360)

These lines reveal how nurses in such situations are not irresponsible as Groenhout implies, but have the desire to participate vocally in the public sphere of their home countries (Ittyipe 2017).

In this respect, a scheme of "rotational migration" has been suggested where caregivers are encouraged to return to their "home countries" with their training abroad with opportunities such as tax benefits and the like (Crozier 2010, 132). In the Indian context, return migration is complex because public sector employment has age limits (30 years for nurses). The private sector also does not pay adequately. Moreover, there have been instances where the private sector has prevented nurses from traveling abroad by confiscating their degrees (which was deemed illegal by the Supreme Court in 2011) or making them sign bonds. Researchers note the unequal relation between health care workers and the public sector is not necessarily evened out by increasing staff (Hazarika 2013, 111). A key issue to be addressed by return migration is the dignity of care work and a public health system that is at the service of the poor. One way to do this would be to increase the responsibility and value of nurses. In India, even experienced nurses are not allowed to prescribe without the guidance of a doctor. This differs considerably from contexts such as the United States,

[22] Kerala exports the largest number of nurses in India. See Abraham (2004) for a detailed account of the gendered and patriarchal aspects underlying this phenomenon.. Also see Dasgupta 2007.

where there are even nurse anesthetists.[23] One of the major reasons for migration is the low social status (in India) of nurses because of the prevalent religious and societal traditions such as the Hindu caste system that looks down on embodied work. Although care work is stigmatized globally, it is much more so in the Indian context. This explains why a large number of Christians from Kerala have joined the nursing profession. Many nurses migrate because Indian society looks down upon care labor and nursing. They prefer to live outside India where they are both economically equipped and can lead a life of dignity. A return migration would have to work toward de-stigmatizing nursing by initiating change at the level of educational institutions.[24] This would enable changing social attitudes by acknowledging the unbounded vulnerability and interdependence of the body. The health care activist movement in India—which is entitlement driven and also nationalistic—would have to address this dimension from the perspective of care.

On the other hand, the private sector in India has a predatory relationship with the public, especially in the context of health. Prime government land is leased to private health clinics at subsidized rates so that some of the patients are treated free of cost (Pandey 2017). However, the latter hardly materializes. There is an exemption from taxes and duties for importing drugs and high-tech medical equipment. Concessions are made to doctors for setting up private practices and nursing homes. All of this should translate into the private sector providing a higher percentage of free service to the poor. These funding practices stem from old government policies, but their intention has not materialized evenly. Hence, a formal process of monitoring health care delivery to the poor could be worked out by the government along with NGOs and the people's health movement.

Such specific suggestions for engaging with care-receivers in the home and host countries, along with migrant care workers, can be theoretically understood through the concept of a decolonized cosmopolitan hospitality.[25] All three sets of entangled players have to be held together without compromising their needs or freedoms. This requires that they are hospitable to each other in the sense of being sensitive to strangers (Hamington 2010a, 22). Such hospitality is a response to the "precari-

[23] See Shetty's comments in IndiaSpend (2017). Also see "What is an Anesthesiologist" 2019.
[24] See Ittyipe (2017) for an account of these problems.
[25] This argument is influenced by Hamington's work on hospitality (2010a, 2010b).

ousness" (Butler 2010, 3; 2017) of human beings, whose inevitable interdependence does not have the comfort or the perils of the familiarity of family bonds. It cannot be understood as an entitlement, since the relationship is non-contractarian. It is not grounded in any specific nation-state, but rests on a domain that is between nations. Hence, citizenship rights to migrant care workers alone cannot remedy the problem. For the relationship between care workers and care-receivers in home and host countries criss-crosses the lines of citizens and guests. It reflects the movement to reside as per the "push" and "pull" factors, which throws human beings together as strangers. Thus, health care workers can visit or reside in their host country and be treated like a citizen/guest. These workers in turn would be hosts of care-receivers in the host country. A similar right of residence could be extended to medical tourists in the home country who would be guests and hosts of those who need care. A decolonized cosmopolitan care, thus, acknowledges the care deficit in the home countries of migrant care workers, as much as, their host countries. It does not privilege either location, since such caring responsibilities emerge from the in between space of having to live together, often as strangers.

The potential for cosmopolitanism in caring practices reveals the limits of the work ethic model dominant in neoliberalism. As Tronto notes this model values individual effort wherein those who work hard can earn the resources to purchase security and care in the market (2013, 84–87). She rightly analyzes such a work ethic framework as positing individuals in competitive, rather than collaborative relationships. Such individual competitiveness is also reflected in nation-states that vie with each other to acquire distinct self-sufficient identities. However, Tronto aptly diagnoses the abstract notion of hard work as sidestepping the social, political and economic constraints underlying it. The opportunity to put in work is based on innumerable forces beyond individual control. More importantly, this model overlooks how individuals are sustained through relationships of care and dependency; care work is performed by family members (mostly by women) or the socially vulnerable, in both the private and public spheres. The all pervasiveness of care worker migration shows how care work brings together caregivers (from the home country) with care-receivers (from both home and host countries) from diverse nationalities. It also indicates that the positions of the care-receiver and caregiver are interchangeable. Caring practices that materialize in a transnational space have a cosmopolitan reach. Moreover, responsibilities to those embedded in such practices are excluded by neoliberalism's individualistic canvas. Rather, these responsibilities are met by acknowledging dependencies that surpass nation-states. To conclude in Tronto's spirit, care acquires a more democratic dimension when its collaborative and cosmopolitan aspects are underscored.

Acknowledgments I thank Petr Urban, Lizzie Ward and Maurice Hamington for their helpful detailed feedback on this chapter. I have benefited from the inputs by Joan Tronto and the participants at the conference "Caring Democracy: Current Topics in the Political Theory of Care" organized by the Institute of Philosophy, Czech Academy of Sciences, Prague, on November 23–24, 2017. I am obliged to Arunima Kaushik and Biraj Mehta for their elaborate discussions on this chapter. My gratitude to Anshu Kulkarni and Aarti Valia for relevant inputs on medical technicalities.

References

Abraham, Binumol. 2004. *Women Nurses and the Notion of their 'Empowerment'*. Discussion Paper No 88 Kerala Research Programme on Local Level Development, Center for Development Studies, Thiruvananthapuram.

Appiah, Anthony Kwame. 2002 [1996]. Cosmopolitan Patriots. In *For Love of Country*, ed. Martha Nussbaum and Joshua Cohen, 21–29. Boston: Beacon Press.

———. 2007. *Cosmopolitanism: Ethics in a World of Strangers*. London: Penguin Books.

Baru, Rama, et al. 2010. Inequities in Access to Health Services in India: Caste, Class and Region. *Economic and Political Weekly* 45 (38): 49–58.

Beck, Ulrich, and Edgar Grande. 2007. *Cosmopolitan Europe*. Cambridge and Malden, MA: Polity Press.

Bhargava, Yuthika. 2018. Medical Tourists Flocking to India. *The Hindu*. https://www.thehindu.com/news/national/medical-tourists-flocking-to-india/article24497896.ece. Accessed 5 January 2019.

Bhuyan, Anoo 2017. *National Health Policy Drops Proposal to Make Health a Fundamental Right*. The Wire (17th March). https://thewire.in/health/national-healthpolicy-fundamental-right-nadda. Accessed 17 July, 2018.

Block, Daniel. 2018. India's Hospitals Are Filling Up with Desperate Americans. *Foreign Policy*, January 2. https://foreignpolicy.com/2018/01/02/indias-hospitals-are-filling-up-with-desperate-americans/. Accessed 5 January 2019.

Butler, Judith. 2002 [1996]. Universality in Culture. In *For Love of Country*, ed. Martha Nussbaum and Joshua Cohen, 45–52. Boston: Beacon Press.

———. 2010. *Frames of War*. London: Verso.

———. 2017. We Are World-less Without One Another: An Interview with Judith Butler. Interviewed by Stephanie Berbec. *The Other Journal: An Intersection of Theology and Culture* 27: 65–75.

Crozier, Gillian K.D. 2010. Care-Workers in the Global Market: Appraising Applications of Feminist Care Ethics. *International Journal of Feminist Approaches to Bioethics* 3 (1): 113–137.

Dasgupta, Shamita Das. 2007. Gender Roles and Cultural Continuity in the Asian Indian Immigrant Community in the US. In *Urban Women in Contemporary India: A Reader*, ed. Rehana Ghadially, 72–86. Los Angeles and New Delhi: Sage Publications.

Deleixhe, Martin, and Sarah-Louise Raillard. 2014. Re-evaluating Kant's Cosmopolitan Law: European Citizenship as a Transition from the Right to Visitation to the Right to Residence. *Revue française de science politique* 64 (1): 77–91.

Groenhout, Ruth. 2012. The "Brain Drain" Problem: Migrating Medical Professionals and Global Health Care. *International Journal of Feminist Approaches to Bioethics* 5 (1): 1–24.

Gupta, Monica Das. 2005. Public Health in India: Dangerous Neglect. *Economic and Political Weekly* 40 (49): 5159–5165.

Gupta, Amit Sen. 2008. Medical Tourism in India: Winners and Losers. *Indian Journal of Medical Ethics* 5 (1). https://doi.org/10.20529/IJME.2008.002. Accessed 15 January 2017.

Hamington, Maurice. 2010a. Toward a Theory of Feminist Hospitality. *Feminist Formations* 22 (1): 21–38.

———. 2010b. The Will to Care: Performance, Expectation, and Imagination. *Hypatia* 25 (3): 675–695.

———. 2012. Care Ethics and Corporeal Inquiry in Patient Relations. *International Journal of Feminist Approaches to Bioethics* 5 (1): 52–69.

———. 2015. Politics Is Not a Game: The Radical Potential of Care. In *Care Ethics and Political Theory*, ed. Daniel Engster and Maurice Hamington, 272–292. Oxford: Oxford University Press.

Hariharan, Githa. 2014. Nursing God's Countries. In *A Clutch of Indian Masterpieces*, ed. David Davidar, 355–360. New Delhi: Penguin.

Hazarika, Indrajit. 2013. Health Workforce in India: Assessment of Availability, Production and Distribution. *WHO South-East Asia Journal of Public Health* 2 (2, April–June): 106–112.

Hooper, Carwyn Rhys. 2008. Adding Insult to Injury: The Healthcare Brain Drain. *Journal of Medical Ethics* 34 (9): 684–687.

IndiaSpend. 2017. India Short of Nearly Two Million Nurses. May 12. https://everylifecounts.ndtv.com/india-short-nearly-two-million-nurses-13129. Accessed 20 December 2018.

Ittyipe, Minu. 2017. Who Cares for the Care-Givers? *Outlook*. https://www.outlookindia.com/magazine/story/who-cares-for-the-care-givers/299151. Accessed 1 November 2017.

Kleingeld, Pauline. 2013. Cosmopolitanism. *Stanford Encyclopedia of Philosophy*. https://plato.stanford.edu/entries/cosmopolitanism/. Accessed 14 November 2017.

Laguipo, Angela. 2016. India Is Europe's Largest Exporter of Doctors and Nurses. *TechTimes*. https://www.techtimes.com/articles/120064/20160101/india-is-europes-largest-exporter-of-doctors-and-nurses.htm. Accessed 5 October, 2017

Miller, Sarah. 2010. Cosmopolitan Care. *Ethics and Social Welfare* 4 (2): 145–157.

———. 2011. A Feminist Account of Global Responsibility. *Social Theory and Practice* 37 (3): 391–412.

National Health Policy. 2017. New Delhi: Ministry of Health and Family Welfare, Government of India. http://cdsco.nic.in/writereaddata/national-health-policy.pdf. Accessed 17 July, 2018

Nussbaum, Martha. 2002a [1996]. Cosmopolitan Emotions. In *For Love of Country*, ed. Martha Nussbaum and Joshua Cohen, ix–xiv. Boston: Beacon Press.

———. 2002b. Patriotism and Cosmopolitanism. In *For Love of Country*, ed. Martha Nussbaum and Joshua Cohen, 3–20. Boston: Beacon Press.

Palriwala, Rajni, and N. Neetha. 2012. Between the State, Market and Family: Structures, Policies and Practices of Care in India. In *Global Variations in the Political and Social Economy of Care: Worlds Apart*, ed. Shahara Razavi and Silke Staab, 176–200. Oxon: Routledge.

Pandey, Kundan. 2017. Government Hospitals on Sale. https://www.downtoearth.org.in/news/health/government-hospitals-on-sale%2D%2D58399. Accessed 5 June 2019.

Percot, Marie, and S. Irudaya Rajan. 2007. Female Emigration from India: Case Study of Nurses. *Economic and Political Weekly* 42 (4): 318–325.

Qadeer, Imrana, and Indira Chakravarthi. 2010. The Neo-liberal Interpretation of Health. *Social Scientist* 38 (5/6): 49–61.

Rao, Mohan, et al. 2011. Human Resources for Health in India. *The Lancet*, January 12. www.thelancet.com. Accessed 23 November 2017.

Razavi, Shahrashoub. 2015. Care and Social Reproduction: Some Reflections on Concepts, Policies and Politics from a Development Perspective. In *The Oxford Handbook of Transnational Feminist Movements*, ed. Rawwida Baksh and Wendy Harcourt, 422–445. Oxford: Oxford University Press.

Reddy, Sunita, and Imrana Qadeer. 2010. Medical Tourism in India: Progress or Predicament? *Economic and Political Weekly* 45 (20): 69–75.

Sengupta, Amit. 2005. The Private Health Sector in India Is Burgeoning, But at the Cost of Public Health Care. *BMJ* 331 (7526): 1157–1158.

Sharma, Rashmi. 2011. Gender and International Migration: The Profile of Female Migrants from India. *Social Scientist* 39 (3/4): 37–63.

Soman, Krishna, and Subhoranjan Dasgupta. 2003. Public Health: Historical Experience. *Economic and Political Weekly* 38 (47): 4942–4944.

Tronto, Joan C. 2005. Care as the Work of Citizens: A Modest Proposal. In *Women and Citizenship*, ed. Marilyn Friedman, 130–145. Oxford: Oxford University Press.

———. 2010. Creating Caring Institutions: Politics, Plurality and Purpose. *Ethics and Social Welfare* 4 (2): 158–171.

———. 2013. *Caring Democracy: Market, Equality, and Justice*. New York and London: New York University Press.

Walton-Roberts, Margaret, et al. 2017. Causes, Consequences and Policy Responses to the Migration of Health Workers: Key Findings from India. *Human Resources for Health* 15: 28.

"What Is an Anesthesiologist". https://www.hss.edu/what-is-an-anesthesiologist.asp. Accessed 10 June 2019.

CHAPTER 11

Understanding the Social Care Crisis in England Through Older People's Lived Experiences

Lizzie Ward, Mo Ray, and Denise Tanner

Introduction

In the final chapter of *Caring Democracy*, Joan Tronto poses the question "how do we go from a society that is primarily concerned with economic production to one that also emphasises care?" (2013, 169). As illustrated in the contributions to this collection, participation in political processes and in decision-making about responsibilities for care are understood as

L. Ward (✉)
School of Applied Social Science, University of Brighton, Brighton, UK
e-mail: E.Ward@brighton.ac.uk

M. Ray
School of Health and Social Care, University of Lincoln, Lincoln, UK
e-mail: Mray@lincoln.ac.uk

D. Tanner
Department of Social Work and Social Care, University of Birmingham, Birmingham, UK
e-mail: D.L.Tanner@bham.ac.uk

P. Urban, L. Ward (eds.), *Care Ethics, Democratic Citizenship and the State*, International Political Theory,
https://doi.org/10.1007/978-3-030-41437-5_11

crucial in answering this question (see chapters by Heier, Bourgaut and White, this volume). Who is excluded from political participation, and how to challenge the power of those who operate from a position of 'privileged irresponsibility' in the allocation of care, are key areas of concern for making democracy more caring and caring more democratic. However, there is a further question concerning participation in how knowledge *about* care is produced? The 'epistemological dimension' of care is recognised in care ethics through the concept of 'responsiveness' in which attention to the care-receiver's experience informs the care process at the micro level. But what counts as 'knowledge' *about* care in political processes and policy decisions at the macro level is also highly significant. Yet, the inclusion of care-receivers at the level of 'knowledge production' is less developed in care scholarship. Within the academic and practice worlds another dimension of participation operates, whereby most knowledge *about* care is produced without the inclusion of care-receivers and with little regard to their lived experiences of care. This chapter draws on empirical research that was co-produced with older people about lived experiences of care within the English social care system. We argue that building knowledge care with those who have lived experience is necessary for the democratisation of care. Knowledge produced from lived experience can make sense of theoretical concepts and consider their relevance to 'everyday life'. But crucially, within the current neoliberal context where only certain types of knowledge are admissible, the actual experiences of care under neoliberalism directly challenge the assumptions that underpin the consumer choice rationale that supports the marketisation of care.

If we are to shift the dominant focus away from the economic domain, Tronto suggests that we need to rethink the relationship between the state and the market (2013, 170). The ascendency and dominance of neoliberalism, as the economic-political system of organising contemporary societies, has resulted in the prioritisation of markets above all human life. This is one of the biggest roadblocks to actualising the 'caring democracy' that Tronto envisages. One starting point for the work that needs to be done to break the neoliberal hold over our thinking is to recognise that neoliberalism began as a man-made (literally) set of ideas which originated in the works of economists, such as Hayek and others, in their mid-twentieth-century fears of centralised state control of the economy (Metcalf 2017). Early neoliberal thought considered the only 'scientific' means of assessing and evaluating all aspects of life is through the market and the price mechanism. Its enduring legacy, and indeed legitimacy, as the underpinning framework of the audit and assessment culture which now dominates many developed welfare societies and public services, merits serious scrutiny. What constitutes knowledge within neoliberal thought is problematic, particularly in relation to care, as the orientation to 'objective' frames of reference relegates lived experiences of care to the realm of opinion or anecdote.

Many have offered critiques on the incompatibility of market mechanisms and equitable health and care provision (Clarke et al. 2007; Fotaki 2009; Mol 2008; Williams and Brennan 2012). But looking at experiences of care can help us understand why these are so incompatible. As we aim to show in this chapter, it is precisely knowledge based on lived experiences—the epistemological dimension of care—that exposes the failures of neoliberalism in meeting care needs. This adds weights to the argument that the current economic domination in human life stands in the way of 'caring democracy'.

The chapter's focus is social care[1] in England where responsibility for the organisation and funding of care has shifted from the state to the individual. It draws on a qualitative research project about the experiences of older people who are paying for their social care.[2] We, as academic researchers, set out to place older people's experiences at the centre of the project, within the research process as well in the empirical data we gathered. We describe this approach as the co-production of knowledge to convey our commitment to prioritising lived experiences and challenging traditional academic knowledge hierarchies.[3] It involves working alongside older people as 'lay' co-researchers and taking the ethical dimensions of participatory research seriously in every aspect of the work. We describe this as 'relational research practice' in which we apply care ethics to the

[1] Care needs related to the activities of daily living, for example, dressing, washing, going to the toilet and eating.

[2] *Ethical issues in self-funded social care: co-producing knowledge with older people* funded by the Wellcome Trust 2017–2020. The research aimed to understand the ethical dimensions related to risk and responsibility in self-funded care by using a 'co-production' approach which centralises older people's lived experiences. See http://www.olderpeopleselffunding-care.com/.

[3] It should be acknowledged that the term 'co-production' in in the UK has become a widely used concept. Arguably its adoption into the mainstream, for example in UK Higher Education Institutes, research funding bodies and so on as part of the 'Impact' agenda, could be understood as the co-option of a more radical understanding of the concept into a neoliberal agenda. A similar move in relation to the involvement of patients and service users in health and care services and in research can also be seen as part of a de-politicisation process linked to forcing individual choice, responsibility and self-care.

ways we *conduct* research as well as conceptually in the analysis (see Ward and Gahagan 2010 for details).

It is important to say at the outset that the research and analysis we offer to illustrate our argument is bounded by the 'local' context and the particular time and place in which it was produced. It comes from a privileged part of the world, where matters concerning social rights and collective responsibilities for care are, largely assumed to be guaranteed by the post-war welfare settlement. Nevertheless, we argue that it offers a case study which illustrates the failures of the neoliberal economic framing in meeting social care needs through a system of marketised care, and this has a wider applicability to different contexts beyond the social care system in England.

Firstly, this chapter offers an overview of the transformations in social care in England. It discusses the implications of neoliberal policy objectives that have driven the changes, primarily individual responsibility and consumer choice, for older people who need care. It then turns to focus on the research we conducted with older people who are paying for their own care and draws on examples from interview data to explore in more depth the disparity between the neoliberal assumptions and actual lived experiences. Finally, we consider what these lived experiences can contribute to understanding the inadequacy of neoliberal thinking in addressing care needs and in democratising care.

Austerity, Welfare and Social Care in England

In November 2018, the UN rapporteur on extreme poverty and human rights, Philip Alston, concluded from his two-week mission to the UK that the government's austerity programme had inflicted 'great misery' on its people. The extent of poverty in the world's fifth largest economy with around 14 million people (20% of the UK population) living in poverty and 1.5 million so destitute that they cannot afford basic essentials was, he argued, the result of "punitive, mean-spirited and often callous" austerity policies driven by a political desire to undertake social re-engineering rather than economic necessity (United Nations 2019, 5).

In gathering his evidence Alston had spent time talking to people who were experiencing the impact of austerity policies: those who use foodbanks for daily needs; those who have lost their homes and have nowhere safe for themselves and their children to sleep; people who sell sex for money or shelter; young people who have joined gangs to survive; and disabled people who have lost the support packages they relied on. He concluded that the scale of austerity measures is so extreme that it represents an abandonment of the values that underpinned the Beveridge post-war social contract and informed the British welfare state:

> The bottom line is that much of the glue that has held British society together since the Second World War has been deliberately removed and replaced with a harsh and uncaring ethos. A booming economy, high employment and a budget surplus have not reversed austerity, a policy pursued more as an ideological than an economic agenda. (United Nations 2019, 4)

Just as shocking as the report was the government response and their "determined state of denial" (ibid., 4), which challenged the report's validity by citing statistics showing increases in the numbers of people in paid work and household income at a record high. The steadfast refusal of the government to encounter the lived experiences of people impacted by its own policies is more than the current trend of 'post-truth' politics. It reflects policymakers and politicians' reliance on 'evidence' framed by narrow outcome measures and quantifiable performance indicators to justify their claims.

The transformation of the welfare state that Alston's report highlighted does, in fact, have a longer history than the financial crises of 2008 and the introduction of the austerity measures that followed. It is part of the longer trajectory of the marketisation, privatisation and outsourcing of health and social care in the UK begun by the Thatcher government at the end of the 1970s[4] and reflected in global shifts of the privatisation of the public realm (Clarke et al. 2007). In the UK, as in many developed welfare societies, this has eroded public funding and provision of health and care which has been replaced by the rhetoric of 'choice' and the belief in the market as the most efficient means to deliver welfare services. For example, within Europe, England has been at the forefront of marketising the social care sector (Ismail et al. 2017), predominantly through the 'personalisation' policy agenda. This introduced a 'cash-for-care' approach whereby those who receive publicly funded care are given a personal bud-

[4] Margaret Thatcher led the UK government between 1979 and 1990. Thatcherism, which extended beyond this period and beyond the UK, was a total rejection of the post-war welfare consensus. Thatcher was inspired by the ideas of Hayek and other neoliberals and was committed to the privatisation of public services and free market principles.

get to purchase their own care through a growing social care market. But since 2010 in the UK, the withdrawal of state responsibility for welfare and care has intensified through austerity politics as a response to the banking crisis and financial meltdown of 2007–2008.

What was essentially a crisis in the financial sector was ideologically reframed by the UK government[5] into one of government debt and public expenditure to justify austerity measures (Clarke and Newman 2012). This was accompanied by a neo-communitarian discourse (Davies 2012) in which 'communities' and 'self-help' were the preferred solutions to the crisis whilst the 'state' was constructed as part of the problem.[6] The combination of the apparent economic necessity of public spending cuts and the elevation of the role of communities has worked to further "deflect and decentralize responsibility for care and welfare" (Clarke and Newman 2012, 303). In spending terms this has resulted in local authorities losing 49.1% of central government funding between 2010 and 2018 (National Audit Office 2018).[7] It is local authorities which provide much of the infrastructure for welfare services, such as schools, libraries, parks, leisure facilities and so on which contribute to civic life as well as social care services.

There are many ways in which these spending cuts have been felt across different groups of people who need care and welfare services, for example, the closure of community transport and meals services, day centres, libraries, which have affected people with needs of all ages. Indeed, the

[5] This reformulation of 'the problem' was promoted by Conservative-led coalition government from 2010 to 2015 and more forcefully from 2015 onwards by the Conservative government.

[6] See Prime Minister Cameron's defining speech on the Big Society: "the size, scope and role of government in Britain has reached a point where it is now inhibiting, not advancing the progressive aims of reducing poverty, fighting inequality, and increasing general well-being. Indeed, there is a worrying paradox that because of its effect on personal and social responsibility, the recent growth of the state has promoted not social solidarity, but selfishness and individualism" (David Cameron, Hugo Young Lecture 10 November 2009. https://conservative-speeches.sayit.mysociety.org/speech/601246 accessed 21/11/18).

[7] Reductions in Local authority funding became a key target for Prime Minister Cameron under the austerity measures, justified as the mechanism to release 'the potential within communities' (DH 2010, 9): "Resource pressures make it even more important to take an approach that changes the relationship between citizen and state. This does mean people and communities playing more of a role in supporting themselves and others. In exchange, they need more freedom to shape their support and public services must remove barriers to this freedom" (DH 2010, 9).

real impact of these public funding cuts was clearly evident to Alston during his UN mission. But it is the provision of social care for older people who have complex needs, where the impacts have been particularly acute. As early as 2014 the National Audit Office (the official body which scrutinises public spending) were warning that the social care system was unsustainable:

> Pressures on the care system are increasing. Providing adequate social care poses a significant public service challenge and there are no easy answers. People are living longer and some have long-term and complex health conditions that require managing through care. Need for care is rising while public spending is falling and there is unmet need. Departments do not know if we are approaching the limits of the capacity of the system to continue to absorb these pressures. (National Audit Office 2014, 11)

The way in which state-supported care is organised in the UK is complex. Healthcare provided universally via the National Health Service (NHS) was from its inception, and still remains, largely free at the point of use,[8] financed and accountable through central government. In contrast, statutory social care is means-tested and administered at a local level, with regional variations in England, Northern Ireland, Scotland and Wales. Local authorities typically only fund the care of those with high needs and limited finances. How 'high needs' and 'limited finances' are defined depends largely on political decisions in the allocation of spending across local authority services, although there are national financial thresholds and eligibility criteria. In England, where the research we draw on was carried out, overall spending on statutory adult social care has fallen substantially as local authorities have made 'budget savings' of over £6 billion since 2010 (ADASS 2017, 4). Unsurprisingly this has resulted in fewer people receiving state-funded care. The Care Quality Commission (CQC), which regulates social care in England, estimated that by 2018, 1.4 million older people did not have access to the care and support they needed (CQC 2018).

[8] From April 2017 NHS staff are expected to check a patient's citizenship before healthcare is given. This move has received criticism, (including from the medical profession) and claims that 'health tourists' are to blame for the funding crisis in the NHS have been viewed as a distraction from the deliberate underfunding from government, linked to the increasing privatisation of the health service and part of the wider policy of creating a 'hostile environment' towards immigration—see Stewart 2017.

We can begin to see here the wide-reaching transformations within the social care system through the longer-term neoliberal restructuring and the more recent, and unprecedented, reductions in government spending for publicly funded social care. Both have led to the further commodification of care framed ideologically by consumer choice and individual responsibility. For older people, who are the focus of the research that this chapter draws on, this has particular impacts. Increasing numbers of older people now need to purchase their own care, rely on family members or simply go without it (Glendinning 2017). But what can the experiences of older people who need care and support services tell us about these fundamental changes to the welfare state? The next section turns to the research we conducted that addressed these questions.

Researching Social Care *with* Older People

After six years of sustained cuts in local authority budgets for social care the Kings Fund reported that "No one has a full picture of what has happened to older people who are no longer entitled to publicly funded care: the human and financial costs to them and those who care for them are mounting" (Humphries et al. 2016, 3). Partly, this is because social care research has focused mainly on publicly funded care; so although the numbers of older people who fall outside of this has increased very little attention is given to their experiences (Tanner et al. 2018). But this lack of attention to lived experiences also reflects the dominance of 'the economics' of social care policy and practice in much social care research despite the drive towards including service-user knowledge through the mainstreaming of 'service-user involvement'.[9]

We had worked previously with older people as co-researchers on projects in designing and conducting research that enables older people to share their lived experiences on their own terms. Our decision to focus on lived experiences of self-funded care in this project was based on the realisation that older people in this situation were completely under the radar in relation to policy and social care practice. Our intention was to get under the political rhetoric that has accompanied the restructuring of welfare services and produce knowledge based in the lived experiences of older people facing the situation of purchasing their own care. Our first

[9] Demonstrating the involvement of patients and service users in research design and development is a requirement of NHS and government research council funding in the UK.

challenge as researchers who want to democratise knowledge production, (and one which is true in relation to 'participation' more generally), is to recognise power differentials that are intrinsic to the research process and find ways to not only acknowledge but actively address these. In working through this challenge, we have developed *relational research practice* which explicitly recognises the value of knowledge from lived experiences of ageing and the issues that older people face. It also means being attentive to the different needs and circumstances of everyone we involve in our work as research participants and co-researchers and building supportive and trusting relationships in our research practice.

We started to explore the issues in a small pilot study where we interviewed older people who were self-funding their care. Having to pay for care can come as something of a shock for the generation of people who have contributed to national social insurance throughout their working lives and who find their contributions do not cover their care needs as they reach a point when social care becomes a necessity in their own lives. But the difficulties are not just a matter of paying and financing care; there is a wider lack of understanding about how to actually go about organising care, assessing what care services are needed, where to find these, who to trust and how much it will cost. In effect people are unprepared for becoming a 'consumer' of care within a market system, and very often this happens at a time of crisis through ill health or following a stay in hospital.

The themes that emerged from the pilot interviews focused around three areas: difficulties in accessing care; finding the *right* help; and managing the care. We could see that our participants were faced with making complex and possibly far-reaching decisions at a point of vulnerability, such as ill health or following discharge from hospital. Their narratives highlighted the difficulty of absorbing information at a time of crisis. There was uncertainty about knowing the right level of services they required, as their care needs were dynamic and changing, and in the absence of any statutory support to help them, they were left trying to work this out on their own.

From this initial work we developed a larger study focused on ethical challenges arising in the transformed care landscape, specifically in relation to risks and responsibilities within care relationships. We expanded the scope of the project to help us understand the relational aspects of older people's experiences by also looking at the perspectives of care providers, practitioners and local authority officials as well as the family and friends supporting older people who are self-funding. The larger study used longitudinal qualitative interviews with older people over a period of eighteen months to explore their care journeys and changes that happened during this time. The study was carried out in three different areas of England and in each research site academic researchers worked with older citizens as co-researchers. The co-researchers were trained in all aspects of research and worked with us on the research design, data collection, analysis and interpretation and dissemination. The research teams also worked with local social care organisations and care providers in 'knowledge exchange' groups which met throughout the project to share emergent themes from the research and create a deliberative space for discussing these from a range of perspectives.

Working in this way allows a different kind of understanding to emerge which encompasses the messy, complex realities of everyday life that cannot be captured within 'objective' measurement techniques. In doing this, it can show the specificities of (in this case) care needs in old age and how these may not have been considered in policy and practice and so can expose a gap in current understanding. The participants in our study revealed many aspects of their lives, such as loss and bereavement, identity, changing relationships as well as health that all form part of the background in which care is negotiated. In the next section we look at some of these experiences by focusing on two participants and themes that emerged in their accounts which illustrate how lived experience can problematise policy assumptions about care in old age.

Two Examples of Lived Experiences of 'Choice'

The promotion of 'choice' is the basis of current English social care policy, with the assumption that choice will empower people who need services:

> people should have the power of choice about what services they receive. … Choice is about empowering people. … incentivising providers to deliver the services that people want and choose for themselves and their families. (HM Government 2014, 1)

Whilst our participants may indeed have valued choice in principle, in line with Barnes (2012), their experiences told a rather different story about the extent and nature of consumer power in the context of needing care in later life. The constraints to exercising their 'choice', not articulated in the policy discourse, entail a combination of personal circumstances and market mechanisms coming into play with the nature of care needs in old age. Here we look in some detail at the accounts of two participants, Brenda and Iris,[10] both of whom were trying to navigate the position of the 'consumer' as they attempted to get their needs for care met. Their stories are illustrative of themes that emerged in many of the experiences of the participants in the study and offer different perspectives on the notion of 'choice'.

Brenda, who was in her early eighties, had lived with physical disability affecting her mobility since her teenage years. As she got older her mobility had worsened and she had also developed a heart condition. She had been widowed for some time and lived on her own. During her working life Brenda had a successful career in financial services. She did not have children but had extended family (siblings, nieces and nephews) who lived close by. We first interviewed Brenda some eighteen months after a serious fall which had resulted in a hospital stay. Following her discharge from hospital, Brenda's care was organised, arranged and paid for by the NHS as part of a six-week rehabilitation process. Without prior warning, she was then left to sort out her ongoing care needs for herself. She described this as being "given a leaflet and expected to get on with it". She was immobile and needed assistance to go to the toilet, wash and dress, make meals and get into bed. She had some prior knowledge of care services, having lived with disability for a long time and had volunteered with a local care charity. She was also well organised and confident in using the Internet to find local care services and research their ratings from inspections carried out by the Care Quality Commission who regulate social care in the UK. In many respects she was comfortable with the process and had clear ideas about what she needed and what was important for her. In other words, she was trying to be an active responsible citizen and she spoke about the importance of remaining 'independent':

> I try to be very independent and try and do things, well after my husband died. ... I was on my own ... and during that time I had one of my knee replacements and I was looking after my mother and working full time and, you know, you learn to be independent as much as possible because you have to be.

[10] These are not real names as we use pseudonyms to protect the anonymity of research participants. This forms part of the ethical approval from the National Social Care Research Ethics Committee which governs the research.

The care package that Brenda had negotiated with a private care company involved a daily care visit of thirty minutes in the morning. The carers set Brenda up for the day ensuring that she had flasks of coffee and food as by this point Brenda was generally able to manage her personal care, although she had bad days where she struggled with dressing. Overall, Brenda was happy with her carers, but she had an ongoing issue over the timing of the care visits. This was the one area in which Brenda indicated strongly that she wanted to feel a sense of control and she had chosen an agency based on this 'choice'. But despite their original assurance that they could provide a call between 7.45 and 8 in the morning in practice this was unreliable and inconsistent, as Brenda explained:

> [*the care package*] ... was ideal for a while but now it's gone completely down the pan ... you know, it goes on, you get a few weeks when it's alright and then all of a sudden it's not.

Brenda had voiced her dissatisfaction about this and had tried to negotiate the times she wanted with the agency that provided the care. However, she expressed feeling at a disadvantage in her dealings with the agency:

> she (*agency manager*) knows that I've got no choice. ... Doesn't matter what I've asked for or that I've been having them for 18 months, you know, they just do what they like, so what do you do?

Brenda had explored the care options available to her and having had care for over eighteen months she had developed relationships with some of her carers. She also had a good understanding of the local care sector. She was very aware that the carers worked for low pay and that the agency that she used was not what she described as a good employer. For example, she knew that the carers were paid only half the amount that she was charged:

> At the moment I'm paying £8.57 for half an hour and the carer gets £4.50. Which is just under half and that's really not very fair is it?

This impacted Brenda in two ways. Firstly, she was reluctant to complain about the carers themselves, even if they were not doing exactly what she required of them. She felt a genuine sympathy and concern for them knowing that as workers they were not treated well. And secondly, she was aware of the issues in relation to recruiting care workers and that the systemic problems in the care sector meant that the unreliable, inconsistent service that she received and lack of choice over the timing of care visits would be a feature in all local care agencies. She was somewhat resigned to paying for a care service that did not meet her needs:

> So I don't know quite honestly. ... of course you do realise that if you try somebody else, everybody's got the same problem. There's not enough carers so, so trying somebody else ... it's probably the devil you know is better than the devil you don't.

As the interview progressed it became clear that Brenda was somehow managing or even tolerating the situation and was quite fearful that her needs would increase. She worried that another fall may mean further hospitalisation, and this impacted on how she was living. She slept in a chair in her living room to avoid going upstairs and getting in and out of her bed. She depended on the sandwiches and flasks of coffee that the morning carers left to avoid standing on her feet and walking to the kitchen. She explained that she needed two lots of surgery on her heart and knee and that she had delayed this as it would most likely mean needing assistance with washing and going to the toilet. In part she was worried about the increased costs of the care she would need but also she had little confidence in the reliability of the agency and feared being left powerless in these circumstances.

Like Brenda, Iris was widowed and lived on her own. She was ninety-two and had severe osteoporosis. She was at risk of breaking bones if she fell and had decreased mobility due to previous fractures. Iris had started having carers three years previously following a heart attack and a series of falls. The carers helped her with daily living tasks and took her out for shopping and social trips as she was unable to go out on her own. She managed her own personal care and bathing with the carers present in case she fell. She had ongoing heart problems for which she needed to take regular medication and the carers helped her with this.

Iris described how she was trying to manage and meet her care needs as something she felt she *should* do without depending on her family. She spoke about the sense of ongoing responsibility she felt for her family and this revealed the complex family dynamics which shaped her decisions. There had been a significant bereavement in the family five years earlier when Iris's daughter died. Her sons and grandchildren lived locally and although she saw them quite often, she did not rely on them to provide care.

> I have never asked for anything and there are not a lot of offers from the family. But it suits me. … we have never really switched from she is looking after us, now we look after her. We haven't ever got there. It's, I don't want to make my two sons sort of feel that they're responsible for my problems and they've got to solve them all, you know.

Iris knew she was struggling to cope with her current situation and following another fall she had begun to worry about being able to remain in her apartment. Like Brenda, she had been researching the options to meet her increasing needs for care. She described herself as 'a planner' always wanting to be prepared and know what was happening next. She had many leaflets and brochures about residential care and care services and had been looking for sources of financial advice. Much of this suggested that she was someone who was organised and who liked to be independent and in control. Yet she also spoke about feeling lonely for the first time in her life, and despite her insistence of not wanting her family to take care of her, there was ambivalence about this. She described how devastated she felt when one of her sons had recently taken up a job offer abroad and moved his family:

> It's all been fairly drastic and dramatic and I'm not quite sure how to deal with it. It was a sort of indirect support, but for me, individually, it was an absolute shock, you know. … But I have to get used to that.

She spoke about how she would love one of her granddaughters to move in with her but did not want her granddaughter to have the responsibility of looking after her. And whilst she was struggling to remain living in her apartment, she was clearly very reluctant to give it up as she regarded it as still the family home and somewhere for the family to gather and a place to stay if they needed to:

> Yes, you see, because they always, always came together here, first in their old home, of course, and then always here, without question, I mean, that was understood that this is where they would be for Christmas … made a big difference to us, when my daughter died.

The themes that emerge in Brenda and Iris's interviews are echoed in many of the accounts of older people who took part in the research who, although living in different individual contexts, were facing similar issues. Their stories illustrate kinds of journeys that we negotiate as we age, involving not only changes in our own capacities but also in our sense of self, of who we are and how we have perceived ourselves during our adult lives. Our feelings about declining independence and needing care from others have to be encountered, and for the people in our study, whilst also trying to work out how to resolve care needs via a market-based system of care. We can see that what apparently guides human behaviour according to neoliberal economic doctrine—maximising self-interest and making 'choices'—bears little relevance in this context. Iris and Brenda, and the other participants in our study, were dealing with far greater complexity. Not only was their capacity to choose bounded by a local social care market but also by the physical and emotional changes that can accompany ageing and by the relational nature of care itself. The enormous emotional, psychological and practical dimensions of these suggest that the economistic logic completely misses so much of what happens in reality. Decisions about care are not rational information-driven ones in the context of old age and ill health where uncertainty about the future and a sense of vulnerability may heavily feature. The assumption that the market provides the mechanism for fair exchange between equal players does not hold true in this context.

For the people in our study, having enough money to pay for care did not in itself guarantee any kind of consumer power. Moreover, their experiences show that their choices were not only, or exclusively, related to the amount and costs of care as they were dealing with difficult personal and interpersonal challenges which had also to be negotiated. They have experienced first-hand what happens when care is commodified, and how this is different from other purchasing decisions. Social care users in England are now expected to adopt the role of 'care consumer' and for self-funders this generally means that the transactions will happen between just them and the care provider with no neutral intermediary who might independently assess their needs. And these decisions are likely to be made at times when the person is already experiencing challenging issues, such as ill health, hospital discharge or other very stressful circumstances, so far from an ideal context in which to be making what are very impactful and possibly far-reaching decisions. Austerity has intensified this situation as local authority cuts mean not just that more people are directly paying for care but that there is less support from reduced community services and diminished oversight from statutory sources, leaving people to negotiate the vagaries of the social care market at a time of potentially substantial and increasing vulnerability.

Towards Caring Democracy: The Epistemological Dimension

The themes that emerged in the experiences of our participants help to expose the fault lines of the current social care system in England. This not only illustrates the flaws in the underlying current assumptions of individual autonomy informing social care policy but also demonstrates how the same assumptions totally fail to understand the nature of care in old age as it is experienced. The key questions are what and how can these experiences contribute to thinking about caring democracy? Tronto's call to shift the focus from economic production to one that is concerned with care will necessarily require challenging the 'knowledge' that is produced by neoliberal systems of audit and measurement as the only legitimate form of knowledge about care. This is crucial as the wider political debate about care has been defined by this same neoliberal economic discourse limiting the boundaries to concerns about growing numbers of older people creating a 'burden' on resources that 'we' cannot afford.

In the current climate it would be easy to construct the welfare state as the golden age of welfare services. The post-war settlement saw the foundation of the NHS and a tax and welfare system based on redistribution. The provision of public services was based on ideals of universal coverage, a commitment to equality and social rights and addressing the inequalities produced by economic growth and market capitalism. But it is crucial to remember that it was always, despite the aspirations of universal coverage, an exclusive system, full of provisos and exceptions, and it was a gendered settlement that promoted traditional gendered norms. From the 1970s, feminist and disability activist movements have exposed and campaigned against these failings and exclusions. Moreover, what became so unavoidably obvious in the 'Windrush scandal' of 2018[11] was the extent to which it was a colonial project (see Gentleman 2019). It was built, and indeed depended on, the labour of migrants from colonised countries who were themselves never truly included in its ideals and entitlements as full citizens. But what appears to have been lost in the UK is a 'public' under-

[11] As part of the UK immigration policy to create a 'hostile environment', thousands of people who had migrated from the Caribbean in the post-war period (known as the Windrush generation after one of the original ships that brought them to the UK) were wrongly classified as 'illegal immigrants'. Many were illegally deported, imprisoned, denied healthcare and lost their jobs and homes. The UK government finally admitted the mistake after many months of media reports by the Guardian in 2018.

standing of collective responsibility for care, although for many of the older generation, like the people who took part in our research, this has been an integral part of their understanding of citizenship. The wider cultural politics of individualism that has taken hold over time, the long game played by neoliberals, has happened insidiously without a full public debate on the democratic implications of these changes. So, the potential of the welfare state to be moving towards 'caring with' (Tronto 2013) is lost along with recognition of the value of 'the public' and collective responsibilities at a societal level.

On the ground the upheavals created by these transformations are evident in a system characterised by volatility and fragmentation, with complex and differing funding arrangements for health and social care. The result is a constantly 'shifting sands' system which is challenging for all who need to navigate it: those who work in it as well those who depend on it for care (National Audit Office 2018). The complexities of these changes have become obfuscated by the dominant neoliberal mantra of 'choice' and the common-sense logic of austerity ideology. This has done little to promote understanding or informed debate amongst a wider public about care, and questions about the division of responsibilities for care that we might aspire to in a democratic society. Indeed, such is the lack of public understanding about the current funding and organisation of social care that a widely held (mistaken) belief persists that the welfare state still provides 'cradle to grave' coverage, collectively funded through social insurance and tax contributions (National Audit Office 2018).[12]

Some have argued that it was the success of the social democratic welfare state that led to its downfall (Hall et al. 2015). Massey (2015) argues that even the limited redistribution and gains in social rights proved intolerable to capitalist interests and the result was the emergence of neoliberalism as a backlash against those gains. To succeed, the neoliberal backlash had to displace the shared 'public' understanding underpinning the welfare state—the commitment to social equality and the role of the state in guaranteeing it—and replace it with a new 'common sense' based on competitive individualism and market relations. Recognising the role that the terminology of neoliberalism plays in shaping our understanding is crucial,

[12] *Ipsos MORI* poll conducted in March 2018 found that large sections of the population wrongly think that social care services are free and provided by the NHS—63% of population thought that NHS provided social care for older people and 49% thought that social care is free at the point of need (NAO 2018).

as Massey argues the "whole vocabulary we use to talk about the economy, while presented as a description of the natural and the eternal, is in fact a political construction that needs contesting" (Massey 2015, 6–7).

A similar point is made by Metcalf (2017) who argues that we need to return to the origins of neoliberalism, to the actual group of men who called themselves 'neoliberals', whose aim and purpose was a 'revolution in economic thought' and trace the intellectual journey of their ideas. We need to be reminded that the 'free market' is a human invention and to see:

> the extent to which a language formerly confined to chalkboard simplifications describing commodity markets (competition, perfect information, rational behaviour) has been applied to all of society, until it has invaded the grit of our personal lives, and how the attitude of the salesman has become enmeshed in all modes of self-expression. (Metcalf 2017 online)

To break through this and 'think differently', what Tronto (2017) has referred to as the need to replace *homo economicus* with *homo politicus*, what counts as relevant knowledge under neoliberalism needs critical examination. If 'caring democracy' requires the dismantling of the neoliberal hold, then a paradigm shift in what constitutes knowledge about care will be needed. An essential part of this is the epistemological dimension of care. Looking at lived experiences of those engaged in the daily giving and receiving of care is to engage with the evidence of what neoliberalism produces on the ground.

Neoliberal logic works through systems and services, including public services of health, education and care services, by audit and measurement of performance indicators. Only things that can be easily counted, (e.g. number of minutes per care visit or number of students registered on a course) are recognised as 'objective facts'. Metcalf (2017) has argued that the founding principles of neoliberalism in Hayek's ideas, that objective truth could only be discovered through the market, have been elevated to a kind of 'social omniscience'. This has penetrated not only the management of the commercial world but public health and care sectors where an audit culture prevails, and measurement based on statistics and performance indicators are the only tools used to produce 'intelligence' about the system. The potential understanding that could be drawn from (in the case of our study) the experience of people with care needs, who are on the receiving end of those systems, is outside of the neoliberal frame. Moreover, efforts to include service user knowledge in policy research and practice tend to be done through a consumerist model which limits this potential.

By contextualising the experiences of our participants as they negotiate the social care market the parameters of the 'crisis' become clear. It is not purely an economic crisis of excessive public expenditure and debt, as the government claims in order to manage the fiscal crisis in the banking sector. Nor is it not just a crisis in care for the lives of the millions of ordinary people who have been impacted by the austerity policies. It is a crisis of care *and* a crisis of democracy in the lack of public debate, agreement and decision-making on major and far-reaching decisions about the basic infrastructure of society.

Neoliberalism, as the doctrine that dominates all spheres of daily life today, impoverishes our capacity to think deeply about the meaning of our actions and experiences. By offering neat and tidy 'answers' (measurable, quantifiable, objective) it makes the complexity of human existence less visible. If we are to *really think* about care and in the case of our study, what care means as in old age and as we approach the end of our life, we must engage with this complexity and lived experience. The kinds of answers that neoliberalism provides are simply not fit for purpose as they are empty and meaningless in this context. To shift public understanding beyond the economic, to enable the political mobilisation of solidarity required for 'caring with' will indeed need breaking the stranglehold on our imagination of what is possible. Listening to the lived experiences of those engaged in the daily struggles of giving and receiving care in a whole range of contexts has the potential power to challenge the neoliberal narrative and how we think about care.

Acknowledgements We thank Beatrice Gahagan and Petr Urban for their detailed feedback on this chapter. We would also like to acknowledge the contribution of all the co-researchers and research teams in the Ethical Issues in Self-funded Social Care: Co-producing Knowledge with Older people project that this chapter draws on. This work was supported by the Wellcome Trust [203363/Z/16/Z].

References

Association of Directors of Adult Social Services (ADASS). 2017. *ADASS Budget Survey 2017*. Leeds: Association of Directors of Adult Social Services.

Barnes, Marian. 2012. *Care in Everyday Life: An Ethic of Care in Practice*. Bristol: Policy Press.

Cameron, David. 2009. *Hugo Young Lecture 10th November 2009*. https://conservative-speeches.sayit.mysociety.org/speech/601246. Accessed 21 November 2018.

Care Quality Commission (CQC). 2018. *State of Health and Adult Social Care in England 2017–18*. Newcastle: Care Quality Commission.

Clarke, John, and Janet Newman. 2012. The Alchemy of Austerity. *Critical Social Policy* 32 (3): 299–319.

Clarke, John, Janet Newman, and Louise Westmarland. 2007. The Antagonisms of Choice: New Labour and the Reform of Public Services. *Social Policy & Society* 7 (2): 245–253.

Davies, William. 2012. The Emerging Neocommunitarianism. *The Political Quarterly* 83 (4): 767–776.

Department of Health (DH). 2010. *Practical Approaches to Improving the Lives of Disabled and Older People through Building Stronger Communities*. London: Department of Health.

Fotaki, Marianna. 2009. Are All Consumers the Same? Choice in Health, Social Care and Education in England and Elsewhere. *Public Money & Management* 29 (2): 87–94.

Gentleman, Amelia. 2019. UK to Pay up to £200m in Compensation to Windrush Victims. *Guardian*, April 3. https://www.theguardian.com/uk-news/2019/apr/03/uk-pay-windrush-victims-200m-compensation-lives-damaged-hostile-environment-policy. Accessed 31 May 2019.

Glendinning, Caroline. 2017. Long-Term Care and Austerity in the UK – A Growing Crisis. In *Long-Term Care for the Elderly in Europe: Developments and Prospects*, ed. Bent Greve, 107–125. Oxford and New York: Routledge.

Hall, Stuart, Doreen Massey, and Michael Rustin, eds. 2015. *After Neoliberalism? The Kilburn Manifesto*. London: Lawrence and Wishart.

HM Government. 2014. *Open Public Services Progress Report*. London: Cabinet Office. https://www.gov.uk/government/publications/open-public-services-2014-progress-report. Accessed 24 March 2019.

Humphries, Richard, Ruth Thorlby, Holly Holder, Patrick Hall, and Anna Charles. 2016. *Social Care for Older People: Home Truths*. London: The King's Fund.

Ismail, Mohamed, Shereen Hussein, Martin Stevens, John Woolham, Jill Manthorpe, Fiona Aspinal, Kate Baxter and Kritika Samsi. 2017. Do Personal Budgets Increase the Risk of Abuse? Evidence from English National Data. *Journal of Social Policy* 46 (2): 291–311.

Massey, Doreen. 2015. Vocabularies of the Economy. In *After Neoliberalism? The Kilburn Manifesto*, ed. Stuart Hall, Doreen Massey, and Michael Rustin, 3–16. London: Lawrence and Wishart.

Metcalf, Stephen. 2017. Neoliberalism: The Idea that Swallowed the World. *Guardian*, August 18. https://www.theguardian.com/news/2017/aug/18/neoliberalism-the-idea-that-changed-the-world. Accessed 21 November 2018.

Mol, Annemarie. 2008. *The Logic of Care: Health and the Problem of Patient Choice*. London: Routledge.

National Audit Office (NAO). 2014. *Adult Social Care in England: On Overview*. London: National Audit Office.

———. 2018. *The Health and Social Care Interface*. Report of the Comptroller and Auditor General, National Audit Office, Ministry of Housing, Communities and Local Government, Department of Health and Social Care.

Stewart, Zoe. 2017. Passport checks for patients is an abandonment of NHS principles. Guardian April 7. https://www.theguardian.com/commentisfree/2017/apr/07/passport-checks-patients-nhs-principles-health-tourists. Accessed 14 August 2019.

Tanner, Denise, Lizzie Ward, and Mo Ray. 2018. 'Paying Our Own Way': Application of the Capability Approach to Explore Older People's Experiences of Self-Funding Social Care. *Critical Social Policy* 38 (2): 262–282.

Tronto, Joan C. 2013. *Caring Democracy: Markets, Equity and Justice*. New York: New York University Press.

———. 2017. There Is an Alternative: Homines Curans and the Limits of Neoliberalism. *International Journal of Care and Caring* 1 (1): 27–43.

United Nations. 2019. *Human Rights Council Visit to the United Kingdom of Great Britain and Northern Ireland: Report of the Special Rapporteur on Extreme Poverty and Human Rights*. A/HRC/41/39/Add.1. United Nations General Assembly. https://documents-dds-ny.un.org/doc/UNDOC/GEN/G19/112/13/PDF/G1911213.pdf?OpenElement. Accessed 14 August 2019.

Ward, Lizzie, and Beatrice Gahagan. 2010. Crossing the Divide Between Theory and Practice: Research and an Ethic of Care. *Ethics and Social Welfare* 4 (2): 210–216.

Williams, Fiona, and Deborah Brennan. 2012. Care, Markets and Migration in a Globalising World: Introduction to the Special Issue. *Journal of European Social Policy* 22 (4): 355–362.

CHAPTER 12

Women's Experiences of Poverty in Japan: Protection and the State

Yayo Okano and Satomi Maruyama

Introduction: The Limits of Social Protection

This chapter tackles a problem in which multiple issues are intertwined, including lower levels of care for the vulnerable, a strong belief in the traditional family, the neoliberal emphasis on self-responsibility, and a new trend of hawkish calls for a strong nation in Japan. The first two issues would be traditionally categorized as private issues and the latter two as public ones. These four issues are discussed by both neoliberals and neoconservatives. How are they interconnected and how are these issues politically influential in Japan? Then, how can we move beyond the connections between them?

The purpose of this chapter is to address these questions by taking our starting point from Joan Tronto's discussion about "assigning responsibility" as a main political agenda (Tronto 2013, 30) and applying her argument to the Japanese socio-political situation.

Y. Okano (✉)
Doshisha University, Kyoto, Japan

S. Maruyama
Kyoto University, Kyoto, Japan

P. Urban, L. Ward (eds.), *Care Ethics, Democratic Citizenship and the State*, International Political Theory,
https://doi.org/10.1007/978-3-030-41437-5_12

From its defeat in World War II until the end of the 1980s, Japan was proud of its miraculous economic growth replacing its former militaristic expansionism. However, its high production and strong consumer culture were supported by the strict sexual division of labor. As Mari Miura, a political scientist of the Japanese welfare system, argues, the Japanese model of social protection[1] can be characterized as 'welfare through work,' which was sustained by the gendered dual system (Miura 2012). This means that the social protection system in Japan aims to protect citizens from poverty, unemployment, illness, injury, disability, and infirmity by offering them stable employment and encouraging a certain type of family.

'Welfare through work,' however, does not function for all types of workers but only for regular workers. While maintaining the breadwinner regime, Japanese employers can enjoy labor market flexibilities. For example, various types of non-regular workers exist outside of the framework of labor law which protects regular workers. They are workers with part-time employment, fixed-term contracts, or indirect employment. During recessions, employers can restrict as well as dismiss those non-regular workers. "Japanese employers essentially have a free hand [...] with respect to the use of non-regular workers, which counterbalances the rigidity of employment protection" (Miura 2012, 26). The coexistence of such totally different ways of employment, in fact, is allowed by the sexual division of labor.

Through this characterization, Miura points out that regular workers are likely to be well protected through the welfare and benefits given by their companies and that the highly protected labor conditions for regular workers are maintained by the large number of potentially irregular workers, who are mostly women with children.

The ideal household created by this social protection system is represented as follows: the husband is an employee, attached to a single company for his entire career and earning the family wage, while the wife is a housewife, as well as potential cheap labor power. The Japanese government once characterized Japan as a 'welfare society,'[2] where both, the

[1] 'Social protection system' is a wider category than 'social security system,' which means the institution of social insurance and pension. The former includes labor regulations, social assistance, community-based services to the vulnerable, child protection, and so on.

[2] According to Katsuhiro Hori, it was 1975 when the notion, 'the Japanese model of welfare society' was first discussed by critics of Japanese social policy and then the LDP published a book as one volume of the policy series, whose title was *The Japanese Model of Welfare Society* in 1979 (Hori 1981, 37). Since then, the theory of 'the Japanese model of welfare

companies to which male citizens belong and the families where female citizens assume unpaid work, were expected to provide them with social protection from poverty and vulnerability. This was in contrast to 'welfare states' such as the UK at the end of the 1970s.

While large companies attracted their male employees with a family wage and better welfare benefits in order to cultivate their loyalties and a sense of belonging, stable families, or good wives and mothers, became the 'home' for a man and his children. Hiroko Takeda acutely points out the 'political' function of family in Japan:

> [T]he family in post-war Japan has constantly shouldered the responsibility of mediating economic and social risk via domestic work by women as a part of the state mechanism of governing the population. Tax and social security were organized from the 1960s onwards so as to 'appreciate' housewives' indirect contribution to the national political economy through unpaid work. (Takeda 2008, 162)

As a result of policies encouraging women to be housewives, which means jobless wives with husbands with a full-time job, the numbers of housewives doubled from 8,900,000 in 1955 to 15,190,000 in 1975 (Honda 2014, 27). Because the family was forced to function "as an 'absorber' of economic and social risks" (Takeda 2008, 161), those who could not fit to this ideal type, such as single mothers, became marginalized and suffered from severe poverty.

However, the Japanese system of social protection, sustained by a happy marriage between employment protection for regular workers and the gender division of labor, has not functioned since the 1990s. Since the bubble economy, where Japanese firms and citizens enthusiastically purchased real estates and stock and widened the gap between real economy and financial economy from 1986 to 1991, collapsed, Japan has struggled with the retrenchment of the economy, stable labor markets and populations, and the growth of social anxiety (Allison 2013, 30).[3]

society' became well known and has been discussed enthusiastically by scholars as well as criticized by feminist scholars.

[3] According to Allison, the sudden change of socioeconomic climate increased the number of suicide deaths dramatically: they reached about 32,000 in 2003. The 2018 white paper on suicide countermeasures indicated that suicide was the first cause of death among young people between 15 and 34 years old. See https://www.mhlw.go.jp/wp/hakusyo/jisatsu/16/dl/1-03.pdf (accessed February 8, 2019).

Dependent on 'welfare through work,' the Japanese government could not immediately offer alternative ways to protect people from poverty, such as heightening social spending or redistribution through taxes, but instead deepened the gap between the highly protected regular workers and the lower paid irregular workers by deregulating labor law to increase levels of irregular jobs. Since the late 1990s, the system of 'welfare through work' itself has created new social risks such as the emergence of the working poor and the lack of adequate safety nets.[4] Now many people, especially women in Japan, suffer from the lack of social protection.

With this socioeconomic background of Japan in mind, this chapter proceeds as follows. The first section discusses the Japanese political situation by focusing on the current argument on the Constitutional amendments, especially Article 9 on the "renunciation of war" and Article 24 on the "equality of the two sexes within the family." In this section, the concepts of "protection pass" and "privileged irresponsibility,"as argued by Joan Tronto, play a critical role. The second section introduces the current situation of the poverty of women in Japan with data and examples. This clearly shows how the family ideologies and social protection system worsen the severe conditions of women and prevent Japanese society from facing the reality of women's sufferings. Ironically, women's poverty is protected from public attention within the family. The third section discusses how the idea of a 'caring democracy' with a radical critique of 'protection pass' can tackle the predicament of poverty and the lack of social protection for women by analyzing a nongovernmental organization's (NGO) activities in Japan. As Joan Tronto argues, the 'protection pass' allows those who engage in protection work, such as the police and military, to be exempted from caring responsibility. We shall find out how the warlike or hawkish appeal by the Japanese Prime Minister disguises and excuses the lack of attentive care to uneasiness and the needs of everyday lives. The notion of 'protection pass' leads us to reconsider the nature of political responsibility. We then conclude that the concept of democratic participation should be transformed, following Tronto's idea of 'caring with' to break the vicious circle of weakening social protection and strengthening military protection in Japanese society.

[4] According to Miura, because of the government's reliance on the conventional system of social protection, social safety nets such as health care insurance or employee pension do not function for "those who work under short-hour contracts and/or fixed-term contracts" (Miura 2012, 91).

Greater Protection for the Nation and Families

Since Shinzo Abe gained his second premiership of the Liberal Democratic Party (hereafter LDP) in September 2012, he has persistently attacked the Constitution.[5] The main target of the attack on the Constitution has been Article 9, which defines the 'renunciation of war' based on the reflection of the defeat in World War II.[6] Yet, it should also be noticed that the issue of family is the focus of today's constitutional controversy. For example, the preamble of a draft of the LDP's Constitution published in April 2012 (hereafter the 2012 draft) reads: "We, the Japanese people, defend our country and territorial land with pride and strong spirit [...] do value harmony and do form a nation where families and the whole society support each other."

According to Abe's understanding of the history of the Constitution, because Article 9 renounces the right of the state to be belligerent, the state of Japan cannot protect its citizens. In his book, Abe asserts that the sentences in the preamble of the current Constitution[7] are "too dependent on others, and strangely humble and petty" (Abe 2013, 126). In fact, Article 9 of the 2012 draft establishes the national defense military force with the Prime Minister as its supreme commander.

On the other hand, Abe also emphasizes family values. Members of the LDP and their sympathizers have criticized the current Constitution for lacking provisions for 'family protection.' They claim that, unless the

[5] Abe won his third leadership election of the LDP in August 2018. Since his second premiership started in December 2012, Prime Minister Abe showed his political strength, especially in his six consecutive victories in national elections, and it has been analyzed by many political scientists in Japan. For example, Koji Nakakita pointed out several reasons of his strength: heightened authority of prime minister by reforms of electoral system, the party subsidies system and the functionality of the Office of the Prime Minister, disappointment of the Democratic Party of Japan government (2009–2012) which started with ardent expectation and ended in failure, winning elections supported by a stable base of affiliated voters under low voting rate conditions in the 50–55% range, and so on (Nakakita 2019). Although Prime Minister Abe repeated that "it is the time to amend the Constitution" on every national election, voters supported Abe government mainly because of its seemingly stable politics or lack of his rivals. See, for another example, the analysis of 2017 snap election (Kingston 2017).

[6] For a more detailed argument about Prime Minister Abe's constitutional attack, see Okano (2018).

[7] The current preamble to the Constitution reflects the postwar sensibility to anti-war beliefs and the urgency of democracy.

family is protected as a fundamental unit of society, the unity of the family is being disintegrated and family values are collapsing.[8]

The current Article 24, which defines respect for individual dignity and the equality of both sexes within the family, has played an important role in remedying the legal and social discrimination against women. Until the end of World War II, there were no legal rights for women, while the patriarch in a family had absolute rights and authority legally under the Constitution of the Empire of Japan. The purpose of the current Article 24 is to deny this pre-war patriarchal system because women's inferiority, or, to say correctly, their rightless position in the family, was regarded as the fetters governing their participation in society.

The simultaneous emphasis on the protection of citizens by the state and that of the family as the foundational unit of society is curious enough when we carefully read Joan Tronto's argument regarding 'passes' out of caring responsibilities. Tronto points out the strict dichotomous boundaries between the feminine/private and the masculine/public structure of our society and mind. These boundaries, therefore, "permit some to bear the burdens (and joys) of care and allow others to escape them" (Tronto 2013, 33). While some—women, foreigners, and the socially disadvantaged—are charged with caring activities, others receive 'passes' out of caring responsibilities because they are engaged in other activities, which are valued as more important than caring activities. These passes are given to those who engage in the activities of 'protection'—such as the military and police—and 'production.'

As we shall discuss more in Section 'Greater Protection for the Nation and Families,' while social protection for poor women has been very weak, society places a high expectation on women to take on a caring responsibility for their families. On the other hand, it seems reasonable to argue that Japan did not provide people with a military 'protection pass' but only a 'production pass,' because Japan substituted its former militaristic

[8]The LDP's Q & A about amendments to the Constitution refers to Article 16 of the Universal Declaration of Human Rights, which asserts that "the family is the natural and fundamental group unit of society and is entitled to protection by society and the State." However, Article 24 of the 2012 draft reads as follows. "Family shall be respected as the natural and fundamental unit of society. Family members must support each other." In a word, the 2012 draft protects the unity of the family in order to emphasize self-responsibility to help each other within a family unit. Unlike the Universal Declaration, there is no mention of social or state responsibility to support families. See https://jimin.jp-east-2.storage.api.nifcloud.com/pdf/pamphlet/kenpou_qa.pdf (accessed January 29, 2019).

expansionism for its economic expansionism. Does it seem that Abe is eager to introduce a new protection pass for people to avoid caring responsibilities?

Focusing on the usage of protection in the Constitutional argument leads us further to rethink Charles Tilly's argument about the 'protection racket.' In his breakthrough essay in 1985, Tilly articulated the ambiguity of the term 'protection.' On the one hand, it literally means protection against fears, threats, and damages. On the other hand, "it evokes the racket in which a local strong man forces merchants to pay tribute in order to avoid damage—damage the strong man himself threatens to deliver" (Tilly 1985, 170). Tilly explored the history of modern nation-states by examining state-making and war-making as "quintessential protection rackets" (ibid., 171).

The dynamic process of state war-making "in essentially the same way as racketeers" (ibid.) reinforces the hierarchical relation between the protector (the state) and the protected (citizens). While citizens must gain from the state protection—no threats from outside, the feeling of security, and a stable livelihood—they have, in fact, no alternative ways to protect themselves without any resources, information, or powers. In this sense, the state as a protector is overwhelmingly powerful and its citizens are literally powerless.

As Tronto argues, the "[p]rotection of the body politic from its enemies, external and internal, has always been an important part of the responsibilities of citizenship" (Tronto 2013, 72). If Tronto's argument is right, then the question is: do the Japanese government and its male citizens gain the protection pass? Is this the reason why the Japanese government, especially Abe, often provokes the threats of external enemies[9] and tries to establish a national defense force?

To explore more implications of the 'protection racket' and the relationship between the attacks on Article 9 and Article 24 of the Constitution, it is also useful to recall the feminist analogy between national security and

[9] J-Alert was introduced in 2007 as a nationwide warning system to inform the public about various threats such as earthquakes, tsunamis, and volcanic eruptions. After North Korea test-fired a new intercontinental ballistic missile, some cities started to conduct a drill for the J-Alert to prepare for the North Korean threat. See, for example, "Fukuoka conducts J-Alert drill to brace for North Korean missile launch," *The Japan Times* (December 1, 2017). https://www.japantimes.co.jp/news/2017/12/01/national/fukuoka-conducts-j-alert-drill-brace-north-korean-missile-launch/#.XE-mY1X7RhE (accessed January 29, 2019).

marriage. Spike Peterson argues that "as protection rackets, states and marriage are implicated in the reproduction of hierarchies and in the structural violence against which they claim to offer protection" (Peterson 1992, 51). In the system of marriage as a 'protection racket,' "apparent gains can mask actual costs in the following four contradictory ways" (ibid., 50).

First, while individual women who choose marriage are rational enough to calculate their own gains and costs, their rational choices systematically reproduce their dependency. Second, because wives try to accumulate their interests and securities through their husbands, it becomes difficult for wives to find and share 'common interests' with other wives and to transform the current system by acting together.

Third, as in the relationship between state protection and citizens, the protectors maintain the power to assess and control the gains and costs of, as well as threats to, their marriage. On the other hand, those who are protected tend to identify themselves with their protectors. Therefore, because they are likely to lose their own particular standpoints and interests, the wives tend to develop attitudes of non-participation in social and political activities.

The fourth issue here represents the most powerful dynamics of the system of marriage as a 'protection racket.' While we can recognize the structural hierarchy, inequality, discrimination, and even violence that marriage contains, "once institutionalized, protection systems render disengagement risky at best, and possibly devastating" (ibid., 52). Especially for the potentially 'protected,' their disengagement in marriage for their protection places a stigma on them and exposes them to social and institutionalized disadvantages. These points bring us back to these questions: what is the relation between Article 9 and Article 24, and why do those who attack Article 9 also target Article 24 with the emphasis of protection?

Abe called Article 9 "strangely humble and petty," and described the state of Japan as appearing 'too dependent' to be a protector from a patriarchal point of view. In this context, the Japanese government and its male citizens cannot gain the protection pass or the superior status as a protector of their vulnerable citizens: that is, women and children. Similarly, Article 24 regulates that any laws related to family and marriage "shall be enacted from the standpoints of individual dignity and the essential equality of the sexes." Therefore, in principle, there should be no legal regulations to force a married couple into the relationship of protector and protected. Moreover, because of the change in the industrial structures and unstable conditions of the labor market under the globalization of the market, marriage and family are losing their capacity to protect their members.

The current socio-political situation in Japan suggests that there is no pass for either protection or production in Japan that enables the evasion of caring responsibility. The Japanese government has not responded to global economic change by reforming its social protection system, but rather by reinforcing the gendered dual system through enhancing the importance of protection, both through national security and through conventional family values.

The following section turns our eyes to more concrete structural situations relating to female poverty in Japan. By closely examining the conditions of poor women and the support provided for them by the NGO Moyai, it should be noticed how the political reintroduction and reinforcement of the gender hierarchy has contributed to worsening and hiding the conditions of poor women.

Women's Hidden Poverty: The Role of Family Ideology

As discussed earlier, Japanese politics today has taken its direction toward reinforcing the gendered hierarchy both within the family and the state. By exploring the data, this section articulates first the situation of Japanese women in general, and then the differences between women's and men's conditions, resulting from their family positions. Analyzing the difficulties that are specific to women will clarify how the reinforcement of gender hierarchy through the ideology of family will have a devastating effect on women and society as a whole. In a word, women are being forced to be the more vulnerable 'protected.'

Statistics show that Japanese women have a lower income than men. An overall 49.8% of women are a part of the labor force: this is relatively lower than that in other Western countries. Even then, 55.5% of working women are in non-regular employment, whereas only 21.9% of men have the same status (Nishi 2017). It is still often too difficult for Japanese women to work, caring for children, and doing housework at the same time. Therefore, 60% of them leave their workplace after marriage, as well as after the birth of their first child (National Institute of Population and Social Security Research 2015), and women's participation rate by age still maintains an M-shaped curve. Moreover, Japan's gender pay gap shows that even full-time female workers earn only 73.4% of the wage of males (Ministry of Health Labor and Welfare 2016): this ratio is the third worst out of all Organisation for Economic Co-operation and Development (OECD) countries (OECD data 2017).

The social security system, which includes pension, social insurance, and taxation, also favors the 'ideal type' of family, which consists of a male breadwinner and a wife who is not working full time. If women living with salaried fathers or husbands earned between $11,800 and $14,500 per year, it would be reasonable to keep their income below $11,800 by adjusting their working hours, as this would enable their household income to be greater after tax and insurance cost deduction.[10] While women individually make rational choices to live with their families, as well as to limit their working hours, this familism of the social security system often prevents wives from being economically independent.

With low incomes and a social security system that privileges male full-time workers, Japanese women tend to stay with their families. Although numbers of unmarried single people are rapidly increasing, the marriage rate is still relatively high and the divorce rate is relatively low compared to that in other Western countries. Unmarried people tend to stay with their parents after graduating from school, and it is estimated that 45.8% of those between 20 years and 34 years of age live in their parents' house (Nishi 2017). In addition, the number of elderly people who live in a three-generation family household is prominently higher than that in other Western countries.

Interestingly, however, the 'feminization of poverty,' which is the phenomenon in which women represent a disproportionate percentage of the poor, is not visible in Japan, even though it has prevailed across the world. In a cross-national study on this phenomenon, June Axinn once stated that "Japan is a special case." "Ironically, Japanese women at this moment are not independent enough to achieve feminization of poverty; they cannot afford divorce and economic independence" (Axinn 1990, 104). In other words, as long as women stay with male breadwinners, their low income cannot be recognized as a problem, even if they are potentially poor. This has remained the case in Japan since the Japanese economy began to be retrenched in the 1990s. For example, more than 30% of solo

[10] This amount used to be lower than it is now. It was between $9300 and $11,800 before 2018, but it was raised after it came under fire for preventing women from earning more.

mothers live with their parents in the hope of gaining financial, housing, and childcare support: this is higher than in Western countries and has been increasing. Since the poverty rate of solo mothers living with their parents is half that of those living without their parents (Tamiya 2018), the family still makes women's poverty invisible.

Familism that covers both the real and potential poverty of women can also be seen in the way in which poverty is socially problematized. Since the late 1990s, the number of homeless people sleeping on the streets had rapidly increased in Japan.[11] In this context, Moyai, one of the most active and well-known NGOs to help poor people, was organized in 2001. Moyai originally began offering guarantors to homeless people who wanted to rent houses but had lost their relationship with their family, because at that time poor people without guarantors were often turned away from rental agreements, even after they secured money from public assistance. Once Moyai started, however, it turned out that people who came to seek assistance were not only homeless but encompassed a wide variety of people who faced difficulties in finding guarantors, such as foreigners living in Japan and women who had suffered from family violence. At this point, Moyai started giving advice to a variety of people living in poverty. In the global financial crisis of 2007–2008, Makoto Yuasa, who is a co-founder of Moyai, organized the 'year-crossing dispatched worker's village'[12] to showcase the existence of poor people to the public, and this received huge media coverage. It triggered the problematization of poverty in Japanese society and Moyai played a central role in this process. However, the symbolic image of poverty at that time was non-regular male workers who had lost their jobs and houses in the financial crisis.

It took more time for poverty among women to attract considerable public attention. In December 2011, a national newspaper posted on its front page that "one-third of single women and 57% of solo-mother households are in poverty" (The Asahi Shimbun 2011). The poverty rate

[11] Most of the homeless people in Japan are males and only 3% are females. For Japanese homeless women, see Maruyama (2018).

[12] In the financial crisis of 2007–2008, many dispatched workers who lived in workers' dormitories lost their jobs and were sent away. Because all the offices and public administration take a holiday for the new year in Japan, there was no place for them to go; therefore a 'dispatched worker's village' was organized by activists in order to offer them food and a place to sleep.

among solo mothers is as high as 50.8%,[13] old single women living mostly on their pension are extremely poor, and the increasing numbers of young women who have no choice but to go into the sex industry have received media coverage recently. However, we should be careful to focus not only on the extreme poverty of female-headed households but also on hidden poverty within households. This is particularly true in the case of Japan where women tend to stay at home in fear of becoming poor and the proportion of female-headed households is relatively low.

Based on these facts, the following examines the data from consultations conducted by Moyai. Through a gender-specific analysis of 3267 consulting cards from 2004 to 2015, it reveals how the family system and intimate relations of women have worsened or, to put it more correctly, have made it more difficult for them to get out of their current situations. Women make up 13.3% of those who consult Moyai. The women are slightly younger than the men and their average age is 42.6 years, whereas the men's average age is 45.8 years. In terms of family structure, almost all of the males are single, while only 56.1% of females are single and they come from a greater variety of households. Women's housing status is more stable than that of men: 27.1% of men and 64.8% of women live in owned[14] or rented housing, while 72.0% of men are homeless. More women have jobs: 21.5% of the men have jobs, compared to 33.2% of the women. Women's employment status is also more stable than that of men. The women who visit Moyai for a consultation have more money than the men: the median amount of money men have is $13, and that of women is $109. The women's health conditions are worse than the men's, especially their mental health: 92.8% of the women have some kinds of health problem, compared to 75.9% of the men. After the consultations, fewer women apply for public assistance: 63.5% of men and 37.5% of women. Women have more experience of being exposed to violence: 2.2% of men and 21.4% of women. According to these data, all indicators imply that the men who seek help with Moyai are poorer than the women.

The observation that the women who seek help are not as poor as the men accords with the discourse that the 'feminization of poverty' is not

[13] Although 81.8% of Japanese solo mothers are working, they are still very poor. One of the reasons for this is that only 24.3% of solo mothers receive child support from their ex-husbands and there is no way to collect it compulsorily in Japan (Ministry of Health Labor and Welfare 2017).

[14] The questionnaire did not include a question on who owns the houses, but in most cases, it is assumed that it is not the women themselves but their fathers or husbands.

visible in Japan. On the one hand, women seem to take the situation of fearing being poor more seriously than men do, and therefore they seek support earlier than men. On the other hand, there are other cases where the women seeking help, even though they may not be regarded as poor as the men, do suffer from hardship that is specific to women. However, the difficulties that women face are not considered to be problems of visible poverty because their hardships are hidden in their families. The following refers to two case studies of people who sought help at Moyai, where women suffered from poverty, but it was concealed within their families.

In case number 1, A is not recognized as poor because poverty levels are usually measured on the household basis. A, a 45-year-old woman, lives with her husband and 13-year-old son. Because A has difficulty in hearing and some health problems, she does not work. She receives $38 disability benefit per month and this is the only money transferred to her own account. Her husband earns $3600 monthly but only gives her $270 per month. She cannot afford to purchase enough food, daily necessities, or pay for their son's educational expenses and medical services fees, while her husband spends much on his hobbies. He is abusive to her as well as their son, and now she is considering getting a divorce. As long as A's husband earns enough to support his family, A and her son are not regarded as poor and she cannot even apply for any benefits until she gets divorced.

In case number 2, B's poverty is caused by an enforced and thus internalized sense of motherhood and responsibility for caring for her son. B, a 61-year-old woman, divorced 23 years ago and currently lives with her 27-year-old son in public housing. B's son worked for several months after finishing high school but quit his job and has stayed in his room all the time since then. He used to hit and kick his mother but has recently never showed up or said anything to his mother, but has eaten the food she leaves at his door. He seems to be obsessive but has never seen a doctor. She earns her living with a part-time job but it is not enough for two adults. She has some health problems and worries about whether she can keep working, but she can hardly make her son leave. If B left her son, B could afford to live on her own, but she retains the role of a mother even for her grown-up son and it is regarded as her voluntary choice. Is her problem just personal?

Both cases A and B show particular difficulty for women in the family. A's poverty is derived from the material control of her husband who is regarded as her protector. As Peterson has clearly pointed out, he obtains the power to assess how much A and their child need. Then why cannot B, who is economically independent, leave her house? This question is open to many interpretations. However, it can be said that familism in Japan makes her situation invisible and that B is afraid of disengagement from her son. These examples of women's difficulties in their family reveal that 'family' in Japan often plays the role of a shield, which prevents women's poverty or other kinds of difficulty from being visible.

Toward a Caring Democracy and Greater Participation

Women in Japan tend to face social hardship because of the gendered dual system and the internalization of family values. On the other hand, by emphasizing the state's responsibility toward national security, the Abe administration has tried to turn attention away from the lack of social protection, while the 2012 draft has tried to force family members to depend on each other further rather than on the state.

If the 2012 draft became the Constitution of Japan, the government could gain 'protection passes' and families would take the burden of caring for each other. Husbands would tend to be protectors, and wives to be the dependent 'protected,' who is, in fact, in charge of taking care of the family members and household. Then the gender hierarchy, the fixed dichotomy of autonomy/dependency and public/private, would be structurally reinforced.

How can we alter the spiral of gendered dual system, whose protection is either economic or military? Here Tronto's idea of a caring democracy provides us with a significant suggestion, especially in terms of 'participation' in the following three points.

First, Tronto's definition of democratic politics is very insightful in rethinking what 'participation' means. She contends that "democratic politics should center upon assigning responsibilities for care, and for ensuring that democratic citizens are as capable as possible of participating in this assignment of responsibilities" (Tronto 2013, 30). As the low fertility rate in Japan has been recognized as a serious social problem since the 1990s, the Abe administration has started to encourage young people to get married. If people's real needs were cared about seriously, it could take measures for spending more on childcare and education, stop stigmatizing 'illegitimate' children, introduce family-friendly regulations in workplaces, and so on. Instead of introducing those policies, however, since 2013 the government has distributed about $28 million annually to local governments, for example, to arrange meeting places for the young under the name of 'grants in aid for regional birthrate.' The policy of encouraging marriage tends to prevent us from rethinking and participating in the assignment of care responsibilities because it emphasizes the family's responsibility to raise children and excludes the responsibilities of others and society as a whole. As the global gender gap index shows,[15] the extreme underrepresentation of female lawmakers offers few opportunities for women's voices to be listened to. As Peterson argued and the two examples in the Section 'Greater Protection for the Nation and Families' showed, because women in their families have difficulty finding their own interests, they are socially invisible or easily neglected. Therefore, most male representatives do not realize that they have to represent women's voices. Thus, the invisibility of the powerless women is reproduced. How can we find a key to break this vicious cycle of the voiceless or the lower participation of the needy? The second implication of Tronto's argument provides us with a key to the answer.

Tronto's idea of caring democracy illustrates the significance of a 'needs' interpretation of democracy. According to her, "needs are defined by more powerful members of the society, rather than those who have the needs themselves" (Tronto 2013, 148). As Section 'Greater Protection for the Nation and Families' mentioned, at first, Moyai did not anticipate female clients because they originally targeted homeless men. However, once female clients came to seek advice, Moyai offered them a place where they could believe that their individual voices were personally listened to. A 'thick needs interpretation' takes place in the interaction between the needy and those who listen to them (cf. Fraser 1989). Through this interaction, the needy might come to realize what they really need. The idea of caring democracy requires us to rethink seriously how the first dimension of caring practice, that is, 'caring about,' is closely linked to the creation of a democratic space where everyone's voice is both valued equally and safely expressed. A thick interpretation of needs also challenges the

[15] See the Report 2018. Political empowerment, especially women in Parliament, is the worst ranking as 130th, compared to other indications such as education and health. http://reports.weforum.org/global-gender-gap-report-2018/data-explorer/#economy=JPN (accessed February 8, 2019).

idealization of family values. On the one hand, emphasizing family values reinforces the existing gendered dual system, which assigns more burden of caring to women, deprives women of resources to participate in society, and social institutions are arranged according to this reality, leading to a worsening situation for women in poverty. In this context, as long as women are within the household, their situation of deprivation is treated as a personal problem. Against this trend, a thick interpretation of needs first encourages the needy to seek help beyond their family, then resituates them in a social structure, and reinterprets their hardship as a structural problem.

Finally, Moyai's example signifies the practice of 'caring with.' Tronto and Fisher once proposed four phases of care as 'four steps in the process of care' (Fisher and Tronto 1990), and then Tronto proposed a fifth phase of 'caring with' (Tronto 2013, 23). 'Caring with,' therefore, appears to be the final step of caring practice. However, Moyai's practice of 'caring with,' in which they open a place to which the needy come, are listened to and treated with equal dignity and respect, and also opens up the place of 'caring about,' as mentioned. The phase 'caring with' in this sense is one of the most important aspects, especially in the case of Japan, where many women are deprived of opportunities to voice their concrete needs through the official representative system.

Conclusion

The case of Japanese women shows that there is a huge gap between the shared understanding of caring responsibilities by the powerful and the reality of the unmet needs of care of the powerless. This dual system of the protectors and the protected politically veils the social risks of the vulnerable. The Japanese government has historically been so indifferent to the problem of poverty that the poverty rate was initially published as late as 2009. However, even today, when we realize that Japanese society faces a serious problem of poverty, women's poverty is still neglected. Strangely enough, the solution proposed by the Abe administration was not policy-based but ideology-based. Does the case of Japan suggest that, if the government forced some people into families, then the social problem of poverty could be easily solved? As Tronto once ironically suggested, "if one wishes to exclude some people from participating in democratic life, then the problems of care are easily solved" (Tronto 2013, 10).

However, an alternative can be clearly seen; "The more people share responsibilities for care publicly, the less they have to fear and the more easily they can trust others." However, "[c]hanging the way we think is hard" (ibid., 146). Moyai exemplifies caring practice, especially 'caring with.' By encouraging caring activities, Moyai enables us to democratize our way of thinking as well as our caring. As Moyai's case shows, interpreting caring needs with others and in a broader social and political context expands caring circles and creates solidarities among those who have their own particular needs. In fact, since Moyai organized the 'year-crossing dispatched worker's village' in 2007, various NGOs such as 'the Single Mothers Forum' and 'the Solidarity Network with Migrants Japan,' associations such as 'the Young Contingent Workers Union' and individuals with different backgrounds have come together under an umbrella association, Anti-Poverty Campaign.[16] It is no exaggeration to say that their movement to 'care about, for and with' the issue of poverty was one of the causes which changed the government party from the LDP to the Democratic Party of Japan in 2009. Caring can democratize not only society but also ourselves.

References

Abe, Shinzo. 2013. *Toward a New Country: Toward a Beautiful Country*, Enlarged ver. Tokyo: Bunshun-shinsho. [安倍晋三『新しい国へ--美しい国へ完全版』(文春新書)]

Allison, Anne. 2013. *Precarious Japan*. Durham: Duke University Press.

Axinn, June. 1990. Japan: A Special Case. In *The Feminization of Poverty: Only in America?* ed. Gertrude Goldberg and Eleanor Kremen, 91–105. New York: Praeger.

Fisher, Berenice, and Joan C. Tronto. 1990. Toward a Feminist Theory of Caring. In *Circles of Care*, ed. Emily Abel and Margaret Nelson, 35–62. Albany: SUNY Press.

Fraser, Nancy. 1989. *Unruly Practices: Power, Discourse, and Gender in Contemporary Social Theory*. Minneapolis: University of Minnesota Press.

Honda, Yuki. 2014. *Reconnecting Society: Education, Work and Family*. Tokyo: Iwanami Shoten. [『社会を結びなおす――――教育・仕事・家族の連携へ』(岩波ブックレット、2014年)]

[16] It was established in October 2007 with the representative, Kenji Utsunomiya, a lawyer and the head of office, Makoto Yuasa. Makoto Kawazoe, the Secretary General of 'the Tokyo Young Contingent Workers Union,' discussed how many associations working for alleviating poverty in Japan met together, see Kawazoe (2008).

Hori, Katsuhiro. 1981. The Japanese Model of Welfare Society. *Quarterly: Social Security Research* 17 (1): 37–50. [堀勝洋「日本型福祉社会論」『季刊 社会保障研究』(1981年)]

Kawazoe, Makoto. 2008. Action Against Poverty: Japan's Working Poor Under Attack. *The Asia-Pacific Journal* 6 (3): 1–10. https://apjjf.org/-M%2D%2DKawazoe/2710/article.pdf.

Kingston, Jeff. 2017. Sinzo Abe Keeps Winning. *The Atlantic*, October 21. https://www.theatlantic.com/international/archive/2017/10/shinzo-abe-japan-military-article-9-north-korea/543546/. Accessed 15 August 2019.

Maruyama, Satomi. 2018. *Living on the Streets in Japan: Homeless Women Break Their Silence*. Melbourne: Trans Pacific Press.

Ministry of Health Labor and Welfare. 2016. *Basic Survey on Wage Structure*.

———. 2017. *National Survey of One Parent Family*.

Miura, Mari. 2012. *Welfare Through Work: Conservative Ideas, Partisan Dynamics, and Social Protection in Japan*. Ithaca: Cornell University Press.

Nakakita, Koji. 2019. Prime Minister Abe Shinzo Heads into Third Consecutive Term as President of the Liberal Democratic Party (Part 2)—Placing Importance on a Strong Base of Support and Obstacles to Creating a Legacy. *Discuss Japan* 51, February 6. https://www.japanpolicyforum.jp/politics/pt20190206070009.html. Accessed 15 August 2019.

National Institute of Population and Social Security Research. 2015. *Marriage and Childbirth in Japan Today: The Fifteenth Japanese National Fertility Survey*.

Nishi, Fumihiko. 2017. Current Situaion of the Unmarried Living with Their Parents. [西文彦『親と同居の未婚者の最近の状況』(2017年)].

OECD data. 2017. *Poverty Rate*.

Okano, Yayo. 2018. Prime Minister Abe's Constitutional Campaign and the Assault on Individual Rights. *The Asia-Pacific Journal* 16 (3): 1–10. https://apjjf.org/2018/5/Okano.html.

Peterson, Spike. 1992. Security and Sovereign States: What Is at Stake in Taking Feminism Seriously? In *Gendered States: Feminist (Re)Visions of International Relations Theory*, ed. Spike Peterson, 31–64. Boulder: Lynne Rienner Publishers.

Takeda, Hiroko. 2008. Structural Reform of the Family and the Neoliberalisation of Everyday Life in Japan. *New Political Economy* 13 (2): 153–172.

Tamiya, Yuko. 2018. Solo Mothers and Their Poverty in *Poverty*, ed. Komamura K. Minervashobo, 79–87. [田宮遊子「母子世帯と貧困」駒村康平編『貧困』(ミネルヴァ書房)]

The Asahi Shimbun. 2011. One-Thirds of Single Women and 57% of Lone Mothers Are in Poverty. December 9.

Tilly, Charles. 1985. War Making and State Making. In *Bringing the State Back In*, ed. Peter Evans, Dietrich Rueschmeyer, and Theda Skocpol, 169–187. Cambridge: Cambridge University Press.

Tronto, Joan C. 2013. *Caring Democracy: Markets, Equality, and Justice*. New York: New York University Press.

CHAPTER 13

Deficit of Democratic Care in the Educational System in Slovakia

Adriana Jesenková

Introduction

This chapter focuses on Slovakia and examines the deficit of care in the Slovak education system in particular. Slovakia is an example of a post-communist country that is still in the process of transformation from a totalitarian to a democratic society. The success of the democratization of Slovak society is largely determined by the formation of democratic citizenship, and education plays an irreplaceable role in this process. Since in the present institutionalized society, the state has a key role in the education system and processes through which it can and does exercise social control, regulate the activities, actions and lives of citizens, the relationship between the state, civil society and the education is very important for democracy.

Why is care ethics a useful tool in the Slovak context and in the field of education? Its application enables understanding and assessment of educational public policies in terms of their effectiveness for care, protection,

A. Jesenková (✉)
Faculty of Arts, Pavol Jozef Šafárik University, Košice, Slovakia
e-mail: adriana.jesenkova@upjs.sk

P. Urban, L. Ward (eds.), *Care Ethics, Democratic Citizenship and the State*, International Political Theory,
https://doi.org/10.1007/978-3-030-41437-5_13

development and flourishing of those concerned. As the rhetoric of caring for citizens, the future of democracy, the future of society and the country (not only) through education is a large part of the current political discourse (in and beyond Slovakia), care ethics can be a useful theoretical tool to identify and differentiate caring educational public policies from those which are an obstacle to, or even the opposite of, caring practices of education.

The concept of democratic care, developed by Joan Tronto (2013), implies that democracy without democratic care cannot survive. In order for care to bring the best possible results, it must be a democratic practice of care. The integrity of good care (practice) lies in mutual, shared care—in caring with others. A good practice of care, based on four principles, that is, attentiveness, responsibility, competence and responsiveness (Fisher and Tronto 1990), cannot be achieved, in accordance with the concept of democratic care, without mutual care with other members of society, with other citizens, that is, without shared mutual care. It means that only if the care is an activity in which others are democratically involved, is it possible to expect and achieve the best outcomes of care. However, not only democracy depends on the democratic practice of care but also the democratic practice of care depends on the democratic political order in which real, ordinary people have an opportunity to express themselves and to be heard by others (Tronto 2013, 55). So, democracy is better for practicing democratic forms of care, and ultimately for better life as a result of better care. It implies that a deficit of democracy in the practice of care determines a deficit of good care and consequently a deficit of good life as its result.

The Slovak education system suffers from several shortcomings, which are generally characterized as deficiencies in the democratic nature of education. Criticism of education deficits is most often focused on unequal access to education. This is considered to be the cause of the deepening of social inequalities and the social exclusion of multiple groups of children and young people. Criticism is less concerned about the content of education, its diversity, the extent to which educational practice is conditioned by the environment in which this practice is democratically implemented, as well as by the participation and inclusion of all actors concerned. Solutions to the democratic deficit in the education system and processes have been proposed in a number of reform initiatives since the foundation of independent Slovak Republic in 1993 and are geared towards an inclusive education system. Although there have been efforts to implement these from the outset, many of the identified shortcomings are still deepening, and attempts to reform and democratize education are still failing or remain inadequate. The issue is that the link between a democratic deficit in education and the lack of care in the education system in Slovakia is not sufficiently reflected.[1] It is necessary to understand the care deficit in the education system as a systemic problem which cannot be solved by individual care activities of individuals alone but by complex interconnected activities of care or transforming care practices based on the responsibility of the community. That means through collective responsibility for education as part of, and a precondition for, caring for a good life. It depends on the understanding of the relation between inclusion and mutual trust as a necessary assumption for the democratic participation of all concerned in the processes of allocating responsibilities. So, it is necessary to think how both trust and care might contribute to forms of social cohesion that can meet standards of inclusive citizenship (Sevenhuijsen 1998, 13).

The first part of the chapter is devoted to care ethics as a basis for distinguishing caring and non-caring forms of education. The focus is on clarifying how ethics of care can be a useful starting point for implementing inclusion in education processes. Then the deficit of democracy and care in education in the Slovak context is outlined and characterized through the case study of the reform of education in Slovakia. In the next section, drawing on care ethics, the risks to inclusive education in Slovakia are outlined, as well as the factors that need to be strengthened in education processes to reduce care deficits and increase its inclusiveness and democratic nature.

Education from Care Ethics Perspectives

In the framework of care ethics, detailed analyses of the educational process have been developed, as well as considerations regarding the structural conditions of educational practice and educational policies (Noddings 1984, 1992, 2002; Held 2006; Tronto 2013). Noddings offers a normative view on education. According to Noddings learning to care and to be cared for is a major developmental task (Noddings 2002). Noddings is very critical of liberal education (defined as a set of traditional disciplines).

[1] I have dealt with the issue of care in relation to the teaching profession in Jesenková (2012), but not from the perspective of care ethics.

She suggests that a morally defensible mission for education necessarily focuses on matters of human caring and the main aim of education should be to encourage the growth of competent, caring, loving and lovable people (Noddings 1984, 1992, 2002). She notices that at the present time the main educational purpose is not the moral one of producing caring people but a relentless drive for academic adequacy. In Noddings' view, the reason for this is the belief that poverty, crime and other evils of current society can be eliminated through better academic training and preparation, and greater numbers of people with greater mathematical and scientific competence. But these social problems are not the consequences of an educational failure, but a moral one. So, Noddings argues, we need to reorder priorities. Education should be organized around themes of care rather than the traditional disciplines. All children, all students should be engaged in general education that guides them in caring for the self, for intimate others, for global others, for animals, for plants, for the environment, for objects and instruments, and for ideas (Noddings 2002, 94–99).

Noddings argues (1) against an ideology of control that forces all students to study a particular, narrowly prescribed curriculum devoid of content they might truly care about; (2) for greater respect for a wide range of human capacities now largely ignored in schools and (3) against the persistent undervaluing of skills, attitudes and capacities traditionally associated with women (Noddings 2002, 95). She suggests that a moral policy for education should recognize a multiplicity of human capacities and interests. Preparation for the world of work, for parenting and for civic responsibility is essential for all students but schools largely ignore the centrality of such interests as intimate relationships in our lives. Noddings does not ignore the intellectual mission of schools. She believes that to put the moral life as the main goal of education does not work against intellectual development or academic achievement but supplies a firm foundation for both.

Held (2006) critically reflects on market expansion into education, arguing that the scope of market activities should be circumscribed by the needs to care. Further she argues that education is a social value that cannot be taken into account from a market perspective, as it lies in something other than the satisfaction of individual consumers or maximizing the profit of the provider. One of the important purposes of education is to produce a sense of community in civil society which depends on political institutions to carry out a shared concern for its vulnerable and dependent members in a caring society (Held 2006, 202).

Both, Noddings and Held, view care relations that connect people with their environment in all its elements—other people, communities, nature—as a fundamental aspect of human life. That is why they argue that the main purpose of education should be to form, develop, cultivate and strengthen human capacity to care for these relations and, through them, for ourselves and others. The relational ontological basis of care ethics implies that relationships are at the heart of ethical considerations. However, this relational ontology means focusing not only on personal relationships but also on the context, and therefore necessarily on the structural relationships and systemic conditions in which any relationships and care exist. In this context, Noddings deals with the organization of schools that take care seriously and the need for changes in the structure of school education (Noddings 1984, 197). Held extends her thinking to the whole of society and considers a caring society in which care values and caring relationships are of high value, supporting the practice of care and receptivity to other people. Thus, a caring society according to her promotes respect for human rights as a fundamental principle for civil society.

However, Tronto's approach highlights the structural conditions for applying ethics of care in practice by individuals, groups of individuals and society as a whole, including education. Tronto (2013) argues against the dominant idea that production and economic life are the most important political and human concerns. Although care is at the centre of human life, it is too often ignored by politics. So, democratic societies need to put the value of care at the centre of their political agenda. It is necessary to conceive care not only as a moral, or a social value, but also as a political value. This rethinking of care depends on a reconceptualization of the public/private division that is analogic to the politics/moral division. So, the reordering of priorities and shifting the value of care to the centre of education and social practice—as Noddings and Held stress—requires challenging and overcoming the borders between morals and politics, the private and the public, care and democracy.

Tronto critically reflects that the market-based approach to education appears to meet the needs of the economy (Tronto 2013). A care approach would stress instead the need for individual development and developing the skills necessary both to care, and to care about, being a citizen in a democratic society (Tronto 2013, 135). Tronto believes that education should be involved in shaping caring citizenship, while noting that any efforts to reform the education system are closely linked to clarifying fundamental issues of values, human rights, justice and morality (Tronto

2013, 134). Thus, education policy and education reform are a part of political and moral value issues in terms of care ethics.

According to Tronto, citizenship in democracy depends on citizens caring about one another and about democracy as well. However, this requires thinking about politics not as an electoral competition but as a collective activity in which we take care of our community and of its future. Democratic policy must then deal with the responsibility we have towards ourselves and other members of the community:

> Democratic policy should focus on the allocation of responsibilities for care and ensuring that democratic citizens are able to participate as much as possible in this allocation of responsibilities for care. (Tronto 2013, 140)

But what does the ability to participate in the allocation of responsibilities for care mean? And how shall we ensure that all citizens are able to participate in this process and are included? And what is our task as individuals, groups, institutions, as part of the community and society as a whole in this process and care practice?

Education for inclusive democratic citizenship requires us to take others as our equals and to care for their inclusion in the processes of allocation of responsibilities of care. It then depends on our mutual recognition and trust. And these elements of caring attitudes can grow only from and through common caring practices. Motivation to reflect upon caring practices of other people around us rises from recognition of our own vulnerability and interdependency. Tronto argues that inclusion consists in our willingness to share our resources and power to participate, and to decide about what is important for a good life and well-being, and ultimately this depends on all of us rethinking ourselves as care-receivers (Tronto 2013, 146–147). "Common caring practices" in this context means doing together, in a common environment, space and time, which makes it necessary to communicate; express opinions, desires, needs, interests, motivations and goals; and negotiate together on ways to achieve them, to avoid conflicts and satisfy the needs of everyone for well-being. So, it is necessary to see practices of voice and listening as crucial citizenship activities and consequently as crucial citizen competencies to learn.

The constitution of common space for common caring practices is very important in this regard. It enables more adequate, detailed and specific experiences and produces knowledge about others, and their forms and relations of caring. This can create the context for changing our perception of others and eliminating stereotypes as a precondition for the trust in others.[2] Trusting in the ability and willingness of others to be attentive to needs and then act carefully and responsibly (in relation to themselves and others) is linked with their recognition and acceptance as equal members of a moral community of mutual trust (Rorty 1997). At the same time, relational ontology and epistemology remind us that, precisely because we are part of complex networks of relationships of connection and interdependence, it is impossible to have absolute control over ourselves and others. Contingency is a necessary aspect of our lives, and so the requirement for absolute trust towards others is not only beyond human forces, but it also sets up unrealistic and unreasonable expectations for trusting relations. Sevenhuijsen (1998) emphasizes, we should acknowledge that we can only get to know others, as well as ourselves, in limited and partial ways. For Sevenhuijsen, we need to know more about micro-practices of trust in order to understand their contribution to democratic practices (Sevenhuijsen 1998, 13). In the context of education, this also means that creating the conditions for the emergence and development of trust through a common area of care must be linked to learning and cultivating critical thinking. This is an important way to distinguish what is trustworthy behaviour in the practice of care for all concerned in education.

From this perspective, understanding and models of protection are important factors effecting the mutual trust and recognition needed for inclusion. Protection is an important dimension of education as a practice of care. Tronto considers rethinking the concept of protection as an essential part of shaping caring democracy (Tronto 2013, 75–80, 171–173). In particular, Tronto draws attention to the link between protection, power and violence. The need to review the understanding of protection in the context of education is also important. Protection discourse appears in public education policies in various forms. It contains challenges to protect children and young people from many real and perceived dangers. But to what extent does the protection provided and declared really protect

[2] A similar point is made by Marian Barnes (2012, 127f.) that space and place are clearly vital to an understanding of individual and collective well-being. Particular spaces and environments can create material and symbolic conditions for developing confidence and critical thinking and thus for more equal and free caring practices or, on the contrary, increase distrust, control and obedience. So that environments, public spaces and institutions can be more or less caring from the democratic care perspective and can be more or less supportive for developing capacity to care inclusively and so democratically.

those who need it? Does education develop vulnerable persons' abilities to differentiate violence and coercion from protection, that is, careful protection from the hegemonic protectionism? Does it give children and young people the skills to be able to protect themselves and others in the future? This question is particularly topical in the context of sex education, for example. This raises the question of whether protection is reduced only to isolation from danger, which is associated with restricting access to information, knowledge and experience. This type of protection may also result in physical segregation, which further deepens ignorance, stereotyped knowledge, dangerous generalizations, fear and hatred.

A narrow understanding of protection as isolation from dangers limits vulnerable people, preventing their growth and development. In fact, this kind of protection results in the growth of vulnerability and powerlessness of "the protected". Truly careful protection seeks to prepare vulnerable persons for the pitfalls and complexities in life, to encounters with differences, disagreement, dissatisfaction, pain and injustice, and provides, shapes and develops competencies to deal with such situations, phenomena and events. Careful protection cultivates the ability to relate and to react to what may be truly dangerous, and respond by transforming relationships with the environment, including the vulnerable being itself (child, pupil, student), as well as other actors (classmates, teachers, parents, other adults). At the same time, careful protection teaches to critically examine and thus differentiate the degree of real danger and identify fictitious and unrealistic hazards. Careful protection thus creates secure relationships and an environment in which it is possible to prepare the currently vulnerable and dependent persons to trust and critically reflect on relationships with the real environment within the complex network of life. So, careful protection should teach us to trust ourselves and others on the basis of critical and a realistic approach to the world. Then education can provide the preparation for a collaborative and caring way of life, not for suspicious and paranoid isolationism.

Such forms of caring education could be one of the key preconditions for every citizen to be able to participate in the processes of determining responsibilities for different forms of care and thus to contribute to making care practice in the most diverse areas of life more just. Therefore, access to education can be conceived as a condition for a full-status citizenship that consists of the inclusive participation in democratic practices of care and care for democracy. Thus, this kind of education is needed by all because better care and better life for everyone depend on citizens caring for democracy and for democratic practices of care.

Reform of Education in Slovakia

The Slovak case of a democratic deficit in education based on the analyses of empirical data, shows causes, factors and mechanisms effecting the success or failure of inclusive processes, and therefore, of democratization (not only) in education. Since Slovakia is affected by global processes, such as the expansion of economism and neoliberalism and the related processes of marketization and commodification, at the same time the Slovak sociocultural and historical-political context has its own specificities. This makes it possible to compare similarities but also differences and particularities with other countries and their education reform activities aimed at democratic inclusion. Care ethics provides the conceptual framework to analyse the reform of the Slovak education from the care perspective. This issue is particularly relevant currently, when the concept of care is becoming an increasingly frequent part of the vocabulary of political actors, not only in Slovakia but in many European countries and across the world.

Education reform was declared as one of the priorities of the democratic transformation process in Slovakia from 1993 as the former Czechoslovakia divided into two independent countries. Efforts to reform education in the first two decades after 1989 are characterized by a centrally managed and externally motivated process, with political consensus on educational policy being attained only at the level of government and state institutions. The strategy of change was conceived without a wide public discussion, often without discussion at all, not only excluding the public but also education professionals. Although later on, the developed strategy was presented for public discussion, it was without sufficient preparation and sufficient time, so public involvement was limited. However, education strategies and programmes mostly responded to strategic policy at transnational level (the Lisbon Strategy and other EU and EC strategies) and had the character of action papers or sub-measures that responded to the priorities set from outside (social inclusion, gender equality, segregation of Roma children). Only gradually and very slowly the strategies have begun to be created on the basis of the field data.[3] On the other hand, with strong civil society and its individual components, especially after the fall of Meciarism in Slovakia (1998) and even more after joining

[3] National Institute for Certified Educational Measurements is a state organization founded in 2008 by the Ministry of Education of the Slovak Republic.

the EU (2004), there have been an increasing number of voices seeking to deepen the democratization reforms in education.

In 2008, the reform of the content of education at primary and secondary schools was initiated by adopting new school legislation. It represented a step towards decentralization of a traditionally prescribed and centrally managed educational system. For example, schools have been given greater freedom and scope for creativity through the possibility of adapting their specific school curricula (within 30%), allowing schools to adapt the educational process in a methodological way and to the specific conditions and needs of individual learning levels. However, reform legislative measures have not brought the expected changes in improving the social status of the teaching profession, which was one of the priorities of the reform. The progressive development of civil society has led to increasing interest and activity from non-governmental organizations and various civil associations and expert communities, pro-reform pedagogues and committed parents who have started to constitute formal and informal institutions supporting next reform changes in education. These institutions also raise the issue of discrimination linked to non-respect for human rights regarding access to education and to segregation, especially in relation to the ethnic Roma minority, as well as in relation to the rights of children and youth with health disabilities and other vulnerable individuals and groups. Insufficient solutions to these problems have contributed to deepening social inequalities and to increasing feelings of injustice. The failure of the reform efforts in education increased dissatisfaction and mistrust in the ability and willingness of competent authorities (state, municipalities, schools) to make the necessary changes. The dissatisfaction with the state of education on the part of teachers over the past decade has gradually resulted in the historically first one-day teacher strike in Slovakia in 2012 and the biggest teacher strike in 2016. Salary increases and education budgets have gained prominence in public debate. However, the public protest of dissatisfied teachers in the country, where governments used to confidently claim that "our people do not strike even when they are dissatisfied", has raised education as an important public issue. The debates concerning the objectives and meaning of education, as well as the values on which it is to be based, have become much more intense. In the demands of the teaching and professional community, which is gradually gaining support from parents and the wider public, there is an increasing call for systemic changes in education, although the consensus on what they are supposed to be is still being shaped.

In this context, a debate on inclusive education has started in Slovakia, which many see as a solution to the unsatisfactory state of Slovak education, and which has been analysed in detail in the *Education Status Report* (2013). The Slovak education system is characterized by a number of serious shortcomings, which to a large extent complicate, or even prevent, inclusion. These include:

- a low number of children in pre-school education;
- pupils of I. and II. grades do not go to one type of school (high selectivity);
- compulsory education does not cover a sufficiently long period of time (from 6 to 17 to 18 years);
- more than 10% of children leave school early;
- grade retention or school exclusion is frequent;
- education of disadvantaged groups is not considered an urgent and important issue in both national and regional school policies[4]; and
- the vast majority (80% or more) of disadvantaged pupils, disabled pupils and pupils with special educational needs are trained in special schools[5] and thus are not pupils of the mainstream education.[6]

Recently, two political documents for better education in Slovakia were published. In 2017, a draft of the National Programme for Education Development entitled *Learning Slovakia* was submitted for public discussion. This comprehensive strategic material was developed as a result of collaboration between experts, consultations and discussions with the public in the regions and it represents a qualitative vision of the

[4]The majority of students in special education are Roma students from a socially disadvantaged environment, especially students diagnosed with mild mental disabilities. Ministry of interior of the Slovak Republic. 2012. The Strategy of the Slovak Republic for Roma Inclusion until 2020. https://www.minv.sk/swift_data/source/romovia/dokumenty/StrategiaSR_integraciaRomov.pdf. Accessed 14 January 2019.

[5]Within European countries, Slovakia ranks first in the share of children educated in special classes or schools, thus, being separated from their peers. There are almost 6% of children in Slovakia special school system, while the European average is 2.3%. Ramberg, Joacim, Lénárt, András, and Watkins, Amanda, eds. 2017. *European Agency Statistics on Inclusive Education: 2014 Dataset Cross-Country Report.* Odense: European Agency for Special Needs and Inclusive Education. www.european-agency.org. Accessed 7 January 2019.

[6]Ministry of Education of the Slovak Republic. 2017. *Learning Slovakia*—National Programme for Educational Development. Proposal for Public Discussion. https://www.minedu.sk/data/files/6987_uciace_sa_slovensko.pdf. Accessed 28 June 2019.

development of Slovak education for one decade. The strategic goal is defined as the quality and availability of education. According to the authors the quality of education and its availability are closely linked. Without adequate availability education cannot be said to ensure quality for all and vice versa; accessibility without high quality is only half the goal. To meet the strategic objective, the document calls for the introduction of individualized learning, with the learner based at the centre, their individual potential and educational needs, and inclusive education, in which teachers, together with other professionals, can work with the diversity of pupils, their diverse potential, talents and disadvantages while perceiving this diversity as a natural phenomenon.[7]

This document was one of the starting points of a strategic political document for educational policy that was adopted by the Slovak government as the National Programme for Education Development 2018–2027, named *Quality and available Education for Slovakia*. The strategic goals of the programme are: (1) to increase the quality of the educational system, (2) to broaden access to quality education for all and (3) to modernize the content of the education system as well as management, funding and evaluation. The government explicitly declares that the Slovak educational system is insufficiently inclusive. So one of the three cross-sectional priorities in state strategy is to achieve inclusive education.[8] However, fully inclusive education is defined as the future goal at which the Slovak society should aim, with a focus on the gradual creation of human resources, material conditions and institutional background.

Undoubtedly, it is good that an effort to achieve inclusion as a prerequisite for the expansion of democracy is declared in such an important strategic policy document. Both documents, in defining the notion of inclusive education, are based on relevant United Nations Educational, Scientific and Cultural Organization (UNESCO) Guidelines on Inclusion in Education (2009) and the recommendations of the Council of Europe and the European Agency for Development in Special Education. But their philosophical assumptions and value background are different. The value basis, which is reflected in the content of *Learning Slovakia*,

[7] Ministry of Education of the Slovak Republic. 2017. "*Learning Slovakia*"—National Programme for Educational Development. Proposal for Public Discussion. https://www.minedu.sk/data/files/6987_uciace_sa_slovensko.pdf. Accessed 28 June 2019.

[8] Ministry of Education of the Slovak Republic. 2018. National programme for the development of education 2018–2027. Quality and available Education for Slovakia. https://www.minedu.sk/data/att/5250.pdf. Accessed 20 January 2019.

accentuates the lifelong learning process of a human being as the core of her human nature and the key to successful life. In particular, success refers to the subjective feeling of success and the joy of achieving the goal, not just a certain performance. This document characterizes human beings as learning beings whose perspectives, ability to solve life and work problems, as well as personal self-realization or meaningful life depend on their attitude to their own development and learning.

The main argument for inclusive education in the government's document is that insufficient inclusion prevents the country from reaching the goals of the Europe 2020 Strategy, which was adopted in 2010 and represents an agenda for providing employment and smart, sustainable and inclusive growth. Its strategic goal is to personally develop pupils and students and to acquire the relevant knowledge and skills needed to successfully apply graduates in the labour market. Implicitly, at the educational policy-making level but also explicitly, there is a neoliberal discourse in which the economic needs of the market and the labour market dominate in the formulation of goals and measures of the educational strategy of the government and the state. Inclusion then acts as an instrumental element for achieving economic and political indicators and goals. Attention is then drawn to education in areas that enable success in the current labour market, which enable the progress and growth of the national economy. According to a government document, education should focus on developing natural science and mathematical literacy. There is no explicit support for education of values such as ethics education or civic education, which marginalizes knowledge of social sciences and humanities.

Inclusive Education: A Care Ethics Perspective

The deficit of democratic care in the Slovak education system and practice, which is manifested by the failure of inclusion, has its causes, factors and mechanisms in its implementation. Insufficient or missing inclusion is generated and reproduced through multiple approaches or combinations thereof. Formalism is an approach that implements inclusion only as mechanical integration, without understanding and taking into account the complexity of inclusion processes. The instrumental approach in education policy uses implementation of inclusion as a tool to achieve other, especially economic and political, objectives. Finally, there is an approach of reducing inclusion to its economic and social aspects, which seeks to implement inclusion only through distributive justice and by ensuring economic and social equality. All these mechanisms and policy strategies fail to implement inclusion, while the problems they were originally supposed to solve are deepening and cumulating.

From the perspective of care ethics, there are a number of related risks that threaten the realization of an inclusive education vision and then for democratic education care practice. Here are just some of them. Resignation to individualized learning means the lack of attention to the specific needs of particular children, including "ordinary" children. The government's strategy is to focus on children with special needs because of exceptional talent or social or health disadvantages. An explicit focus on linking education with the needs of the economy and the labour market requires certain types of knowledge and skills, and thus necessarily leads to uniformity in education. Neglecting the specific needs of the various learners increases the likelihood of increasing dissatisfaction and mistrust. Probably an even greater threat in this case is the indifference and resignation with respect to the responsibility to participate in the formation of educational content, as the content is determined centrally by state authorities based on the demands of the economy, which is perceived to operate on the basis of its own laws. The democratic practice of care fades as it is not needed, and the attitudes, abilities and skills of democratically caring together with others also weaken.

Another risk is reducing inclusion to social or socio-economic inclusion. Our willingness to share the resources is conditioned by our ability to recognize the value of the lives of those with whom we share our resources and to trust them that they will handle them carefully and responsibly. So the measures of distributive justice are therefore inadequate. At the same time inclusion cannot be reduced to inclusion into certain social groups but rather it needs to be inclusion within a shared value framework. Inclusive education cannot simply be identified with desegregation or mechanical integration of different groups of students. While integration is about adapting a child to school, inclusive education seeks to adapt the educational environment to children and their needs. The diversity of children in class and school is perceived as something natural and normal. And this is the challenge of inclusive practice—inclusion necessarily opens the space to change for all agents in the inclusive process, not only those, whom we want to include. Within integration we expect, as active dominant agents, a change in those who are being integrated. The integrated persons are in the position of passive subjects; they are an object from which one activity is expected—adapting to the majority and their norms and patterns. Inclusion is a process where everyone opens up to a possible change because they create a new world in the process of inclusion. What must remain stable in this change are not the subjective identities but the values on which inclusion is grounded—democratic values, the non-hegemonic creation of a mutual world. Ultimately, this means that schools must have sufficient opportunities and competences to create and modify their school curricula in interaction with all stakeholders—children/pupils, teachers, parents, community. Only then can the learning process and practice identify and meet the needs of those concerned.

Neoliberal marginalization of education values threatens the very success of the inclusive education. To achieve social inclusion, cultural inclusion is also needed, and it is done through moral and civic education which includes the forming of attitudes and abilities to collaborate and communicate in a pluralistic social and cultural environment. This requires education to tolerance of differences, the ability to think critically in relation to oneself and others, as well as the ability to understand oneself and others in interdependence and connection. Our willingness to take care of our children's future together with others and to assume collective responsibility for education depends on our trust in others.

Not all the above-mentioned policy strategies and mechanisms pay enough or even any attention to the practice of trust and the creation of its conditions at various levels of the education system, especially at the micro level (classes, schools, communities). However, trust and recognition arising from it are essential prerequisites and thus success factors for inclusive processes. Trusting other people, who are different from us and whose ways of caring can differ from ours, is challenging, and therefore, recognizing their ways of life and care requires the ability to tolerate the differences. The ability to critically assess ourselves is important to be able to perceive and recognize our own shortcomings and to accept good suggestions and advice from others. The ability to critically assess others is important so that we do not fall into absolute trust in others as we are all interdependent, vulnerable, imperfect, and therefore everyone can fail. Absolute trust (in oneself or others) prevents critical judgement and collaboration in achieving common goals and meeting specific needs. So, education can be a very important tool for achieving ability and competence to trust with critical reflection and thus to cooperate with different people for a common goal. Education can contribute to the transformation of cultural and moral value patterns which create attitudes to caring about interests, needs and perspectives of others, variously different beings from ourselves.

The weakest point in the document and the greatest risk of the strategy are that there is no conceptualization of trust and a lack of measures to support, strengthen and create the conditions for the growth of trust in the mutual relations of all concerned actors, that is, teachers, parents, pupils, school founders, municipal or state authorities, and community. Trust is the driving force behind inclusion and consequently the cohesion of the school community. It is not possible to change the opinions of parents of children from socially disadvantaged backgrounds about the value and meaningfulness of education without their participation in the functioning of the educational process and thus in the common practice of care for (their) children. To persuade parents to take responsibility for this practice, the teacher must first recognize them as being able to accept that responsibility and thus recognize them as caring persons. Parents and teachers meeting in common school activities together with shared concern for the success and satisfaction of their children creates the conditions for mutual trust and recognition as equals in the process of caring for children, their future and good life through education. If the founders of schools (municipalities, cities, regions, state) and school management, fail to create systemic conditions for the joint practice of education care, based on different types and forms of activities carried out in common time and space, successfully implementing inclusive education is not possible. It is not that inclusion cannot be performed in a segregated environment, but inclusion processes are likely to fail if desegregation processes are not accompanied. Certainly, these processes in such complex environments require integrated management, which carefully considers and sets processes in the practice of inclusive education in such a way so that trust does not disappear but, on the contrary, becomes strengthened through meeting the needs of all the diverse actors involved.

This raises the question of why trust and recognition are marginalized within the attempt to implement inclusion (not only) in the education system and practice in Slovakia? The reason is the understanding of care and protection as it manifests within the Slovak context. Of particular importance is the implicit and explicit conceptualization of protection as isolation, and the avoidance of outside interference, from a different space or context. Then isolationism is conceived as a form of effective care. However, if democracy and inclusion are important, protection must be re-evaluated as part of educational care and subsequently as part of educational public policy, so that it can be seen as a practice of careful preparation for everyday interaction with a complex environment that will be based on appropriate trust and a critical approach. The rethinking of care and protection is a contextual process. It means it is a necessary task and responsibility of everyone in a particular environment—but in the greatest measure for those with the strongest competencies, abilities and power—to create conditions for joint care practices in which there is an opportunity to form mutual trust and to challenge and change the perception of danger and consequently the strategy of care and protection of those who are needy. The creation of conditions for practices of care—activities, spaces, relations—makes it possible to move from isolation to cooperation, from segregation and formal integration to inclusion and democratic participation in practices of educational care.

Conclusion

The achievement of inclusive education as a democratic practice of educational care depends on the participation of all stakeholders in the process of allocating responsibilities. The Slovak case study shows the importance of care ethics as an analytical tool for identifying and understanding the causes, factors and mechanisms that contribute to the success or failure of inclusive processes in education and, consequently, to the democratization of Slovak society. The example of Slovakia illustrates how the deficits of democratic care in education result in a deficit of inclusive citizenship and so to a deficit of caring democracy. At the same time, the application of care ethics points out the important link between trust and inclusion and the necessity to critically rethink the notion of protection as a dimension of democratic care.

Acknowledgements This work was supported by the Slovak Research and Development Agency under contract No. APVV-15-0234.

References

Barnes, Marian. 2012. *Care in Everyday Life: An Ethic of Care in Practice*. Bristol: Policy Press.

Fisher, Berenice, and Joan C. Tronto. 1990. Toward a Feminist Theory of Caring. In *Circles of Care*, ed. Emily K. Abel and Margaret K. Nelson, 36–54. Albany, New York: SUNY Press.

Held, Virginia. 2006. *The Ethics of Care: Personal, Political, and Global*. New York: Oxford University Press.

Jesenková, Adriana. 2012. Marginalizácia starostlivosti v učiteľskej profesii na Slovensku – faktory, mechanizmy, kontext. *Gender, rovné příležitosti, výzkum* 13 (1): 62–72.

Ministry of Education of the Slovak Republic. 2017. *Learning Slovakia – National Programme for Educational Development*. Proposal for Public Discussion. https://www.minedu.sk/data/files/6987_uciace_sa_slovensko.pdf. Accessed 28 June 2019.

———. 2018. *National Programme for the Development of Education 2018–2027*. https://www.minedu.sk/data/att/5250.pdf. Accessed 20 January 2019.

Ministry of Interior of the Slovak Republic. 2012. *The Strategy of the Slovak Republic for Roma Inclusion Until 2020*. https://www.minv.sk/swift_data/source/romovia/dokumenty/StrategiaSR_integraciaRomov.pdf. Accessed 14 January 2019.

Noddings, Nel. 1984. *Caring: A Feminine Approach to Ethics and Moral Education*. Berkeley: University of California Press.

———. 1992. *The Challenge to Care in Schools: An Alternative Approach to Education*. New York: Teachers College Press.

———. 2002. *Educating Moral People*. New York: Teachers College Press.

Ramberg, Joacim, András Lénárt, and Amanda Watkins, eds. 2017. *European Agency Statistics on Inclusive Education: 2014 Dataset Cross-Country Report*. Odense: European Agency for Special Needs and Inclusive Education. www.european-agency.org. Accessed 7 January 2019.

Rorty, Richard. 1997. Kto sme? Morálny univerzalizmus a ekonomický výber. *ASPEKT* 2: 219–222.

Sevenhuijsen, Selma. 1998. *Too Good to Be True?: Feminist Considerations About Trust and Social Cohesion*. Vienna: Institute for Human Studies. IWM Working Paper No. 3.

Tronto, Joan C. 2013. *Caring Democracy. Markets, Equality, and Justice*. New York: New York University Press.

CHAPTER 14

Organizing the Caring Society: Toward a Care Ethical Perspective on Institutions

Petr Urban

Introduction

The media as well as academia abounds with debates concerning the present-day *crisis of institutions* and the prospects for improving their quality and reputation. Current political and societal changes around the world are characterized by the growing erosion of public trust in institutions. The general public's support for political institutions such as government and parliament has evaporated on a global scale (Edelman Trust Barometer 2019). The crisis in public trust concerns many other institutions of the public sector as well. Over the past decades, even as the public's faith in political institutions was plunging, higher education maintained a high standing. Yet, recent surveys show that public trust in colleges and universities is eroding (cf. Selingo 2017; Pasquerella 2019). Other surveys show decreasing levels of public trust in health care providers (cf. Khullar 2018). The growing erosion of confidence in social and political institutions has been perceived by many social scientists as an impulse for

P. Urban (✉)
Institute of Philosophy, Czech Academy of Sciences, Prague, Czech Republic
e-mail: urban@flu.cas.cz

P. Urban, L. Ward (eds.), *Care Ethics, Democratic Citizenship and the State*, International Political Theory,
https://doi.org/10.1007/978-3-030-41437-5_14

rethinking the role, meaning, design and management of institutions in our societies and polities. It is a goal of this chapter to contribute to this rethinking *from the perspective of a political ethic of care.*

Moreover, in political theory and political science we have recently witnessed what scholars dubbed the *institutional turn.* Fassin (2005), for example, argues that to explore 'the heart of the state' means to penetrate the ordinary functioning of institutions, to present what the agents do when working for it and to consider the values and affects underlying the policies and practices. Focusing on feminist contributions to theorizing institutions, Krook and Mackay (2011) argue that feminist political science has been concerned with institutions from its earliest days (cf. Ferguson 1984; Connell 1987; Franzway et al. 1989; Watson 1990) and maintain that "the 'institutional turn' in feminist and mainstream political science has been well documented" (Krook and Mackay 2011, 1). The argument of this chapter is inspired by the question, whether we can talk about a parallel turn to institutions in *a moral and political theory of care.* I ask in particular whether there is a distinctive care ethical perspective on institutions, and, if there is one, what are its components.

Some scholars have been skeptical about the existence of a care ethical theory of institutions. For example, Frans Vosman recently argued that a weakness of care ethics is that "there are hardly any theories of institutions thus far; and if there are some, they are utterly normative, not analytical, as in the case of the set of requirements towards institutions proposed by Tronto in her book *Caring Democracy*" (Vosman 2016, 50). In what follows, I aim to offer a more complex account of a care ethical perspective on institutions with a special focus on public administration. My argument proceeds as follows. Firstly, by tracing the debates about social and political institutions in the care ethics literature I argue that a theory of institutions is an inherent part of any full-blown moral and political theory of care. In particular, I introduce what I call the 'institutional approach' in care ethics. Secondly, I provide a review of the existing proposals for a care-oriented public administration. I especially concentrate on a recent discussion about the possibility of combining the values of care and bureaucracy in public sector institutions. Thirdly, by drawing on my ongoing fieldwork in the environment of the Czech Ministry of Transport I suggest how a case-study-based, empirically grounded approach to central government institutions can enrich and exemplify a care ethical perspective on institutions and public administration.

The Paths of an Institutional Theory of Care

This section starts by confronting a skepticism about the *possibility* of a care ethical theory of institutions. I discuss how this skepticism relates to the narrow view of caring and institutions proposed by Nel Noddings. Finally, I contrast this view with an 'institutional approach' in care ethics that is characterized by a deep recognition of the role played by social and political institutions for getting us closer to a caring society.

Does Caring Contradict Institutions?

A skepticism about care ethics' capacity to provide a theory of institutions might be easily understood against the background of a critique of 'institutional caring', which certain prominent care ethicists such as Nel Noddings seem to propose. Care ethicists generally agree that realizing good caring in our societies is a desirable goal. Yet, we may ask: Do institutions help us to get closer to this goal? Does good caring need institutions to get done? Or is caring rather bound to concrete persons as a personal attitude, virtue or relationship, which would entail that it is something that cannot be carried out by an institution?

Assume we accept Noddings' classical definition of caring as *a relation between the 'one-caring' and the 'cared-for'* (Noddings 1984, 4) in which "the one-caring is sufficiently engrossed in the other to listen to him and to take pleasure or pain in what he recounts" (Noddings 1984, 19). What can be the role of institutions in getting such caring done? Noddings' answer is quite straightforward. On her account, no institution and organization can "meet the other as one-caring or as one trying to care" (Noddings 1984, 103). Thus, she contends, "it may be a mistake to assume that large impersonal institutions can do an adequate job in the individual's stead. Even when their basic physical needs are met, people often feel uncared for in institutional situations. A better solution is to spread caring, like literacy, over the whole population" (Noddings 2002, 124). In a recent paper, Noddings (2015) consequently warns against the tendency to apply the adjective *caring* to institutions and argues that though institutions can certainly address some particular needs "they cannot *care* in the sense required by care ethics. Assuming that they can do so may lead to a corruption of the concept of care" (Noddings 2015, 72—original emphasis). It is no surprise that based on these and similar expressions of Noddings some have reached a conclusion that Noddings subscribes to "a refusal of any kind of institutionalization of care" (Schües 2016, 254f.).

Yet, as known, since Noddings' early works her theoretical interest in caring has been intimately connected with her efforts in *rethinking and reforming institutions*, in particular educational institutions (Noddings 1984, 1987, 1988). Noddings' seminal book *Caring* (1984), which counts as a foundational work in care ethics, culminates in a section on reorganizing schools for caring. Here, Noddings envisions changing the structure and processes of modern schooling with the goal of making schools more suitable for caring (Noddings 1984, 197f.). Noddings even uses the term '*caring* school' and presents her argument as a reflection on "the possibility of *institutional caring*" (Noddings 1984, 12—emphasis added). The scope of institutional changes envisioned by Noddings is striking. In an earlier paper on education reform, she argues that "if we were to explore seriously the ideas suggested by an ethic of caring for education, we might suggest changes in almost every aspect of schooling: the current hierarchical structure of management, the rigid mode of allocating time, the kind of relationships encouraged, the size of schools and classes, the goals of instruction, modes of evaluation patterns of interaction, selection of content" (Noddings 1988, 221). As early as 1990, Noddings expands her reflection on reorganizing institutions for caring from the domain of education to the one of law and nursing (Noddings 1990) and, finally, in her more recent discussion of public provision of social services such as care for people with mental illness she encourages her readers not to be afraid of the idea of institutions and to join her in examining "how we can reconstruct our institutions so as to reduce opportunities to do harm and increase the possibility of positive human response" (Noddings 2002, 41).

If we don't want to draw the conclusion that there is a striking incoherence in Noddings' thought on caring and institutions, we have to come up with an alternative reading that reconciles Noddings' clearly positive perspective on the possibility of reorganizing institutions to be caring with her skepticism about the possibility of institutions being considered as caring. I argue that the key for such an interpretation lies in paying attention to Noddings' distinction between two different forms of caring: 'caring-for' and 'caring-about'. On her account, to *care-about* means to be concerned about someone or something, to recognize someone's existing needs and rights (Noddings 2013a, xiv), while to *care-for* means to establish a "person-to-person relationship characterized by attention, dialogue, recognition of expressed needs, and immediate response moved by the feeling aroused when people are in direct contact with those in need" (Noddings 2015, 76). In Noddings' view, *institutions can care-about*, they can express their concern about something and recognize existing needs and rights, but *they cannot care-for*, or at least *not directly*. Institutions can facilitate translating their caring-about into caring-for by providing and supporting the conditions under which concrete persons can engage in genuine caring-for (Noddings 2015, 75–83). Thus, Noddings argues, "genuine caring-about should lead us to concentrate on establishing or strengthening organizational structures in which caring-for can flourish" (Noddings 2013b, 207). Against this background one can better understand why Noddings spends so much time theorizing organizational reforms of schools, nursing homes, courts, mental health wards and many other institutions, even if she maintains that institutions cannot care(-for). The aim of these efforts is to suggest how the organizational structures and processes of institutions should be changed so that the institutions can provide suitable conditions for the person-to-person caring.

Let me highlight three aspects of Noddings' account that we need to bear in mind in the context of this chapter: (1) Noddings deploys *a narrow notion of institutions* in terms of large organizations and societal structures; (2) Noddings' definition of caring (in general) is *normatively centered around the notion of 'caring-for'* as a dyadic person-to-person relationship; and (3) as a consequence, Noddings defends *a restrictive view of the role of institutions in caring* as at best providing the conditions under which person-to-person caring relationships can flourish.

In what follows, I argue that none of these three points is representative of what I term the *institutional approach* in care ethics. The advocates of the institutional approach typically claim that creating a caring society demands caring social and political institutions and they urge care ethics to develop "a distinctive *institutional* political theory" (Engster 2004, 113—emphasis added). The institutional approach in care ethics, which I discuss in detail in the next three subsections, can be characterized by (1) *a broader understanding of institutions* (that counts both smaller social structures, such as the family, and broad socio-cultural frameworks as institutions); (2) *a broader definition of caring* (which emphasizes the social and political dimensions of care); and (3) a profound *appreciation of the role of social and political institutions* in approaching the goal of creating a caring society.

Transforming Maternal Practice by Transforming the Institutions of Motherhood

I propose that the beginning of the institutional approach in care ethics is located in Sara Ruddick's groundbreaking paper "Maternal Thinking" (Ruddick 1980). In this essay, Ruddick focuses on *childcaring* (mothering) as a source of a specific style of judging, feeling and reflecting. Ruddick defines childcaring—and caring in general (Ruddick 1980, 361)—primarily as a *practice* and *work*. As a *practice*, childcaring is a human response to a reality that is perceived as presenting certain demands. As a *social* practice, it always takes place in a particular society, under particular social conditions, and thus it is inevitably embedded in particular social, cultural and political contexts (Ruddick 1980, 344–347). This view of caring entails a profound recognition of the role that institutions play in caring. Since Ruddick is especially interested in the practice of childcaring, her focus is primarily on the "institutions of motherhood" and "social conditions of motherhood" (Ruddick 1980, 344, 347, 360). The 'institutions of motherhood' include, in Ruddick's view, not only the institution of the family and the home but also the broad context of social, cultural, political and economic institutions in which the practice of childcaring takes place.

Two points about Ruddick's (1980) analysis of the 'institutions of motherhood' are worth noting. First, Ruddick elaborates on the feminist insight that the institutions of the family and the home are deeply intertwined with the institutions of public life. Though childcaring is always done by individual persons, the way in which it is done is fundamentally affected by the 'public' institutions of political and economic life (cf. Ruddick 1980, 360). Second—and no less in accord with many feminist theorists—Ruddick pays a special attention to the *quality* of institutions by drawing a distinction between *oppressive* and *non-oppressive* institutions. The main cause of the oppressiveness of the 'institutions of motherhood' lies, on her account, in institutional arrangements and social stratifications that install and perpetuate *arrogant or defensive power over others* in sexual, economic and political life. These include for example inequalities of power and privilege and the division between dominating and subordinated people with respect to gender, race and class; separation of public action from private affection; or the division between professional and service labor (Ruddick 1980, 355–359).

Ruddick's analysis of oppressive and non-oppressive institutional contexts of caring has a clearly normative dimension as she contends that good (non-degenerative) forms of caring require non-oppressive institutions. Such a contention may appear similar to Noddings' idea that institutions can care-about by providing conditions in which individual caring-for can flourish. Yet, I suggest, Ruddick's account of caring and institutions is more complex as it shows that the negative effect of an oppressive institutional framework consists primarily in distorting the broader social and economic reality in which caring is situated and which thus affects the very nature of the actual caring activities. Hence, for Ruddick a reflection on the quality of caring concerns not only the relationship between the 'one-caring' and the 'cared-for' (Noddings' 'caring-for') but also, and more fundamentally, the broader web of social, political and economic institutions in which caring is discussed, decided upon, distributed and carried out.

Ruddick's view of caring and institutions entails a transformative element as well. Against the background of her analysis of actual institutional contexts of caring she suggests that creating a caring society would require *serious social reform*, namely refashioning the family, the home, the work-world and politics by recasting the power-gender roles and deconstructing unnecessary social divisions and hierarchies. As an example of such changes with regard to childcaring Ruddick (1980) envisions families, homes and communities that share parental care—practically, emotionally, economically and socially—put in place daycare centers managed by professionals who are themselves engaged in caring activities and involve men and women both inside and outside the home (Ruddick 1980, 360).

Expanding the Institutional Boundaries of Caring

Although in her later work Ruddick (1989/2002) expands the scope of her investigation to caring in general and speaks of a corresponding 'rationality of care', she still considers mothering (childcaring) as "a central instance and symbol of care" and 'maternal thinking' as a "central expression of this rationality" (Ruddick 1989/2002, 46; for a similar view cf. Held 1987, 1990). I suggest that a decisive step in the further development of the institutional approach in care ethics is related to detaching the definition of caring from the emphasis on mothering and the mother-child relationship as a model for rethinking our social and political institutions. This step was famously done by Fisher and Tronto (1990) who define caring as "a species activity that includes everything we do to maintain, continue, and repair our 'world' so that we can live in it as well as possible.

That world includes our bodies, our selves, and our environment, all of which we seek to interweave in a complex, life-sustaining web" (Fisher and Tronto 1990, 40).

A care theory that starts from the broad definition of caring and from the recognition of care as a crucial element in the life of all individuals and communities will sooner or later have to face a set of crucial questions, such as: Who are the actors of caring? How far should the boundaries of caring be expanded? How can we guarantee that groups of people are not unnecessarily privileged in their ability to acquire care? How caring arrangements contribute to meaningful social and political participation? Who should be responsible for the availability and quality of care on a social scale? (cf. Tronto 1987, 1989; Sevenhuijsen 1998; Sevenhuijsen et al. 2003) Drawing on Ruddick's insight that caring is always rooted in the boundaries and structures of our current institutions, Tronto (1993) demonstrates how the traditional boundary between 'private institutions' (the family, the household) and 'public institutions' (the market, the state) has for centuries served as the main vehicle of marginalizing and devaluing care. Over the long history of the West caring was relegated to the domain of close personal relationships in the family and the household, was excluded from political discussions and deliberations, and was gendered as a primary activity of women. Tronto's (1993) analysis of the institutional boundaries of caring begs several important questions: How could our institutions be arranged to expand the conventional understandings of the boundaries of caring? How could the opportunity to provide and receive care be included in the social, political and economic arrangements which structure people's life-plans? The advocates of the institutional approach in care ethics seem to agree on the answer that if caring is to acquire a more important place in the life of communities and polities, caring and the dependence on care must be incorporated into what is said to count as the 'normal' subject of politics (cf. Sevenhuijsen 1998, 150). This view has several ramifications for a care ethical perspective on institutions. First, it implies that we need to rethink the conventional conception of the family as the institution of first resort for caring and examine critically the idea of personal (family) responsibility for caring. Second, it means that we need to rethink the role and responsibility of larger social and political structures, such as the state and its institutions, in securing care as a public value.

Public Ethics of Care and the State's Public Policies

Over the past two decades, care theorists have adopted, roughly speaking, two different strategies in rethinking the institutional boundaries of caring. Some care ethicists maintain that "the family is preeminent among institutions and places where caring projects unfold" (Ruddick 1998, 13; cf. Tronto 2001, 76) and propose to move from the (post-patriarchal) family or the home 'outward' in order to use the caring characteristic of these institutions to "build a public ethic of care" (Noddings 2002, 301; cf. Kittay 1999, 133). On this account, "a social theory (or guide to public policy) that builds from the home outward will require changes in many of our institutions and even in the idea of institutions" (Noddings 1998, 68). Other care theorists, in contrast, propose that "care should be positioned in notions of citizenship rather than family" (Sevenhuijsen et al. 2003, 299) and argue that "the community, as represented by the state, has primary responsibility for care of its citizens, and ... citizens in turn have the right to nonfamily care" (Glenn 2000, 90). On both accounts, however, it is the aim of a 'public ethic of care' to ensure that (1) caring is legitimated as a *collective (public) responsibility*; (2) *access to care-giving and care-receiving* is relatively *equally distributed* and not dependent on economic or social status; and (3) *the responsibility and actual work of caring is shared equitably* and does not fall disproportionally on disadvantaged groups (cf. Glenn 2000, 88).

Now, what does all this mean, if we are to translate this view into the real life of our societies and institutions? First, it means different things in different contexts, since the actual social and political institutions in which caring is discussed, decided upon and done differ with respect to particular social, cultural and political environments. The idea of a 'public ethic of care' has therefore inspired a number of critical analyses of current institutional arrangements of caring in various geographical and cultural contexts worldwide as well as a number of concrete proposals for public policies that are centered around the idea of the collective responsibility for care and the right to the equal access to adequate care-giving and care-receiving (cf. Clement 1996; Ruddick 1998; Sevenhuijsen 1998; Kittay 1999; Glenn 2000; White 2000; Tronto 2001; Noddings 2002; Sevenhuijsen et al. 2003; Hankivsky 2004; Barnes 2006; Held 2006; Engster 2007; Stensöta 2015). With respect to the role of the state and its institutions in realizing a 'public ethic of care', care theorists elaborated in particular on an ethical justification of the welfare state (Sevenhuijsen 1998; Kittay

1999; Glenn 2000; Engster 2007) as well as a criticism of paternalistic and neoliberal forms of the state care provision (White 2000; Tronto 2001; Held 2006; Barnes 2012). Daniel Engster (2015) recently proposed what is perhaps the most comprehensive and detailed account of a public ethic of care so far, which in a systematic way applies care ethics to a number of social policy areas, such as health care, child care, old age, and poverty, and suggests how the basic institutions of a caring welfare state should be designed.

Yet, it is not the aim of this chapter to explore the existing proposals for a public ethic of care in detail. Our previous discussion shall suffice to make the case that any full-blown moral and political theory of care has to deal with the structure and functioning of our social and political institutions. The institutional approach in care ethics sees care as a collective responsibility that needs to be realized through various social and political institutions. To take care as a crucial element in the life of all individuals and communities means to challenge the current institutional arrangements of caring and propose alternative ways of organizing care in our societies and polities. This conclusion puts us in a better position to see the shortcomings of the famous critique proposed by Alison Jaggar who suggests that "care's emphasis on individual responses to immediate needs … encourages what are sometimes called band-aid social work approaches to moral problems rather than efforts to solve them institutionally or prevent their occurrence through social changes" (Jaggar 1995, 196). Such a criticism toward care ethics is not only "overstated", as Hankivsky (2004, 34) noted, but rather completely inadequate when applied to the above-discussed views that represent the institutional approach in care ethics.

Given the care ethical insight that care should be positioned in the notion of citizenship and that the state has primary responsibility for ensuring access to adequate care-giving and care-receiving for all, the state and its institutions that serve this goal must be of prominent interest for care ethicists. In the following section, I want to turn attention to the question of how a care ethics perspective on institutions can be applied to the domain of *public administration*. Hence the chapter shifts its focus from a care ethical discussion of the institutional boundaries of caring and the design of public policies to a care ethical discussion of how the provision of public services and goods should be best administered.

Public Administration and Caring Institutions

Public administration can be defined as a cooperative group effort in a public setting that comprises of those activities that are involved in *implementing* the policies and programs of governments but also have a role in the *formulation* of public policy. Theoretically public administration is an interdisciplinary field of study that examines the structure and workings of institutions that are charged with the administration of governmental functions and studies the behavior of officials responsible for the conduct of these functions. The aim of this section is to take a closer look at existing attempts to apply a care ethics perspective to public administration theory and practice.

Care Ethics and Public Administration

Let us start by taking a quick look at how care ethics was first applied to *educational administration* in the early 1990s. Drawing on Noddings' (1984, 1987) ideas about the educational reform, Starratt (1991) and Beck (1992) argue for introducing care ethics and the values of caring in *educational* leadership and administrative practice. Building on Noddings' (1984) and Gilligan's (1982) view that care ethics should aim at fostering growth, connection and nurturing relationships, Beck argues that care ethics would "lead administrators to listen to and value persons in the context of their communities' schools. It would encourage them to involve students and teachers in problem solving, allowing them 'access to decision-forming arenas'" (Beck 1992, 482). Care ethics, these theorists argue, would reorient educational administration from its current exclusive emphasis on the values of effectiveness and competition to the values of care. It would foster "open, trusting, professional communication" (Starratt 1991, 196), recommend opting for "cooperative strategies" (Beck 1992, 476) and aim at reducing "the artificial separations that cripple caring relations" (Noddings 1987, 27). Davidson (1994) widens the scope of investigation to public administration in general. She identifies, following Noddings (1984), the care perspective as a 'feminine perspective' and argues that deploying this perspective in public administration would "revitalize our demoralized public organizations ... and create opportunities for enhanced interpersonal relationships—both within our bureaucracies and between these bureaucracies and the communities that serve" (Davidson 1994, revised in Scranton and Ranney 2001, 579).

Yet, a problem with these first attempts to apply care ethics to administration lies in deploying the above-discussed narrow view of caring as a nurturing personal relationship. This reduces the perspective of these scholars to a narrow focus on promoting connection and personal growth within the institutional context. Moreover, Davidson's account of 'feminine administrative behavior' is clearly open to the objection of gender essentialism which is related to serious issues identified by early critics of the 'feminine approach' in care ethics (cf. Tronto's 1987 criticism of Noddings).

In contrast, DeLysa Burnier's proposal for a 'care-centered public administration' draws on Tronto's (1993) argument for a *political ethic of care* and takes as a point of departure Fisher and Tronto's (1990) *broad definition of caring* as a social practice which, if fully accomplished, comprises four interrelated phases of caring-about, caring-for, care-giving and care-receiving. Burnier also builds on a feminist approach to public administration developed in the pioneering works of Camilla Stivers (1991, 1993, 1994, 2000). In her groundbreaking 1991 paper, Stivers draws attention to women's historical exclusion from public administration theory and suggests four areas of public administration where a feminist perspective might offer fresh insights: (1) the question of administrative knowledge, (2) the model of the ideal public servant, (3) the nature of administrative discretion and (4) the dimensions of the administrative state. Most importantly, Stivers argues for a feminist rethinking of the very ground of administrative legitimacy, which would base *legitimacy and accountability of administrative discretion* not only on the individual conscience and the internal processes of a particular agency but on *substantive collaboration with affected others* which aims at the *inclusion of a diverse range of perspectives.* A feminist account of administrative practice foregrounds the view of power as a form of "enabling capacity", stresses "the possibility of leadership as facilitation rather than giving orders, and authority as accountable expertise rather than a chain of command" (Stivers 1991, 59).

In what follows, I want to discuss DeLysa Burnier's proposal for a 'care-centered public administration' in detail. On Burnier's view, a care ethics perspective (1) provides an *alternative 'assumptive base' of public administration*; (2) *complicates the conventional founding and historical narrative* of the discipline; (3) *legitimizes a 'relational leadership' approach* in public administration (Burnier 2003, 535–540).

Bureaucracy with its emphasis on the efficient and neutral delivery of public goods and services represents the traditional foundation of public administration. The New Public Management reforms of the 1990s changed this foundation dramatically by replacing bureaucracy with the principles of the market centered around *the value of efficiency*. The governmental delivery of goods and services to citizens was transformed into market transaction where private providers of services compete for customers seeking to maximize their choices. As it is well documented in literature on public administration, the New Public Management reforms deprived the public sector of its more traditional moral values and permitted "a widespread practice of the administration of services to develop that destroys the very idea that the providing organizations could be matters of public concern" (Hirst 1997, 127; cf. Hoggett 2005). Now, given the financial and ethical crisis that resulted from an increased market orientation, Burnier argues, it is not only "imperative that administrators who believe in government's public mission retake center stage and regain control of the public agenda" (Burnier 2009a, 399) but what is needed is "a care transformation of the public sector" which "values care, makes care work visible, and places care values and practices at the center of public administration scholarship and practice" (Burnier 2009a, 396). It is not Burnier's suggestion that care should *replace* the values of bureaucracy and the market, but rather that public administration should *take care as seriously as it has taken bureaucracy and markets.* What would such a transformation entail? How would a care-centered public administration look?

Before answering these questions, let me first draw attention to Burnier's 'interpretative-critical' methodology. It is worth noting that Burnier arrives at the characteristics of a care-centered public administration primarily not from a normative ideal image of public administration but rather from real-life examples (both past and present) of a certain type of administrative practice. Drawing on Stivers (2000), Burnier studies the efforts and activities of the 'settlement women' and identifies behind these activities an "alternative ethos for governance and administrative practice" (Burnier 2009b, 587) which emphasizes *relationality*, viewing situations from *multiple perspectives*, concern for others, *cooperative problem-solving*, care and compassion. Although this alternative construction of administrative reality has never become public administration's dominant construction—Stivers speaks of "public administration's buried heritage" (Stivers 2000, 49)—neither has it disappeared. During her years of teaching public and non-profit administrators in a Master of Public Administration (MPA) university program, Burnier observed that "for many public administrators, especially those working at the street and agency levels, care-centered administration is already at the core of what they do" (Burnier 2009a, 396). Thus, Burnier argues, if we carefully listen to the "everyday talk of government employees and administrators", a fresh discourse might emerge that legitimizes and illuminates "how care as a value and practice is inextricably tied to everyday judgments that clients, citizens, and administrators make about what it means to do a job well or what it means to be a 'good' administrator" (Burnier 2003, 541). Yet, such an inquiry should not only be 'interpretative' but should also be 'critical' in the sense of paying adequate attention to the larger institutional context and its collective meaning structures (Burnier 2005, 398).[1]

What mainly characterizes a care perspective on public administration is the belief that administering is a *situational and relational practice* which seeks to *improve the lives of all individuals and communities.* This further entails several particular beliefs, such as that (1) good administrative processes and outcomes should reflect not only expert judgment but a *collaborative work that takes into account different viewpoints* and lived experiences; (2) good administrators should use their discretionary authority not to accumulate more power but to *reach out to the public* and invite them to join a dialogue; (3) good administrative knowledge should be *situated in experience and dialogical reflection*; and (4) good administrators should be *critically reflexive*, willing to question and challenge their own values, assumptions and professional judgments.

As noted earlier, Burnier does not suggest that a care discourse should be deployed to delegitimize and replace any other normative ground of public administration. In a care-centered public administration, public officials would still be required to apply rules and deliver public goods and services *fairly and equally.* Although public administrators may experience conflicts between bureaucratic requirements of neutrality and objectivity and care requirements of cooperative and contextual problem solutions, 'caring administrators', Burnier argues, would take into consideration

[1] Burnier's call for further work on the everyday care discourse in public administration resonates in Stensöta's (2010) empirical research on the *presence of a care discourse* and care values in the Swedish public sector—yet Stensöta never refers to Burnier's work. Stensöta conducted an extensive empirical study within the administration of sick leave benefits in the Swedish Social Insurance Agency and found out that "a public ethics of care … is a prominent part of the empirical reality of employee public ethics within social insurance administration" (Stensöta 2010, 300).

both as they inevitably work under *multiple ethical contexts* (Burnier 2003, 539–541).[2] Burnier suggests several practical measures that could help a government or an institution become more care-centered. These measures include (1) changing the organizational structure and culture, (2) deploying relational leadership, (3) introducing formal recognition and compensation for care work and emotional labor in the public sector and (4) teaching and training public officials aimed at acquiring knowledge and skills needed for individuals to become caring administrators. Unfortunately, Burnier does not say much about the needed changes concerning the organizational structure and culture, as her focus is mostly on *individual behavior* of public administrators.

As regards the behavior of administrative leaders and managers, Burnier emphasizes a transformative potential of *relational leadership* (cf. Regan and Brooks 1995; Sernak 1998). The relational leader practices *facilitating and reciprocal power* as 'power with' rather than 'power over'. Such a leader promotes collaboration, caring, courage and vision within an organization and remains open to the perspectives of others. The relational leader must "communicate that care is an organizational value to be embraced and practiced by individuals throughout the organization" (Burnier 2003, 538). The emotional labor and care work of relational leaders as well as other employees go often unrecognized in public sector agencies. It is a marginalized and devalued practice, although it can substantially contribute to creating better working conditions in an organization and enhancing the well-being of its clients. Thus, Burnier (2009a) argues, we need to introduce measures of formal recognition and compensation for emotional labor and care work in organizations (such as alternative modes of evaluation, incorporating this work in job descriptions and audits etc.). Finally, governments and public agencies should bear the responsibility for providing public administrators with quality education and training aimed at acquiring knowledge and skills needed for individuals to exercise good administrative discretion and navigate through the complex web of multiple ethical contexts of administrative practice.

[2] Burnier (2009a) even assumes that a care discourse in public administration need not be viewed necessarily inconsistent with the requirements for efficiency and performance measurements (cf. Schachter 2008).

Conflict, Power and Bureaucracy in Caring Institutions

Burnier's pioneering work lays the ground for a care-oriented administrative theory and practice. Yet, it leaves many areas of research open for further elaboration. Drawing on Fisher and Tronto's (1990) broad definition of caring and the distinction of four phases of the care process, Burnier (2003) calls for "the task of explicating the four phases of care more systematically in the context of public administration" (Burnier 2003, 541). However, she seems to leave aside an important element of Fisher and Tronto's analysis, namely their emphasis on *the possibility of conflicts and contradictions* arising in the complex process of caring. It is precisely this element which comes to the forefront of Tronto's recent interest in institutionalized caring. "In fact", Tronto argues, "institutional care is better understood in the context of conflict. As such, care institutions need explicit institutional arrangements to help to resolve conflict as it arises" (Tronto 2010, 168). This requires, in Tronto's view, creating an explicit 'political space within institutions', that is, "a political process that considers the needs, contributions, and prospects of many different actors" (Tronto 2010, 169).

Although Tronto (2010) seems to articulate her account of 'caring institutions' with respect to institutions and agencies that serve to directly provide care, I assume, given her broad definition of caring, that Tronto's characteristics of 'caring institutions' do apply to any kind of institution through which government implements its policies and delivers public goods and services.[3] Tronto approaches the question of how to assess whether an institution provides good caring from a perspective of three "critical elements for assessing practices of care" which grow out of an understanding of care as a *relational practice* (Tronto 2010, 161). All forms of caring, Tronto argues, "require that attention be paid to *purpose*, *power*, and *particularity*" (Tronto 2010, 161—emphasis added). It is true about all forms of caring, but it is especially true about the institutional ones, that they take place in the contexts of possible conflicts and disagreements about the ends of care and within unequal power relations. Conflicts and disagreements often concern the key question of the care process, namely *what are the needs that should be addressed* and *how best to address them*. Any institution which suppresses its awareness of existing power

[3] See Stensöta (2015) for a different interpretation of Tronto's (2010) view of care institutions.

relations (both within and outside the institution), the inevitable conflicts about the institution's purposes and the disagreements in needs interpretation will most likely inflict harm to those who are affected by the institution's agency. Hence, Tronto argues, in order to be more caring an institution has to raise its awareness of the three critical elements, "these aspects of care within the institution need to be worked out consciously ... they ... require a deliberate, political process" (Tronto 2010, 162; cf. Tronto 2001).

What does this mean in more practical terms? First, institutions should be "highly deliberate and explicit about how to best meet the needs of the people who they serve" (Tronto 2010, 169). They have to find out ways of an *active needs interpretation process*. This concerns, Tronto argues, not only the needs of the institution's clients but needs at multiple levels including the needs of the employees of the institution: "care institutions have to think about the nature of the caring process as a whole in order to guide their actions. This requirement does not only demand that the 'needs' of the 'customers' come first but also that the needs of care workers, the allocation of responsibility and proper assessment also happen within the organization" (Tronto 2010, 162). Yet, an adequate needs interpretation is a hard task for any institution, since, given the unequal power relations in institutionalized settings, the needs expressed by less advantaged people may be easily manipulated or distorted or simply not heard (Tronto 2010, 164f.).

One of the ways to counter the risk of inadequate needs interpretation is to make the institutions more *democratic*, *inclusive* and *responsive* so that they "take into consideration the needs and perspectives of all within the institution" (Tronto 2010, 168; cf. Tronto 2013, 158–166). Tronto does not say much about the practical measures that would lead to such a transformation of institutions. She touches upon the ideas of changing the institutional culture (cf. Groombridge 2010), of empowering the institution's staff (cf. Koren 2010), of allocating responsibilities and care work more fairly and of flattening hierarchies in institutions (Tronto 2010, 165, 168), but she does not suggest what that would entail in terms of particular changes to the organizational structure, leadership style, skills and knowledge of employees, consultative mechanisms and so on. Tronto does not really elaborate on whether different types institutions at different levels (e.g. local, regional, national) require same or different changes to become more caring, that is, more responsive, inclusive and democratic.

I want to conclude this section by taking a closer look at a recent attempt in theorizing caring institutions that has the potential to overcome some of the shortcomings of the previous proposals for a theory of caring institutions and seems particularly promising with respect to thinking about institutions in the context of public administration. In her 'Prolegomena to a Caring Bureaucracy' (2017), Sophie Bourgault addresses the hard question of whether large bureaucratic institutions can be conducive to good caring. She seems to be fully right in claiming that this question is of "utmost importance for feminist ethics of care" (Bourgault 2017, 203), since, as discussed earlier, any serious attempt to think a 'care politics' has to deal with care policy formulation and implementation which takes place (also) through many large institutions of the administrative state. Bourgault (2017) counters the mainstream feminist criticism of bureaucratic organizations by arguing that (1) the ideal-bureaucratic (Weberian) emphasis on the criteria of competence in hiring and promotion, clear division of responsibilities and just distribution of resources are supportive of many key (care) feminist aims; (2) removing organizational hierarchies and un-structuring institutions may sometimes be counterproductive to the (care) feminist goals of curbing domination and oppression in our societies and polities.[4] Bourgault's point is that it is possible and fruitful to think large institutions capable of embodying both bureaucratic and caring values.

With regard to organizational structure and power allocation within large institutions, Bourgault suggests creating semi-hierarchical power and decision-making structures that combine clear rules and power divisions with good listening and communicative skills. Flattening the decision-making processes and structures through hybrid organizational forms and 'organized dissonance' (Ashcraft 2001) does not amount to removing all hierarchies and power inequalities within an institution (cf. Martin 1990, 2013).

Bourgault follows previous care theorizing about institutions by stressing that institutions need to become more *attentive* and *responsive.* Inspired by Fricker's (2007) reflection on 'epistemic injustice', Bourgault elsewhere (2020) draws attention to the epistemic injustices that often occur in institutional contexts, such as "discursive dysfunctions that

[4] Bourgault's defense of bureaucratic values in the context of large institutions resonates with several attempts to rethink the importance of the values of bureaucracy in the aftermath of New Public Management reforms (cf. du Gay 2005).

regularly take place in our judicial system, hospitals, schools, workplaces and social service counters" or public officials' prejudices that "compromise the way in which they exercise judgement, the way in which they listen (or rather *fail* to listen)" (Bourgault 2020, 92, 94). This may, as a consequence, harm the client's "capacity as an epistemic subject, that is, as a giver of information and a partner in discursive exchanges" (Bourgault 2020, 94). Fricker (2007) suggests countering such epistemic injustices by 'virtuous hearing' which incorporates a critical awareness of the impact that our social power and identities have and an upward compensation of attention and credibility with respect to marginalized communities and individuals. Bourgault rightly stresses that above Fricker's suggested ways of 'virtuous hearing' we also ought to consider a downward correction of credibility by taking into account "the unduly high levels of credibility and attention offered to the very privileged or powerful (that is, credibility *excesses*)" (Bourgault 2020, 95).

What does that require from an institution in practical terms? A caring institution, Bourgault argues, should ensure that it (1) has administrators with solid listening and communicative skills (personal attentiveness) and (2) puts in place extensive institutional consultation processes that enable reflective ways of defining and addressing the needs of all affected groups (institutional attentiveness). One of the most important questions here is the question of how to facilitate ***good administrative discretion***. On the one hand, administrators should be encouraged to exercise discretion; on the other hand some measures must be in place to ensure that discretion is exercised "without falling into illegitimate arbitrariness" (Bourgault 2017, 208). The point is that these measures do not have to be reduced to adopting more institutional rules and stronger control mechanisms. It is possible to facilitate good discretion by hiring and promoting administrators with good communicative and listening skills, providing administrators with adequate training and support in acquiring needed cognitive and emotional skills combined with professional expertise and developing an organizational culture that recognizes and values good discretion. If an institution seeks to create such a culture, Bourgault argues, it must also pay adequate attention to the issue of time, as bad discretion often occurs under the circumstances of a lack of time. With a special regard to large public sector institutions we need to "think critically about the impact of neoliberal management practices and social acceleration, for these weigh heavily on institutional responsiveness and our ability to offer particularized and non-prejudicial public services" (Bourgault 2020, 95).

Concerning the question of good discretion, the importance of both bureaucratic and caring values comes into play again. Good discretion requires being attentive to particulars (judging on the basis of situational and relational knowledge), but it also often requires 'veiling particulars' and anonymizing concrete cases and affected groups or individuals. Similarly, to Burnier (2003) and in line with some recent research on public administration and public ethics (Dubois 2010; Hoggett 2005; Zacka 2017), Bourgault (2017) notices a *dissonance* which is frequently experienced in the everyday practice of public administrators. It is a dissonance between the principles that guide good administrative practice but, at the same time, *pull in different directions*, that is, toward greater neutrality and impartiality on the one hand and toward more attentiveness and responsiveness on the other hand. Bourgault's argument is that we should think of this dissonance as "healthy and (often) interesting" rather than dangerous and unproductive (Bourgault 2017, 209). Yet, Bourgault contends that "one cannot *simultaneously* seek both the unveiling and the veiling of particulars: in any given situation, one will have to choose which policy one wishes to pursue—and each choice will face significant trade-offs" (Bourgault 2020, 103). In her critical discussion of the trade-offs of the recent attempts to reduce administrative discretion by digitalizing administrative tasks and interactions between citizens and the state, Bourgault arrives at the conclusion that 'caring bureaucracies' should "hold on to face-to-face encounters whenever possible (and pertinent), and to consider carefully the long-term losses that might be incurred by addressing epistemic marginalization/injustices via more 'quick-fix' veiling measures" (Bourgault 2020, 101).

Let me conclude this section by pointing out three elements of Bourgault's reflections on the possibility of large caring bureaucratic institutions that call for further work. First, Bourgault's focus is mainly on the relationships between the institution and clients. Yet it is, in my view, no less important to look at the intra-organizational dimension of a 'caring bureaucracy' as well, since there seems to be a profound connection between the practices and relationships outside and within the institution. Second, Bourgault (as well as Stensöta 2010, 2015) considers primarily institutions operating on the street- and frontline-level. I think it is important to develop a parallel reflection on institutions operating on higher levels of public administration, including central government institutions, since these institutions play a significant role in drafting and interpreting public policies. Finally, to render the idea of a 'caring bureaucracy' more concrete and examine their applicability, we need to open up the theory to more practice-oriented approaches and deploy research with 'ethnographic sensibility' (cf. Herzog and Zacka 2017). It is the aim of the last section of this chapter to provide an example of such a research, which I have been conducting at the Ministry of Transport of the Czech Republic.

A Case Study from the Czech Republic

Since June 2018, I have realized, together with Alice Koubová and Juraj Hvorecký, an applied research project 'Measures for Developing an Ethical Culture in Czech Civil Service'. The 'application guarantor' of the project is the Ministry of Transport of the Czech Republic, a central government institution which comprises about 400 public officials. The project's aims are (1) to describe the current state of civil service ethics at the ministry, (2) to propose suitable tools for developing a sound ethical culture at the ministry and (3) to provide guidelines for implementing the recommended tools and measures at the ministry. The project is planned for three years (until May 2021) and it is designed as a pilot study whose results may be relevant also to other ministries and government institutions in the Czech Republic. It should be noted that while a number of other European countries as well as many other developed democracies across the globe have made important steps forward toward creating sound ethical culture in government institutions over the past two decades, the Czech Republic has stayed back and been almost inactive in this area until very recently.

Though the project is a work in progress and its results are only preliminary, I want to suggest a couple of ideas about how our particular research may both enrich and exemplify a care ethical perspective on institutions and public administration. Let me first draw attention to the question of methodology.

Our applied research project on civil service ethics at a Czech ministry *contextualizes* a care ethics perspective on institutions by focusing on a particular level of administration, in a particular country, at a particular time. All institutions exist, as care theorists noted (cf. Ruddick 1995), in a particular time and space. Hence, all institutions have specific histories and are embedded in specific socio-cultural and political contexts. Our case study calls for paying attention to the socio-cultural and political context of a small post-communist country in the East-Central European region at the beginning of the twenty-first century. This means for example that when discussing the relationships of trust between the Czech ministry and the general public we must bear in mind the high levels of distrust that existed between the institutions of the communist state and its citizens over the second half of the twentieth century. They continue to affect the attitudes of Czech citizens toward the state and its institutions. This highly contextualized approach to institutions which concentrates around a case study bears a close resemblance to the 'empirically grounded ethics of care' and the 'N=N case studies' approach recently proposed by Timmerman et al. (2019). Moreover, by focusing on the central government level of public administration our project both contextualizes a care ethics perspective and moves beyond the one-sided focus on street-level agencies that characterize most previous proposals by care ethicists.

Furthermore, our applied research at the Czech Ministry of Transport *exemplifies* the 'interpretative-critical methodology' developed by Burnier in her account of care-oriented public administration. At the methodological heart of our project lies a combination of *qualitative empirical research* and *philosophical reflection* which enters a dialogue with many disciplines in the field of public administration. Through interviews and focus groups we gather narratives and real-life stories about the everyday practice of public officials at the ministry. In our reflections on these narratives, we try to trace the values that are embodied in the actions, decisions and thoughts of public officials; the normative requirements that they experience; and the ethical issues and dilemmas that they face while working for the ministry as public officials. This analysis is followed by a more normatively oriented reflection through which we formulate our recommendations about what should be done to reach a sound ethical culture at the ministry. This reflection draws from a *critical* interpretation of what we find expressed or tacitly contained in the everyday practice and discourse of the employees of the ministry.

Finally, our project focuses on both the *intra- and extra-institutional dimension* of civil service ethics, that is, on the relationships and interactions which public officials have both within and outside the ministry. Whereas Bourgault (2017, 2020) and Stensöta (2010, 2015) examine the ethical aspects of the interactions between public officials and their clients, we contend that the moral life of institutions has two intertwined dimensions that influence each other. For example, good listening and communicative skills of public officials toward their clients seem to go hand in hand with solid listening and communicative skills toward their colleagues at an institution, and vice versa. Moreover, it is often the case at a ministry as well as other central government institutions that public officials have only a rare face-to-face contact with citizens. From a care ethics perspective this complicates the issue of institutional attentiveness and responsiveness, since we have to take into account different ways of how a ministry can be attentive and responsive, for example, in the processes of drafting legislation. It is our assumption that a solid intra-institutional ethical culture at a ministry makes a substantive contribution to institutional attentiveness and responsiveness of the ministry toward the public.

Let us take a look at some preliminary results of our project. The interviews and focus groups that we conducted with the employees of the Czech Ministry of Transport have clearly shown that the employees work under *multiple normative contexts* which include the requirements of impartiality, effectiveness, efficiency and care. Most employees of the ministry perceive the different normative requirements as legitimate and try to navigate through the situations in which it is hard or even impossible to fulfill all the requirements at the same time. What the employees lack with respect to such situations is sufficient time to think about what is the right thing to do. They often complain about too hectic working pace which forces them to focus too narrowly on the timely completion of their work tasks. These narratives of the public officials working at the Czech Ministry of Transport confirm two above-discussed insights of care ethicists, namely that (1) public administrators necessarily work under different ethical frameworks, which may result into a perceived dissonance between the guiding values of their practice, and (2) good administrative practice and direction requires enough time to navigate through the network of different requirements.

Another finding of our project which resonates with a care ethical perspective on institutions and public administration concerns the issue of *trust and cooperation*. There is a striking lack of cooperation between the units and departments of the ministry. For example, some departments do not share information that is required for smooth functioning of other departments, some teams fuel hostile and competing attitudes toward other teams and so on. When asked about achieving the standards of civil service ethics the employees are often positive about their own team but utterly negative about the rest of the ministry. Our hypothesis is that the lack of cooperation goes hand in hand with a lack of trust and good communication within the ministry as well as with a poor awareness of a common mission and purpose of the work of the ministry. The communication between the departments and employees across the ministry is often extremely formalized. We contend that despite the relatively large size of the ministry and the nature of its agenda it is possible to establish more informal and humane ways of communication and interpersonal contact which would result into higher levels of trust and cooperation. This requires, for example, introducing more opportunities for informal meetings, open discussions and debates among employees, better listening and communication between superiors and subordinates and empowering participation in the debates about the mission and core values of the institution.

Our findings finally show that creating and developing a sound ethical culture at a ministry is a process which *cannot be imposed hierarchically from above* based on a decision made by managers. There is no doubt that the behavior, and communicative and listening skills of leaders are of great importance for successfully changing an institution's ethical culture. Yet, our research at the Czech Ministry of Transport reveals that top-down attempts to improve civil service ethics at the ministry, however well intended, may encounter a hostile reception from subordinate employees as they can perceive these initiatives of the management as yet another burden of requirements on their shoulders or even as an attempt to gain more *control and power over employees.* Now, this negative view is to be contrasted with the interest of individual employees to discuss ethical issues, to improve institutional culture and to become better public servant. We realized that many subordinate employees of the ministry are keen to initiate changes themselves, but they know from experience or they fear that their initiative will not be met with a positive acknowledgment from the management. Thus, we contend that an important step forward consists in empowering public servants and ensuring that their initiatives, appeals and voices will be heard and acted upon. In other words, in a hierarchically structured central government institution there should be not only relational leaders and listening bureaucrats who are skilled in relational and situational needs interpretation but also stable mechanisms and processes that empower subordinate employees and other affected parties and encourage them in their initiatives and own proposals for transforming the institutional culture.

Conclusion

In this chapter, I argued that there is a distinctive care ethical perspective on institutions, which starts from a broader definition of caring as a social practice and views caring as a collective responsibility that needs to be realized through various social and political institutions. The 'institutional approach' in care ethics provides tools for challenging the current institutional arrangements of caring with respect to the idea that the access to care-giving and care-receiving should be relatively equally distributed and that the responsibility and actual work of caring should not fall disproportionally on disadvantaged sections of the society. I further argued that a care ethics perspective can be fruitfully applied to public administration and serve as an alternative ground for rethinking the role, meaning, design and management of public sector institutions. Drawing on the pioneering work of DeLysa Burnier and Sophie Bourgault, I more specifically argued that a care ethical emphasis on attentiveness, responsiveness and inclusiveness, together with a revaluation of bureaucracy, offers an alternative normative ground for public administration in the aftermath of the neoliberal New Public Management reforms. Finally, by discussing a case study from the Czech Ministry of Transport, I showed how the conceptual framework of a care ethical perspective on institutions can be applied in a 'real-world' setting of a contemporary central government institution. The case study also illustrated an empirically grounded approach in a care theory of institutions which can be brought into a fruitful dialogue with the recent proposals for a political theory equipped with 'ethnographic sensibility'.

Acknowledgments My warmest thanks for thoughtful comments on the manuscript of this chapter go to Sophie Bourgault and Lizzie Ward. I am indebted for great discussions over the previous versions of this chapter to Fiona Robinson, Mirko Alagna, Brunella Casalini, Elena Pulcini, Alice Koubová, Martin Nitsche and my wonderful audiences at the University of Florence (November 2018), the University of Ottawa (April 2019) and the 2018 Care Ethics Research Consortium (CERC) Biennial Conference at the Portland State University (September 2018). This chapter is an outcome of the research project 'Measures for Developing an Ethical Culture in the Czech State Administration' (No. TL01000430, Technology Agency of the Czech Republic) realized at the Institute of Philosophy of the Czech Academy of Sciences in Prague.

References

Ashcraft, Karen. 2001. Organized Dissonance: Feminist Bureaucracy as Hybrid Form. *Academy of Management Journal* 44 (6): 1301–1322.

Barnes, Marian. 2006. *Caring and Social Justice*. Basingstoke: Palgrave Macmillan.

———. 2012. *Care in Everyday Life. An Ethic of Care in Practice*. Bristol: Policy Press.

Beck, G. Lynn. 1992. Meeting the Challenge of the Future: The Place of a Caring Ethic in Educational Administration. *American Journal of Education* 100: 454–495.

Bourgault, Sophie. 2017. Prolegomena to a Caring Bureaucracy. *European Journal of Women's Studies* 24 (3): 202–217.

———. 2020. Epistemic Injustice, Face-to-Face Encounters and Caring Institutions. *International Journal of Care and Caring* 4 (1): 91–107.

Burnier, DeLysa. 2003. Other Voices/Other Rooms: Towards a Care-Centred Public Administration. *Administrative Theory and Praxis* 25 (4): 529–544.

———. 2005. Making It Meaning Full: "Postmodern Public Administration" and Symbolic Interactionism. *Administrative Theory and Praxis* 27 (3): 498–516.

———. 2009a. Markets No More: Toward a Care-Centered Public Administration. *Administrative Theory and Praxis* 31 (3): 396–402.

———. 2009b. The Shock of Recognition: Reflections on Bureau Men, Settlement Women. *Administrative Theory and Praxis* 31 (4): 586–589.

Clement, Grace. 1996. *Care, Autonomy, and Justice: Feminism and the Ethic of Care*. Boulder: Westview Press.

Connell, W. Raewyn. 1987. *Gender and Power: Society, the Person, and Sexual Politics*. Cambridge: Polity Press.

Davidson, Anneka. 1994. Gender Differences in Administrative Ethics. In *Handbook of Administrative Ethics*, ed. Terry L. Cooper, 415–433. New York: Marcel Dekker.

du Gay, Paul, ed. 2005. *The Values of Bureaucracy*. Oxford: Oxford University Press.

Dubois, Vincent. 2010. *The Bureaucrat and the Poor: Encounters in French Welfare Offices*. Trans. J.-Y. Bart. Farnham: Ashgate.

Edelman Trust Barometer. 2019. *Edelman Trust Barometer*. Executive Summary. https://www.edelman.com/sites/g/files/aatuss191/files/2019-02/2019_Edelman_Trust_Barometer_Executive_Summary.pdf. Accessed 1 December 2019.

Engster, Daniel. 2004. Care Ethics and Natural Law Theory: Toward an Institutional Political Theory of Caring. *The Journal of Politics* 66 (1): 113–135.

———. 2007. *The Heart of Justice: Care Ethics and Political Theory*. Oxford: Oxford University Press.

———. 2015. *Justice, Care, and the Welfare State*. Oxford: Oxford University Press.

Fassin, Didier, ed. 2005. *At the Heart of the State. The Moral World of Institutions*. London: Pluto Press.

Ferguson, Kathy. 1984. *The Feminist Case Against Bureaucracy*. Philadelphia: Temple University Press.
Fisher, Berenice, and Joan C. Tronto. 1990. Toward a Feminist Theory of Caring. In *Circles of Care: Work and Identity in Women's Lives*, ed. Emily K. Abel and Margaret K. Nelson, 35–62. Albany: SUNY Press.
Franzway, Suzanne, Dianne Court, and Raewyn W. Connell. 1989. *Staking a Claim: Feminism, Bureaucracy and the State*. Sydney: Allen and Unwin.
Fricker, Miranda. 2007. *Epistemic Injustice. Power and the Ethics of Knowing*. Oxford: Oxford University Press.
Gilligan, Carol. 1982. *In a Different Voice. Psychological Theory and Women's Development*. Cambridge, MA: Harvard University Press.
Glenn, Evelyn Nakano. 2000. Creating a Caring Society. *Contemporary Sociology* 29 (1): 84–94.
Groombridge, Brian. 2010. Better Government with Older Citizens: A Test of Democracy. *Political Quarterly* 81 (1): 131–140.
Hankivsky, Olena. 2004. *Social Policy and the Ethic of Care*. Vancouver: UBC Press.
Held, Virginia. 1987. Non-Contractual Society: A Feminist View. In *Science, Morality and Feminist Theory*, ed. Marsha Hanen and Kai Nielsen, 111–137. *Canadian Journal of Philosophy* (Suppl. 13). Calgary: The University of Calgary Press.
———. 1990. Feminist Transformations of Moral Theory. *Philosophy and Phenomenological Research* 50: 321–344.
———. 2006. *The Ethics of Care. Personal, Political, and Global*. New York: Oxford University Press.
Herzog, Lisa, and Bernardo Zacka. 2017. Fieldwork in Political Theory: Five Arguments for an Ethnographic Sensibility. *British Journal of Political Science* 49 (2): 763–784.
Hirst, Paul. 1997. *From Statism to Pluralism: Democracy, Civil Society and Global Politics*. London: Routledge.
Hoggett, Paul. 2005. A Service to the Public: The Containment of Ethical and Moral Conflicts. In *The Values of Bureaucracy*, ed. Paul du Gay, 165–190. Oxford: Oxford University Press.
Jaggar, M. Alison. 1995. Caring as a Feminist Practice of Moral Reason. In *Justice and Care: Essential Readings in Feminist Ethics*, ed. Virginia Held, 179–202. Boulder: Westview Press.
Khullar, Dhruv. 2018. Do You Trust the Medical Profession? *The New York Times*. https://www.nytimes.com/2018/01/23/upshot/do-you-trust-the-medical-profession.html. Accessed 1 December 2019.
Kittay, Eva Feder. 1999. *Love's Labor. Essays on Women, Equality, and Dependency*. London: Routledge.
Koren, Mary Jane. 2010. Person-Centered Care for Nursing Home Residents: The Culture-Change Movement. *Health Affairs* 29 (2): 312–317.

Krook, Mona Lena, and Fiona Mackay, eds. 2011. *Gender, Politics and Institutions: Towards a Feminist Institutionalism*. Basingstoke: Palgrave Macmillan.

Martin, Patricia Yancey. 1990. Rethinking Feminist Organizations. *Gender and Society* 4 (2): 182–206.

———. 2013. Sociologists for Women in Society: A Feminist Bureaucracy? *Gender and Society* 27 (3): 281–293.

Noddings, Nel. 1984. *Caring. A Feminine Approach to Ethics and Moral Education*. Berkeley: University of California Press.

———. 1987. Creating Rivals and Making Enemies. *Journal of Thought* 22 (3): 23–31.

———. 1988. An Ethic of Caring and Its Implications for Instructional Arrangements. *American Journal of Education* 96 (2): 215–230.

———. 1990. Feminist Critiques in the Professions. *Review of Research in Education* 16: 393–424.

———. 1998. Feminist Morality and Social Policy. In *Norms and Values: Essays on the Work of Virginia Held*, ed. Joram G. Haber and Mark S. Halfon, 61–71. Lanham: Rowman and Littlefield.

———. 2002. *Starting at Home: Caring and Social Policy*. Berkeley: University of California Press.

———. 2013a. Preface to the 2013 Edition. In *Caring: A Relational Approach to Ethics and Moral Education*, ed. Nel Noddings, xiii–xx. Berkeley: University of California Press.

———. 2013b. Afterword. In *Caring: A Relational Approach to Ethics and Moral Education*, ed. Nel Noddings, 203–208. Berkeley: University of California Press.

———. 2015. Care Ethics and "Caring" Organizations. In *Care Ethics and Political Theory*, ed. Daniel Engster and Maurice Hamington, 72–84. Oxford: Oxford University Press.

Pasquerella, Lynn. 2019. In an Era of Fake News and Growing Public Distrust, Institutions Must Reframe the Narrative. *HigherEdJobs*. https://www.higheredjobs.com/articles/articleDisplay.cfm?ID=1874. Accessed 1 December 2019.

Regan, B. Helen, and Gwen H. Brooks. 1995. *Out of Women's Experience: Creating Relational Leadership*. Thousand Oaks: Corwin Press.

Ruddick, Sara. 1980. Maternal Thinking. *Feminist Studies* 6 (2): 342–367.

———. 1995. Injustice in Families: Assault and Domination. In *Justice and Care: Essential Readings in Feminist Ethics*, ed. Virginia Held, 203–223. Boulder: Westview Press.

———. 1998. Care as Labor and Relationship. In *Norms and Values: Essays on the Work of Virginia Held*, ed. Joram G. Haber and Mark S. Halfon, 3–25. Lanham: Rowman and Littlefield.

———. 2002 [1989]. *Maternal Thinking: Toward a Politics of Peace*. Boston: Beacon Press.

Schachter, Hindy Lauer. 2008. Feminist Theory and the Political Dimensions of Performance Measurement: A Preliminary Analysis. *Public Performance and Management Review* 32: 263–274.

Schües, Christina. 2016. Ethik und Fürsorge als Beziehungspraxis. In *Praxis der Achtsamkeit. Schlüsselbegriffe der Care-Ethik*, ed. Elisabeth Conradi and Frans Vosman, 251–271. Frankfurt: Campus Verlag.

Scranton, Anneka Marina, and Molly J. Ranney. 2001. Gender Differences in Administrative Ethics. In *Handbook of Administrative Ethics*, ed. Terry L. Cooper, 2nd ed., 555–582. New York: Marcel Dekker.

Selingo, J. Jeffrey. 2017. Americans Love Higher Education, Just Not Their Universities. *The Washington Post*. https://www.washingtonpost.com/news/grade-point/wp/2017/07/18/americans-love-higher-education-just-not-their-universities/. Accessed 1 December 2019.

Sernak, Kathleen. 1998. *School Leadership: Balancing Power with Caring*. New York: Teachers College Press.

Sevenhuijsen, Selma. 1998. *Citizenship and the Ethics of Care. Feminist Considerations on Justice, Morality and Politics*. Trans. Liz Savage. London: Routledge.

Sevenhuijsen, Selma, Vivienne Bozalek, Amanda Gouws, and Marie Minnaar-Mcdonald. 2003. South African Social Welfare Policy: An Analysis Using the Ethic of Care. *Critical Social Policy* 23 (3): 299–321.

Starratt, J. Robert. 1991. Building an Ethical School: A Theory for Practice in Educational Leadership. *Educational Administration Quarterly* 27 (2): 185–202.

Stensöta, Olofsdotter Helena. 2010. The Conditions of Care: Reframing the Debate About Public Sector Ethics. *Public Administration Review* 70 (2): 295–303.

———. 2015. Public Ethics of Care – A General Public Ethics. *Ethics and Social Welfare* 9 (2): 183–200.

Stivers, Camilla. 1991. Toward a Feminist Perspective in Public Administration Theory. *Women & Politics* 10 (4): 49–65.

———. 1993. *Gender Images in Public Administration: Legitimacy and the Administrative State*. London: Sage.

———. 1994. The Listening Bureaucrat: Responsiveness in Public Administration. *Public Administration Review* 54 (4): 364–369.

———. 2000. *Bureau Men, Settlement Women: Constructing Public Administration in the Progressive Era*. Lawrence: University Press of Kansas.

Timmerman, Guus, Andries Baart, and Frans Vosman. 2019. In Search of Good Care: The Methodology of Phenomenological, Theory-Oriented 'N=N Case Studies' in Empirically Grounded Ethics of Care. *Medicine, Health Care and Philosophy* 22 (4): 573–582.

Tronto, C. Joan. 1987. Beyond Gender Difference to a Theory of Care. *Signs: Journal for Women in Culture and Society* 12 (4): 644–663.

———. 1989. Women and Caring: What Can Feminists Learn About Morality from Caring? In *Gender/Body/Knowledge: Feminist Reconstructions of Being and Knowing*, ed. Alison M. Jaggar and Susan R. Bordo, 172–187. New Brunswick: Rutgers University Press.

———. 1993. *Moral Boundaries. A Political Argument for an Ethic of Care.* London: Routledge.

———. 2001. Who Cares? Public and Private Caring and the Rethinking of Citizenship. In *Women and Welfare: Theory and Practice in the United States and Europe*, ed. Nancy J. Hirschmann and Ulrike Liebert, 65–83. New Brunswick, NJ: Rutgers University Press.

———. 2010. Creating Caring Institutions: Politics, Plurality, and Purpose. *Ethics and Social Welfare* 4 (2): 158–171.

———. 2013. *Caring Democracy. Markets, Equality, and Justice.* New York: New York University Press.

Vosman, Frans. 2016. Kartographie einer Ethik der Achtsamkeit – Rezeption und Entwicklung in Europa. In *Praxis der Achtsamkeit. Schlüsselbegriffe der Care-Ethik*, ed. Elisabeth Conradi and Frans Vosman, 33–51. Frankfurt: Campus Verlag.

Watson, Sophie, ed. 1990. *Playing the State: Australian Feminist Interventions.* Sydney: Allen and Unwin.

White, Anne Julie. 2000. *Democracy, Justice, and the Welfare State. Reconstructing Public Care.* University Park: The Pennsylvania State University Press.

Zacka, Bernardo. 2017. *When the State Meets the Street: Public Service and Moral Agency.* Cambridge: Harvard University Press.

Index[1]

A

B

[1] Note: Page numbers followed by 'n' refer to notes.

P. Urban, L. Ward (eds.), *Care Ethics, Democratic Citizenship and the State*, International Political Theory,
https://doi.org/10.1007/978-3-030-41437-5

R

S

The manufacturer's authorised representative in the EU is Springer Nature Customer Service Centre GmbH, Europaplatz 3, 69115 Heidelberg, Germany. If you have any concerns regarding our products, please contact ProductSafety@springernature.com

Printed and bound by CPI Group (UK) Ltd, Croydon, CR0 4YY

22/09/2026

02221058-0003